5

FOCUS
ON
GRAMMAR

AN INTEGRATED SKILLS APPROACH

THIRD EDITION

JAY MAURER

PEARSON
Longman

FOCUS ON GRAMMAR 5: An Integrated Skills Approach

Pearson Education, 10 Bank Street, White Plains, NY 10606

Vice president, multimedia and skills: Sherry Preiss
Executive editor: Laura Le Dréan
Development editor: John Barnes
Production supervisor: Christine Edmonds
Production editor: Diana P. George
Art director: Ann France
Marketing manager: Timothy Benell
Senior manufacturing manager: Nancy Flaggman
Photo research: Aerin Csigay
Cover design: Rhea Banker
Cover images: Large shell, Nick Koudis, RF; background, Comstock Images, RF
Text design: Quorum Creative Services, Rhea Banker
Text composition: ElectraGraphics, Inc.
Text font: 11/13 Sabon, 10/13 Myriad Roman

Illustrators: Chris Gash pp. 2, 70, 99, 244; Burmar Technical Corporation pp. 11, 241;
Brian Hughes p. 51; A. J. Garces pp. 221, 259; David Klug p. 321; Jock MacRae p. 320;
Suzanne Mogensen pp. 175, 176; Andy Myer p. 349; Thomas Newsom pp. 110, 111,
393, 401, 402, 414, 415, 442; Dusan Petricic pp. 9, 28, 86, 141, 216, 335, 336; Susan
Scott pp. 52, 207, 253, 254, 293, 351; Meryl Treatner pp. 73, 81.

Photo credits: p. 16 AP/Wide World Photos; p. 26 Keri Pickett/Getty Images; p. 30 Printed by permission of the Norman Rockwell Family
Agency. Copyright © 1930 the Norman Rockwell Family Entities; p. 33 Getty Images; p. 56 Jack Hollingsworth/Getty Images; p. 57
Ron Chapple/Getty Images; p. 68 China Tourism Press/Getty Images; p. 89 Getty Images; p. 90 Steve Wood/Getty Images; p. 101 Hugh
Sitton/Getty Images; p. 114 Getty Images; p. 128 Art Wolfe/Getty Images; p. 139 SuperStock, Inc./SuperStock; p. 153 AP/Wide World Photos;
p. 165 Bettmann/Corbis; p. 180 (left) Martin Ruegner/Getty Images, (right) Joel Creed/Ecoscene/Corbis; p. 195 Photofest; p. 196 (top)
Photofest, (middle) New Line Cinema/The Kobal Collection, (bottom) Photofest; p. 231 AP/Wide World Photos; p. 233 (left) Dale
O'Dell/SuperStock, (right) AP/Wide World Photos; p. 235 (left) Wolfgang Kaehler/Corbis, (right) Royalty-Free/Corbis; p. 246 (left) Eric
Schaal/Getty Images, (left) ARPL/HIP/The Image Works; p. 247 (left) David Turnley/Corbis, (right) Gianni Dagli Orti/Corbis; p. 272 2002
Rick London and Rich Diesslin; p. 285 Julian Hirshowitz/Corbis; p. 296 Pearson Education; p. 308 Pearson Education; p. 310 Syracuse
Newspapers/Dick Blum/The Image Works; p. 311 David Young-Wolff/PhotoEdit; p. 324 AP/Wide World Photos; p. 326 AP/Wide World
Photos; p. 326 AP/Wide World Photos; p. 340 Digital Vision/Getty Images; p. 352 Bonnie Kamin/PhotoEdit; p. 353 The Art
Archive/Kunsthistorisches Museum Vienna; p. 378 Bettmann/Corbis; p. 406 SuperStock, Inc./SuperStock; p. 422 Erik Dreyer/Getty Images.

Library of Congress Cataloging-in-Publication Data

Focus on grammar. An integrated skills approach — 3rd ed.
    p. cm.
  ISBN 0-13-147466-9 (v. 1 : student book : alk. paper) — ISBN 0-13-189971-6 (v. 2 : student book : alk.
paper) — ISBN 0-13-189984-8 (v. 3 : student book : alk. paper) — ISBN
0-13-190008-0 (v. 4 : student book : alk. paper) — ISBN 0-13-191273-9 (v. 5 : student book : alk. paper)
  1. English language—Textbooks for foreign speakers. 2. English language—Grammar—Problems,
exercises, etc.
PE1128.F555 2005
428.2'4—dc22

                                                                                          2005007655

Printed in the United States of America

ISBN: 0-13-191273-9 (Student Book)
3 4 5 6 7 8 9 10—WC—12 11 10 09 08 07 06

ISBN: 0-13-191275-5 (Student Book with Audio CD)
` 4 5 6 7 8 9 10—WC—12 11 10 09 08 07

CONTENTS

PART III   NOUNS

PART IV   ADJECTIVE CLAUSES

PART V   PASSIVE VOICE

PART VIII NOUN CLAUSES

PART IX CONDITIONALS AND THE SUBJUNCTIVE

APPENDICES

ABOUT THE AUTHOR

Jay Maurer has taught English in binational centers, colleges, and universities in Portugal, Spain, Mexico, the Somali Republic, and the United States; and intensive English at Columbia University's American Language Program. In addition, he has been a teacher of college composition and literature at Santa Fe Community College and Northern New Mexico Community College. Mr. Maurer holds M.A. and M.Ed. degrees in Applied Linguistics and a Ph.D. degree in The Teaching of English, all from Columbia University. He is the co-author of the three-level *Structure Practice in Context* series; co-author with Irene Schoenberg of the five-level *True Colors* series and *Focus on Grammar 1: An Integrated Skills Approach*; co-author of the *True Voices* video series; co-author of *Teen Zone II*; and author of *Focus on Grammar 5: An Integrated Skills Approach*. Currently he writes and teaches in Seattle, Washington. *Focus on Grammar 5: An Integrated Skills Approach*, Third Edition, has grown out of the author's experiences as a practicing teacher of both ESL and college writing.

INTRODUCTION

The *Focus on Grammar* series

Written by ESL/EFL professionals, ***Focus on Grammar: An Integrated Skills Approach*** helps students to understand and practice English grammar. The primary aim of the course is for students to gain confidence in their ability to speak and write English accurately and fluently.

The **third edition** retains this popular series' focus on English grammar through lively listening, speaking, reading, and writing activities. The new ***Focus on Grammar*** also maintains the same five-level progression as the second edition:

- Level 1 (Beginning, formerly Introductory)
- Level 2 (High-Beginning, formerly Basic)
- Level 3 (Intermediate)
- Level 4 (High-Intermediate)
- Level 5 (Advanced)

What is the *Focus on Grammar* methodology?

Both controlled and communicative practice

While students expect and need to learn the formal rules of a language, it is crucial that they also practice new structures in a variety of contexts in order to internalize and master them. To this end, ***Focus on Grammar*** provides an abundance of both controlled and communicative exercises so that students can bridge the gap between knowing grammatical structures and using them. The many communicative activities in each Student Book unit provide opportunity for critical thinking while enabling students to personalize what they have learned in order to talk to one another with ease about hundreds of everyday issues.

A unique four-step approach

The series follows a four-step approach:

Step 1: Grammar in Context shows the new structures in natural context, such as articles and conversations.

Step 2: Grammar Presentation presents the structures in clear and accessible grammar charts, notes, and examples.

Step 3: Focused Practice of both form and meaning of the new structures is provided in numerous and varied controlled exercises.

Step 4: Communication Practice allows students to use the new structures freely and creatively in motivating, open-ended activities.

Thorough recycling

Underpinning the scope and sequence of the *Focus on Grammar* series is the belief that students need to use target structures many times, in different contexts, and at increasing levels of difficulty. For this reason, new grammar is constantly recycled throughout the book so that students have maximum exposure to the target forms and become comfortable using them in speech and in writing.

A complete classroom text and reference guide

A major goal in the development of *Focus on Grammar* has been to provide students with books that serve not only as vehicles for classroom instruction but also as resources for reference and self-study. In each Student Book, the combination of grammar charts, grammar notes, a glossary of grammar terms, and extensive appendices provides a complete and invaluable reference guide for students.

Ongoing assessment

Review Tests at the end of each part of the Student Book allow for continual self-assessment. In addition, the tests in the new *Focus on Grammar* Assessment Package provide teachers with a valid, reliable, and practical means of determining students' appropriate levels of placement in the course and of assessing students' achievement throughout the course. At Levels 4 (High-Intermediate) and 5 (Advanced), Proficiency Tests give teachers an overview of their students' general grammar knowledge.

What are the components of each level of *Focus on Grammar*?

Student Book

The Student Book is divided into eight or more parts, depending on the level. Each part contains grammatically related units, with each unit focusing on specific grammatical structures; where appropriate, units present contrasting forms. The exercises in each unit are thematically related to one another, and all units have the same clear, easy-to-follow format.

Teacher's Manual

The Teacher's Manual contains a variety of suggestions and information to enrich the material in the Student Book. It includes general teaching suggestions for each section of a typical unit, answers to frequently asked questions, unit-by-unit teaching tips with ideas for further communicative practice, and a supplementary activity section. Answers to the Student Book exercises and audioscripts of the listening activities are found at the back of the Teacher's Manual. Also included in the Teacher's Manual is a CD-ROM of teaching tools, including PowerPoint presentations that offer alternative ways of presenting selected grammar structures.

Workbook

The Workbook accompanying each level of *Focus on Grammar* provides additional exercises appropriate for self-study of the target grammar for each Student Book unit. Tests included in each Workbook provide students with additional opportunities for self-assessment.

Audio Program

All of the listening exercises from the Student Book, as well as the Grammar in Context passages and other appropriate exercises, are included on the program's CDs. In the book, the symbol ⌒ appears next to the listening exercises. Another symbol ⌒, indicating that listening is optional, appears next to the Grammar in Context passages and some exercises. All of these scripts appear in the Teacher's Manual and may be used as an alternative way of presenting the activities.

Some Student Books are packaged with a separate Student Audio CD. This CD includes the listening exercise from each unit and any other exercises that have an essential listening component.

CD-ROM

The *Focus on Grammar* CD-ROM provides students with individualized practice and immediate feedback. Fully contextualized and interactive, the activities broaden and extend practice of the grammatical structures in the reading, writing, speaking, and listening skills areas. The CD-ROM includes grammar review, review tests, score-based remedial practice, games, and all relevant reference material from the Student Book. It can also be used in conjunction with the *Longman Interactive American Dictionary* CD-ROM.

Assessment Package (NEW)

An extensive, comprehensive Assessment Package has been developed for each level of the third edition of *Focus on Grammar*. The components of the Assessment Package are:

1. Placement, Diagnostic, and Achievement Tests

- a Placement Test to screen students and place them into the correct level
- Diagnostic Tests for each part of the Student Book
- Unit Achievement Tests for each unit of the Student Book
- Part Achievement Tests for each part of the Student Book

2. General Proficiency Tests

- two Proficiency Tests at Level 4 (High-Intermediate)
- two Proficiency Tests at Level 5 (Advanced)

These tests can be administered at any point in the course.

3. Audio CD

The listening portions of the Placement, Diagnostic, and Achievement Tests are recorded on CDs. The scripts appear in the Assessment Package.

4. Test-Generating Software

The test-bank software provides thousands of questions from which teachers can create class-appropriate tests. All items are labeled according to the grammar structure they are testing, so teachers can easily select relevant items; they can also design their own items to add to the tests.

Transparencies (NEW)

Transparencies of all the grammar charts in the Student Book are also available. These transparencies are a classroom visual aid that will help instructors point out important patterns and structures of grammar.

Companion Website

The companion website contains a wealth of information and activities for both teachers and students. In addition to general information about the course pedagogy, the website provides extensive practice exercises for the classroom, a language lab, or at home.

What's new in the third edition of the Student Book?

In response to users' requests, this edition has:

- a new four-color design
- easy-to-read color coding for the four steps
- new and updated reading texts for Grammar in Context
- post-reading activities (in addition to the pre-reading questions)
- more exercise items
- an editing (error analysis) exercise in each unit
- an Internet activity in each unit
- a Glossary of Grammar Terms
- expanded Appendices

References

Alexander, L. G. (1988). *Longman English Grammar.* White Plains: Longman.

Biber, D., S. Conrad, E. Finegan, S. Johansson, and G. Leech (1999). *Longman Grammar of Spoken and Written English.* White Plains: Longman.

Celce-Murcia, M., and D. Freeman (1999). *The Grammar Book.* Boston: Heinle and Heinle.

Celce-Murcia, M., and S. Hilles (1988). *Techniques and Resources in Teaching Grammar.* New York: Oxford University Press.

Firsten, R. (2002). *The ELT Grammar Book.* Burlingame, CA: Alta Book Center Publishers.

Garner, B. (2003). *Garner's Modern American Usage.* New York: Oxford University Press.

Greenbaum, S. (1996). *The Oxford English Grammar.* New York: Oxford University Press.

Leech, G. (2004). *Meaning and the English Verb.* Harlow, UK: Pearson.

Lewis, M. (1997). *Implementing the Lexical Approach.* Hove East Sussex, UK: Language Teaching Publications.

Longman (2002). *Longman Dictionary of English Language and Culture.* Harlow, UK: Longman.

Willis, D. (2003). *Rules, Patterns and Words.* New York: Cambridge University Press.

TOUR OF A UNIT

Each unit in the *Focus on Grammar* series presents a specific grammar structure (or two, in the case of a contrast) and develops a major theme, which is set by the opening text. All units follow the same unique **four-step approach**.

Step 1: Grammar in Context

The **conversation** or **reading** in this section shows the grammar structure in a natural context. The high-interest text presents authentic language in a variety of real-life formats: magazine articles, web pages, questionnaires, and more. Students can listen to the text on an audio CD to get accustomed to the sound of the grammar structure in a natural context.

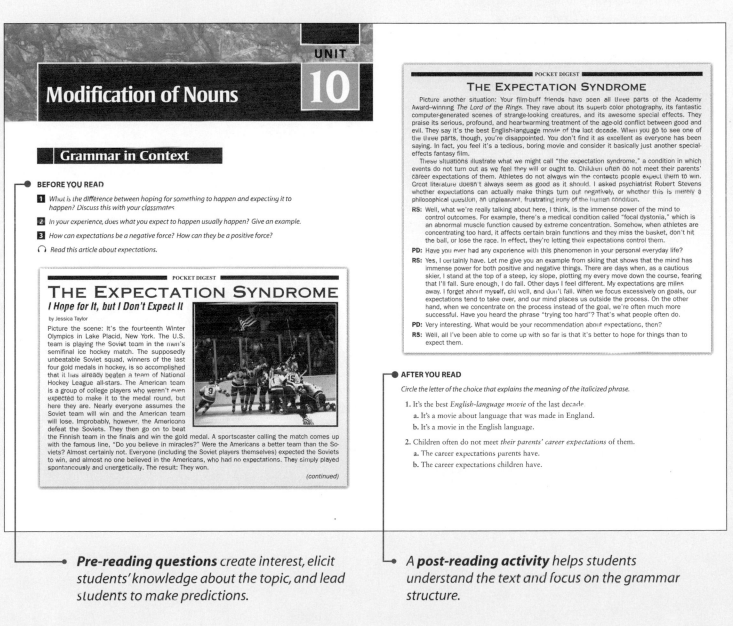

Pre-reading questions *create interest, elicit students' knowledge about the topic, and lead students to make predictions.*

A **post-reading activity** *helps students understand the text and focus on the grammar structure.*

Step 2: Grammar Presentation

This section is made up of grammar charts, notes, and examples. The **grammar charts** focus on the forms of the grammar structure. The **grammar notes** and **examples** focus on the meanings and uses of the structure.

*Clear and easy-to-read **grammar charts** present the grammar structure in all its forms and combinations.*

*Each **grammar note** gives a short, simple explanation of one use of the structure. The accompanying **examples** ensure students' understanding of the point.*

Grammar Presentation

PAST TIME

PAST TIME: GENERAL OR SPECIFIC (DEFINITE)

Simple Past
Weinlick **needed** to find a bride.
He **advertised** on the Internet.

Past Progressive
Was / Were + Base Form + *-ing*
He **was looking** for someone special.

PAST TIME: NOT SPECIFIC (INDEFINITE)

Present Perfect
Has / Have + Past Participle
The couple **has chosen** the date for the party.
They **have** already **sent** the invitations.

PAST TIME: HABITUAL OR REPEATED

Used To + Base Form
She **used to be** a pharmacist.

Would + Base Form
Some days she **would work** 12 hours.

PAST TIME: BEFORE A TIME IN THE PAST

Past Perfect
Had + Past Participle
He **had met** her before the wedding.

Past Perfect Progressive
Had been + Base Form + *-ing*
He **had been planning** the wedding for months.

PAST TIME: AFTER A TIME IN THE PAST BUT BEFORE NOW ("FUTURE IN THE PAST")

Was / Were Going To + Base Form
He knew he **was going to marry** soon.

Would + Base Form
He knew when the wedding **would be**.

GRAMMAR NOTES

1. Use the **simple past** to express an action, event, or state completed at a general or specific time in the past.

Remember that many of the most common verbs have irregular past forms and past participles.

2. Use the **past progressive** to express an action that was in progress (= not finished) at a time in the past.

3. Use the **present perfect** to express an action, event, or state completed at an indefinite time in the past.

▶ **BE CAREFUL!** Don't use the present perfect with a past-time expression.

NOTE: The simple past is the definite past. The present perfect is the indefinite past.

Remember that the present perfect also connects the past and the present. (See Unit 1.)

4. Use **used to** + base form to show a habitual action, event, or state that was true in the past but is no longer true.

You can also use **would** + base form to express actions or events that occurred regularly during a period in the past.

▶ **BE CAREFUL!** *Used to* and *would* are similar in meaning when they express past actions. However, only *used to* can show past location, state, or possession.

EXAMPLES

- Runze **wanted** to get married. *(general)*
- She **filled out** an application form several days before the wedding. *(specific)*
- Weinlick and Runze **met** five days before they **got** married.

- Runze **was studying** pharmacy at the University when she decided to get married.

- How many Americans **have** ever **considered** an arranged marriage?
- Weinlick **got married a few years ago**.
  Not Weinlick ~~has gotten married~~ a few years ago.
- The two **met** on June 8, 1998.
- They **have** already **met**.
- I **have attended** many weddings since then.

- Kayoko **used to play** tennis a lot.

- When we were children, we **would spend** every summer in Maine.

- I **used to live** in Chicago.
- Sarah **used to be** a marriage counselor.
- We **used to have** a summer home.
  Not I ~~would live in~~ Chicago.
  Sarah ~~would be a~~ marriage counselor.
  We ~~would~~ have a summer home.

(continued)

__Be careful notes__ alert students to common errors made by students of English.

__Notes__ provide guidelines about meaning, usage, and level of formality.

Step 3: Focused Practice

This section provides students with a variety of contextualized **controlled exercises** to practice both the forms and the uses of the grammar structure.

Focused Practice *always begins with a "for recognition only" exercise called* **Discover the Grammar**.

Exercises are **cross-referenced** *to the appropriate grammar notes to provide a quick review.*

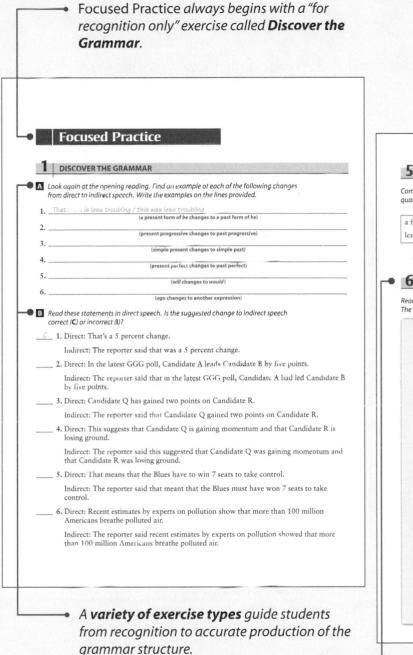

Focused Practice

1 DISCOVER THE GRAMMAR

A Look again at the opening reading. Find an example of each of the following changes from direct to indirect speech. Write the examples on the lines provided.

1. _That . . . is less troubling / this was less troubling_
   (a present form of *be* changes to a past form of *be*)
2. _____
   (present progressive changes to past progressive)
3. _____
   (simple present changes to simple past)
4. _____
   (present perfect changes to past perfect)
5. _____
   (*will* changes to *would*)
6. _____
   (*ago* changes to another expression)

B Read these statements in direct speech. Is the suggested change to indirect speech correct (**C**) or incorrect (**I**)?

_C_ 1. Direct: That's a 5 percent change.

   Indirect: The reporter said that was a 5 percent change.

____ 2. Direct: In the latest GGG poll, Candidate A leads Candidate B by five points.

   Indirect: The reporter said that in the latest GGG poll, Candidate A had led Candidate B by five points.

____ 3. Direct: Candidate Q has gained two points on Candidate R.

   Indirect: The reporter said that Candidate Q gained two points on Candidate R.

____ 4. Direct: This suggests that Candidate Q is gaining momentum and that Candidate R is losing ground.

   Indirect: The reporter said this suggested that Candidate Q was gaining momentum and that Candidate R was losing ground.

____ 5. Direct: That means that the Blues have to win 7 seats to take control.

   Indirect: The reporter said that meant that the Blues must have won 7 seats to take control.

____ 6. Direct: Recent estimates by experts on pollution show that more than 100 million Americans breathe polluted air.

   Indirect: The reporter said recent estimates by experts on pollution showed that more than 100 million Americans breathe polluted air.

A ***variety of exercise types*** *guide students from recognition to accurate production of the grammar structure.*

5 A PERSONAL INVENTORY
Grammar Notes 5–6

Compare your life now to your life five years ago. Write eight sentences, using each of the quantifiers in the box.

a few	a little	a lot	fewer
less	many	more	much

Example: I have **more friends** now than I did five years ago.

6 EDITING

Read this excerpt from a president's speech. There are 12 mistakes in the use of quantifiers. The first one is already corrected. Find and correct 11 more.

> My fellow citizens: We are at a time in our history when we need to make some real
> _a great many_
> sacrifices. Recent presidents have made ~~a great deal of~~ promises they didn't keep. You may
> not like everything I tell you tonight, but you deserve to hear the truth. On the economy,
> we've made little progress, but we still have a great many work to do, so there are several
> measures I'm proposing. First, I want to raise taxes on the very wealthy because a few of
> them are really paying their share. Second, many of members of the middle class are
> carrying an unfair tax burden, so I'm asking for a tax cut for the middle class. If I'm
> successful, most of you in the middle class will be paying 10 percent less in taxes next year,
> though few of you in the higher-income group may see your taxes rise little.
>
> How do I intend to make up the lost revenue? The problem with the national income
> tax is that there are much loopholes in the current law which allow any people to avoid
> paying any taxes at all; I want to close these loopholes. My additional plan is to replace the
> lost revenue with a national sales tax, which is fairer because it applies to every people
> equally. Third, we have no money to finance health care reform, and we've made a little
> progress in reducing pollution and meeting clean air standards. Therefore, I am asking for
> a 50-cent-a-gallon tax on gasoline, which will result in many more people using public
> transportation and will create additional revenue. Thus, we will have enough of money to
> finance our new health care program and will help the environment at the same time.

Focused Practice ***always ends with an editing*** *exercise to teach students to find and correct typical mistakes.*

Step 4: **Communication Practice**

This section provides open-ended **communicative activities** giving students the opportunity to use the grammar structure appropriately and fluently.

*A **listening** activity gives students the opportunity to check their aural comprehension.*

*Many exercises and activities are **art-based** to provide visual cues and an interesting context and springboard for meaningful conversations.*

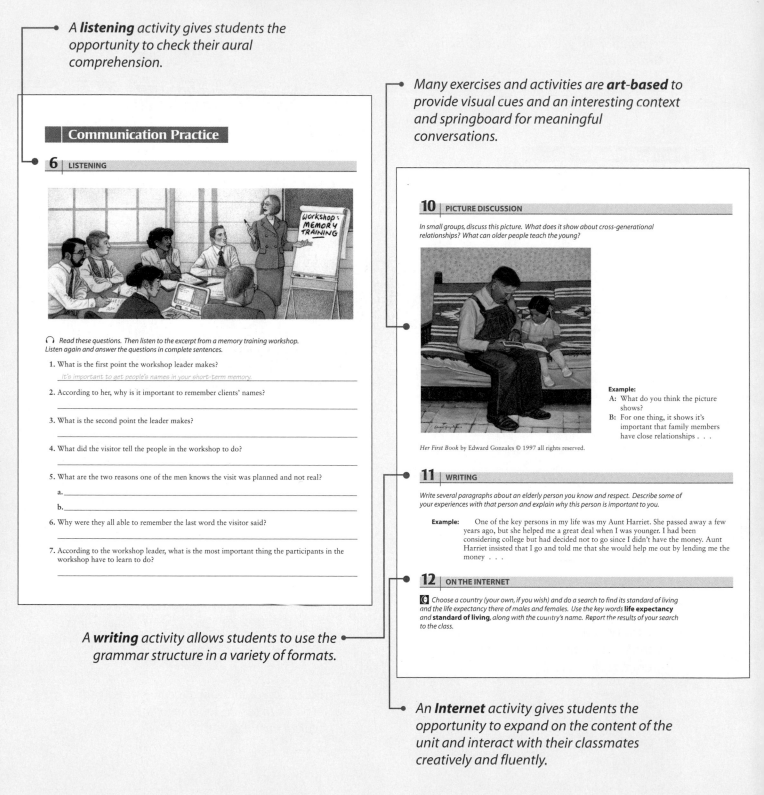

Communication Practice

6 | LISTENING

☊ *Read these questions. Then listen to the excerpt from a memory training workshop. Listen again and answer the questions in complete sentences.*

1. What is the first point the workshop leader makes?

   It's important to get people's names in your short-term memory.

2. According to her, why is it important to remember clients' names?

3. What is the second point the leader makes?

4. What did the visitor tell the people in the workshop to do?

5. What are the two reasons one of the men knows the visit was planned and not real?

   a.
   b.

6. Why were they all able to remember the last word the visitor said?

7. According to the workshop leader, what is the most important thing the participants in the workshop have to learn to do?

10 | PICTURE DISCUSSION

In small groups, discuss this picture. What does it show about cross-generational relationships? What can older people teach the young?

Example:
A: What do you think the picture shows?
B: For one thing, it shows it's important that family members have close relationships . . .

Her First Book by Edward Gonzales © 1997 all rights reserved.

11 | WRITING

Write several paragraphs about an elderly person you know and respect. Describe some of your experiences with that person and explain why this person is important to you.

Example: One of the key persons in my life was my Aunt Harriet. She passed away a few years ago, but she helped me a great deal when I was younger. I had been considering college but had decided not to go since I didn't have the money. Aunt Harriet insisted that I go and told me that she would help me out by lending me the money . . .

12 | ON THE INTERNET

🌐 *Choose a country (your own, if you wish) and do a search to find its standard of living and the life expectancy there of males and females. Use the key words **life expectancy** and **standard of living**, along with the country's name. Report the results of your search to the class.*

*A **writing** activity allows students to use the grammar structure in a variety of formats.*

*An **Internet** activity gives students the opportunity to expand on the content of the unit and interact with their classmates creatively and fluently.*

TOUR BEYOND THE UNIT

In the *Focus on Grammar* series, the grammatically related units are grouped into parts, and each part concludes with a section called **From Grammar to Writing** and a **Review Test** section.

From Grammar to Writing

This section presents a point which applies specifically to writing, for example, combining sentences with time words. Students are guided to practice the point in **a piece of extended writing**.

Activities focus on issues **important for successful writing**.

Activities focus on issues **important for successful writing**.

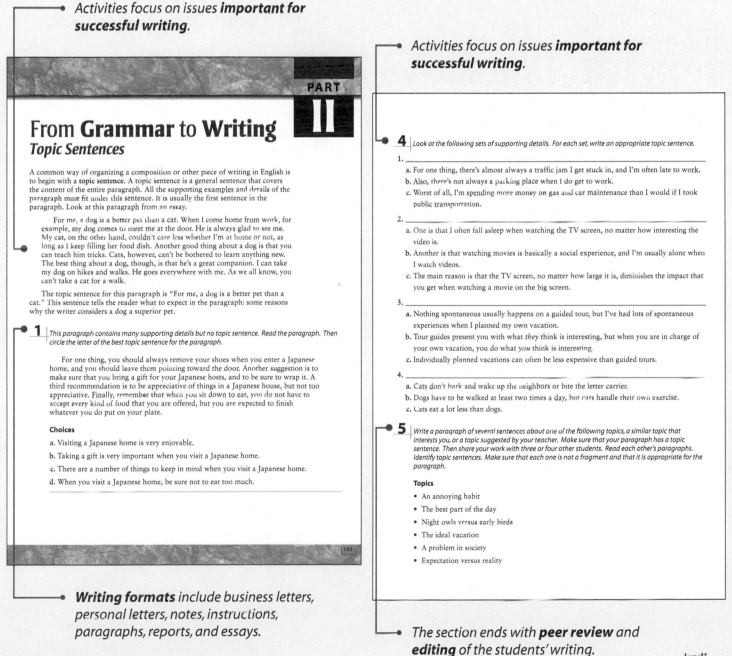

PART II

From **Grammar** to **Writing**
Topic Sentences

A common way of organizing a composition or other piece of writing in English is to begin with a **topic sentence**. A topic sentence is a general sentence that covers the content of the entire paragraph. All the supporting examples and details of the paragraph must fit under this sentence. It is usually the first sentence in the paragraph. Look at this paragraph from an essay.

For me, a dog is a better pet than a cat. When I come home from work, for example, my dog comes to meet me at the door. He is always glad to see me. My cat, on the other hand, couldn't care less whether I'm at home or not, as long as I keep filling her food dish. Another good thing about a dog is that you can teach him tricks. Cats, however, can't be bothered to learn anything new. The best thing about a dog, though, is that he's a great companion. I can take my dog on hikes and walks. He goes everywhere with me. As we all know, you can't take a cat for a walk.

The topic sentence for this paragraph is "For me, a dog is a better pet than a cat." This sentence tells the reader what to expect in the paragraph: some reasons why the writer considers a dog a superior pet.

1 | *This paragraph contains many supporting details but no topic sentence. Read the paragraph. Then circle the letter of the best topic sentence for the paragraph.*

For one thing, you should always remove your shoes when you enter a Japanese home, and you should leave them pointing toward the door. Another suggestion is to make sure that you bring a gift for your Japanese hosts, and to be sure to wrap it. A third recommendation is to be appreciative of things in a Japanese house, but not too appreciative. Finally, remember that when you sit down to eat, you do not have to accept every kind of food that you are offered, but you are expected to finish whatever you do put on your plate.

Choices

a. Visiting a Japanese home is very enjoyable.

b. Taking a gift is very important when you visit a Japanese home.

c. There are a number of things to keep in mind when you visit a Japanese home.

d. When you visit a Japanese home, be sure not to eat too much.

4 | *Look at the following sets of supporting details. For each set, write an appropriate topic sentence.*

1. _____

a. For one thing, there's almost always a traffic jam I get stuck in, and I'm often late to work.

b. Also, there's not always a parking place when I do get to work.

c. Worst of all, I'm spending more money on gas and car maintenance than I would if I took public transportation.

2. _____

a. One is that I often fall asleep when watching the TV screen, no matter how interesting the video is.

b. Another is that watching movies is basically a social experience, and I'm usually alone when I watch videos.

c. The main reason is that the TV screen, no matter how large it is, diminishes the impact that you get when watching a movie on the big screen.

3. _____

a. Nothing spontaneous usually happens on a guided tour, but I've had lots of spontaneous experiences when I planned my own vacation.

b. Tour guides present you with what *they* think is interesting, but when you are in charge of your own vacation, you do what *you* think is interesting.

c. Individually planned vacations can often be less expensive than guided tours.

4. _____

a. Cats don't bark and wake up the neighbors or bite the letter carrier.

b. Dogs have to be walked at least two times a day, but cats handle their own exercise.

c. Cats eat a lot less than dogs.

5 | *Write a paragraph of several sentences about one of the following topics, a similar topic that interests you, or a topic suggested by your teacher. Make sure that your paragraph has a topic sentence. Then share your work with three or four other students. Read each other's paragraphs. Identify topic sentences. Make sure that each one is not a fragment and that it is appropriate for the paragraph.*

Topics

• An annoying habit

• The best part of the day

• Night owls versus early birds

• The ideal vacation

• A problem in society

• Expectation versus reality

[103]

Writing formats include business letters, personal letters, notes, instructions, paragraphs, reports, and essays.

The section ends with **peer review** and **editing** of the students' writing.

Review Test

This review section, covering all the grammar structures presented in the part, can be used as a test. An **Answer Key** is provided at the back of the book.

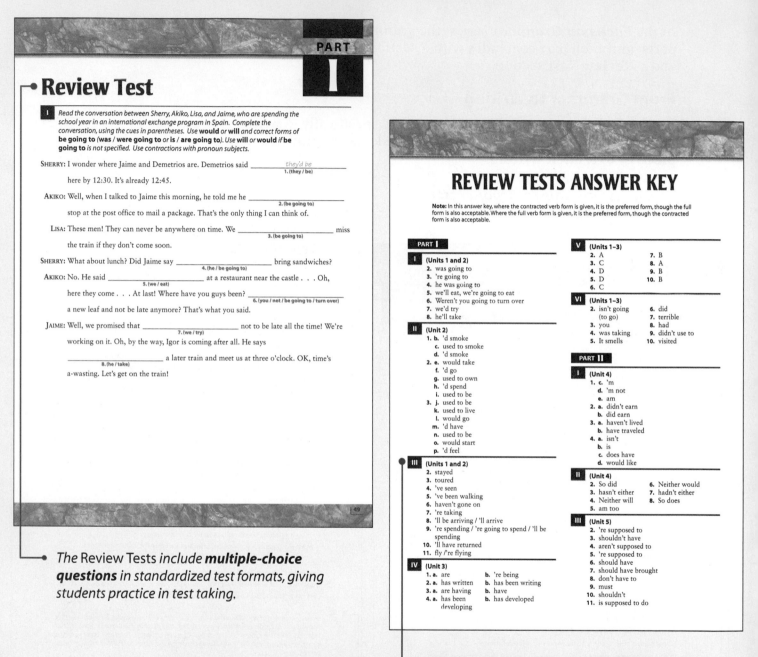

The Review Tests *include **multiple-choice questions** in standardized test formats, giving students practice in test taking.*

The Answer Key to the Review Tests *provides **cross-references** to the appropriate unit(s) for easy review.*

ACKNOWLEDGMENTS

Writing the Third Edition of *Focus on Grammar 5* has been even more interesting and challenging than the first two times. I'm indebted to many people who helped me in different ways. Specifically, though, I want to express my appreciation and gratitude to:

- My students over the years.

- Françoise Leffler, for her excellent editing work in the early stages of the project.

- Marjorie Fuchs, Margo Bonner, Miriam Westheimer, and Irene Schoenberg—the other members of the FOG author team—for their support and encouragement.

- That genius, whoever he or she is, who created the joke about the parrot that has been floating around in cyberspace for some time now. The same for the unknown authors of the bumper stickers.

- Nancy Blodgett and Kathleen Silloway for their expertise in moving the project along.

- Jane Curtis, whose experience and many excellent comments were invaluable in reframing the grammar charts and notes and the From Grammar to Writing exercises. Many thanks.

- Laura Le Dréan, for her confidence and excellent direction of the entire project. Thanks very much.

- John Barnes, my editor, for his patience with me, his excellent eye for detail, and his overall vision. He has been instrumental in making this a better book.

Above all I am grateful to:

- My friends at West Side who have encouraged me.

- My wife Priscilla for her love and wonderful support.

- My best friend.

I am also grateful to the following reviewers:

Mary Ann Archbold, South Bay Adult School, Redondo Beach, CA; **Sheila Badanic,** Douglas College, New Westminister, BC; **John T. Campbell,** Southeast Missouri State University, MO; **Tony Carnerie,** Allaint International University–San Diego, CA; **Amelia Chávez Ruiz,** Lake Forest School, Mexico State, Mexico; **Elizabeth Clemente,** Instituto Tecnológico de Estudios Superiores de Monterrey, Atizapan, Mexico State; **Susanna Eguren,** Instituto Cultural Peruano Norteamericano, Lima, Peru; **Shirley Freeden,** University of Saskatchewan, Saskatoon, Saskatchewan; **Stegan Haag,** Langara College, Vancouver, BC; **Martha Hall,** The New England School of English, Cambridge, MA; **Molly Hashman,** Calgary, AB; **Vicki L. Holmes,** University of Nevada, Las Vegas, NV; **Silvia Icela**

Espinoza Galvez, Colegio Lux, Hermosillo, Sonora; **Elena Lattarulo,** Cuesta College, San Luis Obispo, CA; **Louise Mavalankar,** Truman College, Chicago, IL; **Brian McDonald,** English Language Program, Grossmont College; **Martha McGaughey,** Language Training Institute, NJ; **Myo Myint,** Mission College, Santa Clara, CA; **Georgina Orozco,** Instituto Cumbre, Ciudad Obregón, Sonora; **Kathleen Pierce,** Bell Language School, Brooklyn, NY; **Rhonda Ramirez,** Garland High School, TX; **Ernesto Romo,** Lake Forest School, Mexico State, Mexico; **Fiorilla Ruggiero,** Penn Valley Community College, MO; **Fernando Rujeles,** Centro Colombo Americano, Bogotá, Colombia; **René Sandoval,** Martin Luther King, Jr. School, Guadalajara, Jalisco; **Rusten Seven,** Dokuz Eylul University School of Languages, Izmir, Turkey; **María Elena Vera de la Rosa,** Lake Forest School, Mexico State, Mexico; **Magneli Villanueva Morales,** Universidad Regiomontana, Monterrey, Nuevo León; **Carolyn Vizcaya,** Colegio Villa Rica, Boca del Río, Mexico

CREDITS

Pages 2–3: Based on Rich Beattie, "How to Bargain for Anything . . . Anywhere," *Travel Holiday*, September 1998, pp. 56, 58, 60.

Pages 9–10: David Holmstrom, "This Man's Been Nearly Everywhere." John Clouse. *Christian Science Monitor*, March 10, 1998, p. 1. Copyright 1998. The Christian Science Publishing Society. Reproduced with permission. All rights reserved. For permission to reprint, fax your request to 617-450-2031 or e-mail to copyrt@cps.com.

Pages 16–17: Based on information in "A Match Made in the Mall: Minnesota Anthropology Student Weds Bride Chosen by Family and Friends," *Dallas Morning News*, June 14, 1998, p. 7A, copyright: The Associated Press; "Here Come the Bridal Candidates: Society: Friends of 28-year-old will vote to select his mate. As election day nears, Dad is not so sure of the plan," Home Edition; *Los Angeles Times*, June 8, 1998, p. A-19.

Page 26: Adapted from Phil McCombs, *Washington Post*. In *Lakes Area News*. brainerddispatch.com. Web posted February 24, 2001.

Pages 56–57: Based on "Born First or Last: Does It Matter?" by Carol Kramer, Internet. OCP General Research, http://www.eisa.net.au/-santeri/fbol.html.

Pages 69–70: John Rosemond, "Asian Parents Differ on Childrearing." *Albuquerque Journal*, July 1, 1993. Family psychologist John Rosemond is the author of eight best-selling parenting books and is one of America's most popular speakers. For more information, see his website at www.rosemond.com.

Pages 72–74: Based on information in Rex Shelley, *Culture Shock: Japan* (Portland, OR: Graphic Arts Publishing, 1993).

Page 81: Based on information in Norine Dressler, *Multicultural Manners: New Rules of Etiquette for a Changing Society* (New York: John Wiley & Sons, 1996), pp. 94, 98–99.

Pages 89–90: Based on information in "St. Brendan's Isle," www.castletown.com/brendan.htm and "Who the Heck Did 'Discover' the New World?" by Donald Dale Jackson. *Smithsonian*, September 1991, pp. 76–85.

Pages 98–99: Based on information in David Feldman, *Imponderables: The Solution to the Mysteries of Everyday Life.* (New York: William Morrow, 1986, 1987).

Page 100: For riddle 1: Eric Elfman, *Almanac of the Gross, Disgusting, and Totally Repulsive* (New York: Random House, 1994); for riddles 2 and 3: Louis G. Cowan, *The Quiz Kids, Questions and Answers* (Akron, Ohio: Saalfield Publishing, 1941); for riddle 4: Ann Elwood and Carol Orsag Madigan, *The Macmillan Book of Fascinating Facts* (New York: Macmillan, 1989).

Pages 114–115: Based on Emma Duncan, "A Survey of Food," *The Economist*, December 13, 2003.

Page 121: Charlyn Fargo, "Fusion Cooking Melds Cultures and Tastes," Copley News Service (San Diego, CA), August 5, 1998, p. F5.

Pages 128–129: Based on Jared Diamond, "Twilight at Easter," *The New York Review of Books*, Volume 51, Number 5, March 25, 2004.

Page 134: Some information taken from *The World Almanac and Book of Facts 2004* (New York: World Almanac Education Group, Inc., 2004), pp. 183, 192.

Page 135: Excerpted from "Earthweek: A Diary of the Planet," by Steve Newman, ©Chronicle Features 2004. In *The Seattle Times*, February 27, 2004, p. A3.

Page 149: *The World Almanac and Book of Facts, 2004* (New York: World Almanac Education Group, Inc., 2004), p. 13.

Page 164: Adapted from the introduction to *Appointment in Samarra*, by John O'Hara. New York: Harcourt, Brace, and Company, 1934. Story originally written by W. Somerset Maugham in his play *Sheppey*.

Pages 180–181: Adapted from "What's Your Personality Type?" *New Woman*, August 1998, pp. 68–71, by Barbara Barron-Tieger and Paul D. Tieger, authors of *Do What You Are, Nurture by Nature*, and *The Art of SpeedReading People*.

Pages 206 and 209: *A Beautiful Mind*, copyright © 2002 by Leonard Maltin, from *LEONARD MALTIN'S 2003 MOVIE & VIDEO GUIDE*, by Leonard Maltin. Used by permission of Dutton Signet, a division of Penguin Putnam, Inc.

Pages 220–221: Based on information in Mark McGwire, "15 Minutes of Fame," *Biography Magazine*, September 1998; and Richard Severn, "D. B. Cooper: Perfect Crime or Perfect Folly?" *Seattle Times*, November 17, 1996.

Pages 235–236: Adapted from Patricia Hughes, "The Sacred Rac," in *Focusing on Global Poverty and Development* by Jayne C. Millar (Washington, D.C.: Overseas Development Council, 1974).

Page 250: Adapted from E. Randall Floyd, *Great American Mysteries* (Little Rock: August House Publishers, 1990).

Pages 252: Adapted from Kenneth C. Davis's *Don't Know Much About History?* (New York: Avon Books, 1990), pp. 13–14.

Pages 258–259: Based on Judith Viorst's essay "Friends, Good Friends, and Such Good Friends." in Alfred Rosa and Paul Eschholz, eds., *Models for Writers: Short Essays for Composition*, 3rd ed. New York: St. Martin's Press, 1989.

Pages 317–318: Based on information in Tamim Ansary, "What Makes a Sport Olympic?" www.encnet/features/column/?page=tamimhome.

Page 318, Exercise 4: Alex Salkever, Special to *The Christian Science Monitor*, "When Sports Become Too Extreme," *The Christian Science Monitor*, March 24, 1998, p. 1. Reprinted by permission of the author.

Pages 326–327: Based on information in Brad Darrach, "Journey: A Brave Family Changes Horror into Healing after a Child Dies," *Life*, October 1, 1995, pp. 42+.

Page 333: Sutapa Mukerjee, "A Caring Elephant That Died of Grief," *The Seattle Post-Intelligencer*, May 6, 1999, Copyright: The Associated Press.

Pages 340–341: Based on information in Emily Yoffe, "How Quickly We Forget," *U. S. News & World Report*, October 13, 1997, p. 52.

Pages 364–365: Author unknown. The story is adapted from one that has been circulating on the Internet for a number of years.

Page 372: Includes material adapted from "Humor," *The World Book Encyclopedia*, Volume H. (Chicago: World Book, 1998), pp. 435–436; and "Humour and Wit," *Encyclopedia Britannica*, Macropaedia (Chicago: Encyclopedia, 1998), p. 686.

Page 373: Some items from *Funny Bumper Stickers. The Canonical List of Bumper Stickers.* www.ruighaver.net/bumperstickers/list.htm.

Page 376: David Field, "They Do Have a Sense of Humor," *USA Today*, September 22, 1998. Reprinted with permission.

Pages 378–379: Adapted from Project for Excellence in Journalism, *Five Common Mistakes Journalists Make with Numbers*. Washington, D. C. journalism.org. Web posted October 2002.

PART I

Past, Present, and Future

1 Present and Future Time

Grammar in Context

BEFORE YOU READ

1 *Where do you like to travel?*

2 *Look at the picture. When you travel, do you ever bargain to get a better price?*

3 *Is it fair to try to get a lower price for an item, or is it better to pay the price the seller wants?*

🎧 *Read this article about learning how to bargain.*

WORLD TRAVELER

It's a Bargain!

by Tammy Samuelson

ONE THOUSAND
SIX HUNDRED

In an open-air market in Turkey, a tourist is admiring the beautiful oriental rugs on display. She finds one she likes and asks the price. "One thousand dollars," the vendor says. Knowing she shouldn't pay the full price, she says, "Six hundred!" "Nine hundred!" the vendor counters. The woman throws up her hands in mock frustration and walks away. The vendor goes after her. Not long afterwards, both vendor and buyer agree on eight hundred dollars, a 20 percent reduction. Both vendor and customer are smiling and happy. They've just participated in a ritual that has existed worldwide for centuries.

So you're visiting another country this year? You already have your tickets, and you leave next Tuesday at 4 P.M. A week from now you'll be relaxing in the sunshine or visiting famous landmarks. By the end of the summer, of course, you'll have been traveling for several weeks, and it'll be time to think about bringing back some souvenirs for friends and family. Souvenirs cost money, though, so maybe if you do some bargaining, you'll be able to get some good buys. . . . What? You

WORLD TRAVELER

don't know how to bargain? You're afraid to? Relax. In my capacity as the *Times* travel editor, I've been making trips abroad since 1997, and I've visited 38 countries. I take a trip every year, so bargaining is one thing I've learned to do. In this week's column I'm going to give you some tips on how to perform this most enjoyable activity. Once you learn to bargain, I think you'll like it.

Many people are used to paying fixed prices for items and are reluctant to bargain. Some may be afraid to hurt the vendor's feelings by offering too low a price. Others are afraid of being assertive. Some may even avoid bargaining because they want to give the impression they can afford anything. Bargaining is not too big a deal in some countries, but even in North America a certain kind of bargaining goes on whenever someone goes to a yard or garage sale and tries to get the seller to lower the price. Vendors in much of the world expect you to bargain and will be disappointed if you don't. So here are some bargaining tips.

FIRST TIP Find out how much something is worth. When you bargain with someone, the object of the game is not to beat the vendor. It's to pay a fair price for whatever you want to buy. So do some research. Get a good idea of the general price range for an item. That way you'll be able to bargain with confidence.

OK. You've done your research. You know how much things cost, so you can go shopping.

SECOND TIP Never accept the first offer. You'll make a counter-offer when the vendor says the price. Remember: The vendor expects this.

THIRD TIP Treat the vendor with respect. Keep in mind that the bargaining experience should not be a competition; it should be a game. Stick to your guns, but have fun with the process. If the vendor insists it's impossible to go any lower on the price, show her how much money you have. But be polite.

FOURTH TIP Be prepared to walk away if you don't get a fair price. Don't get angry. Just make it clear you're not going to buy if the vendor doesn't come down. If he doesn't, start to walk away. As soon as you do this, he will most likely come running after you.

THE FINAL TIP Be sure to wear sunglasses. For centuries people of many cultures have regarded the eyes as "the windows of the soul." If you're nervous or intimidated, this will show in your eyes. Wear dark glasses to conceal your anxiety. You'll feel more confident if you do.

Well, have I persuaded you? Do you feel a little more confident, or at least a little less nervous? By the time you get home, you'll have seen a lot of wonderful things. If you haven't bargained, though, you'll have missed out on one of life's most interesting experiences. Give it a try. Have a great trip, and have no fear!

AFTER YOU READ

What does each sentence mean or imply? Circle the correct answer.

1. So you're visiting another country this year?
   a. You're already visiting another country.
   b. You're going to visit another country in the near future.

2. I've been making trips abroad since 1997.
   a. The author certainly won't make any more trips abroad.
   b. The author may make some more trips abroad.

3. When you make it clear you're not going to buy, the vendor will lower the price.
   a. Neither action is in the future.
   b. Both actions are in the future.

Grammar Presentation

PRESENT AND FUTURE TIME

PRESENT TIME: IN GENERAL OR NOW

Simple Present
Tourists often **spend** a lot of money.

Present Progressive
Be + Base Form + *-ing*
A tourist **is looking** for a souvenir.

PRESENT TIME: FROM A TIME IN THE PAST UNTIL NOW

Present Perfect
Have + Past Participle
We **have visited** 11 countries so far.

Present Perfect Progressive
Have been + Base Form + *-ing*
We**'ve been traveling** for three weeks.

FUTURE TIME: A TIME IN THE FUTURE

Simple Future
Will / Be going to + Base Form
You**'ll like** the hotel. You**'re going to like** the hotel.

Future Progressive
Will be + Base Form + *-ing*
A week from now, you**'ll be relaxing** in the sun.

Simple Present
The tour **starts** tomorrow at 4:00 P.M.

Present Progressive
Be + Base Form + *-ing*
We**'re visiting** our friends later this summer.

Two Actions in the Future
I'**ll call** you as soon as we **land**.

Future Perfect
Will have + Past Participle
We'**ll have arrived** by 4:00 P.M.

Future Perfect Progressive
Will have been + Base Form + *-ing*
We **will have been flying** for hours by then.

GRAMMAR NOTES

EXAMPLES

1. Use the **simple present** to show actions, events, or states that are true in general or happen habitually.

   We also use the simple present to narrate events in sequence.

- Vendors **work** long hours. *(true in general)*
- We **spend** every August at the beach. *(habitual)*
- A tourist **finds** a beautiful dress and **asks** how much it costs.

2. Use the **present progressive** to show actions or events that are in progress at the moment (not finished).

   ▶ **BE CAREFUL!** Don't use the progressive with non-action verbs.

- A tourist **is admiring** the rugs. *(right now)*

- She **likes** that rug.
  NOT She's liking that rug.

3. The **present perfect** and the **present perfect progressive** connect the past and the present. Use them to show actions and states that began in the past and continue until now.

   Note that they are often used with *for* + a length of time and *since* + a starting point.

   ▶ **BE CAREFUL!** Don't use the simple present for actions or events that began in the past and are continuing now.

- Bargaining **has existed for** centuries.
- She's **been writing** her travel column **since** 1997.

- I've **been** here for three months now.
  NOT I'm here for three months now.

4. Use the **present perfect**, not the present perfect progressive, to describe completed actions with a connection to the present.

- I've **visited** Italy four times.
  NOT I've been visiting Italy four times.

(continued)

5. Use the **present perfect progressive** to show that an action with a connection to the present is unfinished or temporary.	• They**'ve been touring** Italy. *(They're still touring.)* • He**'s been studying** in Boston but will soon return home.

6. Use *will* or *be going to* to say what you think will happen in the future. ▶ **BE CAREFUL!** Use *will*, not *be going to*, to express an unplanned future action. ▶ **BE CAREFUL!** Use *be going to*, not *will*, to talk about a future situation that is planned or already developing.	• I think I**'ll enjoy** the trip. OR • I think I**'m going to enjoy** the trip. • Call me next week. Maybe I**'ll be** free. NOT Maybe ~~I'm going to~~ be free. • We**'re going to take** our vacation in June this year. NOT ~~We'll take~~ our vacation in June this year.

7. Use *will* in the **progressive** to describe an action that will be in progress at a certain time in the future. **USAGE NOTE:** We often use the **future progressive** informally to talk about a **future intention**.	• Next week at this time we**'ll be climbing** Kilimanjaro. • We**'ll be visiting** Florence on our Italy trip.

8. You can use the **present progressive** to talk about a future action or event that has already been arranged.	• We**'re traveling** to Japan in August. We already have our tickets.

9. You can use the **simple present** to talk about a future action, state, or event that is part of a schedule or timetable.	• We **leave** on Saturday at 8:00 P.M. • The plane **arrives** in Rome at 8:30 A.M.

10. To talk about two separate actions in the future, use *will* or *be going to* in the independent clause and the simple present in the dependent clause.	independent clause dependent clause • We**'ll rent** a car when we **get** to Italy. NOT We'll rent a car when we ~~will get~~ to Italy.

11. Use the **future perfect** to show an action, state, or event that will happen before a certain time in the future.	• By the end of our trip, we**'ll have seen** a lot of wonderful things.
You can also use the future perfect in the **progressive**.	• By the end of the summer, we**'ll have been traveling** for several weeks.
NOTE: We often use the future perfect with *by* and *by the time*.	• *By the time* we finish our trip, we**'ll have visited** 18 countries.

Reference Notes

For definitions and examples of **grammar terms**, see Glossary on page G-1.

For a list of **non-action verbs**, see Appendix 2 on page A-2.

For a list of **non-action verbs sometimes used in the progressive**, see Appendix 3 on page A-3.

For a list of **words that begin dependent clauses**, see Appendix 20 on page A-9.

Focused Practice

1 | DISCOVER THE GRAMMAR

A *Refer to the article and follow the instructions.*

1. Read the first paragraph of the opening reading. Which verbs are used to:

   a. narrate events in sequence?

   b. show an action in progress?

2. In the last line of paragraph 1, what form is the verb phrase "has existed"? Why does the author use that form here?

3. In paragraph 2, the future is expressed in several different ways. Underline the verbs and label the ways.

B *Look at these sentences. Does the underlined verb refer to present time or future time?*

1. A tourist <u>is admiring</u> the beautiful oriental rugs. _____*present*_____

2. A tourist <u>finds</u> a rug she likes. _____

3. She <u>asks</u> the price. _____

4. So <u>you're visiting</u> another country this year. _____

5. You <u>leave</u> next Tuesday at 4:00 P.M. _____

6. When you <u>do</u> some bargaining, you'll get some good buys. _____

7. You'll make a counter-offer when the vendor <u>announces</u> the price. _____

8. After you <u>make</u> it clear you're not going to buy, the vendor will come down. _____

2 | A LETTER HOME

Grammar Notes 1–3, 7

Nancy Osborne is traveling in Europe. Complete her letter to her friend Evelyn with the correct forms of the verbs in the box. Use only the forms presented in this unit. Use a verb more than once if necessary.

be	get	go	love	shine	stay	visit

London Towers Hotel

Sunday, July 19
Hi Evelyn,

   Well, I _____'ve been_____ in London for a week now,
        1.
and the sun _____ every day since I got here.
              2.
What a surprise! I _____ my favorite
                    3.
museums and all the usual attractions—went to the British Museum yesterday

and had such a good time that I _____ again today. Also went
                                  4.
to the Tower of London. I really _____ a kick out of those
                                  5.
guides in their funny hats.

   I _____ in a bed and breakfast that is really nice, but it's
      6.
also pretty expensive, so I _____ to a hostel tonight. I don't
                            7.
think I'll mind staying there, since I don't need luxury.

   The British people _____ so friendly and helpful! And I
                        8.
really _____ the accent.
        9.
   That's it for now. Hope things _____ OK with you. I'll write
                                    10.
again soon.

Best,
Nancy

3 | A WORLD TRAVELER

Read this article about John Clouse. At the time the article was written, Clouse had visited more countries than anyone else in the world. Complete the passage by circling the correct verb forms.

This Man's Been Nearly Everywhere

John Clouse (has) / is having the thickest, most dog-eared passport in the world. Turn
1.

to page 16 of the 1996 *Guiness Book of World Records* and you are going to find / 'll find
2.

the reason. He will hold / holds the record for traveling to all 192 of the globe's inde-
3.

pendent countries, and to all but a few of the other territories that existed in early 1996.

Clouse, who has spent about $1.25 million roaming from A to Z in the past 40 years,

says he travels for the love of it, not to outrun anybody else who may be keeping a list. He

is now down to just three remote islands to visit.

Clouse has continued / continued his journeys since making the record book, and not
4.

only has he visited every country in the world, but some two or three times. Now he

focuses / is focusing on the remaining three islands.
5.

"Yeah, I 've been trying / try to get to three places: one is the Paracel Islands, owned
6.

by China in the South China Sea," he says. "And on two occasions the weather

has kept / has been keeping me from reaching Bouvet, an island in Norwegian Antarctica.
7.

No. 3 is Clipperton, a French island about 700 miles west of Acapulco."

After all his traveling he says / will say, "I don't believe there are evil empires and evil
8.

people. Yes, there are some bad leaders in the world, but seeing people as individuals has

taught me that they are all basically alike. You can be in some terrible place and someone

will extend hospitality to you."

Clouse is traveling / travels light, with a small suitcase, and seldom goes / will go
9.   10.

first class. His collection of *National Geographic* magazines is his source for research.

(continued)

Years ago he stopped taking photos and now <u>has kept / keeps</u> a journal of his travels.

　　　　　　　　　　　　　　　　　　　　　　　　　　11.

He has crossed the Atlantic Ocean at least 100 times, and the Pacific Ocean

40 or 50 times.

Clouse <u>concludes / will conclude</u> that the right attitude is synonymous with the

　　　　　　12.

lightness of his suitcase. "Travel without a lot of mental baggage," he says. "Try not to go

with preconceived notions that the place will be dirty or hostile, and if it is, go with the

flow and make the best of it."

"Learn a few words like *please* and *thank you*," he suggests. "That really

<u>is going to please / pleases</u> people."

　　13.

---

4 | A TRIP TO EAST AFRICA   *Grammar Notes 4–6, 8–10*

Study the Lamonts' itinerary for their trip to East Africa. Then complete the sentences with the correct present or future form of the verbs in parentheses.

East Africa Trip Itinerary

Date	Destination
June 5	Land in Nairobi, Kenya, at 12 noon
June 5–6	Stay in Nairobi; tour the city
June 7	Visit Treetops resort in Kenya; stay the night there
June 8–9	Take the train to Dar Es Salaam, Tanzania; tour the city; travel to Mombasa on the afternoon of June 9; stay there that night
June 10	Tour Mombasa; take the boat to Zanzibar; stay there that night
June 11	Tour Zanzibar; return to Mombasa late afternoon; take the bus to Moshi at 5 P.M.; stay in Moshi that night
June 12–16	Climb Kilimanjaro
June 16	Take the bus to Ngorongoro Crater; stay there that night
June 17	Tour Ngorongoro Crater in a land rover until mid-afternoon
June 17	Stay in Arusha that night
June 18	Take the bus to Nairobi; arrive Nairobi 4 P.M.
June 18	Fly to New York, 9 P.M.

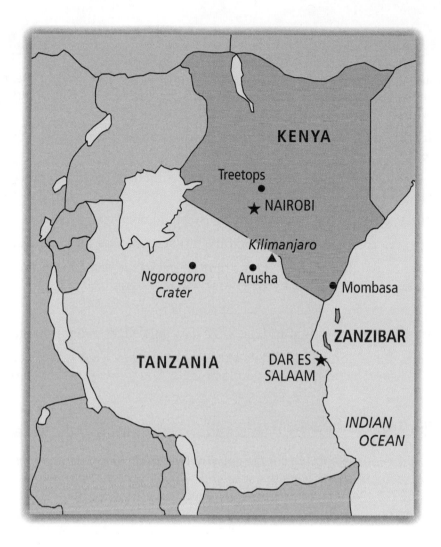

have visited

It is Tuesday, June 11, about 6 P.M. So far, the

Lamonts _____ three large cities:
               1. (visit)

Nairobi, Dar Es Salaam, and Mombasa.

They _____ at a
              2. (also stay)

5 | THE FLEA MARKET

Grammar Notes 6, 10, 11

*Read this dialogue. Number the sentences in the correct order. Then work with a partner to decide which sentences Student A and Student B say. Mark the sentences **A** or **B**. Read the dialogue aloud with your partner.*

_____ Take it easy. We'll be there in a few minutes—as soon as we cross the big bridge coming up. See it?

_____ I'll have a splitting headache by the time we get there if you don't stop complaining. There'll still be some bargains!

_____ Next time you go to the flea market, I'm staying home!

_____ Yes, you are. You're making me nervous. Just stop making all that noise!

_1/A_ Can't you drive a little faster? By the time we get to the flea market, they'll have sold all the best items. Those antique vases I love will be all gone.

_____ Well, excuse me for living! But I'm not complaining!

_____ Yes. But we're *already* an hour late. We'll have missed all the best bargains.

_____ Next time, we're going to leave home two hours earlier. That way, even if we get lost, we'll still have time to get some good bargains. You know how I love to bargain.

6 | BY THIS TIME NEXT YEAR . . .

Grammar Notes 10–11

*Write three sentences about your future plans, using **when** or **after**. Use the simple present and future in these sentences. Then write three sentences about what you will have accomplished by this time next year. Use the future perfect in these three sentences. Share your sentences with a partner.*

Examples: When / After I **graduate** from college, I'll **apply** for a job.

By this time next year, I'll **have traveled** to India.

1. _____

2. _____

3. _____

4. _____

5. _____

6. _____

7 | EDITING

Read this travel log. There are 14 mistakes in the use of present and future verbs. The first mistake is already corrected. Find and correct 13 more.

Travel Log

I am writing these words in English because I need the practice. At this moment I am on an airplane over the Pacific Ocean, on my way to a year of study at Columbia University in the United States. I am looking forward to being there, but I am also a little afraid. What ~~do~~ *will* I find when I will get to America? Will the Americans be arrogant and violent? Will I make any friends? Am I happy?

These were the words I wrote in my diary on the airplane last month. But I'm here for a month now, and I've found that things are a lot different from what I expected. I've found that the majority of people here are friendly. They are going out of their way to help you if you need it.

On television, the news programs are speaking a lot about bad events like accidents, murders, diseases, and fights. But I don't see as much violence in my life as I do on television. I have not been mugged, and I don't worry all the time about my safety.

Two of the ideas I had about the United States, however, will seem to be true. One is that Americans aren't paying much attention to rules. One of my best American friends says, in fact, "Rules are made to be broken." The other idea I had is about the American family. In Asia the family is very important, but some Asian people are thinking that the family is meaning nothing in the United States. I'm not knowing if this is true or not. But I think it might be true, since my American friends almost never are mentioning their parents or their brothers and sisters. Anyway, I am going to have a chance to see a real American family. I go with my roommate Susan to spend Thanksgiving break with her family in Pennsylvania. When I will see her family, I will understand more.

Communication Practice

8 | LISTENING

🎧 *The Foster family is traveling in Canada. Listen to their conversation. Then listen again and mark the sentences* **T** *(true) or* **F** *(false).*

_T_ 1. Tim is still in bed.

_____ 2. The Fosters are going to the mall this morning.

_____ 3. Amy and Tim want to go to the museum.

_____ 4. Dad thinks the children can learn something at the museum.

_____ 5. The Fosters are on the tour bus now.

_____ 6. The Fosters will miss the bus if they don't hurry.

_____ 7. Tim and Amy like tours.

_____ 8. Tim thinks it's important to learn new things.

_____ 9. Amy and Tim would rather go to the museum by themselves than go on a tour.

_____10. The Fosters are going to the mall before they go on the tour.

_____11. The tour will end after 12:30.

9 | SMALL-GROUP DISCUSSION

Work in small groups. Read this quote from "This Man's Been Nearly Everywhere." Do you agree or disagree with Clouse? Why or why not? Give examples from your own experiences to support your viewpoint.

Clouse says, "I don't believe there are evil empires and evil people. Yes, there are some bad leaders in the world, but seeing people as individuals has taught me that they are all basically alike. You can be in some terrible place and someone will extend hospitality to you."

Example: **A:** I disagree with Clouse. I believe there are evil empires and evil people. Maybe there aren't many, but there are some.

B: What's an example of an empire you think is evil?

10 | WRITING

*Write two or three paragraphs on one of the following topics, using present and future
verbs.*

- What is your response to the quote by Clouse in Exercise 9? Give examples from your own experience to support your viewpoint.

- What is your dream vacation?

Example: For most of my life, my idea of a dream vacation has been to visit China. This dream is finally going to come true. I leave next Friday for a two-week trip to China with a group from work. We're going to visit Beijing, Shanghai, and the Great Wall. We're even going to . . .

11 | ON THE INTERNET

Work in small groups. Choose a vacation spot that you might like to visit. Look it up on the Internet and find out a number of facts about it. Then describe your place to the class, describing what you'll do there, but don't say its name. The rest of the class must guess your vacation spot.

2 | Past Time

Grammar in Context

BEFORE YOU READ

1 *What do you think the term "arranged marriage" means?*

2 *Would you rather find your own person to marry or have someone else select that person for you?*

3 *Do you think an arranged marriage is likely to be a happy marriage?*

⌒ *Read this article about an unusual marriage.*

LIFESTYLES

A *Marriage* Made on the *Internet?*

*H*ow many Americans have ever considered asking friends or relatives to select their spouse for them? Not very many, apparently. Yet this is exactly what David Weinlick did.

Weinlick had apparently long been considering marriage and had known for quite some time that he was going to get married in June of 1998. When the wedding would take place and who would be invited he already knew. He just didn't know whom he would be marrying. You see, he hadn't met his bride yet.

It all started some years ago. Friends would repeatedly ask Weinlick, an anthropology student at the University of Minnesota, when he was going to tie the knot. He would say he didn't know. Eventually he got tired of these questions, so he just picked a date out of the blue: June 13, 1998. As this date was getting closer and closer, Weinlick, 28, knew he had to do something. His friend Steve Fletcher came up with the idea of a democratic selection process. Weinlick liked the idea, so he advertised for a bride on the Internet on a Bridal Nomination Committee website.

He created an application form and asked friends and relatives to interview the candidates and select the winner. They did this at a bridal candidate party before the ceremony on the day of the wedding.

Internet *Marriage*

Weinlick's friends and relatives took the request quite seriously. Though Weinlick wasn't sure who his bride would be, he did want to get married. He said he thinks commitment is important and that people have to work at relationships to make them successful. Weinlick's sister, Wenonah Wilms, said she thought that all of the candidates were nice but that she was looking for someone really special. Wilms added that it was important for her brother to marry someone who would fit into family celebrations like at Christmas.

So who won the election? It was Elizabeth Runze, a pharmacy student at the University of Minnesota. Runze hadn't met Weinlick before she picked up a candidate survey on the Monday before the wedding. They talked briefly on that day and again on Tuesday when Runze turned in the completed survey about her career plans and hobbies. However, neither Weinlick nor Runze knew who would ultimately be chosen by Weinlick's friends and family on Saturday, the day of the wedding. After her Saturday selection by the committee, Runze said the day was the most incredible she had ever experienced.

Weinlick was happy too. After the selection, the groom said the plan had turned out almost exactly as he had hoped.

By the time the wedding day arrived, Weinlick had prepared everything: the rings, the musicians, his tuxedo, and the reception afterwards. The two took their vows at the Mall of America in Minneapolis while about 2,000 shoppers looked on from the upper levels of the mall.

Probably few Americans would do what Weinlick and Runze did. There have been reports, however, that the newlyweds are doing well. Weinlick and Runze's union qualifies as an "arranged marriage," a phenomenon that has traditionally not been popular in America. Arranged marriages are common in many other parts of the world, though, or at least they used to be. Maybe they're not such a bad idea.

AFTER YOU READ

Read these pairs of sentences. In each pair of sentences, only one is true. Circle the letter of the true statement.

1. **a.** Weinlick didn't consider marriage for a long time before his wedding.
   b. Weinlick considered marriage for a long time before his wedding.

2. **a.** Weinlick and Runze met for the first time when Elizabeth picked up a candidate survey.
   b. They met several months before the wedding.

3. **a.** Weinlick knew who his bride would be before the day of the wedding.
   b. Weinlick didn't know who his bride would be until the day of the wedding.

Grammar Presentation

PAST TIME

PAST TIME: GENERAL OR SPECIFIC (DEFINITE)

Simple Past
Weinlick **needed** to find a bride. He **advertised** on the Internet.

Past Progressive
Was / Were + Base Form + *-ing*
He **was looking** for someone special.

PAST TIME: NOT SPECIFIC (INDEFINITE)

Present Perfect
Has / Have + Past Participle
The couple **has chosen** the date for the party. They **have** already **sent** the invitations.

PAST TIME: HABITUAL OR REPEATED

Used To + **Base Form**
She **used to be** a pharmacist.

Would + **Base Form**
Some days she **would work** 12 hours.

PAST TIME: BEFORE A TIME IN THE PAST

Past Perfect
Had + Past Participle
He **had met** her before the wedding.

Past Perfect Progressive
Had been + Base Form + *-ing*
He **had been planning** the wedding for months.

PAST TIME: AFTER A TIME IN THE PAST BUT BEFORE NOW ("FUTURE IN THE PAST")

Was / Were Going To + **Base Form**
He knew he **was going to marry** soon.

Would + **Base Form**
He knew when the wedding **would be**.

GRAMMAR NOTES	**EXAMPLES**
1. Use the **simple past** to express an action, event, or state completed at a general or specific time in the past. Remember that many of the most common verbs have irregular past forms and past participles.	• Runze **wanted** to get married. *(general)* • She **filled out** an application form several days before the wedding. *(specific)* • Weinlick and Runze **met** five days before they **got** married.
2. Use the **past progressive** to express an action that was in progress (= not finished) at a time in the past.	• Runze **was studying** pharmacy at the University when she decided to get married.
3. Use the **present perfect** to express an action, event, or state completed at an indefinite time in the past. ▶ **BE CAREFUL!** Don't use the present perfect with a past-time expression. **NOTE:** The simple past is the definite past. The present perfect is the indefinite past. Remember that the present perfect also connects the past and the present. (See Unit 1.)	• How many Americans **have** ever **considered** an arranged marriage? • Weinlick **got married a few years ago**. NOT Weinlick ~~has gotten married~~ a few years ago. • The two **met** on June 8, 1998. • They **have** already **met**. • I **have attended** many weddings since then.
4. Use *used to* + base form to show a habitual action, event, or state that was true in the past but is no longer true. You can also use *would* + base form to express actions or events that occurred regularly during a period in the past. ▶ **BE CAREFUL!** *Used to* and *would* are similar in meaning when they express past actions. However, only *used to* can show past location, state, or possession.	• Kayoko **used to play** tennis a lot. • When we were children, we **would spend** every summer in Maine. • I **used to live** in Chicago. • Sarah **used to be** a marriage counselor. • We **used to have** a summer home. NOT I ~~would live~~ in Chicago. Sarah ~~would be~~ a marriage counselor. We ~~would have~~ a summer home.

(continued)

5. Use the **past perfect** to show an action, event, or state that happened before a certain time in the past.	• By June 13, the family **had interviewed** dozens of candidates.
Use the past perfect with the simple past to show which of two past actions, events, or states happened first. The past perfect is often used with *by the time* and conjunctions such as *when*, *before*, *after*, and *because*.	• **By the time** the wedding day arrived, Weinlick **had prepared** everything. • Weinlick and Runze **had known** each other for five days **when** they got married.
▶ **BE CAREFUL!** In such sentences with *when*, notice the difference in meaning between the **past progressive** and the **past perfect progressive**.	• When I left, it **was snowing**. *(It was still snowing.)* • When I left, it **had been snowing**. *(It had stopped snowing.)*

6. Use the **past perfect progressive** to express an action that was in progress before another past event.	• She **had been working** when she got married.

7. Use *was / were going to / would* + base form to describe an action, event, or state that was planned or expected in the past (before now). Sentences with *was / were going to / would* are sometimes called **future in the past**.	• Weinlick knew that he **was going to get** married on June 13, 1998. • He knew where the wedding **would be**.

Reference Note
For a list of **verbs with irregular past forms and past participles**, see Appendix 1 on page A-1.

Focused Practice

1 | DISCOVER THE GRAMMAR

A 1. *List the simple past irregular verbs in the opening reading. Write the base form of each one next to the past form.*

2. *Find a sentence in the reading that shows two past actions, one happening before the other. What forms are used? Why?*

B *Look at these sentences based on the reading. Write the earlier-occurring action or state on the left and the later-occurring action or state on the right.*

1. Weinlick had known for a long time that he was going to get married on June 13, 1998.

   Weinlick had known for a long time / he was going to get married on June 13, 1998.

2. He just didn't know whom he would be marrying.

3. Friends would repeatedly ask Weinlick when he was going to tie the knot.

4. Runze hadn't met Weinlick before she picked up a candidate survey.

5. By the time the wedding day rolled around, Weinlick had prepared everything.

C *Look at these sentences containing* **would**. *Is the meaning of* **would** *future in the past* **(F)** *or habitual action in the past* **(H)**?

___F___ 1. He already knew when the wedding would be and who would be invited.

_____ 2. He just didn't know who the bride would be.

_____ 3. Friends would repeatedly ask Weinlick when he was going to tie the knot.

_____ 4. He would say he didn't know.

_____ 5. Weinlick's sister added that it was important for her brother to marry someone who would fit in at Christmas.

_____ 6. Neither Weinlick nor Runze knew who would be chosen by his friends and family.

2 | DO OPPOSITES ATTRACT?

Complete this story by circling the correct verb forms.

Ellen Rosetti and Mark Stevens <u>were married</u> / (<u>have been married</u>) for almost
1.
a year now. Their marriage almost <u>didn't happen</u> / <u>wasn't happening</u>, though.
2.
They <u>were meeting</u> / <u>met</u> on a blind date when Ellen's friend Alice <u>had</u> / <u>has had</u>
3. **4.**
two extra tickets for a concert.

At first, Ellen <u>thought</u> / <u>was thinking</u> Mark was the most opinionated man
5.
she'd ever met. A couple of weeks after the concert, Mark <u>called up</u> / <u>was calling</u>
6.
up and <u>had asked</u> / <u>asked</u> Ellen out. Ellen <u>wanted</u> / <u>has wanted</u> to say no, but
7. **8.**
something <u>made</u> / <u>was making</u> her accept. After that, one thing <u>had led</u> / <u>led</u> to
9. **10.**
another. Today Mark says, "Ellen is unique. I <u>'ve never met</u> / <u>didn't meet</u> anyone
11.
even remotely like her."

Ellen says, "At first glance you might have trouble seeing how Mark and I
could be married. In certain ways, we're as different as night and day. I'm an
early bird; he's a night owl. He's conservative; I'm liberal. He <u>was always loving</u> /
12.
<u>has always loved</u> sports and I <u>'ve never been able</u> / <u>was never able</u> to stand them.
13.
I guess you might say we're a case of opposites being attracted to each other."

3 | BEFORE AND AFTER

*Jim Garcia and Mark Stevens both got married fairly recently. Fill in the blanks in their conversation with the correct forms of **used to** or **would** and the verbs in parentheses. Use **would** if possible. If **would** occurs with a pronoun subject, use a contraction.*

MARK: So, Jim, how does it feel to be an old married man? Been about six months, hasn't it?

JIM: Yep. It feels great. It's a lot different, though.

MARK: Yeah? How so?

JIM: Well, I guess I'd say I _____*used to have*_____ a lot more freedom. Like on
  1. (have)

Saturdays, for example. I _____ until 11 or even noon. Then,
  2. (sleep)

when I got up, my buddies and I _____ out for breakfast at a
  3. (go)

restaurant. Now Jennifer and I get up at eight at the latest. She's really an early bird.

And I either make her breakfast or she makes it for me. And then on Saturday nights I

_____ out with the guys and stay out till all hours of the night.
  4. (go)

Now it's just the two of us. Sometimes we go out on Saturday night, and sometimes we

don't.

MARK: Does that bother you?

JIM: You know, it doesn't. Life actually _____ kind of lonely. It's
  5. (be)

not anymore. What about you? Have things really changed?

MARK: They sure have. For one thing, the neighborhood is totally different. Remember the

apartment I _____ in, right north of downtown? Well, Ellen
  6. (live)

and I just bought a house in the suburbs. That's a trip, let me tell you.

JIM: I'll bet.

MARK: Yeah. My weekends _____ my own. I
  7. (be)

_____ all day Saturday working on my car or going mountain
  8. (spend)

biking. Now I have to cut the grass and take care of the yard.

JIM: So would you change anything?

MARK: I sure wouldn't. You know how everyone says how great it is to be single? Well, I

_____ so too. Not now. Now I'd say "been there, done that."
  9. (think)

JIM: Me too. I wouldn't change a thing.

4 | THE REST IS HISTORY

Grammar Notes 1, 5

Complete the story of how Jim Garcia and Jennifer O'Leary got married. Combine each pair of sentences into one sentence. Begin the new sentence with the connecting word or phrase in parentheses. Use the simple past and past perfect.

1. Jim Garcia and Jennifer O'Leary graduated from high school. They knew each other for three years. (when)

   When they graduated from high school, Jim Garcia and Jennifer O'Leary had known each other for

   three years.

2. Jim completed four years of military service, and Jennifer graduated from college. They both returned to their hometown about a year ago. (by the time)

   _____

   _____

3. Jennifer started teaching, and Jim took a job as a computer programmer. They saw each other again. (before)

   _____

   _____

4. Neither went out on any dates. They ran into each other in a drugstore one morning. (when)

   _____

   _____

5. Jim drove to Olson's Drugstore. He woke up with a splitting headache. (because)

   _____

   _____

6. Jennifer's younger sister fell and hurt herself and needed medicine. Jennifer also went to Olson's. (because)

   _____

   _____

7. A week passed. Jim asked Jennifer out on a date. (before)

   _____

   _____

8. Jim and Jennifer dated for three months. They got married. (when)

   _____

   _____

5 | PLANS AND EXPECTATIONS

Grammar Note 6

Before Jim got married, he jotted down some of his plans and expectations, which are given below on the left. Some of them came true, and some didn't. On the right, complete Jim's thoughts now about those plans and expectations. Use the future-in-the-past constructions **was / were going to** *+ base form or* **would** *+ base form.*

Jim's Plans and Expectations	**Jim's Thoughts Now**
1. I think it'll be quite a while before we have any children.	*I thought it would be quite a while* _____ *before we had any children* _____, but that's not true. Our first baby is due in four months.
2. I think I'll probably feel just a little bit trapped.	_____ _____, but I haven't felt that way at all.
3. I think we're going to live in an apartment.	_____ _____, and we do.
4. I expect that there won't be as much money to spend.	_____ _____, but that's not true. Jennifer really knows how to keep our lifestyle economical.
5. I hope that we'll be happy.	_____ _____, and we are. Tremendously.
6. I'm sure that we're going to have a lot of fun together.	_____ _____, and we do. It's a blast.
7. I don't think I'll see as much of my buddies.	_____ _____, and I don't. That's OK, though.
8. I figure that we're going to be taking a lot of trips.	_____ _____, but we haven't taken any yet.

6 | WEINLICK AND RUNZE: AN UPDATE

Grammar Notes 1–5, 7

How are David and Elizabeth Weinlick doing several years after getting married? Read this update. Then answer the questions in complete sentences.

About three years after they got married at the Mall of America in Minneapolis, David and Elizabeth Weinlick's marriage was still going strong. When telephoned in February 2001, David Weinlick was in good spirits and said their marriage was doing wonderfully. He was finishing a student teaching program in a local high school, and Elizabeth had switched to nursing school because she felt she would have more of a chance to help people as a nurse than as a pharmacist. David said they were expecting their first child in June 2001. When called a day later, Elizabeth echoed what David had said, adding that the due date for their first child was June 13, 2001—the third anniversary of their marriage. Both David and Elizabeth stressed that commitment is the thing that makes a marriage work. The feelings came later, they said. "The day we got married we had no relationship. Zero. Nothing!" Elizabeth commented. Feelings of love developed after they got to know each other. Asked how they handle conflict, Elizabeth said, "We laugh." In other words, they don't let conflict develop.

Here's an interesting postscript to their story: It turns out that David's great-grandparents went through a similar situation. His great-grandfather was scheduled to become a missionary in Alaska, but his church felt he would need a wife to stand alongside him in his work. They recommended a woman in New York State who they thought would make him a good wife. The two did in fact get married after a very short courtship. Forty-three years later, David's great-grandparents said they had never regretted the way in which they wed. An observer commented that "many young people today might have happier married lives if they got acquainted more after marriage instead of so much before."

There may well be some truth in this.

1. When David and Elizabeth were telephoned, what occupations were they pursuing?

   _____

2. What did Elizabeth use to do?

   _____

3. Why had she switched career plans?

   _____

4. In what way is David and Elizabeth's situation similar to that of David's great-grandparents?

   _____

   _____

5. Where was David's great-grandfather going to do missionary work?

_____

6. Why did the committee recommend a woman in New York State?

_____

7. What was unusual about the date June 13, 2001?

_____

7 | EDITING

Read Jennifer Garcia's journal entry. There are 11 mistakes in the use of verb constructions. The first mistake is already corrected. Find and correct 10 more.

> May 20
>
>   *have been*
>
>   I just had to write today. It's our six-month anniversary. Jim and I ~~are~~
>
> married six months as of today. So maybe this is the time for me to take
>
> stock of my situation. The obvious question is whether I'm happy I get
>
> married. The answer is "Absolutely." When I remember what my life has
>
> been like before we're getting married, I realize now how lonely I've been
>
> before. Jim is a wonderful guy. Since we both work, we took turns doing the
>
> housework. He's really good about that. When we have been dating, I wasn't
>
> sure whether or not I'll have to do all the housework. But I wasn't having
>
> any reason to worry. Today we split everything 50 / 50. The only complaint I
>
> was having is that Jim snores at night. When I tell him that, he only says,
>
> "Well, sweetie, you snore too." I don't believe it. But if this is our only
>
> problem, I guess we're pretty lucky.
>
>   Well, I would have a long and tiring day, but it's almost over. It's time to go
>
> to sleep.

Communication Practice

8 | LISTENING

🎧 *Read these questions. Listen to the news broadcast. Then listen again and answer each question in a complete sentence containing a past-time verb.*

1. What did Samantha Yang and Darrell Hammer hire Reverend Martinez to do?

   They hired him to marry them while they were

   parachute jumping from a plane.

2. To date, how many jumps have Samantha and Darrell each made?

   _____

   _____

3. How long have they been members of the jumping group?

   _____

   _____

4. How were they originally going to get married?

   _____

   _____

5. Why did they decide not to do this? (first reason)

   _____

   _____

6. Why did they decide not to do this? (second reason)

   _____

   _____

7. Had Reverend Martinez ever done this kind of wedding before?

   _____

   _____

UNUSUAL WEDDINGS

9 | INFORMATION GAP: BETTER THAN IT USED TO BE

Work with a partner to complete the text. Each of you will read a version of the same story. Each version is missing some information. Take turns asking your partner questions to get the missing information.

Student A, read the story about Jack Strait. Ask questions and fill in the missing information. Then answer Student B's questions.

Student B, turn to page 32 and follow the instructions there.

Example: **A:** What kind of company did he use to work for?
B: He used to work for a large, impersonal company. How long would he stay on the road?
A: He would stay on the road for two or three weeks at a time.

Jack Strait's life is quite different now from the way it used to be. He used to work for _____ company. His job required him to do a lot of traveling. He would stay on the road for two or three weeks at a time. It was always the same: As soon as he pulled into a town, he would look for _____. The next morning he'd leave his business card at a lot of different establishments, hoping that someone would agree to see him. If he'd been lucky enough to arrange an appointment in advance, he'd show them _____. Occasionally they would buy something; most often they wouldn't.

Jack's marriage began to suffer. He missed his wife a lot, but there wasn't much he could do about the situation. And when he was on the road, he hardly ever saw his children. He would try to call them _____ if he had a spare moment, but usually it was so late that they had already gone to bed. They were growing up without him. Finally, his wife laid down the law, saying, "Why should we even be married if we're never going to see each other?" Jack decided she was right. He took a risk. He quit his job and started his own business. Things were difficult at first, but at least the family was together.

That was five years ago. Things have changed a lot since then. Jack and his family used to live in a small apartment. Now they own a house. Life is good.

Compare your story with your partner's. Are they the same? Now discuss these questions: What did Jack's occupation use to be? Is it important to take risks in life as Jack did? Can you think of an example of a risk you have taken in your life?

10 | PICTURE DISCUSSION

With a partner, discuss the picture. Describe the situation. What is happening?
Approximately how long do you think these people have been married? Do you think their
relationship is less interesting or satisfactory than it used to be, or is it just different?
Present your opinions to the class.

11 | WRITING

Choose one of the following topics and write two or three paragraphs about it.

1. Describe a situation that has turned out differently from what you expected—for example, a marriage or other relationship, or college plans. First talk about what you thought would happen; then talk about what actually happened.

2. Did marriages use to be arranged in your culture or a culture you are familiar with? How would young people meet their mates when your parents or grandparents were young? Ask an older person you know about the situation.

Example: I've been happily married for some time now, but when I was introduced to the man who is now my husband, it never occurred to me that we would end up husband and wife. In fact, when I met Dave, I thought he was the most arrogant man I had ever met. Here's how it happened . . .

12 | ON THE INTERNET

Use the Internet to find five interesting statistics about marriage. Share your information with the class.

Examples: • the country with the highest percentage of married adults

• the country with the lowest percentage of married adults

• the longest marriage on record

INFORMATION GAP FOR STUDENT B

Student B, read the story about Jack Strait. Answer Student A's questions. Then ask your own questions and fill in the missing information.

Example: **A:** What kind of company did he use to work for?
B: He used to work for a large, impersonal company.
How long would he stay on the road?
A: He would stay on the road for two or three weeks at a time.

Jack Strait's life is quite different now from the way it used to be. He used to work for a large, impersonal company. His job required him to do a lot of traveling. He would stay on the road for _____. It was always the same: As soon as he pulled into a town, he would look for a cheap motel to stay in. The next morning he'd leave _____ at a lot of different establishments, hoping that someone would agree to see him. If he'd been lucky enough to arrange an appointment in advance, he'd show them his samples. _____ they would buy something; most often they wouldn't.

Jack's marriage began to suffer. He missed his wife a lot, but there wasn't much he could do about the situation. And when he was on the road, he hardly ever saw his children. He would try to call them _____ if he had a spare moment, but usually it was so late that they had already gone to bed. They were growing up without him. Finally, his wife laid down the law, saying, "Why should we even be married if we're never going to see each other?" Jack decided she was right. He took a risk. He quit his job and started his own business. Things were difficult at first, but at least the family was together.

That was five years ago. Things have changed a lot since then. Jack and his family used to live _____. Now they own a house. Life is good.

Compare your story with your partner's. Are they the same? Now discuss these questions: What did Jack's occupation use to be? Is it important to take risks in life as Jack did? Can you think of an example of a risk you have taken in your life?

Simple and Progressive: Action and Non-Action Verbs

Grammar in Context

BEFORE YOU READ

1 *What are some benefits that technology provides us? Write down several.*

2 *What are some problems caused by technology?*

Read this article about the effects of technology on our lives.

TRENDS MAGAZINE

What Is Technology Doing to Us?

Technology is such a major part of our lives today that it's difficult to think of life without its products. Where would we be without such things as cell phones, CD players, automobiles, and computers? There's no doubt that technology serves us and enriches our lives. The trouble is, technology has a downside also. Are there ways to gain the benefits of technology without being at the mercy of it? Let's look at the pros and cons of three technological products.

The telephone

Pros: Since its invention in 1876, the telephone has become more important to people's lives with each passing year. It's hard to imagine life without it, as we learn when we move and don't have phone service for a day or two. The telephone is just about everywhere these days. If we want to go to a popular movie but are afraid it will be sold out when we get to the theater, all we have to do is call in advance and order tickets. Telephones save lives;

if there's an emergency, we call 911. The telephone allows us to stay in touch with people who live on the other side of the street, the country, or the world.

Cons: Consider the cell phone; it's a wonderful technological product. We carry a cell phone with us in case our car breaks down. We use it to talk with our friends at our convenience and to take care of business matters when we can't get to a regular phone. But the downside is that cell phones can be troublesome and even dangerous. Increasingly these days, teachers are having problems with students who

(continued)

bring cell phones to class and insist on using them. Teachers try to prohibit cell phone use in class, but students feel strongly about their right to use their cell phones, and school districts are often reluctant to forbid them. Much more significantly, many serious and even fatal accidents are caused by people talking on their cell phones while driving. A few cities and states have passed laws against using hand-held devices in cars, but they are few and far between.

The automobile

Pros: As with the telephone, there are countless benefits of cars. Let's assume you just bought a new one, and today you're driving it for the first time. Everyone says it looks good, and you're discovering that it performs beautifully. It takes you places speedily. It gives you freedom and mobility. Together with the telephone, it can save a life if someone is in an accident or is sick and has to get to a hospital quickly. It allows you to go places at speeds undreamed of in the past. This week you're working at a job that is far from your home, but your car will get you there fast. And the manufacture of cars provides millions of jobs worldwide.

Cons: The automobile is a victim of its own success because almost everyone wants one. It does its job so well that cars are everywhere—and that's the problem. We have built freeways to handle the steadily increasing traffic generated by the car's popularity. As soon as a new freeway is built or lanes are added to an existing freeway, however, traffic simply increases to the point that it often takes longer to get somewhere by freeway than on city streets. There are other negatives: Cars are the major cause of air pollution, and each year in the United States over 40,000 people are killed in auto accidents—more than from diseases such as kidney failure.

The computer

Pros: We live in the Information Age, and the computer is the key element of it. Let's say you have a new computer, and you love it. The music you listen to on it sounds wonderful. Your computer gives you access to the world: you e-mail your friends, do research on the Internet, create documents and edit them easily, check up on sports scores, and read news articles without even having to subscribe to a daily paper. What a marvelous

invention technology has provided us. How could we do without it?

Cons: Yesterday your computer was working fine, but today it's being difficult. You don't know much about fixing computer problems, so you call for technical support. The technician determines that you have two computer viruses. You download and install anti-virus protection, and everything is fine for a while. It's a good thing, because you're working at home today. But you've also agreed to take a friend to a doctor's appointment, and you're printing a document to take along and work on. You have just enough time to print the document and jump into the car, but the printer chooses this moment to stop functioning. By the time you've figured out how to fix the printer and you pick up your friend, you're late. You feel bad about this, but what can you do?

Technology is so important that our world would have difficulty surviving without its constant advances. If a technological product is there, people will use it. Our problem is over-dependence on it. We need to learn how to use technology moderately, and we'll explore ways of doing that in next month's issue.

AFTER YOU READ

What does each sentence mean? Circle the correct answer.

1. Your car performs beautifully.
   a. It does a good job.
   b. It looks beautiful.

2. You feel bad about getting your friend to the appointment late.
   a. You're unhappy about this.
   b. You're ill because of this.

3. Your computer is being difficult today.
   a. It is difficult for you to understand how to use it.
   b. Your computer is not doing what you want it to do.

Grammar Presentation

ACTION AND NON-ACTION VERBS

Action Verbs	
Simple Form	**Progressive Form**
They normally **drive** to work.	Today they**'re taking** the bus.

Most Non-Action Verbs
Simple Form
People **know** he is a good employee. They **want** to understand his problem. This building **belongs** to the company.

Some Non-Action Verbs	
Simple Form (Stative Use)	**Progressive Form (Active Use)**
I **have** a new cell phone. She **appears** very happy about the job. They **think** they need a new car.	I**'m having** problems with it. She is **appearing** in a new play. Please don't bother me; I'm **thinking**.

Action Verbs
+ Adverb
He **works constantly**. The computer **is working well** today.

(continued)

Some Non-Action Verbs	
+ Adjective (Stative Use)	**+ Adverb (Active Use)**
Your car **looks good**.	He **looked thoughtfully** at the message.
The soup **tastes delicious**.	You should **taste** that **carefully**—it's hot!
She **feels bad** about what she said.	The doctor **felt** the bruise **gently**.

THERE + BE

Simple Form
There were many requests for a new version.
There are some problems with the invention.
There won't be an alternative technology.
There appears to be a need for a simple device.

GRAMMAR NOTES

EXAMPLES

1. Action verbs describe actions. Use **simple** verb forms (without *-ing*) to describe all of an action—the action in general. Use **progressive** verb forms (with *-ing*) to describe part of an action—in progress at a specific time.	• Computers **perform** tasks quickly. • Martha **works** for a high-tech company. • The mechanic **is fixing** my car.

2. Non-action verbs describe states, such as appearance *(seem)*, emotions *(love)*, mental states *(know)*, perceptions *(hear)*, possession *(own)*, and wants *(need)*. They are often called **stative** verbs. These verbs are generally used in the simple form and not in the progressive. Some stative verbs can be used to describe either states or actions. When they are used to describe actions, they usually have different meanings.	• The boss **seems** angry. • I **know** my co-workers very well. • Sam **owns** three cell phones. • We **need** a new car. NOT We ~~are needing~~ a new car. • People **are** basically equal, or should **be**. *(a state)* • The children **are being** difficult today. *(an action—behaving)* • I **see** what you mean. *(a state—understand)* • Two of my co-workers **are seeing** each other. *(an action—dating)*

3. We normally use adverbs with **action verbs**. Remember that many adverbs end in **-ly**. There are a few irregular adverbs such as *well*, *hard*, and *fast*.	• Bill always **drives carefully**. • The children **speak** Chinese **well**. • Sarah **works hard**.

4. We normally use the verbs *look*, *sound*, *feel*, *smell*, and *taste* to show states, in which case they are used with adjectives, not adverbs. ▶ **BE CAREFUL!** These verbs are sometimes used to show actions, in which case they are used with adverbs. When they are used to describe actions, these verbs usually have different meanings.	• Sarah **doesn't look good** today. Is she depressed? • Your idea **sounds good** to me. • I don't **smell well** when I have a cold. *(an action—using one's nose).* • The fire alarm **sounded** a warning **loudly**. *(an action—making a noise).*

5. To show the existence of something, we often use *there* + *be*. The verb can be past, present, or future. **NOTE:** *There* is used with simple, not progressive, verb forms. Verbs like *seem* and *appear* can also be used with *there*. ▶ **BE CAREFUL!** The verb in a *there* construction agrees in number with the noun following it.	• **There was** no other option. • **There won't be** anywhere to park. • **There seems** to be a problem with the TV. • **There have been** several accidents here. • NOT ~~There's been~~ several accidents here.

Reference Notes
For a list of **non-action verbs**, see Appendix 2 on page A-2.
For a list of **non-action verbs sometimes used in the progressive**, see Appendix 3 on page A-3.

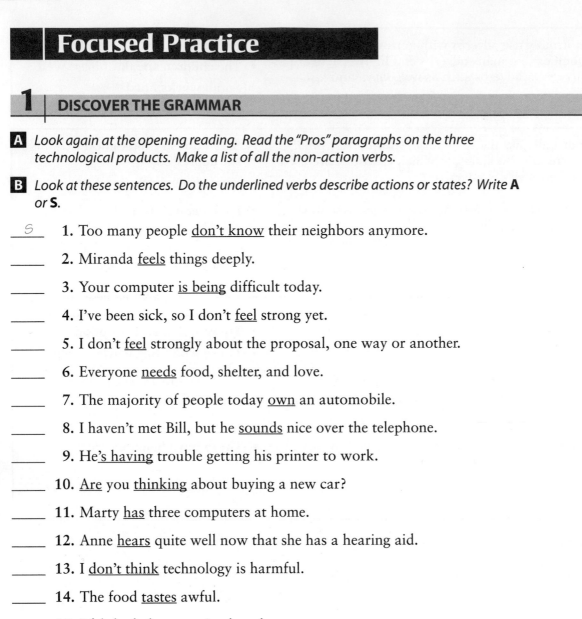

Focused Practice

1 | DISCOVER THE GRAMMAR

A *Look again at the opening reading. Read the "Pros" paragraphs on the three technological products. Make a list of all the non-action verbs.*

B *Look at these sentences. Do the underlined verbs describe actions or states? Write **A** or **S**.*

___S___   **1.** Too many people <u>don't know</u> their neighbors anymore.

_____   **2.** Miranda <u>feels</u> things deeply.

_____   **3.** Your computer <u>is being</u> difficult today.

_____   **4.** I've been sick, so I don't <u>feel</u> strong yet.

_____   **5.** I don't <u>feel</u> strongly about the proposal, one way or another.

_____   **6.** Everyone <u>needs</u> food, shelter, and love.

_____   **7.** The majority of people today <u>own</u> an automobile.

_____   **8.** I haven't met Bill, but he <u>sounds</u> nice over the telephone.

_____   **9.** He<u>'s having</u> trouble getting his printer to work.

_____   **10.** <u>Are</u> you <u>thinking</u> about buying a new car?

_____   **11.** Marty <u>has</u> three computers at home.

_____   **12.** Anne <u>hears</u> quite well now that she has a hearing aid.

_____   **13.** I <u>don't think</u> technology is harmful.

_____   **14.** The food <u>tastes</u> awful.

_____   **15.** I <u>felt</u> bad about getting here late.

C *Look again at the reading. Underline the six sentences that use* there *to show existence.*

2 | STATEMENTS WITH ACTION AND NON-ACTION VERBS   *Grammar Notes 2–3*

Complete these statements with a non-action verb in the simple present or an action verb in the present progressive. Use the verbs in the box.

be	have	hear	see	smell	taste	think

1. Some consider the computer to be a machine that _____*thinks*_____.

2. People who are dating are said to be _____ each other.

3. One _____ with one's nose.

4. One _____ with one's eyes.

5. The bald eagle is a large North American bird that _____ a white head and neck.

6. One _____ with one's ears.

7. A person who _____ is using his or her brain.

8. One _____ primarily with one's tongue.

9. That child _____ normally well-behaved.

10. But at the moment, he _____ difficult and causing lots of trouble.

11. Your day has gone badly so far; you _____ a bad day.

3 | EFFECTS OF TECHNOLOGY   *Grammar Note 3*

Complete these sentences about the effects of technology. Use adverbs with action verbs and adjectives with non-action verbs. Circle the correct word.

1. Freeways throughout the world look (similar) / similarly.

2. Democracy gives us the opportunity to use technology free / freely.

3. In theory, technology helps us to perform tasks simple / simply.

4. Technology allows food to be prepared and distributed rapid / rapidly.

5. An attraction of fast food is that it smells and tastes good / well.

6. Technology has many benefits. Eyeglasses help people see clear / clearly.

7. Hearing aids help people hear good / well.

8. Computers help people communicate quick / quickly.

9. Freeways are designed to help drivers get places easy / easily.

10. Unfortunately, they also cause people to feel angry / angrily when they're stuck in traffic.

4 | THE WORLD: PAST, PRESENT, AND FUTURE

Grammar Note 4

Look at the chart. Write a sentence using **there** *(meaning existence) plus the time word to describe each phenomenon. Make the sentences negative if it is logical to do so. Use the correct form.*

Phenomenon	Time
1. taxes	always
2. complete peace in the world	never
3. between 200 and 300 million people on the Earth	in 1 A.D.
4. automobiles	after 1910
5. television	before 1920
6. humans on other planets	now
7. deaths from smallpox	before the 20th century
8. personal computers	before 1950
9. DVD players	since the 1990s
10. just under 8 billion people on the Earth	by 2025

1. *There have always been taxes.*

2. _____

3. _____

4. _____

5. _____

6. _____

7. _____

8. _____

9. _____

10. _____

5 | **A PERSONAL INVENTORY**   *Grammar Notes 2–4*

Complete each sentence according to your own experience. Use adjectives or adverbs, depending on the type of verb.

1. do / bad / on written tests

   I do badly on written tests.

2. play / a sport / good

   _____

3. a food / taste / good

   _____

4. feel / bad / when

   _____

5. do / good / in / a school subject

   _____

6. feel / strong / about

   _____

7. look / good in / a color

   _____

8. a vacation / sound / interesting

   _____

9. something / smell / awful

   _____

10. a place / look / beautiful

   _____

6 | EDITING

Read this student essay. There are 13 mistakes in the use of verbs, adjectives, and adverbs.
The first mistake is already corrected. Find and correct 12 more.

No Cell Phone Restrictions!

It seems ~~It's seeming~~ that I constantly hear the same thing: "Cell phones are dangerous. We're needing to severely restrict them. People are dying because of cell phones." Well, I'm thinking cell phones themselves aren't the problem. I'm completely opposed to restrictions on them, and here's why.

First, people say cell phones are dangerous to health, so they should be limited. Supporters of this idea ~~say~~ *are saying* there are being studies showing that cell phones produce radiation that is harmful to users. I ~~think~~ *thinks* this is nonsense. There ~~hasn't been~~ *haven't being* any real proof. It's ~~sounding~~ *sound* like just another study that ultimately isn't meaning anything.

Second, a lot of teachers are proposing that we *are* not allow cell phones in classes because they're a ~~distraction~~ *distracting/ning.* I feel pretty ~~angrily~~ *angry* about this. Here's a good example. Two weeks ago in my history class, one of the students ~~was having~~ *had* her cell phone on because her mother was really sick and might need a ride to the hospital. The student's mother couldn't contact anyone else. In fact, the student's mother did call, and the student found someone to help her mother. What if her cell phone ~~hadn't~~ *hasn't* been on? The teacher would have felt pretty badly.

Third, people argue that *are* using a cell phone while driving is dangerous. I *m* disagree. It's no more ~~dangerously~~ *dangerouse* than turning on the car radio or eating a sandwich. People do those things when they *are* drive *ing.* The law says *m* you must have one hand on the steering wheel. It's possible to use a cell phone correct with one hand. I ~~use~~ *am using* my cell phone careful; I *carefully* always keep *keeping* one hand on the wheel. Maybe there *s* should be training in ways to use a cell phone *am* good, but we shouldn't prohibit using cell phones in *the* cars.

This has always been a free country. I hope it stays *s* that way.

Communication Practice

7 | LISTENING

🎧 *Read these questions. Listen to the conversation. Then listen again and answer the questions in complete sentences.*

1. How are things going for Mary?

Things aren't going well for her.

2. What kind of problem is Mary having?

3. What is wrong?

4. What is this a good example of?

5. How much money is involved?

6. How did this probably happen?

7. When are people supposed to report problems like this?

8. When did Mary report the problem?

9. Why?

10. According to Jim, what is the downside of the Internet?

8 | SMALL-GROUP DISCUSSION

Look at the chart. Fill it out for yourself, adding two other inventions not mentioned. Then discuss your answers in a small group. Talk about which inventions are important for your life and which are not. Share your conclusions with the class.

Example:
A: I have a good bicycle, but it's not really important in my life.
B: Why not?
A: Well, it works well, and it's a great way to exercise, but I seldom ride it.
C: Why don't you ride it more often?
A: It's too dangerous because there aren't any bike trails in my neighborhood.

Invention	Have one	Don't want one	Works well	Often use it	Seldom use it	Pros	Cons
bicycle	✓		✓		✓	great way to exercise	too dangerous
car							
TV set							
dishwasher							
cell phone							
computer							
other							
other							

9 | WRITING

What do you consider the most important invention of the last 200 years? Write two or three paragraphs about it, explaining your choice. Talk about the invention's benefits and disadvantages. Use one of these topics or develop your own.

the airplane	the automobile	the computer	photography	television

Example: In my opinion, the most important invention in the last 200 years is the automobile. It's obvious that cars have changed the way people live. They have created jobs. They've given us mobility and freedom. They've changed the way towns and cities are built. . . .

10 | ON THE INTERNET

 Look at the following list of inventions. When were they invented? By whom? Use the Internet to find the answers. Compare your answers with those of the rest of the class.

the bicycle	the microscope	the telescope	the VCR	the X-ray machine

From **Grammar** to **Writing**
The Sentence

In formal English a sentence must have a subject and a verb that shows person, number, and time. Only one type of sentence has no subject: an imperative sentence. In imperative sentences, the subject *you* is understood.

Word groups that contain a subject or a verb but are not sentences are called **fragments**.

Look at the sentences. The complete subjects are underlined once and the complete verbs twice.

Examples: Sherry and her friends are students.

They are spending a year studying in Spain in an exchange program.

All of the students in the program arrived a month ago.

Most of them will stay for the entire year.

Sherry's sister Martha has received three letters from her.

The letters were written over a period of three months.

Write soon.

Are exchange programs good learning experiences?

These word groups are fragments:

Sherry sitting and writing a letter. (no verb)

Were taking the train to Barcelona. (no subject)

Such an exciting year. (no subject or verb)

1 On the line below each of the word groups, write **sentence** if the group is a sentence. If the word group is not a sentence, write **fragment** and explain why by writing **no subject**, **no verb**, or **no subject and no verb**.

1. Sherry at the library doing research.

fragment—no verb

2. All afternoon.

_____

3. Akiko and Lisa were at home.

_____

4. Has been an exciting year.

_____

5. A worthwhile experience meeting students from many nations.

_____

6. They would do it again.

_____

7. Akiko waiting at the bottom of the stairs.

_____

8. Think about this question.

_____

2 | *Read the description of a trip to Barcelona. There are eight sentences and eight groups of words that are not sentences. Underline the eight sentences.*

In late December. Sherry, Akiko, and Lisa took a one-day trip to Barcelona. Not knowing anyone there. They stayed in a youth hostel for a very reasonable price. On their one day in the city. They visited the Sagrada Familia, Gaudí's famous church. All three girls were impressed by the church's beauty. And decided to climb to the top instead of taking the elevator. Nearing the top, Akiko began to feel dizzy and had to start down again. Sherry and Lisa continued climbing. However, even Sherry, who had done a great deal of mountain climbing in Canada. Felt nervous and unprotected at the summit. Both she and Lisa agreed that the view was magnificent. And the climb well worth it. The three decided to return to Barcelona. As soon as they could.

Now rewrite the paragraph, eliminating all the word groups that are not sentences by combining them as necessary.

The first word of a sentence begins with a capital letter. A sentence ends with some punctuation, most commonly a period. Question marks are used at the end of direct questions. Exclamation points are placed at the end of sentences that express very strong feelings. Commas are used within sentences to show short pauses or to separate single things in a list or parts of a sentence.

capital (upper-case) letter	T	question mark	?
small (lower-case) letter	t	exclamation point	!
period	.	comma	,

Examples: They met in Spain.

Who knows the answer?

Leave me alone or I'll call the police!

She visited Singapore, Malaysia, and Thailand.

In late August, he got a new job.

French food is very delicious, and it is known all over the world.

3 | *Read this description of an experience in Morocco. It contains 16 sentences. Find the sentences and insert initial capitalization and end punctuation in the appropriate places. Do not add or eliminate any commas.*

last summer when my wife and I were traveling in Morocco, we had one of the most interesting bargaining experiences ever. we were in an open-air market in Rabat, and I really wanted to buy a Moroccan *jellaba*, a long, heavy, ankle-length garment there were several different shops where jellabas were sold, but Heather and I were drawn to one shop in particular I tried one jellaba on it fit perfectly, and I knew it was the one I wanted, so I asked the merchant how much it was he said it was $200 now I've always been uncomfortable about bargaining, so I was ready to pay his price Heather took me aside, however, and said that was too much and that he expected me to bargain when I said I couldn't bargain, she told me that bargaining was part of the game and that I should offer him less I sighed, tried to swallow the lump in my throat, and suggested $100 he smiled and asked for $150, whereupon I offered $110 he looked offended and shook his head Heather grabbed my hand and we started walking away I thought that was going to be the end of the experience, but then the merchant came running after me, saying he'd accept $125 I ended up buying the jellaba for that amount, and I still have it since then I've never been afraid to bargain

4 | *Write two paragraphs about an experience you have had while traveling. Be careful to avoid sentence fragments. Then work with a partner. Your partner will check your paragraph, and you will check your partner's. Try to discover and correct any fragments.*

Review Test

I *Read the conversation between Sherry, Akiko, Lisa, and Jaime, who are spending the school year in an international exchange program in Spain. Complete the conversation, using the cues in parentheses. Use **would** or **will** and correct forms of **be going to** (**was / were going to** or **is / are going to**). Use **will** or **would** if **be going to** is not specified. Use contractions with pronoun subjects.*

SHERRY: I wonder where Jaime and Demetrios are. Demetrios said _____*they'd be*_____
1. (they / be)

here by 12:30. It's already 12:45.

AKIKO: Well, when I talked to Jaime this morning, he told me he _____
2. (be going to)

stop at the post office to mail a package. That's the only thing I can think of.

LISA: These men! They can never be anywhere on time. We _____ miss
3. (be going to)

the train if they don't come soon.

SHERRY: What about lunch? Did Jaime say _____ bring sandwiches?
4. (he / be going to)

AKIKO: No. He said _____ at a restaurant near the castle . . . Oh,
5. (we / eat)

here they come . . . At last! Where have you guys been? _____
6. (you / not / be going to / turn over)

a new leaf and not be late anymore? That's what you said.

JAIME: Well, we promised that _____ not to be late all the time! We're
7. (we / try)

working on it. Oh, by the way, Igor is coming after all. He says

_____ a later train and meet us at three o'clock. OK, time's
8. (he / take)

a-wasting. Let's get on the train!

II *Read the conversations. Fill in the blanks with the correct forms of the words in parentheses. Use* **would** *if possible; otherwise, use* **used to**. *Use contractions with pronoun subjects.*

1. A: You _____*used to smoke*_____, didn't you?
a. (smoke)

 B: Yeah, sometimes I _____ after meals, but I quit six months ago.
b. (smoke)

 A: Good. I _____ too. It was terrible. When I was a serious smoker, I
c. (smoke)

 _____ two packs a day. I'm glad I stopped.
d. (smoke)

2. A: When I was a child, my family spent every summer at a lake in the mountains. We kids

 _____ a hike every morning. In the afternoon, we
e. (take)

 _____ swimming.
f. (go)

 B: Yeah, our summers were like that too. My parents _____ a cottage
g. (own)

 on the beach. They sold it after we grew up, but when I was a kid, we

 _____ every July there. Ah, those were the good old days! Life
h. (spend)

 _____ carefree. Now it's just hectic.
i. (be)

3. A: Did you play many sports when you were growing up?

 B: Well, I _____ an avid softball player when I was in elementary
j. (be)

 school. There was a park near where we _____, and the kids from
k. (live)

 my neighborhood _____ there almost every weekend from May to
l. (go)

 October.

 A: How about high school?

 B: I was on the football team. I remember how tough the practices were.

 A: How so?

 B: We _____ daily practices in the summer before the fall season, and
m. (have)

 it _____ really hot. Not only that, but practices
n. (be)

 _____ at 6:30 in the morning, so we _____
o. (start)   p. (feel)

 really tired when we began and even worse when we finished.

 A: Well, I never had to worry about the heat; my sport was ice hockey!

III *Read the itinerary for the Mendozas' Italian tour. Today is the morning of July 20. Fill in the blanks with the correct forms of the verbs in parentheses. Use negative forms where necessary.*

Fred and Alice Mendoza	**Itinerary**	Italy Trip, July 15–23

Date	Destination
July 15	Arrive at Rome airport; check in at hotel in Rome
July 16	Tour Vatican City, including Sistine Chapel
July 17	Day trip to Pompeii; return to Rome to spend night
July 18	Visit other attractions in Rome: Colosseum, Forum, Trevi Fountain; stay in Rome that night
July 19	Take train to Venice; arrive in Venice late afternoon
July 20	Take walking tour of Venice, morning; go on gondola ride, afternoon; tour St. Mark's Cathedral; take evening train to Florence; arrive early morning
July 21	Tour Florence
July 22	Another day touring Florence; late afternoon: take train to Pisa; spend night there
July 23	Tour Pisa; return to Rome late afternoon; take 11:00 P.M. flight home

1. The Mendozas ___*have been*___ in Italy since the night of July 15.
   (be)

2. They _____ the first four nights in Rome.
   (stay)

3. On their first full day in Rome, they _____ Vatican City.
   (tour)

4. Since touring the Vatican, they _____ Pompeii, the Colosseum, the Forum, the
   (see)

   Trevi Fountain, and some of Venice.

5. Right now it's 11:00 A.M. They _____ around Venice since 9:00 this morning.
   (walk)

6. They _____ on a gondola ride yet.
   (go)

7. Tonight they _____ the train to Florence.
   (take)

8. They _____ in Florence early tomorrow morning.
   (arrive)

9. They _____ two days in Florence and one night in Pisa.
   (spend)

10. By the evening of July 23, they _____ to Rome.
    (return)

11. They _____ home at 11:00 P.M. on the 23rd.
    (fly)

IV *Look at the pictures. Complete each pair of sentences. Use a simple verb form in one sentence and a progressive verb form in the other. Use the verbs develop, taste, be, have, and write.*

1. Mr. Schoenberg's students _____ usually well
   _{a.}
   behaved. Today, for some reason, they _____
   _{b.}
   difficult.

2. Amy Tanaka is a novelist. She _____ five
   _{a.}
   novels already. She _____ a sixth novel since
   _{b.}
   last October and expects to complete it in July.

3. The employees of Excelsior Computer _____
   _{a.}
   their annual holiday party this evening. They always

   _____ it sometime in December.
   _{b.}

4. Excelsior Computer _____ an amazing new
   _{a.}
   software program since last summer and expects to release it
   in four months. In the past ten years, the company

   _____ 15 major software programs.
   _{b.}

V | *Circle the letter of the one underlined word or phrase in each sentence that is not correct.*

1. Just before the telephone <u>rang</u>, I <u>was hoping</u> someone <u>called</u>
   A   B   C
   and <u>suggest</u> going somewhere.
   D

   A   B   Ⓒ   D

2. Igor <u>doesn't go</u> with us to Toledo today; <u>he's</u> <u>staying</u> home because
   A   B   C
   he <u>has to</u> finish a term paper.
   D

   A   B   C   D

3. <u>I'll</u> <u>have returned</u> to Barcelona by the time <u>you'll</u> <u>get</u> to Manila.
   A   B   C   D

   A   B   C   D

4. I <u>promised</u> <u>to be</u> ready, but when he <u>arrived</u>, I <u>took</u> a shower.
   A   B   C   D

   A   B   C   D

5. I <u>hope</u> dinner <u>is going to</u> <u>be</u> ready soon. <u>It's smelling</u> delicious.
   A   B   C   D

   A   B   C   D

6. I <u>didn't</u> even <u>think</u> there would be a party. Akiko and Jaime <u>have done</u>
   A   B   C
   a great job, and last night's get-together <u>was</u> great.
   D

   A   B   C   D

7. Sherry <u>felt</u> <u>terribly</u> when she <u>forgot</u> Lisa's birthday and <u>had</u> no present.
   A   B   C   D

   A   B   C   D

8. The plane <u>has</u> just <u>taken off</u> when I <u>realized</u> I had <u>given</u> my parents the
   A   B   C   D
   wrong arrival date.

   A   B   C   D

9. <u>There</u> <u>didn't used to</u> <u>be</u> a factory on this corner, <u>did</u> there?
   A   B   C   D

   A   B   C   D

10. We <u>haven't</u> <u>been visiting</u> Venice since 2001. <u>Wouldn't</u> it be
    A   B   C
    fun <u>to go</u> there again?
    D

    A   B   C   D

VI | *Go back to your answers to Exercise V. Write the correct form for each item that you believe is incorrect.*

1. _____ *would call* _____   6. _____

2. _____   7. _____

3. _____   8. _____

4. _____   9. _____

5. _____   10. _____

▶ *To check your answers, go to the Answer Key on page RT-1.*

PART II

Modals and Other Auxiliaries

4 *Be* and Auxiliaries in Additions, Tags, and Short Answers

Grammar in Context

BEFORE YOU READ

1 *In your view, can people change their character, or is it basically determined at birth?*

2 *Do you think the order in which children are born determines their character? Explain your answer.*

⌒ *Read this article about birth order.*

Psychology Monthly

DOES IT MATTER *WHEN* YOU WERE BORN?

Dear Reader,

Let's see if you can answer the following question: There are two men, one named Sam and the other named Jerry. They're pretty similar: Sam is a perfectionist; so is Jerry. Jerry, always a high achiever, was president of his high school class. So was Sam. Neither man went to college. Both did become successful businessmen, though. Jerry has been a leader in most of his enterprises. So has Sam. Sam always tries to obey rules. Jerry does too. Jerry has never liked liberal ideas. Neither has Sam. The question is, why are they so similar?

"Wait!" you say, "I know what the explanation is: They're identical twins. That's why they're so similar." Well, dear reader, I'm sorry to disappoint you, but that isn't it. They're not twins, or even related to each other. But they are both firstborns. Sam and Jerry are examples of what researchers are calling the birth-order theory. According to this theory, the order in which children are born plays a significant role in the formation of their personalities and in the way they ultimately turn out. Does this sound like some crazy new theory? It isn't. It's been around for a while.

Psychology Monthly

The main idea behind the birth-order theory is quite simple: Firstborn children enjoy a special relationship with their parents simply because they were there before any other children were. When other children come along, firstborns understand that these new arrivals represent a challenge to their special relationship. For this reason, firstborns tend to be conservative, rule-oriented, and opposed to change. They want to keep things as they are. Later borns have a different challenge. They must somehow find a place in their parents' affections. They sense that they have to become different from the oldest child, so they do.

One of the main supporters of the birth-order theory is Frank Sulloway, a researcher who did a 26-year study about 7,000 famous people in history. The results of the computer analysis led Sulloway to develop his theory that first, second, and later borns often have very different characteristics. According to Sulloway, firstborns are usually self-confident, assertive, conscientious, and conservative. They can also be jealous, moralistic, and inflexible. Winston Churchill, John Wayne, Oprah Winfrey, and Joseph Stalin were all firstborns. Based on this idea, we might expect powerful political figures, such as U.S. presidents, to be firstborns. They generally are, says Sulloway.

Last borns, Sulloway observes, are usually more social, more agreeable, and more open to new and even revolutionary ideas. This is because, sensing the power of the already established relationship between the oldest sibling and the parents, they have to turn outward to establish their place in the world. Famous last borns are Joan of Arc, Thomas Jefferson, and Leon Trotsky.

What about families in which there are more than two children, or only one? If there are three children in a family, the middle child is usually more flexible than the other two and often has a talent for compromise. And a family in which there's only one child is the least predictable configuration, Sulloway says. Only children aren't as inflexible as firstborns. Like firstborns, they do identify with their parents, however.

Perhaps you're saying to yourself, "But this is all just too much of a generalization, isn't it?" Yes, maybe it is. Sulloway is the first to acknowledge that there are many exceptions to the birth-order theory. A child's temperament has a great deal to do with how he or she turns out. Shy children, for example, may not become leaders even if they are firstborns. And, as Sulloway notes, there have been a lot of famous firstborns who became revolutionaries, as well as later borns who became conservatives. Still, the theory of birth order does appear to be generally valid.

Assuming that there is some validity to the birth-order theory, what can parents do to achieve the best possible relationships with their children? In Sulloway's view, they should give each child unique time and attention. If they do, they probably won't significantly change the influences of birth order, but they will maximize the quality of those relationships.

AFTER YOU READ

1 *Look at these two sentences. Based on them, which is true, **a** or **b**? Circle the letter of the answer.*

Sam always tries to obey rules. Jerry does too.

a. Jerry normally obeys rules.

b. Jerry normally doesn't obey rules.

2 *Look at these two sentences. Based on them, which is true, **a** or **b**? Circle the letter of the answer.*

Jerry has never liked liberal ideas. Neither has Sam.

a. Sam is a liberal.

b. Sam is not a liberal.

3 *Look at these two sentences. What does* do *at the end of the second sentence stand for? Circle the letter of the answer.*

They must somehow find a place in their parents' affections. They sense that they have to become different from the oldest child, so they do.

a. become different from the oldest child

b. find a place in their parents' affections

Grammar Presentation

BE AND AUXILIARIES IN ADDITIONS, TAGS, AND SHORT ANSWERS

ADDITIONS REFERRING TO PRECEDING INFORMATION

Statement	Addition
You might think this **is** crazy.	It **is**.
It sounds like it**'s** a ridiculous idea.	It **isn't**.
You wonder if he might **be** wrong.	He **is**.
Some people **believe** in you.	I'm not sure I **do**.
See if you **can solve** it.	Michael thinks you **can**.
He **is working** on this problem right now.	At least he says he **is**.
Many of us **have worked** on this.	All my friends **have**.

ADDITIONS OF SIMILARITY WITH *So, Too, Neither, Not Either*

Statement	Addition
Michael **is** a good leader.	**So is** Dennis.
	Dennis **is too.**
Carolyn **isn't** jealous of her siblings.	**Neither is** Alice.
	Alice **isn't either.**
Annie **doesn't play** sports.	Karen **doesn't either.**
George **can't ski**.	**Neither can** Martin.
George **is studying** engineering.	**So is** Martin.
Annie **has visited** Japan several times.	Karen **has too.**

ADDITIONS OF CONTRAST AND EMPHASIS

Statement	Addition
They**'re not** rich,	**but** they **ARE*** successful.
They**'re** rich;	**however**, they **AREN'T** powerful.
She**'s never studied** Italian,	**but** she **CAN speak** it fairly well.
He**'s had** many years of German;	he **CAN'T speak** it, **though.**
I **don't have** a computer at home,	**but** I **DO use** one at work.
We **have** a lot of money;	**still**, we **DON'T manage** to be happy.
My mother **is never** home;	she **DOES keep** in touch, **however.**
They **didn't go** to college;	they **DID become** successful, **though.**

*Capital letters are used here to show which words are stressed for emphasis.

TAG QUESTIONS

Statement	Tag		Short Answers	
That**'s** a good idea,	**isn't** it?			it **is.**
You**'re working** with Sam,	**aren't** you?			I **am.**
Jeff **has worked** hard for this,	**hasn't** he?	Yes,		he **has.**
We **can visit** your office,	**can't** we?			you **can.**
Annie **works** at the lab,	**doesn't** she?			she **does.**
That**'s not** a good idea,	**is** it?			it**'s not.**
I**'m not doing** well,	**am** I?			you**'re not.**
Jason **hasn't called**,	**has** he?	No,		he **hasn't.**
They **can't come** now,	**can** they?			they **can't.**
Megan **didn't study**,	**did** she?			she **didn't.**

GRAMMAR NOTES	EXAMPLES

1. Auxiliaries are helping verbs (HV) that are used with main verbs (MV) to make negative statements, questions, progressive forms, and perfect forms, and to express meanings such as possibility and advice.

-       HV   MV
  It **doesn't** make sense to me.
- HV   MV
  Does this sound like a crazy theory?
-     HV   MV
  He **might** be a last born.

2. Auxiliaries can be used:

  a. without a main verb in additions to statements

  b. in the tags of tag questions

  c. in short answers

The main verb **be** is also used in additions, tags, and short answers.

- Let's see if you can understand this. I think you **can**. *(addition)*

  A: She went to college, **didn't** she? *(tag)*

  B: Yes, she **did**. *(short answer)*
- You might assume presidents are firstborns. They usually **are**.

  A: Sulloway is a last born, **isn't** he?

  B: Yes, he **is**.

3. In **additions** that refer to previous information, we use **be** if it is present or implied in the previous statement.

If *be* is not present in the previous statement, **other auxiliaries** are used to refer to previous information.

- We might think firstborns are conservative. They often **are**.
- Frank seems like a good parent. In fact, he **is**.
- Jerry owns a company. Or at least he says he **does**.
- Alice says we've solved the problem. I'm not sure we **have**.

4. To make an affirmative addition to an affirmative statement, use *so* or *too*.

To make a negative addition to a negative statement, use *neither* or *not either*.

▶ **BE CAREFUL!** When you make additions with *so* and *neither*, place these words at the beginning of the sentence, and invert the subject and the auxiliary.

- Sam is a perfectionist. **So is** Jerry.

            OR

  Jerry **is too**.
- Jerry has never liked liberal ideas. **Neither has** Sam.

            OR

  Sam **hasn't either**.
- Martha got married last year. **So did Helen**.

  NOT So ~~Helen did~~.
- Sam didn't go to college. **Neither did Jerry**.

  NOT Neither ~~Jerry did~~.

5. Use auxiliaries to make a contrast with a preceding statement. Use a negative addition to make a contrast to an affirmative statement. Use an affirmative addition to make a contrast to a negative statement.

NOTE: In additions of contrast, there is sometimes a contrast word such as *but*, *though*, *however*, or *still*.

To place special emphasis on a word, pronounce it with stress. To emphasize a verb in the simple present or simple past, use *do*, *does*, and *did* in affirmative sentences.

To emphasize a verb with *be* and other auxiliaries, use full forms, not contracted forms.

- Some think all leaders are firstborns. They **aren't, though**.
- They're not twins, **but** they **are** both firstborns.
- I don't have any children of my own. **Still**, I **do** love children.
- Neither of them got a college education. They **did** have successful careers.
- He's not a conservative. He **is** a Republican.
- I've never read Sulloway's book. I **have** read two of his articles.

6. In **tag questions**, use a negative tag after an affirmative statement. Use an affirmative tag after a negative statement.

Use tag questions to check information or to comment on a situation. You expect the listener to agree with you, and your voice falls on the tag.

Use tag questions to get information. You expect an answer, and your voice rises on the tag.

- The birth-order theory **makes** sense, **doesn't it**?
- Young children **shouldn't** be left alone, **should they**?

A: You're an only child, **aren't you**?
B: Uh-huh. So was my dad.
A: That's an interesting idea, **isn't it**?
B: Yeah. It's fascinating.

A: You have a sister, **don't you**?
B: No. Actually, I have a brother.

(continued)

7. Use **auxiliaries without main verbs** in short answers.

- Sulloway is a writer, isn't he? Yes, he **is**.
- Have you read his book? No, I **haven't**.
- Is she an only child? Yes, she **is**. NOT Yes, ~~she's~~.

▶ BE CAREFUL! Use full forms, not contractions, in affirmative short answers. You can use contracted forms or full forms in negative short answers.

A: Had you heard about the birth-order theory previously?

B: No, I hadn't.

OR

No, I **had not**.

Focused Practice

1 | DISCOVER THE GRAMMAR

A *Look at these sentences. The verbs that are circled refer to a preceding word or phrase. Find and underline the preceding word or phrase referred to by the circled verbs. Draw an arrow between the two.*

1. Let's see if you can <u>answer the following question</u>. No doubt you can.

2. Sam is a perfectionist; so is Jerry.

3. Jerry, always a high achiever, was president of his high school class. So was Sam.

4. Jerry has been a leader in most of his enterprises. So has Sam.

5. Sam always tries to obey rules. Jerry does too.

6. Jerry has never liked liberal ideas. Neither has Sam.

7. Does this sound like some crazy new theory? It isn't.

8. They were there before any other children were.

9. They sense that they have to become different from the oldest child, so they do.

10. Based on this idea, we might expect powerful political figures, such as U.S. presidents, to be firstborns. They usually are, says Sulloway.

11. But this is perhaps too much of a generalization. Yes, maybe it is.

B Look again at the reading. Read the first two and the last three paragraphs. Find six sentences in which auxiliaries are used to show contrast or emphasis. Write the main parts of those sentences here and underline the auxiliary.

1. *Both _did_ become successful businessmen, though.* _____

2. _____

3. _____

4. _____

5. _____

6. _____

2 | ADDITIONS   Grammar Notes 2–5

Match the statements on the left with the correct additions on the right.

_f_	1. Jefferson was a last born,	**a.** Neither had my wife.
_____	2. My favorite cousin is an only child,	**b.** Everyone in my family has.
_____	3. Does her idea sound silly?	**c.** He won't be, though.
_____	4. Everyone expected the plan to fail.	**d.** but she does read it well.
_____	5. Most people support that plan.	**e.** It isn't.
_____	6. Tim hasn't done the work.	**f.** and so was Joan of Arc.
_____	7. Sarah can't speak Japanese,	**g.** I'm not sure I do.
_____	8. Dan thinks he'll be successful.	**h.** and I am too.
_____	9. I've graduated from college.	**i.** It didn't, however.
_____	10. I'd never heard of birth order.	**j.** He says he hasn't, anyway.

3 | FAMILY DYNAMICS

*Read a dinner table conversation in the Grant family. Complete the conversation with
verbs or verb phrases to show contrast and emphasis or to refer to what was said before.*

MRS. GRANT: Kids, come on, now. You need to eat your asparagus.

SAMANTHA: Do I have to, Mom? I don't like asparagus.

MOLLY: Neither _____*do I*_____, Mom.
1.

MRS. GRANT: Yes, you _____ have to eat it. It's good for you.
2.

MOLLY: Mom, if I eat it, it'll make me sick. I know it _____.
3.

MRS. GRANT: No, _____. Don't be silly.
4.

MR. GRANT: Steve, what about your homework? You promised me you were going to do it

before dinner.

STEVE: I _____ it, Dad.
5.

MR. GRANT: You _____? When? While you were watching TV?
6.

STEVE: From 5:00 to 5:30. It only took me a half hour.

MR. GRANT: What about you, girls? Have you finished your homework? We need to be leaving

for the concert pretty soon.

SAMANTHA: I _____, Dad.
7.

MOLLY: So _____.
8.

MRS. GRANT: What was that you said about a concert, John?

MR. GRANT: You know, the big Shania Twain concert—the one we've had tickets to for a month.

MRS. GRANT: It's not tonight, is it?

MR. GRANT: Yes, _____, Helen. You forgot, didn't you?
9.

MRS. GRANT: Oh, no! I'm not ready. Come on, now. Everyone needs to help. Who'll clear the table?

STEVE: I _____, Mom.
10.

MR. GRANT: What about loading the dishwasher?

SAMANTHA: Can't we just leave the dishes in the sink if we're in such a hurry?

Mr. Grant: No, _____. Now, who'll do it?
                              11.

Steve: Sam _____, Dad.
                        12.

Samantha: Thanks a lot, pal!

Mr. Grant: Come on, kids. Let's get going.

4 | SENTENCES ABOUT FAMILIES   *Grammar Notes 4–5*

Read these sentences. Use the words in parentheses to write additions of similarity or contrast.

1. The kids don't like to eat vegetables. (my husband / similarity)

   My husband doesn't either. **OR** *Neither does my husband.*

2. My cousin is an only child. (I / contrast)

   _____

3. I don't work in the field of pediatrics. (my brother and sister / contrast)

   _____

4. I'd never read anything about family dynamics. (anyone else in my family / similarity)

   _____

5. Some parents favor one child over another. (should / contrast)

   _____

6. Our family has taken a vacation every year for 10 years. (my brother's family / contrast)

   _____

7. My daughter doesn't read or write Spanish. (speak / contrast)

   _____

8. Our son hasn't been accepted at the university. (daughter / similarity)

   _____

9. Bob has always been an excellent student. (Katie / similarity)

   _____

10. Steve doesn't want to leave home. (Theresa / contrast)

    _____

5 | LET'S TALK IT OVER

🎧 *Listen to Brent Washburn's conversation with his thirteen-year-old son, Jeremy, about Jeremy's recent behavior. As you listen, read the tapescript and pay special attention to the use of stress for contrast and emphasis. There are ten auxiliary verbs that show emphasis or make a contrast with a preceding statement. The first one is circled. Find and circle the other nine.*

BRENT: Jeremy, come on into the living room. There are some things we need to talk about.

JEREMY: Dad, if it's about the broken window in the bathroom, I can explain. I guess I did break it, but I didn't mean to. It was an accident, really.

BRENT: It wasn't the window I wanted to talk about. I was wondering how it got broken, though.

JEREMY: It's not the window? What do you want to talk about, then?

BRENT: Well, for one thing, I got a letter from your teacher, Ms. Hammond. She says you haven't been studying and you might fail. You do want to pass the seventh grade, don't you?

JEREMY: Of course, Dad. And I have been studying. I just keep forgetting to turn in my homework.

BRENT: She says you don't pay attention in class, either, and you're always staring out the window.

JEREMY: Dad, she just doesn't like me. I do pay attention. Just because I'm not looking at Ms. Hammond doesn't mean I'm not paying attention to what she's saying . . . She's boring, too.

BRENT: Jeremy, I've known Ms. Hammond for a long time. Her classes may not always be fun, but she does know how to teach. From now on, I want you to study every evening from 7:00 until 9:00, and I'm going to call Ms. Hammond every week to see if you're turning in your homework. And I will call every week. Don't think I won't.

JEREMY: Do I still get to watch TV and play video games?

BRENT: Not during the week until your grades improve. You can't have any of your friends over during the week either. Of course, you can read a book if you've finished your homework. OK. Now, let's talk about the window. What did happen to the window?

6 | EDITING

Read this letter from Jeremy Washburn's seventh-grade teacher to Jeremy's parents, reporting on his progress at school. There are ten mistakes in the making of additions and the use of auxiliaries. The first mistake is already corrected. Find and correct nine more.

MADISON JUNIOR HIGH SCHOOL

February 12

Dear Mr. and Mrs. Washburn,

I'm writing to give you a progress report on Jeremy. In general, I'd say he's doing better than before, though he ~~is~~ *isn't* doing as well as he could. He still has a tendency to daydream a little too much, but he doesn't seem to be paying better attention in class. One of his weak subjects is science; neither is math. He scored high in math on the national achievement tests a month ago, though, so he is have a chance of passing his math class. However, he is passing at the moment. Either is he passing science. He is doing very well in English, though, and he's doing reasonably well in history and art either. The main problem I'm having is getting Jeremy to turn in his work; still, he didn't submit three assignments last week. I appreciate your efforts to monitor his study time in the evenings. Children today have so many distractions, do they? Your son is lucky to have parents who care about education; many don't. Jeremy is doing better; he isn't out of trouble yet. Please keep up the supervised work at home, and call me if you have any concerns.

Sincerely,

Priscilla Hammond
Priscilla Hammond

Communication Practice

7 | LISTENING

🎧 *Listen to a segment of the radio talk show* Do the Right Thing. *Then listen again. Read the statements and check* **True** *or* **False.**

	True	False
1. Sally says she never really loved Bob.	☐	☑
2. Sally thinks a lot of Bob as a person.	☐	☐
3. A few weeks ago Sally tried to tell Bob her feelings.	☐	☐
4. Bob accepted what Sally told him.	☐	☐
5. Sally says she's unsure of her feelings.	☐	☐
6. Mary Mobley says Sally doesn't have to tell Bob the truth.	☐	☐
7. Jerry is rich.	☐	☐
8. Jerry has put money away for his children.	☐	☐
9. Jerry and his children live in the same vicinity.	☐	☐
10. Jerry's son can afford to make the payments on a house.	☐	☐
11. Mary Mobley thinks Jerry's children don't really sound selfish.	☐	☐
12. Mary Mobley thinks not giving the children their inheritance now might be a good thing to do.	☐	☐

8 | GROUP DISCUSSION

A *Read this article about raising children. As you read, think about points you agree or disagree with.*

Example: American parents have lost their way. (disagree)

PARENTING *Monthly*

ASIAN PARENTS DIFFER ON CHILD REARING

by John Rosemond

A man called the other day from Milwaukee with an interesting story that illustrates how much American parents have lost their way.

He and his wife took their three children, ages 6, 4, and 3, to the zoo for what was supposed to be a pleasant afternoon. Instead, it was a disaster. The children ran in three directions at once, requiring that the two parents run even faster. The children's activity levels were matched by their continuous yelling. They demanded everything they saw. The parents saying no resulted in dramatic displays of anger. So, they said yes more often than not. The children then began complaining that their toys and souvenirs were too heavy, so the parents wound up carrying armloads of worthless junk.

"Needless to say, John," he went on, "we didn't have a good time. In fact, my wife and I took the kids home early because we were getting angry at one another."

To many, this story will sound very familiar. Some might even say, "Well, what did they expect, taking three young children to the zoo?"

But that's not where this father's story ends. In the course of all this noise and confusion, he and his wife noticed an Asian woman with three equally young children. But her children were well behaved, calm, quiet, and followed their mother like ducklings. She spoke with her children, but only rarely. It was apparent that this woman was not giving her children many instructions. They seemed to know what she expected of them. Neither the mother nor the kids were carrying any junk, yet everyone seemed to be having a good time.

"What's her secret?" asked my man from Milwaukee.

It just so happens I've had several conversations lately with Asian parents; all of them have arrived here recently. They tell me they are shocked by the behavior of American children, and fear their bad influence. In the course of these conversations, I've discovered that these parents have assumptions about child rearing as different from those of average American parents as China is from the United States.

The first assumption is that children should pay more attention to parents than parents pay to children. These parents understand that you cannot discipline a child who is not paying attention to you. They also understand that the more attention parents pay to children, the less children will pay to parents.

Second, no attempt should be made to persuade children to cooperate. In fact, since cooperation implies a state of equality, these parents don't even seek cooperation. Instead, they expect obedience.

Third, they don't explain themselves to their children. Therefore, their children's questions are about what the world is made of and how it works, rather than

(continued)

ASIAN PARENTS DIFFER ON CHILD REARING

about the "why?" and "why not?" of their parents' rules and expectations. In fact, these parents are amazed at the amount of time American parents waste dealing with such things.

Lastly, these parents do not tolerate misbehavior. Therefore, they do not bribe their children, nor do they threaten them.

The truly sad thing is that most of America's children used to be as well-behaved as those Asian kids. The good news is, it's not too late, however, to save ourselves.

B *Now read the article again. Form small groups and discuss Rosemond's article. In two columns, list points you agree with and disagree with. Say why you agree or disagree in each case. Discuss your points with the class.*

Example: **A:** American parents have lost their way.
　　　　　 B: I basically disagree. Some American parents have lost their way, but not all of them have.

9 | PICTURE DISCUSSION

With a partner, discuss the picture. Compare the American family and the Asian family. What differences do you see? Which family is behaving more like a family in your culture?

Example: **A:** Which family looks more similar to a family in your culture?
　　　　　 B: The Asian family does. They're . . .

10 | WRITING

Is child rearing better when children pay more attention to parents than parents pay to children, or when the opposite is true? Write three or four paragraphs explaining your viewpoint. Give examples to support your ideas.

Example: In my opinion, children should pay more attention to their parents than parents pay to their children. I don't believe that parents should ignore or neglect their children. I do think, however, that many parents these days are too worried that their children won't like them and are not willing to use their parental authority. Let me explain my viewpoint . . .

11 | ON THE INTERNET: FAMOUS PEOPLE AND BIRTH ORDER

Use the Internet to find out information about a famous person you are interested in. Is the person an only child? If the person has siblings, where does he or she come in birth order? Does what you know about this person fit the birth-order theory? Report your findings to the class.

Example: I researched President George W. Bush. He is the oldest of five children in the Bush family. I think he fits the birth-order theory because his conservative values are similar to those of his father, President George H.W. Bush.

5 Modals to Express Degrees of Necessity

Grammar in Context

BEFORE YOU READ

1 *Look at the picture on page 73. What are the people doing? Is this a practice in your culture?*

2 *What are some things that should and shouldn't be done in your culture? Make a short list.*

🎧 *Read this article about cultural differences.*

What We Should and Shouldn't Have Done

Recently my wife and I had a cross-cultural experience that taught us about some things we should have done differently. Six months ago my company sent me to work at our branch office in Japan. My Japanese co-workers have been friendly and gracious, and last week one of them invited my wife and me to his house for dinner. We were honored to be invited, and the food was delicious. But even though Masayuki and Yukiko, his wife, were most polite and friendly and never gave an indication that anything was wrong, we felt a bit uncomfortable about the evening. I decided to ask my friend Junichi about it. He's lived in both Japan and the United States, so he knows the differences between the two cultures. He gave me a lot of pointers. Now we know what we should and shouldn't have done.

The first tip was about taking off our shoes. We knew that you're supposed to take off your shoes when you enter a Japanese home, so we did. We didn't know we were supposed to arrange them so they'd be pointing toward the door when we left so that we'd be able to put them on without having to turn around. But this wasn't a big mistake, Junichi said.

The second pointer was about gifts. Helen and I knew you're supposed to take a gift to a Japanese home. Masayuki and Yukiko seemed a little shocked, though, when we pulled the present out of a plastic bag and said, "We thought

What We Should and Shouldn't Have Done

you'd like this CD. It's rock and roll." Junichi chuckled and said, "Well, you should have wrapped the CD. It's OK to bring it in a plastic bag, but the gift itself has to be wrapped. And you mustn't say anything about the gift. Just give it to your hosts. The main problem, though, was the gift itself."

"You mean we should have taken something different?"

"Yes. A rock and roll CD isn't really an appropriate gift."

"Well, what should we have taken?"

"Maybe a box of chocolates. Or you could have taken some flowers."

After that I told Junichi about what happened before dinner. Masayuki and Yukiko had invited us to sit down for some tea and snacks. The tea was delicious, but we had trouble eating the raw sushi. I was able to finish mine, but Helen couldn't finish hers. Masayuki and Yukiko seemed a little puzzled. Junichi chuckled again and said, "Well, in Japan it's considered impolite to leave half-eaten food on a plate."

"You mean you've got to eat everything that's offered to you?" I asked.

"You don't have to. But if you take something, you must finish it."

After we ate, Helen asked Yukiko if she could help her in the kitchen. This is the way we do things back in the United States, but Junichi says you are not to do this in Japan. According to the rules of Japanese culture, visitors aren't allowed to go into the kitchen.

The other thing you probably shouldn't do, he says, is praise pictures or ornaments in the house. If you do, your Japanese

(continued)

What We Should and Shouldn't Have Done

hosts might feel they have to give the object to you. Fortunately, we didn't do that.

At the end of the evening, Masayuki asked us if we'd like to have another drink. We thought it wouldn't be polite to say no, so we accepted and stayed for another half hour. Finally we felt that we absolutely had to leave, so when Masayuki invited us to have an additional drink, I said, "We'd really like to, but it's late. We'd better get going, or we won't be able to get up in the morning." Masayuki and Yukiko seemed relieved. Junichi said, "That's what you should have done in the first place. When a Japanese host invites you to have a drink at the end of the evening, you should refuse gently. Otherwise, you could be there all night. Leaving earlier would have been fine."

I asked what he thought we might do to rectify the situation. "Shall we invite them over?" I asked. He said, "Yes, you ought to do that. Just remember all the things I've told you. But don't invite them to an informal, Western-style party with a lot of loud music. Just make it a simple dinner for the four of you."

Good advice, I thought. What really struck me is how much we all have to learn about other cultures.

AFTER YOU READ

Complete these sentences. Circle the correct answer. Discuss your answers.

1. The author and his wife _____.
   a. followed exactly the Japanese custom of taking your shoes off
   b. should have left their shoes pointing toward the door, but didn't

2. In Japan, it's a good idea to _____.
   a. bring something like a rock and roll CD as a house gift
   b. wrap a gift instead of just bringing it in the original bag

3. In Japan, it's wrong to _____.
   a. talk about a gift when you give it to your host
   b. bring a gift in a plastic bag

4. According to their Japanese friend, the author and his wife should _____.
   a. ask Masayuki and Yukiko to join them for a quiet dinner party
   b. ask Masayuki and Yukiko to a typical Western-style party

Grammar Presentation

MODALS TO EXPRESS DEGREES OF NECESSITY (RANGING FROM OBLIGATION TO NO OBLIGATION)

Obligation (Necessity)							
You	**must** **have to** **have got to**	**call**	them.	You	**must not** **can't** **are not allowed to**		**call**	them.
You	**had to**	**call**	them.	You	**couldn't** **weren't allowed to**		**call**	them.

Advice							
You	**had better** **should** **ought to**	**leave**	early.	You	**had better not** **shouldn't**	**leave**	early.
You	**should have** **ought to have**	**left**	early.	You	**shouldn't have**	**left**	early.

Expectation							
You	**are supposed to** **are to**	**take**	a gift.	You	**are not supposed to** **are not to**	**do**	this.
You	**were supposed to** **were to**	**take**	a gift.	You	**were not supposed to** **were not to**	**do**	this.

Suggestion			
You	**could** **might**	**give**	roses.
You	**could have** **might have**	**given**	roses.

No Obligation (No Necessity)			
You	**don't have to**	**call**	them.
You	**didn't have to**	**call**	them.

Necessity 100%

0%

GRAMMAR NOTES	EXAMPLES
1. Modals are auxiliary verbs. The modals are *can, could, had better, may, might, must, ought to, shall, should, will,* and *would*. Each modal has only one form for all persons.	• I / You / He / She / We / They **could take** some flowers.
Use **simple modals** (modal + base form) for the present and the future.	• We **should invite** Jim to the party tonight.
Use **perfect modals** (modal + *have* + past participle) to show degrees of necessity in the past.	• We **should have invited** Jim to last week's party too.
When referring to degrees of necessity, modals show speakers' attitudes toward the actions they are describing. Modals are used to talk about obligations, advice, expectations, and suggestions.	• You **could invite** them over. • You **should leave** early.

2. Some **modal-like expressions** have meanings similar to modals: *must* *have to* *should* *be supposed to*	• You **must finish** everything on your plate. / You **have to finish** everything on your plate. • You **should take** a gift. / You**'re supposed to take** a gift.

3. Use **must**, **have to**, and **have got to** to show strong necessity. They are similar in meaning.	• You **must / have to / have got to arrive** on time.
USAGE NOTES Use **must** formally to show very strong obligation that can't be escaped.	**A:** You mean you **must eat** everything they offer you?
Use **have to** in all forms and situations, formal and informal.	**B:** No, you **don't have to**.
Use **have got to** informally in conversation. It is rarely used in the negative. Use **don't have to** instead.	
Use **will have to** to show future necessity.	• We**'ll have to invite** them over to our house.
Use **had to** to show past necessity.	• We felt we **had to take** a gift.
▶ **BE CAREFUL!** Don't use *must have* + past participle to show past necessity.	• We **had to leave**. NOT We ~~must have left~~.

4. Use ***must not*** to say that it is necessary not to do something (that it is prohibited).

▶ **BE CAREFUL!** Although *must* and *have to* have similar meanings, *must not* and *don't have to* have very different meanings. For *don't have to*, see note 9.

- You **must not smoke** here.

- We **must not miss** the flight.
  NOT We ~~don't have to~~ miss the flight.

---

5. Use ***had better*** to give a warning that something bad or negative will happen if advice isn't followed.

- We**'d better get going**, or we'll be late.
- You**'d better not discuss** politics during dinner.

---

6. Use ***should*** or ***ought to*** to offer advice. They mean "it would be a good idea if . . ." and are basically the same in most situations. Use *should*, not *ought to*, in questions and negatives.

Use ***should have*** / ***ought to have*** to express advice about past situations. *Should have* and *ought to have* suggest that the action did not happen. *Shouldn't have* and *ought not to have* suggest that it did.

NOTE: We sometimes use ***shall*** in questions to ask for advice. In this meaning, *shall* is used only with *I* or *we*. When it is used with *we*, it is often followed by a sentence with *let's*. In this meaning, *shall* is somewhat similar to *should*.

- You **should** / **ought to refuse** gently.
  A: **Should I invite** a guest?
  B: No, you **shouldn't.**
- You **should** / **ought to have done** that the first time.
- You **shouldn't** / **ought not to have mentioned** your gift.

  A: **Shall** we **get** them some flowers?
  B: Yes, **let's do** that.

---

7. Use ***be supposed to*** to show an expectation. It is used only in the present and the past. In the past, the affirmative suggests that the action didn't happen. The negative suggests that the action did happen.

You can use ***be to*** + base form formally to express a strong expectation.

- You**'re supposed to take off** your shoes when you enter a Japanese home.
- We **were supposed to take** flowers.
- We **weren't supposed to mention** the gift we'd brought.
- All employees **are to attend** the company office party.
- You**'re not to ask** any personal questions.

(continued)

8. Use *could* or *might* to make polite, not-too-strong suggestions about the present or future.

Use *could have* / *might have* + past participle to make polite suggestions about a past opportunity. In this meaning, *might have* and *could have* mean that the action didn't happen.

- You **could** / **might take** them some chocolates.

- You **could have** / **might have taken** some flowers.

9. To say that something is not necessary, use *don't* / *doesn't have to*.

In the past, use *didn't have to* + base form to show that something was not necessary.

- You **don't have to eat** everything offered to you.

- You **didn't have to bring** a gift.

Focused Practice

1 | DISCOVER THE GRAMMAR

Look at these sentences. Each sentence can be said in another, similar way. Circle the letter of the choice that is closer in meaning to the sentence given.

1. We knew that you're supposed to take off your shoes when you enter a Japanese home, so we did.
   a. Japanese people expect guests to remove their shoes.
   b. It doesn't matter whether or not you wear your shoes in a Japanese home.

2. Well, you should have wrapped the CD.
   a. You wrapped the CD, and that was the right thing to do.
   b. You didn't wrap the CD, and that was a cultural mistake in Japan.

3. And you mustn't say anything about the gift.
   a. It's sometimes acceptable to say something about the gift.
   b. It's definitely wrong to say anything about the gift.

4. Or you could have taken some flowers.
   a. Flowers are an acceptable gift in Japan, but the author and his wife didn't take any.
   b. The author and his wife made a cultural mistake by not taking flowers.

5. According to the rules of Japanese culture, visitors aren't allowed to go into the kitchen.
   a. The Japanese expect visitors to stay out of the kitchen.
   b. It's OK for visitors to go into a Japanese kitchen.

6. If you do, your Japanese hosts might feel they have to give the object to you.

    a. Japanese hosts might feel a strong obligation to give the object to you.

    b. Japanese hosts might feel they can choose not to give the object to you.

7. When a Japanese host invites you to have a drink at the end of the evening, you should refuse gently.

    a. The hosts don't expect you to refuse gently.

    b. It's a good idea to refuse gently.

8. Yes, you ought to do that.

    a. It doesn't matter whether you do that.

    b. It would be a good idea to do that.

9. Junichi says you are not to do this in Japan.

    a. People won't care if you do this in Japan.

    b. It's a cultural mistake to do this in Japan.

2 | SHOULD WE LEAVE A TIP?   *Grammar Notes 3, 6–9*

Read this conversation between Fumiko, a visiting exchange student, and her American friend Jane. Complete the conversation with items from the box. Use each item once.

~~are you supposed to leave~~	could have left	don't have to leave	had to worry
ought to have given	should we have left	should you leave	should you tip
supposed to do	were supposed to leave	you're supposed to do	

JANE: Hi, Fumiko. How are things going?

FUMIKO: Really well. But there's something I wanted to ask you about.

JANE: OK. What?

FUMIKO: Tipping. I just don't understand it. ___*Are you supposed to leave*___ a tip
                                          1.

everywhere you eat? This is really bothering me. I've never

_____ about this before. We don't tip in Japan.
                     2.

JANE: You don't?

FUMIKO: No. You're not really _____ that. It's all included in
                                         3.

the service charge.

JANE: Tell me more. Have you had a problem with this?

(continued)

FUMIKO: Yeah. Last week a Chinese friend of mine and I had dinner at a restaurant. We knew

we _____ a tip, but we didn't know how much.

                                    4.

JANE: How much did you leave?

FUMIKO: About 25 percent. _____ more?

                                    5.

JANE: Wow! Twenty-five percent. That's a lot. The service must have been really good.

FUMIKO: Actually, it wasn't. The waiter was pretty rude . . . and slow.

JANE: Well, if you're not really satisfied with the service, you

_____ anything.

                                  6.

FUMIKO: So how much _____ the waiter if you're satisfied?

                                  7.

JANE: Between 15 and 20 percent. Fifteen is the usual.

FUMIKO: Hmmm. OK. Now here's another question. I'm confused about what

_____ if you're sitting at a lunch counter instead of

                                  8.

at a table. _____ anything for the person behind the

                                  9.

counter?

JANE: It's a nice gesture. Why do you ask?

FUMIKO: Yesterday I had lunch at a cafeteria counter. The waitress was really nice and polite. I

felt like I _____ her something.

                                  10.

JANE: Did you?

FUMIKO: No.

JANE: Well, you _____ something. Maybe 5 to 10 percent.

                                  11.

FUMIKO: Oh. OK. Next time I will.

3 | **GIFT GIVING IN TWO OTHER CULTURES**   *Grammar Notes 3, 6–7, 9*

A *Read this short essay about gift giving.*

A Chinese woman had lived in Australia for a few years. On her birthday, she was invited to the home of an Australian friend to celebrate. When she was presented with a gift, she thanked her friend and put the gift away. Her friend asked, "Aren't you going to open it?" The Chinese lady said, "Oh no! I don't want to open it now."

In Chinese culture, one is not expected to open a gift immediately after receiving it. In Australian culture, however, the opposite is true. There are other rules about gift giving in Chinese culture. It is important, for example, to avoid giving umbrellas, knives, scissors, and clocks.

Iranian culture has its rules too. Amanda, a young North American woman, went to the home of her fiancé's sister. She saw a small statue, and when she said she liked it, the sister insisted on giving it to her. Why? Many Middle Easterners feel obligated to give something to someone who admires it. Amanda didn't want to accept the statue, but Fariba, the sister, kept insisting. Amanda should have kept on refusing. Iranians may keep on insisting, but you are under no obligation to accept.

B *Now complete these sentences, using modals or modal-like expressions. Make some sentences negative if necessary.*

1. According to the rules of Australian culture, the Chinese lady _____ opened the gift at the party.

2. In Chinese culture, one _____ open a gift immediately after receiving it.

3. In Chinese culture, one _____ avoid giving umbrellas, knives, scissors, and clocks.

4. Iranians feel one _____ give something to someone if that person admires it.

5. Amanda _____ refused to accept the statue.

6. Even if an Iranian keeps on insisting, you _____ accept.

4 | SHOULDS AND COULDS

Grammar Notes 6, 8

Look again at the opening reading. Write six sentences about what the American couple should have done and shouldn't have done. Then write four sentences about what they could or might have done.

1. *They should have wrapped the CD.*

2. _____

3. _____

4. _____

5. _____

6. _____

7. _____

8. _____

9. _____

10. _____

5 | EDITING

Read this letter from Tong-Li, an international exchange student in Australia, to her friend Masako in Singapore. There are 11 mistakes in the use of modals or modal-like expressions. The first mistake is already corrected. Find and correct 10 more.

Dear Masako,

    Sorry it's taken me so long to write. I ~~shouldn't~~ *should* have gotten to this weeks ago, but I've been so busy. I'm really looking forward to the holidays and seeing all you guys again.

    School is going well. It's tough but really interesting, and I'm sure I should to be studying even more than I have been. Part of the problem is that I'm taking too many classes. You're only suppose to take five a term, but I'm taking six.

Anyway, I've gotten to know a lot of new people, including several Australians. I have this one really good friend, a girl named Jane. She invited me to her house last week for a party. Actually, it was my birthday, but I didn't know she knew that. I thought it was a party like any other. I figured I better take some kind of gift, but I couldn't decide what it must be. Finally I came up with the idea of a bouquet of flowers. As soon as I got to the party, I gave it to Jane, and she was really happy to get it. But then the funniest thing happened. I guess I should expect something was up from the mysterious way Jane was acting, but I didn't. This was a surprise party—for me! As soon as I took off my coat and sat down, a lot of people jumped up from behind sofas and other places where they'd been hiding and shouted "Surprise! Happy birthday!" I was embarrassed, but I might not have been, because everyone was really friendly, and pretty soon I forgot about my embarrassment. Then they gave me presents. I was about to put them away, but Jane said, "Aren't you going to open them?" I didn't know what to do. In China you shouldn't have opened gifts right when you get them, but apparently you are supposed to in Australia. So I opened them. The nicest gift was a new blouse from Jane. She told me I must have gone and try it on immediately, so I did. It's beautiful. Anyway, what a party! I thought I knew all about Australian culture, but I guess I'm not as familiar with it as I thought. The custom of opening up presents in front of the gift giver is a strange one to me.

The weather is kind of chilly. How is it back in Singapore? Nice and warm? Must I bring you something special from Australia when I come?

Well, Masako, I'm running out of space, so I got to sign off. Write soon.

Best,

Tong-Li

Communication Practice

6 | LISTENING

 Listen to the telephone conversation. Read the questions. Then listen again. Complete the answers, using modals or modal-like expressions.

1. Why do Dad and Ray need to get home as soon as possible?

   Mom's surprise party is supposed to start in 15 minutes.

2. What's Bev's opinion about delaying Mom's present, and why?

   _____

3. What does Dad say when Bev reminds him about not putting things off till the last minute?

   _____

4. What's Dad's opinion about Bev's camera suggestion?

   _____

5. What's Bev's opinion about a dress?

   _____

6. What's Bev's blouse suggestion?

   _____

7. What's Bev's scarf suggestion?

   _____

8. What does Bev say about getting home as soon as possible, and why?

   _____

7 | INFORMATION GAP: WHY WON'T THEY WAIT ON US?

Work with a partner to complete this story. Each of you will read a version of the same story. Each version is missing some information. Take turns asking your partner questions to get the missing information.

Student A, read the story. Ask questions and fill in the missing information. Then answer Student B's questions.

Student B, turn to page 88 and follow the instructions there.

Example: A: Where were they supposed to stay?
B: They were supposed to stay at the Grand State Hotel. What should they have gotten?
A: They should have gotten a confirmation number.

A married couple was traveling in Europe and had just entered a new country. They had been having a wonderful time, but now everything was going wrong. The first problem was finding accommodations. They were supposed to stay at _____, but when they got to the hotel there was no record of their reservation. The wife said they should have gotten a confirmation number. They hadn't, unfortunately, so they had to spend the night _____. The next day they finally found a room at a hotel far from the center of town. There were two rooms available: a large one and a tiny one. Since they were on a tight budget, they decided they had better take the tiny one. The second problem was communication. They were starving after spending hours looking for accommodations, so they went into a restaurant. A waiter brought them a menu, but they couldn't understand it. The husband said they should have _____. They hadn't done that, though, so they didn't know what to order.

Time passed. Other people were being served but they weren't. Frustrated, they decided they had to do something. But what? They noticed that a boy about 11 years old seemed to be listening to their conversation. Soon the boy came over to their table. "Excuse me," he said. "You have to _____. Then they'll take your order." The husband and wife were both astonished but grateful. The wife said, "You speak our language very well. Did you study it somewhere?" The boy said, "I lived in Australia for three years. I learned English there." He asked, "Shall I help you order? I can translate the menu."

When they got back home, their friends asked them what they had liked best about the trip. The wife said, "Well, the best part was visiting that country where everything went wrong. At some point, everybody should _____. You don't have to be miserable, but you need a challenge. That's when you learn things. Maybe that's what people mean when they say travel is broadening."

8 | SMALL-GROUP DISCUSSION: IS IT OK IN YOUR CULTURE?

Work in small groups. Decide individually whether each of the behaviors is required, advised, allowed, or unimportant in your culture or another culture you are familiar with. Check the appropriate boxes. Then discuss the results with the others in your group.

Example: **A:** When you're invited to dinner in your culture, are you supposed to take a gift?
B: Absolutely. You must take a gift. And it has to be wrapped. What about in your culture?
A: It's pretty much optional. You should take a gift if it's a birthday party, but . . .

	must	should	mustn't	shouldn't	don't have to	doesn't matter
1. take a gift when invited somewhere	☐	☐	☐	☐	☐	☐
2. ask how old someone is	☐	☐	☐	☐	☐	☐
3. smoke without asking permission	☐	☐	☐	☐	☐	☐
4. hug friends when you see them	☐	☐	☐	☐	☐	☐
5. shake hands when you meet someone	☐	☐	☐	☐	☐	☐
6. remove your shoes at someone's house	☐	☐	☐	☐	☐	☐
7. offer to pay your share at a restaurant	☐	☐	☐	☐	☐	☐
8. ask how much someone weighs	☐	☐	☐	☐	☐	☐
9. ask what someone's occupation is	☐	☐	☐	☐	☐	☐
10. leave a tip in a restaurant	☐	☐	☐	☐	☐	☐
11. call people by their first name	☐	☐	☐	☐	☐	☐

9 | WRITING

Write two or three paragraphs about a past situation that you feel you should have handled differently. Tell what you should or could have done (past) and what you should, could, or might do in a similar future situation.

Example: Two years ago my husband and I were traveling on a train in Europe. It was the middle of the night, and we were the only travelers in a sleeping car. We were both deeply asleep when suddenly our compartment door was loudly opened and several young people came in and began looking for their beds. They were talking very loudly and did not settle down and go to sleep. For a while we tolerated this and tried to go back to sleep but couldn't. Finally, my husband got very angry and started to yell at them. He shouldn't have done this, because the young people just laughed at him. Instead of this, he should have . . .

10 | ON THE INTERNET

⏻ *Use the Internet to find answers to questions you have about what you should and shouldn't do in another culture. Share your questions and answers with the class.*

Examples: In Japanese culture, should you shake hands with someone you meet?

In Lebanese culture, are you supposed to tip in a restaurant?

INFORMATION GAP FOR STUDENT B

Student B, read the story. Answer Student A's questions. Then ask your own questions and fill in the missing information.

Example: A: Where were they supposed to stay?
B: They were supposed to stay at the Grand State Hotel. What should they have gotten?
A: They should have gotten a confirmation number.

A married couple was traveling in Europe and had just entered a new country. They had been having a wonderful time, but now everything was going wrong. The first problem was finding accommodations. They were supposed to stay at the Grand State Hotel, but when they got to the hotel there was no record of their reservation. The wife said they should have gotten _____. They hadn't, unfortunately, so they had to spend the night at the train station. The next day they finally found a room at a hotel far from the center of town. There were two rooms available: a large one and a tiny one. Since they were on a tight budget, they decided they had better _____. The second problem was communication. They were starving after spending hours looking for accommodations, so they went into a restaurant. A waiter brought them a menu, but they couldn't understand it. The husband said they should have brought along a phrase book. They hadn't done that, though, so they didn't know what to order.

Time passed. Other people were being served but they weren't. Frustrated, they decided they _____. But what? They noticed that a boy about 11 years old seemed to be listening to their conversation. Soon the boy came over to their table. "Excuse me," he said. "You have to pay for your meal first. Then they'll take your order." The husband and wife were both astonished but grateful. The wife said, "You speak our language very well. Did you study it somewhere?" The boy said, "I lived in Australia for three years. I learned English there." He asked, "_____? I can translate the menu."

When they got back home, their friends asked them what they had liked best about the trip. The wife said, "Well, the best part was visiting that country where everything went wrong. At some point, everybody should experience difficulty. You don't have to _____, but you need a challenge. That's when you learn things. Maybe that's what people mean when they say travel is broadening."

Modals to Express Degrees of Certainty

Grammar in Context

BEFORE YOU READ

1 *When people say, "Columbus discovered the New World," what do they mean?*

2 *What theories have you heard of as to who besides Columbus might have "discovered" the New World?*

⌒ *Read this article about the discovery of America.*

Who *Really* Discovered America?

A well-known school rhyme goes like this: "In fourteen hundred and ninety-two, Columbus sailed the ocean blue." However, Columbus may not have been the first to visit the Western Hemisphere. So many other groups have been nominated for the honor that the question might almost be rephrased as follows: "Who *didn't* discover America?" But what does the evidence show? Who *really* discovered the New World? Those suggested include the Vikings, the Japanese, the Chinese, the Egyptians, the Hebrews, the Portuguese, and some Irish monks.

The Vikings are perhaps the best-known candidates. Some assume there were several Viking trips to the New World, but the most famous is the voyage of Leif Erickson. Evidence suggests that Erickson and some companions visited the New World in about the year 1000, almost 500 years before Columbus. Viking records and artifacts found in the New World indicate that they arrived at a place they named "Vinland the Good"—the land of grapes. Scholars originally assumed that Vinland must have been present-day Newfoundland. Today, though, the assumption is that Vinland couldn't have been Newfoundland, since that island is too far north for grapes to grow. Could the climate have been warmer in Erickson's day? Perhaps. However, the current theory is that Vinland may have been what is now Rhode Island, Cape Cod, the Boston area, or Nova Scotia.

The Japanese are more recent candidates. In 1956 on the Pacific coast of Ecuador, an amateur archaeologist discovered pottery fragments dating back about 5,000 years. Where did

Christopher Columbus

(continued)

Who *Really* Discovered America?

they come from? Intrigued by the mystery, Betty Meggers of the Smithsonian Institute concluded that individuals may have sailed from Japan across the Pacific to Ecuador about 5,000 years ago. Meggers based her conclusion on the similarity of the pottery found in Ecuador to Japanese pottery of the same era. Besides this, said Meggers, it has been established that there was no pottery in Ecuador in 3000 B.C., so the Japanese may have introduced it. If this theory is true, how could the voyage have happened? Some think Japanese fishermen might have been swept out to sea and carried across the Pacific for 10,000 miles. The theory may sound unlikely and may be disproved eventually, but the pottery evidence must mean something.

One interesting theory is the story of St. Brendan, an Irish monk born in A.D. 484, who made many voyages in northwestern Europe to establish monasteries. Maps of the time of Columbus showed an island far out in the Atlantic called "St. Brendan's Isle." Brendan's journey is mentioned in a document called "Voyage of St. Brendan the Abbot." The journey supposedly took place in the sixth century, and reports of it may have influenced Columbus to believe that there really was a New World. The text says that when Brendan and his fellow monks took this tremendous journey, they saw "sea monsters" and "crystals that rose up into the sky" and described "a rain of bad-smelling rocks." In 1976, British navigation scholar Tim Severin decided to test the theory to see if Brendan and his companions could really have accomplished this voyage. Using the specifications described in the St. Brendan text, they built a curragh, an Irish boat made out of leather, and attempted the journey. On the way, they passed Greenland and wintered in Iceland, where they saw whales, a volcano, and icebergs. They theorized that Brendan's sea monsters could have been large, friendly whales, that the crystals rising to the sky might have been icebergs, and that volcanoes in Iceland might have produced the rain of bad-smelling rocks. Severin's group did eventually get to Newfoundland, proving that a curragh could have made the journey to North America. Religious artifacts and stone carvings showing vocabulary and grammatical constructions from Old Irish have been found in Virginia in the United States. This suggests that other missionaries could have gone to the New World after Brendan's return. So the story may be true.

However, we come back to the original question: Who really "discovered" America? Continued future research should get us closer to an answer. Whatever the results of such future investigations, Columbus did <u>not</u>, of course, really discover America. The Native Americans who migrated across the Bering Strait 10,000 or more years ago were, of course, the real discoverers, and they deserve most of the credit. The statement that Columbus "discovered" the New World really means that he started two-way communication between the Old World and the New. In that sense, therefore, Columbus's reputation is still safe.

Could this boat have made it across the Atlantic?

AFTER YOU READ

What does each sentence mean? Circle the correct answer.

1. Leif Erickson and some companions must have visited the New World around the year 1000.
    a. It's almost certain that they visited it then.
    b. It's absolutely certain that they visited it then.
    c. It's possible that they visited it then.

2. The story of St. Brendan may have influenced Columbus to believe there was a New World.
    a. It's almost certain that it influenced him.
    b. It's possible that it influenced him.
    c. It's absolutely certain that it influenced him.

3. Future research should get us closer to an answer.
    a. It's possible that it will get us closer.
    b. It's absolutely certain that it will get us closer.
    c. It's almost certain that it will get us closer.

Grammar Presentation

MODALS TO EXPRESS DEGREES OF CERTAINTY

Speculations about the Present							
It	**must** **has (got) to**	**be**	true.	It	**can't / couldn't** **must not**	**be**	true.
It	**may / might** **could**	**be**	true.	It	**may not** **might not**	**be**	true.

Speculations about the Past							
It	**must have** **had to have**	**been**	true.	It	**can't have** **couldn't have** **must not have**	**been**	true.
It	**may have** **might have** **could have**	**been**	true.	It	**may not have** **might not have**	**been**	true.

Speculations about the Future								
We	should ought to	solve	it soon.					
We	may might could	solve	it soon.	We	may not might not	solve	it soon.

GRAMMAR NOTES

EXAMPLES

1. We use **modals** and **modal-like expressions** to express different degrees of certainty. With these modals we speculate, or make guesses, about things based on logic and facts as we understand them.

- The story **must** be true. *(approximately 90% certain)*
- The story **might** be true. *(approximately 50% certain)*

Remember that we use modals in progressive as well as in simple forms.

- He **may** be planning another trip.

When we want to state a fact we are absolutely—100 percent—sure of, we don't use modals.

- That story is true.
- He was planning another trip.

2. Use *must / have to / have got to* + base form when you are speculating about the present and are almost certain.

- The evidence **has to / has got to** mean something.

To make a negative speculation, use *can't / couldn't* + base form.

- That theory **can't** be / **couldn't** be right.

Use *must not* + base form when you are slightly less certain.

- It **must not** be right.

NOTE: We usually don't contract *must not* in this meaning of *must*.

- The explorer **must not** be famous. NOT The explorer ~~mustn't~~ be famous.

In questions, use **could / couldn't** + base form.

- **Could** that be the case?
- **Couldn't** that be the explanation?

3. Use *may / might / could* + base form when you are speculating about the present and are less certain.

- We **may / might / could** know the answer.

Use *may not / might not* + base form in the negative.

- They **may not / might not** have any evidence.

  NOT They ~~mayn't~~ have any evidence.

▶ **BE CAREFUL!** We usually do not contract *might not*, and we never contract *may not*.

In questions, use *could / might* + base form.

- **Could / Might** that be correct?

---

4. Use *must have / had to have* + past participle when you are speculating about the past and are almost certain.

- They **must have / had to have** visited America.

In the negative, use *can't have / couldn't have* + past participle.

- That **can't have / couldn't have** happened.

Use *must not have* + past participle when you are slightly less certain.

- He **must not have** made the trip.

In questions, use *can have / could have* + past participle.

- **Can / Could** that **have** been the reason?

---

5. When you are speculating about the past and are less certain (50%), use *may have / might have / could have* + past participle.

- They **may / might / could have** reached the New World.

▶ **BE CAREFUL!** *Could have* + past participle has two meanings.

- He **could have** gone. (*It's a possibility—a degree of certainty*)
- He **could have** gone. (*He didn't—a missed opportunity*)

In the negative, use *may not have / might not have* + past participle.

- They **may / might not have** found what they were looking for.

In questions, use *might have / could have* + past participle.

- **Might / Could** they **have** had trouble?

---

6. Use *should / ought to* + base form when you are almost certain about a future action or event.

- Continued research **should / ought to** get us closer to an answer.

---

7. Use *may / might / could* + base form when you are less certain about a future action or event.

- We **may / might / could** know the answer soon.

In the negative, use *may / might + not / never* + base form.

- However, we **may / might never** know the answer.

Focused Practice

1 | DISCOVER THE GRAMMAR

A *Look again at the opening reading. Read the first three paragraphs. Underline all the modals and modal-like expressions that show a degree of certainty.*

B *Look at these sentences based on the reading. For each sentence, circle the letter of the statement that is closer in meaning.*

1. Columbus may not have been the first to visit the Western Hemisphere.

    a. He might not have been the first.

    b. He could not have been the first.

2. It must have been about the year 1000 when Erickson visited the New World.

    a. I'm almost certain it was about the year 1000.

    b. I think maybe it was about the year 1000.

3. The assumption is that Vinland couldn't have been Newfoundland.

    a. It must not have been Newfoundland.

    b. It can't have been Newfoundland.

4. How could the voyage have happened?

    a. I'd like an explanation of how the voyage was impossible.

    b. I'd like an explanation of how the voyage was possible.

5. Individuals may have sailed from Japan to Ecuador.

    a. It's possible they did it.

    b. It's certain they did it.

6. The pottery evidence must mean something.

    a. I'm almost sure it means something.

    b. I strongly doubt it means something.

7. Other missionaries could have gone to the New World after Brendan's return.

    a. It's possible that they went.

    b. They had the opportunity to go but didn't.

8. Continued research should get us closer to an answer.

    a. It's possible that it will.

    b. It's almost certain that it will.

2 | WHERE'S HARRY?

Read this conversation. Complete it with modal constructions from the box.

could be working	~~could have gotten~~	may have had to	might be
might be meeting	must have	must have been visiting	should be

BLAKE: I wonder what's keeping Harry. He's usually on time for office parties. I suppose he

_____*could have gotten*_____ stuck in traffic.
　　　　　　1.

SAMANTHA: Yeah, that's a possibility. Or he _____ work late. I've never
　　　　　　　　　　　　　　　　　　　2.

known him to be late for a party.

BLAKE: You know, I've always felt there's something a little puzzling—or even mysterious—

about Harry.

SAMANTHA: What makes you say that?

BLAKE: Well, he never says much about his past. He's really an interesting guy, but I don't

know much about him. For all I know, he _____ an
　　　　　　　　　　　　　　　　　　　　　　3.

international spy.

SAMANTHA: I think I know what you mean. Or he _____ as a government
　　　　　　　　　　　　　　　　　　　　4.

agent.

BLAKE: Something tells me this is a case of *cherchez la femme*.

SAMANTHA: What does that mean?

BLAKE: It means "look for the woman." I figure he _____ a girlfriend
　　　　　　　　　　　　　　　　　　　　　5.

that he doesn't want us to know about.

SAMANTHA: Yeah, maybe so. You know, now that I think of it, he always leaves work early on

Friday afternoons. I see him go to the parking garage about 4:00, and it always seems

like he's trying not to be seen. He _____ his secret love.
　　　　　　　　　　　　　　　　　　6.

[The doorbell rings.]

BLAKE: Oh, wait a minute. There's the doorbell. Everyone else is here. That

_____ him.
　　　7.

(continued)

HARRY: Hi, folks. Sorry I'm late. Had some business to take care of.

SAMANTHA: Business, huh. You mean romantic business?

HARRY: Romantic business? What are you talking about?

BLAKE: We figure you _____ your lady love. After all, we see you
                                    8.
leave early every Friday afternoon.

HARRY: Pretty funny. Well, there is a lady, and I love her. But it's not what you think.

SAMANTHA: What is it, then?

HARRY: My mother. She's 88 years old, and she lives in a retirement home. I go to see her
every Friday.

---

3 | MYTH, LEGEND, OR REALITY?   *Grammar Notes 3–5*

*Read this article about past cultures. Complete the sentences, using the words in
parentheses. Be careful to put the verbs in the past or present form.*

World Review

Where do we draw the line between myth or legend and reality? How much is true

and how much invented? What happens to groups or cultures when they disappear?

We at *World Review* decided to explore some of these questions.

Let's first consider the saga of the ancient Pueblo people of the U.S. Southwest.

Scholars think that these people, called the Anasazi or "ancient ones" by the Navajo,

_____ *may have settled* _____ about A.D. 100 in the Four Corners area, where today
     1. (may / settle)
the corners of the states of Arizona, Utah, Colorado, and New Mexico come together.

The Anasazi are known to have developed agriculture and to have built impressive

cities and spectacular cliff dwellings. About the year 1300, however, something

happened to the Anasazi. They abandoned their dwellings and migrated to other

locales, such as the Rio Grande Valley in New Mexico and the White Mountains in

Arizona. What _____ this?
              2. (could / cause)

Today many anthropologists assume that the present-day Pueblo peoples in

the Southwest _____ the descendents of the Anasazi.
                          3. (must / be)

However, for other scholars, questions remain: What _____
                                                    4. (might / bring)

an end to their flourishing culture? Drought? Attacks by unfriendly tribes? Are

certain present-day Native Americans really the descendants of the Anasazi? Or

_____ they actually _____?
                               5. (could / disappear)

Next, let's turn our attention to the story of Atlantis, the famed "lost continent"

which is said to have existed in the Atlantic Ocean thousands of years ago.

Atlantis was supposedly located west of the Strait of Gibraltar. Is Atlantis a myth, or

_____ it _____? Plato wrote about Atlantis in two of his
                            6. (could / exist)

dialogues, describing it as a fabulous island, larger than Libya and Turkey. He believed

that Atlantis _____ about 9,000 years before his time. The
                       7. (had to / exist)

Atlanteans were reputed to have conquered many lands around the Mediterranean

and, he thought, _____ evil and greedy in the process. Their
                           8. (must / become)

island or continent was supposed to have sunk into the sea after being hit by

earthquakes. _____ an Atlantis? Certain writers think the
                      9. (Could / there really / be)

present-day Basques _____ the descendants of survivors of the
                           10. (might / be)

catastrophe, if there was one. Is the Atlantis story just an entertaining legend invented

by Plato? Or, if Atlantis was real, is the problem simply that it existed so long ago that

traces of its memory are all that remain? Many scholars think that reports of a disaster

on the island of Thíra _____ the Atlantis legend. Thíra, in the
                        11. (may / influence)

Mediterranean Sea north of Crete, was destroyed about 1500 B.C. by volcanic eruptions

and accompanying earthquakes, which also devastated civilization on nearby Crete.

Perhaps the Thíra disaster was the basis for the Atlantis legend, or the descendants of

Atlanteans _____ still _____ among us. At this point, we
                           12. (might / be)

simply don't know.

4 | PREDICT YOUR FUTURE

Grammar Notes 6–7

Think for a few minutes about things you might accomplish or are likely to accomplish in the next 10 years. Write 10 sentences describing these potential accomplishments. Use **should**, **ought to**, **may**, **might**, *and* **could**. *Then compare your sentences with a partner's.*

Examples: I **might get married** within three years.

I **should finish** my college education by 2010.

5 | EDITING

Read this student essay. There are nine mistakes in the use of modals. The first mistake is already corrected. Find and correct eight more.

WHY WE ITCH

One ~~must~~ *might* think that with all the scientific progress that has been made in the last century, researchers would be able by now to answer this very simple question: Why do we itch? Unfortunately, scientists can't answer this question with any certainty. They simply don't know.

There are some clear cases involving itching. If a patient goes to her doctor and complains of terrible itching and the doctor finds hives or some other kind of rash, the doctor will probably say that she must eat something she was allergic to—or that she must not have been stung or bitten by some insect. This kind of case can be easily explained. Most itching, however, does not have an obvious cause.

Here's what scientists do know: Right under the surface of the skin there are sensory receptors that register physical stimuli and carry messages to the brain. These receptors detect pain and let the brain know about it. If there is a high level of physical stimulation to the body, the sensory receptors might carried a message of pain to the brain. If the level of physical stimulation is low, the sensors might be report it as itchiness.

There has been a lot of speculation about the function of itching. Some researchers think it's possible that the function of itching has to be to warn the body that it is about to have a painful experience. Others theorize that early humans might developed itching as a way of knowing that they needed to take insects out of their hair. Still others believe that itching could have been a symptom of serious diseases such as diabetes and Hodgkin's disease.

One of the most interesting aspects of itching is that it may have be less tolerable than pain. Research has shown, in fact, that most of us tolerate pain better than itching. Many people will allow their skin to be painfully broken just so they can get rid of an itch.

Communication Practice

6 | LISTENING

🎧 *Listen to a discussion in a biology class. Then listen to certain statements made during the discussion. For each statement, choose the sentence, **a** or **b**, that gives the same information.*

1. **a.** It's almost impossible that it was me on the tape.
   b. It's possible that it was me on the tape.

2. **a.** There's probably a mistake.
   b. There's possibly a mistake.

3. **a.** It's possible that all of you have had this experience before.
   b. It's almost certain that all of you have had this experience before.

4. **a.** You have probably figured out the answer.
   b. You will probably be able to figure out the answer.

5. **a.** It's probably because we hear the sound in a different way.
   b. It's possibly because we hear the sound in a different way.

(continued)

6. **a.** It's possibly because the sound travels through different substances.

   b. It's almost certainly because the sound travels through different substances.

7. **a.** It's certain that it's a combination of the two things.

   b. It's possible that it's a combination of the two things.

8. **a.** It's almost certain that the sound others hear is the real sound.

   b. It's unlikely that the sound others hear is the real sound.

9. **a.** The sound we heard was probably the real sound.

   b. The sound we hear is probably the real sound.

10. **a.** It's certain that internal hearing is more accurate than external hearing.

    b. It's almost certain that internal hearing is more accurate than external hearing.

7 | SOLVE THE PUZZLE

Work with a partner to solve these puzzles. Using past modals, suggest several possible solutions to each puzzle and write them down—from most likely to least likely—and label them accordingly.

1. On November 22, 1978, an 18-year-old thief broke into a lady's house and demanded all her money. She gave him all she had: $11.50. The thief was so angry that he demanded she write him a check for $50. Two hours later, the police caught the thief. How?

   Example: **A:** The thief might have given the lady his real name for the check.

   B: It could be that the lady just recognized him.

   A: Or there may have been a security camera in the building.

2. A dog owner put some food in a pan for her cat. Then, because she didn't want her dog to eat the cat's food, she tied a six-foot rope around his neck. Then she left. When she came back, she discovered that the dog had eaten the cat's food. What happened?

3. A young girl named Michelle decided to ride her bicycle from her own town to a town 10 kilometers away. After a while she reached a crossroads where she had to change direction. She discovered that the signpost with arrows pointing to different towns in the area had blown down. She didn't know which road was the right one. Nevertheless, she was able to figure out which road to take. What do you think she did?

4. Roy Sullivan, a forest ranger in Virginia, had several experiences in his life in which he was struck by a powerful force. Two times his hair was set on fire. He had burns on his eyebrows, shoulder, stomach, chest, and ankle. Once he was driving when he was hit and was knocked 10 feet out of his car. What do you think happened to him?

8 | SMALL-GROUP DISCUSSION

Form small groups. Look again at the story of Atlantis in Exercise 3. Which explanation do you think is the most likely? Which do you like best? Discuss your opinions with your partners. Report your opinions to the class.

Example: A: Which explanation do you like best about Atlantis?
B: Well, the one I like best is that the Basques are descendants of the Atlanteans. But I don't think it's the most likely explanation.
A: What is it, then?
B: I think it must have been . . .

9 | PICTURE DISCUSSION

Look at the photograph of Stonehenge, located on the Plain of Salisbury in southern England. With a partner, discuss the photograph. Who do you think built it? What do you think it was used for? Use modals in your discussion.

Example: It might have been used for religious ceremonies.

10 | WRITING

Write about an important world mystery you have heard of. Using present and past modals of certainty, speculate on the causes and possible explanations. Use one of the following topics or choose your own.

- How were the great pyramids in Egypt built?
- Who or what is making the crop circles in Britain?
- Does the Loch Ness monster really exist?
- How did the great statues get to Easter Island?

Example: Does the Loch Ness monster really exist? I've always wanted to believe it does, and for years I did believe that. Recently, however, I've come to a different conclusion. Reports of seeing the monster might be from people's imaginations. Or they could just be tricks. But the legend can't be true. Here's why I think this . . .

11 | ON THE INTERNET

Use the Internet to find information about a mystery that intrigues you. You may choose a topic mentioned in this unit or create your own topic. Share your information with the class.

From **Grammar** to **Writing**
Topic Sentences

A common way of organizing a composition or other piece of writing in English is to begin with a **topic sentence**. A topic sentence is a general sentence that covers the content of the entire paragraph. All the supporting examples and details of the paragraph must fit under this sentence. It is usually the first sentence in the paragraph. Look at this paragraph from an essay.

> For me, a dog is a better pet than a cat. When I come home from work, for example, my dog comes to meet me at the door. He is always glad to see me. My cat, on the other hand, couldn't care less whether I'm at home or not, as long as I keep filling her food dish. Another good thing about a dog is that you can teach him tricks. Cats, however, can't be bothered to learn anything new. The best thing about a dog, though, is that he's a great companion. I can take my dog on hikes and walks. He goes everywhere with me. As we all know, you can't take a cat for a walk.

The topic sentence for this paragraph is "For me, a dog is a better pet than a cat." This sentence tells the reader what to expect in the paragraph: some reasons why the writer considers a dog a superior pet.

1 | *This paragraph contains many supporting details but no topic sentence. Read the paragraph. Then circle the letter of the best topic sentence for the paragraph.*

> For one thing, you should always remove your shoes when you enter a Japanese home, and you should leave them pointing toward the door. Another suggestion is to make sure that you bring a gift for your Japanese hosts, and to be sure to wrap it. A third recommendation is to be appreciative of things in a Japanese house, but not too appreciative. Finally, remember that when you sit down to eat, you do not have to accept every kind of food that you are offered, but you are expected to finish whatever you do put on your plate.

Choices

a. Visiting a Japanese home is very enjoyable.

b. Taking a gift is very important when you visit a Japanese home.

c. There are a number of things to keep in mind when you visit a Japanese home.

d. When you visit a Japanese home, be sure not to eat too much.

Remember that an English sentence must contain a subject and a verb in at least one independent clause. The following groups of words are potential topic sentences, but they are fragments (they are not independent clauses, or they lack a subject or verb):

Reasons why the birth order theory makes sense. (not an independent clause)

Correction: There are several reasons why the birth order theory makes sense.

Relaxing and doing nothing. (no verb)

Correction: Relaxing and doing nothing can be beneficial sometimes.

2 *Each of the following word groups is a fragment but is also a potential topic sentence. Make necessary additions to each.*

1. A city where exciting and mysterious things happen.

_____

2. Reasons why college isn't for everybody.

_____

3. Wild animals not making good pets.

_____

4. Regular exercise and its benefits.

_____

3 *Read this paragraph. Then look at the four possible topic sentences. With a partner, discuss which one is the best. Why? What is wrong with each of the other choices?*

One reason is that when commercial flights began, all pilots were male. Men were hired because they had flight experience obtained in combat. Women, not having been in combat, had no flight experience. A second reason is simply prejudice: The powers in the airline industry presumably believed the stereotype that there are certain jobs that women cannot do as well as men. A third reason is inertia and the status quo—flying has mostly been a male-dominated profession since it began, and it takes time to change things. Eventually we will see more and more female commercial airline pilots, but for the present, old ideas die hard.

Choices

a. Why there are so few women commercial pilots today.

b. There are three principal reasons why there are so few women commercial pilots today.

c. Women pilots in aviation.

d. Men are still prejudiced about women's capabilities.

4 Look at the following sets of supporting details. For each set, write an appropriate topic sentence.

1. _____

    a. For one thing, there's almost always a traffic jam I get stuck in, and I'm often late to work.

    b. Also, there's not always a parking place when I do get to work.

    c. Worst of all, I'm spending more money on gas and car maintenance than I would if I took public transportation.

2. _____

    a. One is that I often fall asleep when watching the TV screen, no matter how interesting the video is.

    b. Another is that watching movies is basically a social experience, and I'm usually alone when I watch videos.

    c. The main reason is that the TV screen, no matter how large it is, diminishes the impact that you get when watching a movie on the big screen.

3. _____

    a. Nothing spontaneous usually happens on a guided tour, but I've had lots of spontaneous experiences when I planned my own vacation.

    b. Tour guides present you with what *they* think is interesting, but when you are in charge of your own vacation, you do what *you* think is interesting.

    c. Individually planned vacations can often be less expensive than guided tours.

4. _____

    a. Cats don't bark and wake up the neighbors or bite the letter carrier.

    b. Dogs have to be walked at least two times a day, but cats handle their own exercise.

    c. Cats eat a lot less than dogs.

5 Write a paragraph of several sentences about one of the following topics, a similar topic that interests you, or a topic suggested by your teacher. Make sure that your paragraph has a topic sentence. Then share your work with three or four other students. Read each other's paragraphs. Identify topic sentences. Make sure that each one is not a fragment and that it is appropriate for the paragraph.

Topics

- An annoying habit
- The best part of the day
- Night owls versus early birds
- The ideal vacation
- A problem in society
- Expectation versus reality

Review Test

I *Read the conversations between a job interviewer and various applicants. Fill in the blanks using the cues in parentheses. Use full forms for auxiliaries used to emphasize or show stress; use contracted forms for all other auxiliaries.*

1. A: What languages are you familiar with, Ms. Suzuki? Do you speak Mandarin?

    B: No, I _____ *don't speak* _____ Mandarin. I _____ *do speak* _____ Japanese
                     a. (not / speak)   **b. (speak)**
    and Spanish, though.

    A: Are you fluent in those languages?

    B: I _____ fluent in Japanese. I _____ fluent
                 c. (be)   **d. (not / be)**
    in Spanish, but I _____ conversant in it.
                      e. (be)

2. A: Mr. Quinn, your résumé says that you attended college. Did you earn a bachelor's degree?

    B: No, I _____ a B.A. I _____ an associate
                 a. (not / earn)   **b. (earn)**
    degree, though.

3. A: Ms. Liu, this job requires overseas experience. Have you lived abroad?

    B: I _____ abroad, but I _____ extensively in
                 a. (not / live)   **b. (travel)**
    Europe and Eastern Asia.

4. A: Mr. Travolta, this _____ a full-time position. It
                         a. (not / be)
    _____ a three-quarter-time job, however, and it
         b. (be)
    _____ an extensive benefits package. Are you interested?
         c. (have)
    B: The job sounds interesting. I _____ some time to think it over,
                                 d. (would like)
    though. Could I let you know by next Monday?

II *Complete the conversations using* **so**, **neither**, **too**, *or* **not either** *plus the appropriate auxiliary to make additions. Use contractions whenever possible.*

1. A: Avocados have a disgusting texture, I think. I can't stand them.

   B: _____*Neither can*_____ I. They're at the bottom of my list.

2. A: What did you think of *The Lord of the Rings*? I thought it was pretty neat.

   B: _____ I. I really liked Viggo Mortenson and Elijah Wood.

3. A: Janice has never been to Mexico City.

   B: Joe _____. He wants to go this summer, though.

4. A: Helena won't be able to come to the party Wednesday afternoon.

   B: _____ Josh. He has a doctor's appointment.

5. A: How do you feel about hunting whales? I'm against it.

   B: I _____. I can understand both sides of the issue, but it still seems cruel to
   the whales.

6. A: Did you hear that Bill spent $2,000 on a new bicycle? I wouldn't spend that much.

   B: _____ I. There are better things to do with your money.

7. A: Can you believe it? Mandy had never heard of Peter Jackson.

   B: Well, I _____ before *The Lord of the Rings* came out. You just can't know
   everything.

8. A: I can't believe it! My mother says she believes in UFOs.

   B: Really? _____ my mother. She says she saw one once.

III *Complete this letter to a columnist and the columnist's response. Circle the correct modals and modal-like expressions.*

Dear Pamela:

   My wife, Jeannine, and I invited a Japanese colleague to dinner last week. We'd invited her once

before, but she'd (had to)/ must decline because of other commitments. This time, she was able to
          1.

come. Things were going well at first. Yoko, my co-worker, seemed a little nervous, but that was

understandable. I thought she was probably trying to remember how you 'd better / 're supposed to
                                                                          2.

act when you visit an American home. She brought a beautifully wrapped present, which my wife

opened right away. Yoko seemed to think Jeannine shouldn't have / must not have done that,
                                                              3.

(continued)

because she looked upset. I thought maybe in Japan you <u>don't have to / aren't supposed to</u> tear the
_{4.}
paper. Maybe you <u>could / 're supposed to</u> take it off gently and fold it, or something. Anyway, my
_{5.}
wife tore it off and pulled out a box of excellent chocolates. She <u>should have / might have</u> waited
_{6.}
until after dinner, but she insisted on passing them around and having everyone eat some of them.
Before dinner! Yoko was embarrassed. She said she thought she <u>should bring / should have brought</u>
_{7.}
something else for a gift. Pamela, what went wrong? It think it was all Jeannine's fault.

Puzzled in Pittsburgh

Dear Puzzled:

You <u>aren't allowed to / don't have to</u> blame anybody for this problem. It's a clear case of cultural
_{8.}
misunderstanding. What you <u>must / are to</u> understand is that in Japan when someone takes a gift to a
_{9.}
friend's house, the friend <u>shouldn't / doesn't have to</u> open it in front of the visitor. It is more polite to
_{10.}
wait until later to open it, so it was probably something of a shock to your Japanese friend to see your
wife make such a big scene. That's not what one <u>might have done / is supposed to do</u> in Japan.
_{11.}

Don't be too concerned about it. I'm sure your friend will understand when you explain to her
and apologize.

Pamela

IV *Read the story. Fill in the blanks with modals or modal-like expressions.*

One of the most puzzling experiences I've ever had happened last winter. It was one of those
typical dark and stormy nights that you read about in mystery novels. Sitting on the sofa in the
living room, I could hear thunder and see an occasional flash of lightning. It ____*must have*____
_{1.}
been at least 1:00 A.M. I was reading an exciting mystery novel. Suddenly the phone rang, startling
me out of my wits. I picked up the receiver, muttering to myself something like, "Who
_____ that be at this hour of the night? Someone _____ died." But
_{2.}   _{3.}
no. There were a few seconds of silence; then a low, scary voice said, "Help me. Help me." "Who
are you?" I asked. "Who is this?" No answer. The phone went dead.

The next morning it all seemed like a bad dream. I was troubled enough by the experience to tell my friend Josh about it. "It _____ been a crank call," he said. "Or it
4.
_____ been one of your friends playing a joke on you."
5.

"What do you think I _____ do?"
6.

"Do? Why do anything? It won't happen again."

It did happen again, though, the following night. At precisely 1:12 A.M. (I looked at my watch this time) the phone rang, waking me out of a sound sleep. The same deep, scary voice was on the other end of the line. I responded in the same way, but the voice just said, "Help me, help me." Then there was silence, and the line went dead as before.

The next day I told Josh about it again. "I still say it _____ to be some friend of
7.
yours playing a joke. Don't you recognize the voice?"

"Not at all," I said. "It _____ be anyone I know."
8.

"Well, call the phone company. They _____ have an idea about what to do."
9.

I never did call the phone company, for some reason. This experience went on for the next five nights. At precisely 1:12 A.M., the phone would ring, and I would pick it up, only to hear the same thing: "Help me, help me." After that, it stopped. Since then I haven't stopped wondering if I
_____ called the police.
10.

I wonder if it _____ been someone who needed help. Or was it just a joke? I
11.
_____ never find out.
12.

V *Look at the pictures. Write a sentence using the modal or modal-like expression in parentheses to describe each situation, making sure to use the correct form.*

1.

(should)

They should all be

wearing their seat belts.

2.

(must)

_____

_____

3.

(had better)

_____

_____

4.

MAY I SEE YOUR DRIVER'S LICENSE, PLEASE?

SORRY, SIR, I DON'T HAVE IT.

(be supposed to)

_____

_____

5.

GATE 40C

WHERE'S JERRY?

(might)

_____

_____

6.

WHY DIDN'T YOU CALL?

SORRY, MOM. I JUST DIDN'T THINK OF IT.

(could)

_____

_____

7.

(may)

_____

_____

8.

(should)

_____

_____

VI *Circle the letter of the one underlined word or phrase in each sentence that is not correct.*

1. I think we <u>ought</u> <u>look into</u> a nice guided tour—that is, if we
    A B
   <u>can find</u> one that <u>won't bankrupt</u> us.
   C   D   (Ⓐ) B C D

2. Fortunately, I was <u>able to get</u> a scholarship to attend college, and my
   A
   sister was <u>either</u>; otherwise, we never <u>could have</u> <u>afforded</u> it.
   B   C   D   A B C D

3. You <u>had better</u> <u>to set</u> your alarm, or you <u>might not</u> <u>wake up</u> on time.
   A   B   C   D   A B C D

4. The only idea I <u>have</u> as to why Joe <u>isn't</u> here is that he might <u>have been</u>
   A   B   C
   <u>working</u> late.
   D   A B C D

5. All employees <u>were to</u> <u>attend</u> the company party on Saturday, and
   A   B
   everyone <u>should</u> <u>bring</u> a present for the gift exchange.
   C   D   A B C D

6. Frank <u>has</u> always <u>been</u> against capital punishment, and <u>so</u> <u>had</u> I.
   A   B   C   D   A B C D

7. We <u>ought to</u> <u>take</u> some extra cash along on the trip, but we
   A   B
   absolutely <u>don't have to</u> <u>forget</u> our passports.
   C   D   A B C D

8. Joe called to say that he won't <u>be able to</u> <u>get here</u> by seven o'clock,
   A   B
   but he <u>shouldn't</u> <u>manage to be</u> here by eight.
   C   D   A B C D

(continued)

9. If <u>you want</u> flowers from your rose bushes, you'll <u>have to</u> <u>water</u>   **A B C D**
A B C

them, <u>haven't</u> you?
D

10. I suppose they <u>could be</u> <u>working</u> late at the office, but Amy didn't   **A B C D**
A B

mention it, and <u>either</u> <u>did</u> Mary.
C D

VII   *Go back to your answers to Exercise VI. Write the correct form for each item that you believe is incorrect.*

1. _____ *ought to* _____   6. _____

2. _____   7. _____

3. _____   8. _____

4. _____   9. _____

5. _____   10. _____

▶ *To check your answers, go to the Answer Key on page RT-1.*

PART III

Nouns

7 Count and Non-Count Nouns

Grammar in Context

BEFORE YOU READ

1 *Do you think food today is basically safe and nutritious, or do you have concerns about it?*

2 *What do you think the most important food issues are today?*

3 *Do you believe diets are effective?*

🎧 *Read this transcript of part of a TV presentation by a food and nutrition expert.*

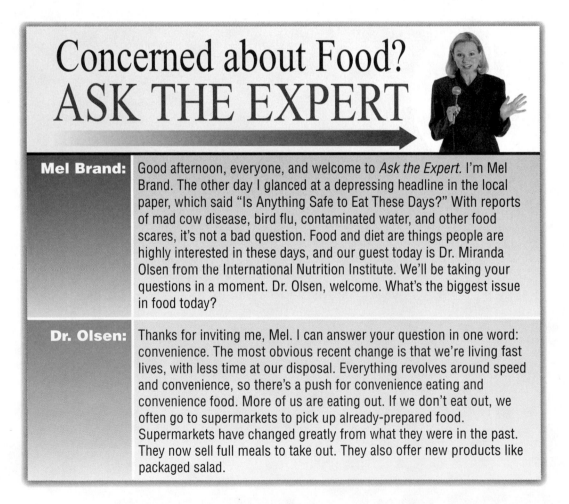

Concerned about Food?
ASK THE EXPERT

Mel Brand:	Good afternoon, everyone, and welcome to *Ask the Expert*. I'm Mel Brand. The other day I glanced at a depressing headline in the local paper, which said "Is Anything Safe to Eat These Days?" With reports of mad cow disease, bird flu, contaminated water, and other food scares, it's not a bad question. Food and diet are things people are highly interested in these days, and our guest today is Dr. Miranda Olsen from the International Nutrition Institute. We'll be taking your questions in a moment. Dr. Olsen, welcome. What's the biggest issue in food today?
Dr. Olsen:	Thanks for inviting me, Mel. I can answer your question in one word: convenience. The most obvious recent change is that we're living fast lives, with less time at our disposal. Everything revolves around speed and convenience, so there's a push for convenience eating and convenience food. More of us are eating out. If we don't eat out, we often go to supermarkets to pick up already-prepared food. Supermarkets have changed greatly from what they were in the past. They now sell full meals to take out. They also offer new products like packaged salad.

Mel Brand:	All right, Dr. Olsen. Thanks for that overview. Now let's have some questions from our audience. Please give your name and tell us where you're from. Yes, the gentleman in the back.
Bob:	I'm Bob Gonzales from Tampa, Florida. My question is about school lunches. My three children are all in high school, and they take lunches from home, which is OK. What I'm really concerned about, though, are the vending machines in the schools. They sell soda, candy, and snacks. I'm worried that the kids are filling up on sodas and chips and not eating what they should. Is there any nutrition in that kind of stuff? Am I worrying for nothing?
Dr. Olsen:	No, you're not, Bob. You have reason to be concerned. There's very little nutrition in soda and snacks. Soda is loaded with sugar, and most snacks are just empty calories. School vending machines have become a big problem in many places. What usually happens is that big companies pay school districts to have vending machines there. The districts find it difficult to turn down the money. There's more and more opposition to having these machines in schools, though, and you <u>can</u> get rid of them.
Mel Brand:	OK. Another question? Yes, ma'am—in the third row.
Maria:	Yes, good morning, Dr. Olsen. I'm Maria Spring from Toronto, Ontario. My question is about diets. In my family we're really concerned about losing weight, so we've started using low-fat or fat-free food. The trouble is, we all hate it because it tastes so bland. Can you give me any advice?
Dr. Olsen:	Well, there's evidence that a nonfat or low-fat diet can actually lead to weight gain. My advice is to stay away from such diets. You can eat regular food in moderate quantities. Avoid sodas. Drink plenty of water and juice, and minimize your intake of salt and sugar. Make sure you eat five to eight servings a day of fruits and vegetables. And exercise at least three times a week. Play a couple of games of tennis. Take brisk walks. That should help your family to lose weight.
Mel Brand:	All right. Next question? Yes, the man in the back …

AFTER YOU READ

What does the underlined word refer to? Circle the correct answer.

1. People are highly interested in <u>food</u>.

    a. food in general   **b.** a specific type of food

2. There's very little nutrition in <u>soda</u>.

    a. an individual serving of soda   **b.** soda in general

3. My question is about <u>diets</u>.

    a. diets in general   **b.** particular diets

Grammar Presentation

NOUNS

Proper Nouns
Professor Lee heads the **Nutrition Institute**.

Common Nouns
The **professor** teaches **nutrition**.

COUNT AND NON-COUNT NOUNS

Count Nouns			
Article or Number	Noun	Verb	
A One	**snack**	is	refreshing.
The Two	**snacks**	are	

Non-Count Nouns		
Noun	Verb	
Rice	is	nourishing.
Nutrition		important.

NOUNS WITH COUNT AND NON-COUNT MEANINGS

Count Meaning
There's **a hair** in my soup!
A chicken escaped from the henhouse.
My favorite **works** of art are from China.

Non-Count Meaning
Sandra has black **hair**.
We had **chicken** for dinner.
It takes **work** to prepare a meal.

NON-COUNT NOUNS IN COUNTABLE FORM

Non-Count Noun
I'll have **tea**.
You need **advice**.
Let's play **tennis**.
The stew needs more **spice**.
Fruit is nutritious.

Countable Form
I'll have **a cup of tea**.
Let me give you **a piece of advice**.
Let's play **a game of tennis**.
There are several **spices** in this stew.
Many different **fruits** are grown in California.

USES OF NON-COUNT NOUNS

Non-Count Nouns in Uncountable Use
I'd like some **coffee**.
Cheese is produced in France.
The sun provides **light**.

Non-Count Nouns in Countable Use
Please bring us **two coffees**.
Brie is **a soft cheese**.
I see **a light** in the window.

GRAMMAR NOTES   **EXAMPLES**

1. **Nouns** represent persons, places, and things. There are two types of nouns: proper nouns and common nouns.	
Proper nouns name particular persons, places, or things. They are usually unique and are capitalized in writing.	• Dr. Olsen, Ichiro Suzuki, São Paulo, China, the Empire State Building, Harrod's
Common nouns refer to people, places, or things but are not the names of particular individuals.	• scientist, athlete, city, country, building, department store

2. There are two types of **common nouns**: count nouns and non-count nouns.	
Count nouns refer to things that you can count separately. They can be singular or plural. You can use *a* or *an* before count nouns.	• one **woman**, nine **planets** • This **sandwich** is delicious. • Some **vegetables** are tasty. • That's **an** interesting **question**.
Non-count nouns refer to things that you cannot count separately. They usually have no plural form. We usually do not use *a* or *an* with non-count nouns, though they are often preceded by *some* or *the*.	• I bought **rice**. NOT I bought a rice. • Let me give you **some advice**. NOT Let me give you an advice.
▶ **BE CAREFUL!** Many nouns have both count and non-count meanings. Check your dictionary to avoid mistakes.	• She heard **a noise** in the attic. • **Noise** can be harmful to health. NOT A noise can be harmful to health.
We normally use a **singular verb** with a non-count noun. We use a **singular pronoun** to refer to the noun.	• **Rice feeds** millions. NOT Rice feed millions. • **It** feeds millions.

(continued)

3. Notice the following categories and examples of **non-count nouns**.

Abstractions	• chance, energy, honesty, love
Activities	• basketball, dancing, tennis
Diseases	• AIDS, cancer, influenza, malaria
Foods	• beef, bread, fish, fruit, meat
Gases	• air, carbon dioxide, oxygen, smoke
Liquids	• coffee, gasoline, milk, tea, water
Natural phenomena	• electricity, heat, rain, thunder
Occupations	• dentistry, nursing, teaching
Particles	• dust, pepper, salt, sand, sugar
Solid elements	• gold, iron, plutonium, silver
Subjects	• Chinese, English, physics, science
Others	• equipment, furniture, money, news

4. We frequently **make non-count nouns countable** by adding a phrase that gives them a form, a limit, or a container.

NON-COUNT NOUN	COUNTABLE FORM
furniture	a piece of furniture
lightning	a bolt / flash of lightning
meat	a piece of meat
rice	a grain of rice
tennis	a game of tennis
thunder	a clap of thunder
water	a cup of water

5. We use many **non-count nouns** in a **countable sense** without the addition of a phrase (such as "a piece of"). We can use these nouns with *a / an* or in the plural to mean *kind / type / variety of*.

A / an and plurals can also be used to indicate discrete amounts.

- Do you like **pasta**?
- In Italy, I tasted **a** new **pasta**.

- I drink **tea** every morning.
- That shop has many different **teas**.

- I drank **a soda**.
- Please bring us two **orange juices**.

6. When **non-count nouns** are preceded by *some* or occur alone, they refer to things that don't have any particular boundaries.	• I drank **some soda**. • **Orange juice** is produced in Florida.

7. Some nouns are irregular.
 	
   a. A few **non-count nouns** end in *-s*.
 	
   b. A few **count nouns** have **irregular plurals**.
	
	• news, mathematics, economics, physics
	
	• criterion, phenomenon, nucleus
	  (singular count nouns)
	• criteria, phenomena, nuclei
	  (their irregular plural forms)

8. **BE CAREFUL!** In its normal usage, the word *people* is **plural** and means "more than one person." In this meaning, it does not have a singular form, and it takes a plural verb. The word *people* meaning "a particular group (or particular groups) of human beings" can have a singular and a plural form.	• Hawaiian **people use** food in unusual ways. NOT Hawaiian people ~~uses~~ food in unusual ways. • The Hmong are **a people** of southern China and nearby areas. • Many different **peoples** have settled in Hawaii.

Reference Notes
For a list of **non-count nouns,** see Appendix 5 on page A-4.
For a list of phrases for **counting non-count nouns,** see Appendix 6 on page A-5.
For a list of **irregular plurals,** see Appendix 4 on page A-3.

Focused Practice

1 DISCOVER THE GRAMMAR

Read the sentences based on the opening reading. Underline the count nouns. Circle the non-count nouns.

1. With <u>reports</u> of (mad cow disease,) bird (flu,) contaminated (water,) and food <u>scares</u>, it's not a bad <u>question</u>.

2. Food and diet are things people are interested in these days.

3. What's the biggest issue in food today?

4. We're living fast lives with less free time, so we seek convenience.

5. I'm concerned about the vending machines that sell soda, candy, and snacks.

6. Is there any nutrition in that kind of stuff?

7. My family is concerned about losing weight, so we've started using low-fat or fat-free food.

8. There's evidence that a nonfat or low-fat diet can actually lead to weight gain.

2 NON-COUNT NOUNS IN COUNTABLE FORM

Grammar Note 4

Complete each sentence with the correct phrase to give the non-countable noun a countable form. Refer to Appendix 6 on page A-5 for help in completing this exercise if necessary.

1. When we moved to the new office, we lost _____*a piece of*_____ equipment.
   (a piece of / a pound of)

2. Let me give you _____ advice: don't buy that item.
   (a speck of / a piece of)

3. The floor was so clean that there wasn't _____ dust anywhere.
   (a speck of / a piece of)

4. Please get _____ sugar when you're at the store.
   (a pound of / a piece of)

5. Our office bought several new _____ furniture.
   (pieces of / matters of)

6. There hasn't been _____ rain here for over a month.
   (a drop of / a grain of)

7. We heard an interesting _____ news on the radio last night.
   (amount of / piece of)

8. In our family it's customary to have _____ tea late in the afternoon.
   (a kilo of / a cup of)

9. What you order at a restaurant is _____ choice.
   (a piece of / a matter of)

10. You've had a reasonable _____ time to finish the job.
    (branch of / period of)

3 | **BLENDING** *Grammar Notes 3, 5*

Read the article about fusion cooking and complete it with words from the box.

century	chefs	~~cooking~~	cuisines	flavoring	foods
fusion	menu	rolls	rules	spices	ways

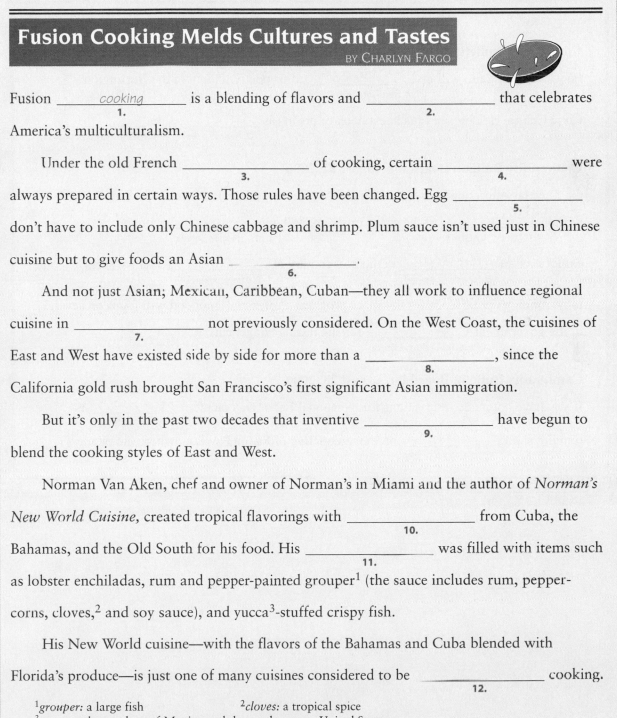

Fusion Cooking Melds Cultures and Tastes
BY CHARLYN FARGO

Fusion _____cooking_____ is a blending of flavors and _____ that celebrates
          1.   **2.**
America's multiculturalism.

Under the old French _____ of cooking, certain _____ were
                              3.   **4.**
always prepared in certain ways. Those rules have been changed. Egg _____
                                                                              5.
don't have to include only Chinese cabbage and shrimp. Plum sauce isn't used just in Chinese

cuisine but to give foods an Asian _____.
                                         6.

And not just Asian; Mexican, Caribbean, Cuban—they all work to influence regional

cuisine in _____ not previously considered. On the West Coast, the cuisines of
              7.

East and West have existed side by side for more than a _____, since the
                                                                8.
California gold rush brought San Francisco's first significant Asian immigration.

But it's only in the past two decades that inventive _____ have begun to
                                                              9.
blend the cooking styles of East and West.

Norman Van Aken, chef and owner of Norman's in Miami and the author of *Norman's*

New World Cuisine, created tropical flavorings with _____ from Cuba, the
                                                            10.
Bahamas, and the Old South for his food. His _____ was filled with items such
                                                    11.
as lobster enchiladas, rum and pepper-painted grouper[1] (the sauce includes rum, pepper-

corns, cloves,[2] and soy sauce), and yucca[3]-stuffed crispy fish.

His New World cuisine—with the flavors of the Bahamas and Cuba blended with

Florida's produce—is just one of many cuisines considered to be _____ cooking.
                                                                        12.

[1]*grouper:* a large fish   [2]*cloves:* a tropical spice
[3]*yucca:* a desert plant of Mexico and the southwestern United States

4 | COMMUNITY BULLETIN BOARD

Grammar Notes 5–8

Interactive websites on the Internet give people information about entertainment, cultural events, and the weather. Fill in the blanks in the bulletin board messages, choosing the correct count or non-count form in parentheses. Refer to Appendices 4 and 6 on pages A-3 and A-5 for help in completing this exercise if necessary.

COMMUNITY BULLETIN BOARD

[Follow Ups] [Post a Reply] [Message Board Index]

Community Bulletin Board for August 26, 2006

Poet Jefferson Saito will give ___*a reading*___ of his poetry tonight in the Burlington
          1. (reading / a reading)

Civic Center. He describes his latest book of poems as _____ in _____.
                                              2. (work / a work)   **3. (progress / a progress)**

Community Bulletin Board for August 27, 2006

On Tuesday afternoon at 4 PM at City Hall, Professor Helen Hammond, who has

written _____ of the space program, will give _____ on the
       4. (history / a history)   **5. (talk / a talk)**

exploration of _____ in the 21st century at _____ when we seem
            6. (space / a space)   **7. (time / a time)**

to be running out of funds for the space program. Professor Hammond will focus on several

of the government's _____ for suggesting budget cuts.
                 8. (criterion / criteria)

Community Bulletin Board for August 28, 2006

If you have not made reservations for the annual Labor Day picnic, _____ is
                                                        9. (time / a time)

running short. _____ on the remodeling of Patton Pavilion, where the picnic
        10. (Work / A work)

```
┌──────────────────────────────────────────────────────────────────────┐
│ ▣            ════════ COMMUNITY BULLETIN BOARD ════════          ▣▣    │
├──────────────────────────────────────────────────────────────────────┤
```

will be held, is complete. All residents of Burlington are invited, but you must have a ticket,

which will cover the price of dinner. The menu will include _____, meat, and
                                                            11. (fish / a fish)

pasta as main courses. _____ and _____ are free.
                       12. (Soda / A soda) **13. (milk / a milk)**

Community Bulletin Board for August 29, 2006

On Friday evening at 8:00 P.M. in the Civic Auditorium, Professor Mary Alice Waters will

present a program on the Hmong, _____ of China and Laos. Professor Waters
                                 14. (peoples / a people)

will show _____ about marriage customs of the Hmong and other
          15. (film / a film)

_____ of Eastern Asia.
16. (people / peoples)

---

5 | A PIECE OF ADVICE   *Grammar Notes 3–6, 8*

*Write your own sentence for each of the nouns and noun phrases in the box. Then share
your sentences with a partner. Discuss and correct them if necessary.*

a people	a piece of advice	a soda	a TV	fruits
furniture	peoples	pieces of furniture	spices	time

Example: My boss gave me a great piece of advice: Check your e-mail just three times a day.

1. _____

2. _____

3. _____

4. _____

5. _____

6. _____

7. _____

8. _____

9. _____

10. _____

6 | EDITING

Read this letter. There are 12 mistakes in the use of count and non-count nouns. The first mistake is already corrected. Find and correct 11 more.

Miramar Ipanema Hotel

Dear kids,

    Your mom and I are having a wonderful time in Brazil. We landed in Rio de Janeiro on Tuesday as scheduled and made it to our hotel without any problems. On Wednesday we walked and sunbathed on Copacabana and Ipanema beaches. The only problem was that I dropped my camera and got ~~sands~~ *sand* in it, and now it's not working. Actually, there's one other problem: We don't have enough furnitures in our hotel room. There's no places to put anything. But everything else has been great. We went to a samba show, and even though it was intended for tourist, it was a lot of fun.

    The Brazilian people is very friendly and helpful. On Friday we had a flight to São Paulo scheduled for 9:00 A.M., and we missed the bus and couldn't get a taxi. But we were saved by one of the hotel employee, who gave us a ride to the airport. We got there just in time. Now we're in São Paulo. It's an exciting place, but I can't get over the traffics. It took two hour to get from our hotel to the downtown area. Yesterday we had lunch at a famous restaurant where they serve feijoada, which is typical Brazilian foods. It had so much spice in it that our mouths were on fire, but it was delicious. Tonight we're going to have dinner at another restaurant where they serve all kinds of meat. They raise a lot of cattle in Brazil, and meats are very popular. This restaurant is one of the most famous ones.

    The other thing about Brazil that's really interesting is the amount of coffee the Brazilians drink. They have little cups of coffees several times a day—called caffezinho. We tried it; it's very strong and sweet.

    That's all for now. Your mom hasn't had a time to go shopping yet, which is good. You know how much I hate shopping.

Love,

Dad

Communication Practice

7 | LISTENING

🎧 **A** *Read the sentences. Then listen to the cooking show.*

1. Pelmeni is ___a (traditional) Russian___ dish.
   (national origin)

2. The principal ingredient of pelmeni is _____.
   (type of meat)

3. Other meats that can be used to make pelmeni are _____.
   (types of meat)

4. You need _____ meat to make pelmeni.
   (amount)

5. You need _____ egg _____ to make pelmeni.
   (number) **(item)**

6. You need _____ water for the meat mixture.
   (amount)

7. You need _____ salt for the meat mixture.
   (amount)

8. To make the dough, you need _____ flour.
   (amount)

9. Each dough circle should be approximately _____ in diameter.
   (size)

10. One person can easily eat _____ pelmeni at a meal.
    (number)

🎧 **B** *Now listen again. Complete the sentences. Refer to the clues in parentheses.*

8 | INFORMATION GAP: A GRAIN OF SAND

Student B, turn to page 127 and follow the instructions there. Student A, read statements 1–5 aloud. Student B will read the best completion for each statement, including a phrase from the box below in each statement. Then reverse the process for statements 6–10. Refer to Appendix 6 on page A-5 for help in completing this exercise if necessary.

a branch of	a clap of	a flash of	a game of
a grain of	a piece of	a speck of	an article of

Student A's statements

1. A particle of a cereal grown in Asia is called . . .

2. A small piece of powdery material is called . . .

3. An athletic competition played on a field and using a ball is called . . .

4. A part of the science that studies planets and stars is called . . .

5. A loud sound that usually comes with a sudden light from the sky is called . . .

(continued)

Student A's completions

f. jewelry

g. sand

h. lightning

i. furniture

j. advice

9 | WRITING

Write two or three paragraphs about the best or worst meal experience you have ever had. Your essay can be serious or funny. Describe the kind of meal it was and what was good, bad, interesting, or funny about it.

Example: The worst meal experience I've ever had happened about a year ago. I'd been studying French for three years, and I guess I wanted to show my parents how much I'd learned about French culture and language. It was my mother's birthday, so I made reservations at a very nice French restaurant in town. The trouble started right after we got there . . .

10 | ON THE INTERNET

 Use the Internet to research one of the following.

- the preparation of an exotic dish

- a particular diet you are interested in

Then report your findings to the class. If you learn about the preparation of a dish, tell the class how the dish is made. If you learn about a particular diet, explain what the diet is and discuss its advantages and disadvantages.

Examples: A: I learned how to make Mexican *mole*. It's a traditional dish with 20 ingredients: turkey or some other kind of meat, chili peppers, peanuts, chocolate, and . . .

B: I learned about the Atkins diet. It's a high-protein, low-carbohydrate diet. The advantages of it are that you can lose weight on it and eat foods like beef, chicken, fish . . .

INFORMATION GAP FOR STUDENT B

Listen as Student A reads statements 1–5. Read aloud the best completion for each statement, including a phrase from the box below. Then read statements 6–10. Student A will read the best completion for each statement. Refer to Appendix 6 on page A-5 for help in completing this exercise if necessary.

a branch of	a clap of	a flash of	a game of
a grain of	a piece of	a speck of	an article of

Student B's completions

a. soccer

b. astronomy

c. rice

d. thunder

e. dust

Student B's statements

6. A statement of recommended behavior is . . .

7. A particle of a material found on beaches is called . . .

8. A sudden light from the sky is called . . .

9. An object on which one sits or sleeps is called . . .

10. A decorative object worn on the body or the clothes is called . . .

8 Definite and Indefinite Articles

Grammar in Context

BEFORE YOU READ

1 *What is an example of an environmental problem that you consider serious?*

2 *Do you think people exaggerate the seriousness of hazards to the environment? What would be an example?*

3 *How can serious environmental problems be remedied?*

Read this article about an environmental disaster.

The Real Mystery of EASTER ISLAND

Most of us have seen pictures of the gigantic statues of Easter Island, and a big mystery has been this: Who built the statues, and how were they moved? Recently, however, we've become aware of an even greater mystery: What happened to Easter Island? What changed it so drastically?

Easter Island lies in the South Pacific about 2,300 miles west of Chile, the country to which it belongs. According to current estimates, it was settled about the year 900 by Polynesians. If you go to Easter Island today and visit Rano Raruku, the quarry where the statues were carved, you'll see almost 400 statues in various stages of disrepair. On roads leading

This area was once a subtropical forest

out from Rano Raruku, a volcanic crater about 600 yards across, there are about 100 more statues. Many if not most of these statues are toppled over and damaged. Elsewhere on the island you'll see more than 100 gigantic platforms on which the statues stood.

Easter Island was discovered by Dutch explorer Jacob Roggeveen on April 5, 1722— Easter day. When Roggeveen landed, he saw the island much as it is today: a rather desolate place covered mostly by grassland, with no trees taller than 10 feet. It is clear today, however, that Easter Island was once much different: Most of it was a subtropical forest. At one time, the island was home

The Real Mystery of EASTER ISLAND

to as many as 15,000 people, while today there are only about 200. What occurred to cause such drastic changes?

Explorer Thor Heyerdahl theorized that the building and moving of the statues was somehow linked with the activities of the Incas and with the Egyptians and their Pyramids. Author Erich Von Däniken proposed that extraterrestrials made and moved the statues. However, it is believed today that the Easter Islanders did all the work themselves. But how could they have done this? They didn't have cranes, metal tools, large animals, or wheels. (The wheel had been invented long before, but the Easter Islanders didn't have access to it.) One very convincing explanation is that they invented their own devices, called canoe rails, which are ladders with parallel wooden logs connected by crosspieces. The islanders used the rails to drag the statues. But large trees would have been required to build the rails, along with other kinds of trees to provide bark to make rope to pull the statues. Had such trees ever existed there?

Botanist John Flenly and anthropologist Paul Bahn have concluded that these trees did exist. Studies have established that the island was once covered with forests. One of the principal trees was the Chilean wine palm, which grows as high as 65 feet and as wide as 3 feet. The assumption is that the trunks of the wine palm were used to lift and move the statues and that the bark of other trees was used to make rope for hauling. But what happened to the trees?

Today some consider the deforestation of Easter Island one of the greatest environmental disasters of all time. The disaster was almost certainly caused by humans. No one knows for sure how or why it happened, of course, but it seems likely that a few hundred years after it was settled, the island began to experience a decline. It came to be ruled by 11 chiefs, who apparently constructed the statues as competitive demonstrations of their power. As the population increased, competition among the chiefs became fiercer. More and more land was cleared to grow crops to feed the people, and more and more trees were cut down to provide firewood and wood for use in moving and raising the statues. This deforestation led to the drying of the land, the loss of nutrients in the soil, and eventually less and less rainfall. In effect, the climate was changed.

Why did the Easter Islanders allow the disaster to happen? Did they simply fail to recognize an eventual problem? Was the problem too far advanced to do anything about it when they figured out what was happening? Perhaps more significantly for us, are there parallels today? Are we acting as the Easter Islanders did, but on a global scale? For example, does the push to cut down trees (such as in the Amazon rain forest) in the name of jobs and economic development make environmental sense? Are we over-fishing the ocean in our current belief that the supply of seafood is limitless? Are future catastrophes in the works? We mustn't shy away from these questions.

AFTER YOU READ

What does the underlined phrase refer to? Circle the correct answer.

1. Most of it was covered with <u>a subtropical forest</u>.

   a. subtropical forest in general   **b.** one particular subtropical forest

2. <u>The wheel</u> had been invented millennia before.

   a. one particular wheel   **b.** wheels in general

3. Tree bark provided <u>the rope</u> used to raise the statue.

   a. one particular rope   **b.** rope in general

Grammar Presentation

INDEFINITE AND DEFINITE ARTICLES

A/An: INDEFINITE ARTICLE

	Non-Specific	Generic
SINGULAR COUNT NOUNS	He saw **a statue** at **an exhibition**.	**A statue** is **a** three-dimensional **figure**.

ZERO ARTICLE (NO ARTICLE)

	Non-Specific	Generic
PLURAL COUNT NOUNS	Easter Island has impressive **statues**.	**Statues** are made in all shapes and sizes.
NON-COUNT NOUNS	The statues are made of **stone**.	**Stone** is an important building material.
PROPER NOUNS	**Ms. Johnson** spent a year on **Easter Island**. She worked in **Egypt** and **Hawaii**. She now lives in **New York City**.	

THE: DEFINITE ARTICLE

	Specific	Generic
SINGULAR COUNT NOUNS	He finally got a computer. **The computer** he got is good. It's **the best computer** in **the world**.	**The computer** is a great invention.
PLURAL COUNT NOUNS	**The rain forests** in South America are being cut down.	**The rain forests** are in danger everywhere.
NON-COUNT NOUNS	**The stone** from that quarry is very soft.	
PROPER NOUNS	She crossed **the Sahara**, visited **the Pyramids**, and sailed down **the Nile**.	

GRAMMAR NOTES	EXAMPLES
1. When speakers do not have a particular person, place, or thing in mind, the nouns they use are **non-specific**. Use the indefinite article, *a / an*, with non-specific singular count nouns.	• He wants to buy **a statue**. • She wants to be **an anthropologist**.
2. A noun is often **indefinite** the first time a speaker mentions it. It is usually **definite** after the first mention.	• I heard of **an** interesting **mystery**. • **The mystery** is about Easter Island.
3. Use **zero article** (no article) with non-specific plural count nouns, non-specific non-count nouns, names of people, names of most countries, and habitual locations.	• The island used to have tall **trees**. • **Platinum** and **gold** are valuable minerals. • **Mr. Flenly** is a botanist. • Many **statues** have been found in **Egypt**. • People spend most of their time at **work**, at **school**, or at **home**.
4. A noun is **generic** when it represents all members of a class or category of persons, places, or things. In other words, generic nouns talk about things in general. Three common ways to use nouns generically are: **a.** zero article + plural count noun **b.** indefinite article + count noun **c.** zero article + non-count noun ► **BE CAREFUL!** Don't use *the* before a non-count noun used generically. **NOTE:** You can also make a generic statement with the definite article + adjective. A head noun such as *people* or *individuals* is implied. The adjective is plural in meaning and takes a plural verb.	 • **Computers** are **machines** that do calculations and process information. • **A computer** is **a machine** that does calculations and processes information. • **Water** is essential for survival. • **Rainfall** is essential for crops. NOT ~~The rainfall~~ is essential for crops. • **The rich are** fortunate. **They need** to help **the poor**, who **are** not so fortunate. (= the rich people, the poor people)

(continued)

5. A noun is **definite** when the speaker and listener both know which particular person, place, or thing is being talked about. Use the definite article, *the*, with non-count nouns and singular and plural nouns that are definite for you and your listener.

NOTE: A noun or noun phrase is normally definite if you can ask a *which* question about it. Nouns of this type are often followed by a phrase with *of*.

- **The food** we had for lunch was terrible.
- **The island** used to be covered by forests.
- **The statues** were made by tribal chiefs.
- **The population** of the island has declined a great deal.

6. Use the **definite article** with nouns that describe something unique.

An adjective can often make a noun represent something unique. Examples of such adjectives are *first, last, only, right, wrong,* and the comparative and superlative form of adjectives.

- **The sun** gives us light and heat.

- It's one of **the worst disasters** in the world.

7. You can use the **definite article** generically in two ways:

a. in the singular: We often use this construction with inventions and musical instruments.

b. in the plural: We often use this construction with the names of peoples and of animal species.

- **The wheel** was invented thousands of years ago.

- She plays **the harp**.

- **The Hawaiians** are a resourceful people.
- There are many attempts today to save **the whales**.

8. Note these other uses of the **definite article** with nouns and noun phrases:

a. with public places

b. with the names of many geographical regions or features

c. with the names of a few countries

d. with the names of ships

- the bank, the post office, the library, the movies
- the Middle East, the Grand Canyon, the Colorado River, the Pacific Ocean
- the Netherlands, the United States, the Dominican Republic
- the *Titanic*, the *Queen Mary*

Reference Note
For more complete lists of **nouns used with the definite article,** see Appendices 7–9 on pages A-5–A-6.

Focused Practice

1 | DISCOVER THE GRAMMAR

A *Read the sentences based on the opening reading. For each sentence, classify the underlined word or phrase as indefinite (**I**), definite (**D**), or generic (**G**).*

_I_ 1. We've become aware of <u>an even greater mystery</u>.

_____ 2. Chile is <u>the country</u> to which Easter Island belongs.

_____ 3. There are gigantic <u>platforms</u> all over the island.

_____ 4. The building and moving of the statues was somehow linked with the activities of <u>the Incas</u> and the <u>Egyptians</u>.

_____ 5. Von Däniken thought the statues had been made by <u>extraterrestrials</u>.

_____ 6. <u>The wheel</u> had been invented long before.

_____ 7. <u>Canoe rails</u> are <u>ladders</u> with parallel wooden logs connected by crosspieces.

_____ 8. <u>The Chilean wine palm</u> grows as high as 65 feet.

_____ 9. Did they simply fail to recognize <u>an eventual problem</u>?

_____ 10. Is <u>the supply</u> of seafood limitless?

B *Read the sentences based on the reading. Circle the letter of the statement that correctly explains the meaning of each sentence.*

1. Who built the statues there, and how were they moved?
   a. Who built some of the statues there?
   b. Who built all of the statues there?

2. The island was settled by Polynesians.
   a. Some of the Polynesians settled the island.
   b. All of the Polynesians settled the island.

3. One of the principal trees in the forest was the Chilean wine palm.
   a. There was one Chilean palm tree in the forest.
   b. There were many Chilean palm trees in the forest.

4. But what happened to the trees on the island?
   a. What happened to all of the trees on the island?
   b. What happened to some of the trees on the island?

5. Trees were cut down to provide firewood.
   a. All of the trees were cut down.
   b. Some of the trees were cut down.

2 | DISASTERS

Read the descriptions of two notable environmental disasters that have occurred in recent decades. Fill in the blanks with the correct article in parentheses (— means no article is needed).

CHERNOBYL DAMAGE WIDER THAN PREVIOUSLY REPORTED

DETAILS ARE FINALLY EMERGING. On April 26, 1986, _____ fires and explosions following
1. (— / The)

_____ unauthorized experiment caused _____ worst accident in _____ history of
2. (an / the)   3. (a / the)   4. (— / the)

nuclear power at the nuclear power plant in Chernobyl, Ukraine. At least 31 people were

killed in _____ disaster itself, and _____ radioactive material was released into
5. (— / the)   6. (—, the)

_____ atmosphere. Approximately 135,000 people were evacuated from _____
7. (an / the)   8. (a / the)

vicinity. _____ scientists warned of _____ possible future cancer deaths and birth
9. (— / The)   10. (— / the)

defects.

MASSIVE OIL SPILL IN ALASKA

MARCH 24, 1989. _____ oil tanker *Exxon Valdez* struck Bligh Reef in Prince William
1. (An / The)

Sound, Alaska, tonight, causing _____ worst oil spill in _____ U.S. history. More
2. (a / the)   3. (— / the)

than 10 million gallons of _____ oil were spilled, causing the deaths of _____ many
4. (an / —)   5. (— / the)

animals and resulting in _____ great environmental catastrophe. The captain of
6. (— / a)

_____ *Valdez* was not present in _____ wheelhouse at _____ time of _____
7. (— / the)   8. (a / the)   9. (— / the)   10. (an / the)

accident; _____ ship was being piloted by _____ first mate, who was inexperienced.
11. (a / the)   12. (— / the)

It was determined that _____ captain, rather than _____ first mate, should have been
13. (a / the)   14. (— / the)

piloting _____ vessel. _____ Exxon agreed to pay for _____ cost of cleaning up
15. (a / the)   16. (— / The)   17. (— / the)

_____ spill.
18. (— / the)

3 | EARTHWEEK: A DIARY OF THE PLANET

Read the two excerpts from the article "Earthweek: A Diary of the Planet." Fill in the blanks with the articles needed. Leave a blank if no article is necessary.

Permafrost Warning

___The___ melting of permafrost in Sweden's sub-Arctic region due to global warming is
1.

believed to be releasing vast quantities of the greenhouse gas methane into _____
2.

atmosphere. _____ research team, led by _____ GeoBiosphere Science Center at
3. **4.**

Lund University, said their research shows _____ part of _____ soil that thaws
5. **6.**

during summer has become deeper since 1970, and the permafrost has disappeared entirely

in some locations. "This has led to significant changes in the vegetation and to a subsequent

increase in emission of the greenhouse gas methane," _____ team announced. They
7.

added that methane is 25 times more damaging to _____ atmosphere than _____
8. **9.**

carbon dioxide and often is overlooked in _____ discussion of greenhouse gases.
10.

Plastic Pollution

_____ German magazine *Geo* published _____ report that said _____ plastic
1. **2.** **3.**

trash has created _____ environmental hazard that stretches across _____ Pacific
4. **5.**

from California to Hawaii, resulting in more plastic than plankton on _____ water's
6.

surface. _____ March issue quotes biologist Charles Moore of the Algalita Marine
7.

Research Foundation as saying: "Most plastic floats near _____ sea surface where some
8.

is mistaken for _____ food by birds and fishes." The masses of plastic find their way
9.

into _____ Pacific from _____ western United States and _____ Canada after
10. **11.** **12.**

storms flush the debris downstream and ultimately into _____ ocean. Maritime
13.

observers have witnessed areas of floating plastic that stretch as far as the eye can see in

_____ central Pacific.
14.

4 | INVENTIONS AND INSTRUMENTS

Grammar Notes 4, 8

Write two sentences about each invention or instrument. In the first sentence, write about the item's characteristics. In the second sentence, use the definite article to say when the item was invented.

> **Example:** computer / electronic device / process information and perform high-speed calculations / 1944
>
> A computer is an electronic device that processes information and performs high-speed calculations. / Computers are electronic devices that process information and perform high-speed calculations.
>
> The computer was invented in 1944.

1. television set / electronic device / receive electromagnetic waves, convert waves into images, display them on a screen / 1920s by Farnsworth and Zorinsky

   _____

   _____

2. wheel / circular device / turn around central point / 5,000 to 6,000 years ago

   _____

   _____

3. clarinet / woodwind instrument / use a reed / around 1700

   _____

   _____

4. guitars / stringed instruments / typically have six strings / in the 1400s in Spain

   _____

   _____

5. automobiles / self-powered traveling vehicles / 1874 by Siegfried Marcus in Vienna

   _____

   _____

6. telephones / communication devices / convert sound signals into waves and reconvert them into sounds / 1878 by Alexander Graham Bell

   _____

   _____

5 | EDITING

Read this composition about genetic engineering and the environment. There are 15 mistakes in the use of articles. The first mistake is already corrected. Find and correct 14 more.

Genetic Engineering

People say we are now able to perform ~~a~~ genetic engineering. I am against this for several reasons. First, it is dangerous to tamper with the nature because we don't know what will happen. We could upset balance of nature. For example, people are against a mosquito because it carries malaria. Suppose we change the DNA of the mosquito so that it will die off. That will stop a malaria, but it will upset ecological balance because certain other species depend on mosquito. If we destroy it, these other species won't be able to survive. This will have serious effect on environment.

Second, genetic engineering will take away people's control over their own lives. Suppose scientists develop the capability to isolate gene for violent behavior and they eliminate this gene from future generations. This may eliminate a violence, but I believe that behavior is matter of choice, and this type of genetic engineering will eliminate choice. It will make people behave as others have determined, not as they have determined, and it will take away an individual responsibility.

Third, genetic engineering will remove chance from our lives. Part of what makes the life interesting is unpredictability. We never know exactly how someone, or something, is going to turn out. It's interesting to see what happens. As far as I am concerned, we should leave genetic engineering to Creator.

Communication Practice

6 | LISTENING

🎧 *Read the statements. Then listen to the conversation between a husband and a wife. Listen again and circle the answer that correctly completes each sentence.*

1. According to the husband, the newspaper is on the side of _____.
   a. the Indians   **(b.)** the environmentalists

2. Whose point of view does he think is ignored?
   a. the Indians'   **b.** the environmentalists'

3. The husband supports the point of view of _____.
   a. the Indians   **b.** the environmentalists

4. The wife supports the point of view of _____.
   a. the Indians   **b.** the environmentalists

5. The issue is whether _____ can hunt whales.
   a. one particular group of Indians   **b.** all Indians

6. The husband is in favor of allowing hunting because _____.
   a. it will reduce the surplus of whales   **b.** it will allow the Indians to support themselves

7. The wife thinks it's cruel to hunt _____.
   a. some whales   **b.** all whales

8. She says _____ animals are raised for food.
   a. all   **b.** some

9. The wife thinks it's acceptable to use _____ animals for food.
   a. all   **b.** some

10. The wife thinks _____ are intelligent.
    a. some whales   **b.** all whales

7 | PICTURE DISCUSSION

Form small groups and discuss this picture. Identify the items you see. Then discuss the situation. How can we dispose of items we no longer need or want? Are there solutions to this problem?

Example: **A:** I see an electric skillet and two axes.
B: How do you think we should dispose of things like those?
C: Well, I think each city should send trucks to pick up things people don't want.
D: They could sell the items at special centers.

Yard sale

8 | WRITING

Work in small groups. Choose an environmental issue from the list below or develop your own idea. Write about the topic you select. Say why you think the issue is important and what should be done about it. Exchange papers with another group and correct any mistakes in the use of articles.

Possible Issues

- saving endangered animals

- improving air quality

- getting rid of nuclear weapons

- disposing of garbage

- ensuring the supply of clean water

Example: Laws against air pollution have been in effect for decades now, but we haven't seen much progress in reducing air pollution. Actually, air pollution has gotten worse in many areas. If we want to make real progress, we need stricter laws, and we need to enforce them. There are three areas where we can improve: automobiles, factories, and the burning of forests. Let's look at each of these separately.

The automobile . . .

9 | ON THE INTERNET

Form teams of four or five. Each team creates five questions about the environment, inventions, or musical instruments. Use the Internet to find answers to your questions. Then play a game in class. Teams take turns asking their questions. A team responding with the correct answer receives one point. The team with the most points at the end of the game is the winner.

Quantifiers

Grammar in Context

BEFORE YOU READ

1 *Do you pay for most things with cash, with credit cards, or by some other means?*

2 *What would be the advantages and disadvantages of living in a cashless society?*

🎧 *Read this article about money.*

AUGUST 6, 2006   BUSINESS TODAY

What's Happening to CA$H?

How did money originate, and where? The Babylonians were the first to develop actual "money" when they started to use gold and silver about 2500 B.C. The practice of using pieces of silver and gold as units of value gradually spread through much of the ancient world. In the following centuries, other items came to be used as money, for example, jewelry, land, and even cattle.

In the last two centuries, however, there has been a movement away from physical money and toward a more abstract system. One good example of an abstract type is fiat money, which is normally paper currency issued by a government. Fiat money isn't based on gold or silver; it has value only because the government says it does. Its value depends on trust in the government. Perhaps the most abstract type of money is electronic. E-money involves the electronic transfer of funds from one bank account to another. In such a financial transaction, no actual money is transferred. The balance in one account is simply increased, and the bal-ance in the other account is correspondingly decreased.

Does this mean that there are no longer any advantages to cash? Not at all. Suppose, for example, that you're walking down a

(continued)

DO YOU TAKE ANY CREDIT CARDS?

What's Happening to CA$H?

street and suddenly remember you need to buy some flowers. You see a flower vendor and decide this is the time to buy a dozen roses. What do you do? Write a check, or pull out your bank card? At this writing, few flower vendors take checks, and even fewer take plastic. Most of them prefer cash. If you've got some money, you simply pull out a few bills, hand them to the vendor, and happily walk away with your flowers. Pretty easy, huh? It wouldn't be that easy without cash.

Or suppose you'd like to give a little money as a gift. It's a lot more personal and pleasing to receive a few crisp bills in a birthday card than a check, which can seem rather cold and mechanical. Suppose you're at a food fair, and you feel like getting a couple of hot dogs. It's much easier to pull out cash to pay for them. In restaurants these days, it's become common to pay with a credit or debit card and to include the tip in the total amount. Sometimes, though, you might want to leave your server some actual money in appreciation of particularly good service. It seems to make a better emotional connection.

So cash has its advantages. Of course, it has a number of disadvantages as well. For example, you might be robbed. Also, cash can be heavy. Carrying a lot of coins can make holes in your pockets. It's inconvenient to take a great deal of money with you to pay for large purchases; imagine trying to carry enough cash to pay for a house or a car—or even a sofa. Besides that, cash has been handled by many different people and is covered with germs.

Then there's the matter of paying bills. Traditionally, most people in North America have paid their bills with checks, but the recent trend is to pay bills electronically. The Japanese, among others, have been doing this for years. In Japan, payment for such things as heat, electricity, and water is handled by automatic deduction from a bank account. It's much easier than writing out several checks to different agencies. And since it's automatic, people don't have to worry about whether they've forgotten to pay their bill.

There are a number of disadvantages to electronic money, however. Some people have little use for credit cards, saying that using them encourages us to live beyond our means. Others say that using electronic money places too much control of our personal finances in the hands of strangers. Mistakes are easily made and hard to correct.

The jury is still out on whether the trend toward less and less use of cash is good or bad. What seems clear is that it's definitely growing.

$

AFTER YOU READ

What does each sentence mean? Circle the correct answer.

1. Few flower vendors take checks.
   a. Some flower vendors take checks.
   b. Not many flower vendors take checks.

2. It's inconvenient to take a great deal of money with you.
   a. It's inconvenient to take a lot of money.
   b. It's inconvenient to take some money.

3. Some people have little use for credit cards.
   a. They like them.
   b. They don't like them very much.

Grammar Presentation

QUANTIFIERS

Quantifiers	With Count Nouns	With Non-Count Nouns
ONE EACH EVERY	**One store** is open. **Each coin** is valuable. **Every bank** is closed.	∅* ∅ ∅
TWO BOTH A COUPLE OF SEVERAL	**Two stores** are open. **Both stores** are nearby. She bought **a couple of gifts**. She bought **several gifts**.	∅ ∅ ∅ ∅
FEW A FEW MANY A GREAT MANY	They have **few investments**. She has **a few investments**. Does he own **many buildings**? He owns **a great many buildings**.	∅ ∅ ∅ ∅
LITTLE A LITTLE MUCH A GREAT DEAL OF	∅ ∅ ∅ ∅	They have **little money**. She has **a little money**. Does he have **much property**? He owns **a great deal of property**.
NO ANY SOME ENOUGH A LOT OF / LOTS OF PLENTY OF MOST ALL	They have **no bonds**. They don't have **any bonds**. They have **some stocks**. You have **enough stocks**. He has **a lot of** / **lots of clients**. He has **plenty of clients**. **Most banks** are safe. **All banks** are insured.	They have **no insurance**. They don't have **any insurance**. They have **some cash**. You have **enough cash**. He has **a lot of** / **lots of patience**. He has **plenty of patience**. **Most work** is useful. **All work** is tiring.

*∅ = quantifier not used

GRAMMAR NOTES

EXAMPLES

1. Quantifiers state the number or amount of something. Quantifiers can be single words or phrases.	• I bought **a dozen tulips**. • There's **some money** in my account.
Quantifiers are used with both nouns and pronouns.	• **A lot of people** vacation in the summer. • **Most of us** are going on the trip.
Quantifiers are often used alone if the noun or pronoun has just been mentioned, as in a question.	**A:** Have you made **many friends** here? **B:** Yes, I've made **a lot**.

2. Quantifiers are used with different types of nouns:	
a. with singular count nouns: *one, each, every,* etc.	• I took **each item** back to the store. • We were able to solve **every problem**.
b. with plural count nouns: *two, both, a couple of, a dozen, several, few, a few, many, a great many, a number of,* etc.	• We visited **a couple of countries**. • We bought **a few souvenirs**.
c. with non-count nouns: *a little, little, much, a great deal of, a great amount of,* etc.	• I only make **a little money** at that job. • She earns **a great deal of money**.
d. with both plural count nouns and non-count nouns: *no, any, some, enough, a lot of / lots of, plenty of, most, all,* etc.	• She has **no plans** to travel. • We took **no cash** on the trip.

3. Use *a few / few* with count nouns and *a little / little* with non-count nouns.	• Mary has **a few investments**. • She has saved **a little money**.
Note the difference between *a few* and *few* and between *a little* and *little*. Use *a few* and *a little* to make positive statements.	• I have **a few** good **friends**. • We have **a little food** at home.
Use *few* and *little* to make negative statements.	• Jerry has **few friends**. • Mary has **little self-confidence**.
▶ **BE CAREFUL!** In comparison, use *fewer* with count nouns and *less* with non-count nouns. Use *more* with both count and non-count nouns.	• I have **fewer problems** than I used to. • I also earn **less money**, though. • I have **more friends**. • I also have **more self-confidence**.

4. Use *many* with count nouns and *much* with non-count nouns.

In spoken affirmative statements, native speakers usually prefer *a lot of* or *lots of* to *much* and *many*, which sound more formal. This is especially true of *much*.

However, *much* and *many* are common in questions and negatives in spoken and written English.

Use *a great many* with count nouns and *a great deal of* with non-count nouns. These quantifiers are rather formal and found more in writing than in speech.

- He doesn't have **many friends**.
- I don't have **much trouble** getting to work.
- There are **a lot of accidents** on this road.
- There's **lots of construction** going on.
- Did they spend **much money**?
- She does not read **many magazines**.
- The government has **a great many responsibilities**.
- Presidents are under **a great deal of stress**.

5. Use *some* and *any* with count nouns and non-count nouns.

Use *some* in *affirmative* statements.

Use *any* in *negative* statements.

Use both *some* and *any* in questions. In general, use *some* in offers and *any* in negative questions.

- Did you make **some / any purchases**?
- Do you have **some / any cash** with you?
- Bill bought **some souvenirs**.
- He borrowed **some money** from me.
- Alice didn't take **any trips**.
- She didn't have **any money**.
- Did you buy **some / any clothes**?
- Would you like **some soda**?
- Didn't you send **any postcards**?

(continued)

6. Many **quantifiers** appear in phrases with the preposition *of*. Use *of* + *the* or another determiner when you are specifying particular persons, places, things, or groups.

- **Most of the EU countries** are using the euro.
- We saw **many of her films**.

We generally use quantifiers without *of* when we have no particular person, place, thing, or group in mind.

- **Most people** don't understand the economy.
- **Many restaurants** take credit cards.

▶ **BE CAREFUL!** Quantifiers with *of* can be used only with plural count nouns and non-count nouns.

- **Most of the coins** were very old.
- **Most of the gold** was pure.
- NOT ~~Most of the~~ coin was very old.

NOTE: Quantifiers like ***most of*** and ***many of*** can be followed by a singular or a plural verb, depending on the noun that follows *of*.

- Most of the **food has** been eaten. *(non-count noun + singular verb)*
- Most of the **people have** arrived. *(plural noun + plural verb)*

Reference Note
For more information on **count and non-count nouns,** see Unit 7.

Focused Practice

1 | DISCOVER THE GRAMMAR

Look at these sentences based on the opening reading. Could they be rewritten using the words in parentheses without changing the basic meaning or creating an incorrect sentence?

_____no_____ **1.** This is a trend that has been developing for *many* years now. (much)

_____ **2.** Are there still *any* advantages to cash? (some)

_____ **3.** You suddenly remember you need to buy *some* flowers. (any)

_____ **4.** At this writing, *few* flower vendors take checks. (a few)

_____ **5.** *Few* vendors take plastic. (little)

_____ **6.** Suppose you'd like to give *a little* money as a gift. (little)

_____ **7.** It's *much* easier to pull out cash to pay for them. (a lot)

_____ **8.** Cash has *some* disadvantages as well. (any)

_____ **9.** Cash has been handled by *many* different people. (a lot of)

_____**10.** *Most* people have paid their bills with checks. (a great deal of)

_____**11.** It's easier than writing out *several* checks. (a little)

_____**12.** Some people have *little* use for credit cards. (a little)

2 | **OUR SECOND EUROPEAN TRIP**   *Grammar Notes 2–5*

Complete the sentences by choosing the correct quantifier.

1. We just got back from our second trip to Europe. This time we visited _____*fewer*_____
   countries. (less / fewer)

2. We didn't visit _____ of the Scandinavian countries this time. (some / any)

3. We spent _____ money this time too. (less / fewer)

4. We did buy _____ wonderful souvenirs, though. (some / any)

5. Last time we rented a car and were amazed by the _____ cars on the
   roads. (amount of / number of)

6. This time we traveled by train. We expected _____
   people to be traveling that way. (much / a lot of)

7. However, there weren't very _____. (much / many)

8. We had _____ problems finding seats in the railroad cars. We never had
   to stand. (few / a few)

9. That's a good thing. My husband has _____ patience when it comes to
   competing with other passengers. (little / a little)

10. The trip was so economical that we had _____ extra money at the
    end. (little / a little).

3 | SAVING FOR A TRIP

Ron and Ashley Lamont are trying to save money for a trip to South America. They are examining their budget. Complete their conversation with quantifiers from the box, using each expression once.

a couple of	a few	~~a lot of~~	both of	enough
every	few	fewer	$40	less
more	most of	much	one of	some

ASHLEY: Ron, we're still spending _____a lot of_____ money on things we don't really need.
1.

    After I pay the bills this month, we're going to have _____ cash left over
    2.

    than we did last month. We're supposed to be saving for the trip to South America,

    remember? We're not saving _____ money. If we don't start saving
    3.

    _____, we won't be able to go.
    4.

RON: What have we bought that we don't need?

ASHLEY: That exercise machine, for one thing. We've only used it _____ times.
5.

    We could get a year's membership at the gym for what it cost and still have something

    left over.

RON: You mean _____ us could get a membership, don't you?
6.

ASHLEY: No, _____ us could. That's what I'm saying. The machine cost $500,
7.

    and memberships are $150 each. Let's sell the thing and go to the gym.

RON: Hmmm. Maybe you're right. What else?

ASHLEY: Well, we're spending about _____ extra a month on those premium
8.

    cable channels. We'd have _____ channels to choose from if we went
    9.

    back to the basic coverage, but we don't watch _____ TV anyway.
    10.

RON: Yeah, you're right . . . And you know, I'd say we could get rid of call waiting on the

    phone. We've used it very _____ times, and _____ my
    11.   12.

    friends say they hate it when they call, and then another call comes in while we're

    talking.

ASHLEY: Uh-huh. Let's cancel it, then. And here's one more suggestion. We should start taking a

sack lunch to work _____ times a week instead of going out at noon. If
                              13.

we did these four things, we'd have _____ money left over
                                                          14.

_____ month that could go into our trip fund.
         15.

RON: Oh no! Not my lunches with the boys! Lunchtime is when I get to see them.

ASHLEY: Invite them over to play volleyball. Then think of Rio de Janeiro.

---

4 | WORLD NUMBERS   *Grammar Notes 4–6*

Look at the table. Then complete each sentence with the appropriate quantifier from the box. Use each quantifier once.

	The world in 1960	**The world in 2000**
Population	3,020,100,000	6,052,800,000
Birth rate per thousand people	31.2	21.5
Death rate per thousand people	17.7	9.0
Female life expectancy at birth	51.9 years	68.5 years
Male life expectancy at birth	48.6 years	64.6 years
Electricity use per person	1,445 kilowatt hours	2,175 kilowatt hours
Television sets per thousand people	112.8	272.4
Gross domestic product per person	$2,607	$5,666

a great deal of	~~a great many~~	few	fewer
less	many	more	much

1. ___*A great many*___ people were born between 1960 and 2000.

2. There were _____ births per thousand people in 2000 than in 1960.

3. There were _____ deaths per thousand people in 1960 than in 2000.

4. The life expectancy of men is _____ than that of women.

5. On the average, _____ females lived to be older than 52 or males older than 49 in 1960.

6. There was _____ growth in the use of electricity between 1960 and 2000.

7. There were more than twice as _____ TV sets in the world in 2000 as in 1960.

8. The gross domestic product was more than twice as _____ in 2000 as in 1960.

5 | A PERSONAL INVENTORY   *Grammar Notes 5–6*

Compare your life now to your life five years ago. Write eight sentences, using each of the quantifiers in the box.

a few	a little	a lot	fewer
less	many	more	much

Example: I have **more friends** now than I did five years ago.

6 | EDITING

Read this excerpt from a president's speech. There are 12 mistakes in the use of quantifiers. The first one is already corrected. Find and correct 11 more.

My fellow citizens: We are at a time in our history when we need to make some real

sacrifices. Recent presidents have made ~~a great deal of~~ *a great many* promises they didn't keep. You may

not like everything I tell you tonight, but you deserve to hear the truth. On the economy,

we've made little progress, but we still have a great many work to do, so there are several

measures I'm proposing. First, I want to raise taxes on the very wealthy because a few of

them are really paying their share. Second, many of members of the middle class are

carrying an unfair tax burden, so I'm asking for a tax cut for the middle class. If I'm

successful, most of you in the middle class will be paying 10 percent less in taxes next year,

though few of you in the higher-income group may see your taxes rise little.

How do I intend to make up the lost revenue? The problem with the national income

tax is that there are much loopholes in the current law which allow any people to avoid

paying any taxes at all; I want to close these loopholes. My additional plan is to replace the

lost revenue with a national sales tax, which is fairer because it applies to every people

equally. Third, we have no money to finance health care reform, and we've made a little

progress in reducing pollution and meeting clean air standards. Therefore, I am asking for

a 50-cent-a-gallon tax on gasoline, which will result in many more people using public

transportation and will create additional revenue. Thus, we will have enough of money to

finance our new health care program and will help the environment at the same time.

Communication Practice

7 | LISTENING

🎧 *Read the questions. Then listen to a conversation in a restaurant. Listen again and answer the questions.*

1. Which restaurant has fewer menu choices?
   a. this restaurant (circled)   **b.** the last restaurant

2. At which restaurant does the food cost less?
   a. this restaurant   **b.** the last restaurant

3. How much money does Bill have?
   a. none at all   **b.** a few dollars

4. Does Bill have enough money to pay the bill?
   a. yes   **b.** no

5. How much is the bill?
   a. $55   **b.** $15

6. How many credit cards does Bill have?
   a. one   **b.** none at all

7. Do Mary and Bill have enough money together to pay the bill?
   a. yes   **b.** no

8. Are there any ATM machines nearby?
   a. Yes, there are.   **b.** No, there aren't.

8 | THE QUANTIFIER GAME: WORLD FACTS

Form two teams. Each team uses its prompts to construct eight questions about world facts with quantifiers. Then each team creates two questions of its own, for a total of ten questions. The other team answers each question.

Example: country / more / people / China / India
       A: Which country has more people, China or India?
       B: China has more people.

Team A's Prompts

1. country / fewer / people / Canada / Mexico

2. country / more / land area / Canada / the United States

(continued)

3. country / produce / less / oil / Venezuela / Mexico

4. country / no / snowfall / Somalia / Tanzania

5. country / fewer / rivers / Libya / Nigeria

6. country / smaller number / people / Monaco / Cyprus

7. country / produce / large amount / gold / Nigeria / South Africa

8. city/ little / rainfall / Aswan, Egypt / Athens, Greece

Team B's Prompts

1. country / fewer / people / Great Britain / Spain

2. country / more / land area / Australia / Brazil

3. country / produce / less / oil / the United States / Saudi Arabia

4. country / no / military / Colombia / Costa Rica

5. country / fewer / rivers / Yemen / Turkey

6. country / smaller number / people / San Marino / Kuwait

7. country / use / larger amount / nuclear energy / the Netherlands / France

8. city / little / rainfall / Antofagasta, Chile / Nairobi, Kenya

9 | WRITING

Write about an interesting experience you have had with money. Choose one of these topics or create your own topic.

- a time when you ran out of money

- a time when you tipped too much or too little

- a time when you lost your wallet or purse

Example: The most interesting experience I've ever had with money was three years ago when I was visiting New York City. I had gone to a restaurant and ordered a large, expensive meal. I thought I had more than enough money to pay for the meal, but I had a big surprise. Here's how it happened . . .

10 | ON THE INTERNET

Assume that you are going to take a trip to Europe. Use the Internet to compare the currency of your country to the euro. What is the current exchange rate? Find out if any members of the European Union are not using the euro. Also find out which European countries are not members of the EU. Report your findings to the class.

Modification of Nouns

Grammar in Context

BEFORE YOU READ

1 *What is the difference between hoping for something to happen and expecting it to happen? Discuss this with your classmates.*

2 *In your experience, does what you expect to happen usually happen? Give an example.*

3 *How can expectations be a negative force? How can they be a positive force?*

🎧 *Read this article about expectations.*

POCKET DIGEST

THE EXPECTATION SYNDROME
I Hope for It, but I Don't Expect It

by Jessica Taylor

Picture the scene: It's the fourteenth Winter Olympics in Lake Placid, New York. The U.S. team is playing the Soviet team in the men's semifinal ice hockey match. The supposedly unbeatable Soviet squad, winners of the last four gold medals in hockey, is so accomplished that it has already beaten a team of National Hockey League all-stars. The American team is a group of college players who weren't even expected to make it to the medal round, but here they are. Nearly everyone assumes the Soviet team will win and the American team will lose. Improbably, however, the Americans defeat the Soviets. They then go on to beat the Finnish team in the finals and win the gold medal. A sportscaster calling the match comes up with the famous line, "Do you believe in miracles?" Were the Americans a better team than the Soviets? Almost certainly not. Everyone (including the Soviet players themselves) expected the Soviets to win, and almost no one believed in the Americans, who had no expectations. They simply played spontaneously and energetically. The result: They won.

(continued)

POCKET DIGEST

THE EXPECTATION SYNDROME

Picture another situation: Your film-buff friends have seen all three parts of the Academy Award–winning *The Lord of the Rings*. They rave about its superb color photography, its fantastic computer-generated scenes of strange-looking creatures, and its awesome special effects. They praise its serious, profound, and heartwarming treatment of the age-old conflict between good and evil. They say it's the best English-language movie of the last decade. When you go to see one of the three parts, though, you're disappointed. You don't find it as excellent as everyone has been saying. In fact, you feel it's a tedious, boring movie and consider it basically just another special-effects fantasy film.

These situations illustrate what we might call "the expectation syndrome," a condition in which events do not turn out as we feel they will or ought to. Children often do not meet their parents' career expectations of them. Athletes do not always win the contests people expect them to win. Great literature doesn't always seem as good as it should. I asked psychiatrist Robert Stevens whether expectations can actually make things turn out negatively, or whether this is merely a philosophical question, an unpleasant, frustrating irony of the human condition.

RS: Well, what we're really talking about here, I think, is the immense power of the mind to control outcomes. For example, there's a medical condition called "focal dystonia," which is an abnormal muscle function caused by extreme concentration. Somehow, when athletes are concentrating too hard, it affects certain brain functions and they miss the basket, don't hit the ball, or lose the race. In effect, they're letting their expectations control them.

JT: Have you ever had any experience with this phenomenon in your personal everyday life?

RS: Yes, I certainly have. Let me give you an example from skiing that shows that the mind has immense power for both positive and negative things. There are days when, as a cautious skier, I stand at the top of a steep, icy slope, plotting my every move down the course, fearing that I'll fall. Sure enough, I do fall. Other days I feel different. My expectations are miles away. I forget about myself, ski well, and don't fall. When we focus excessively on goals, our expectations tend to take over, and our mind places us outside the process. On the other hand, when we concentrate on the process instead of the goal, we're often much more successful. Have you heard the phrase "trying too hard"? That's what people often do.

JT: Very interesting. What would be your recommendation about expectations, then?

RS: Well, all I've been able to come up with so far is that it's better to hope for things than to expect them.

AFTER YOU READ

Circle the letter of the choice that explains the meaning of the italicized phrase.

1. It's the best *English-language movie* of the last decade.

   a. It's a movie about language that was made in England.

   b. It's a movie in the English language.

2. Children often do not meet *their parents' career expectations* of them.

   a. The career expectations parents have

   b. The career expectations children have

3. Focal dystonia is an *abnormal muscle function* caused by extreme concentration.

    a. The function of a particular muscle is abnormal.

    b. A particular muscle is abnormal.

Grammar Presentation

MODIFICATION OF NOUNS

	Adjective Modifier	Noun Modifier	Head Noun
I remember the		Winter	Olympics.
	wonderful		athletes.
	amazing	hockey	games.
	unexpected	U.S.	victory.

Order of Adjective Modifiers								
	Opinion	Size	Age	Shape	Color	Origin	Material	
I saw a	great		new			French		movie.
I met its	fascinating		young			Chinese		director.
She had		large		round			jade	earrings.
She wore a		long			red		silk	dress.

Several Adjective Modifiers	
Different Modifier Categories	**Same Modifier Category**
A **great new epic** movie	A **serious, profound, and heartwarming** movie A **serious, profound, heartwarming** movie A **heartwarming, profound, serious** movie

Compound Modifiers		
The movie has lots of	**computer-generated** **strange-looking**	scenes. creatures.
The main character is a	**10-year-old** **long-haired, short-legged**	girl. boy.

GRAMMAR NOTES	EXAMPLES
1. Nouns can be modified both by adjectives and by other nouns. **Adjective** and **noun modifiers** usually come before the noun they modify. The noun that is modified is called the head noun.	• Yao Ming is a **famous Chinese** (adjective modifiers) **basketball player**. (noun modifier + head noun)
2. Noun modifiers usually come directly before the nouns they modify. When there are both adjective and noun modifiers, the noun modifier comes closer to the head noun.	• **Milk chocolate** is chocolate made with milk. • **Chocolate milk** is milk that has chocolate in it. • Pelé is a **famous soccer player**. (adj. mod. / noun mod. / head noun)
3. Two common types of **adjective modifiers** are present participles and past participles (also called **participial adjectives**). Remember that participial adjectives that end in *-ing* describe someone or something that causes a feeling. Participial adjectives that end in *-ed* describe someone who experiences a feeling.	• It was a **boring** movie. • The **bored** viewers left. • The result of the game was **shocking**. • The news is **exciting**. • We were **shocked** by the result. • Everyone is **excited** by the news.

4. When there is **more than one modifier** of a noun, the modifiers generally occur in a **fixed order**. The following list shows the usual order of common adjective and noun modifiers. The order can be changed by the emphasis a speaker wants to give to a particular adjective.

POSITION	CATEGORY OF MODIFIER	
1	Opinions	• ugly, beautiful, dull, interesting
2	Size	• big, tall, long, short
3	Age or temperature	• old, young, hot, cold
4	Shapes	• square, round, oval, diamond
5	Colors	• red, blue, pink, purple
6	Origins, nationalities, or social classes	• computer-generated, Brazilian, Chinese, middle-class
7	Materials	• wood, cotton, denim, silk, glass

5. When a noun has **two or more modifiers** in the same category, we separate the adjectives with a comma. If the modifiers are in different categories, do not separate the adjectives with a comma.

NOTE: The order of adjectives in the same category can vary.

- He is a **serious, hardworking** student.
- I bought a **beautiful denim** shirt.

- He is a **serious, hardworking** student.
- He is a **hardworking, serious** student.

6. Compound modifiers are constructed from more than one word. Here are four common kinds:

  a. number + noun

  b. noun + present participle

  c. noun + past participle

  d. adjective + past participle

When compound modifiers precede a noun, they are generally hyphenated.

▶ BE CAREFUL! Plural nouns used as modifiers become singular when they come before the noun.

- I work in a **10-story** building.
- It's a **prize-winning** film.
- It's a **crime-related** problem.
- The actor plays a **long-haired, one-armed** pirate in the movie.

- Her daughter is 10 years old.
- She has a **10-year-old** daughter.
  NOT She has a ~~10-years-old~~ daughter.

7. BE CAREFUL! In written English, avoid having more than two noun modifiers together. Using too many noun modifiers in sequence can be confusing. Look at the example: Is Jerry a student who won an award for painting portraits? Is Jerry a painter who won an award for painting students? Is the award given by the students?

To avoid confusing sentences like this, break up the string of noun modifiers with prepositional phrases or rearrange the modifiers in some other way.

There is no similar problem with adjective modifiers.

- Jerry Gonzales won the **student portrait painter** award.

- Jerry Gonzales won the award for painting portraits of students.
  OR
- Student Jerry Gonzales won the award for painting portraits.
- The **clever little brown-and-white** fox terrier impressed us all. (*All the adjectives clearly modify* fox terrier.)

Focused Practice

1 | DISCOVER THE GRAMMAR

Read these sentences based on the opening article. Circle all head nouns that have noun or adjective modifiers before them. Underline adjective modifiers once, noun modifiers twice, and compound modifiers three times.

1. It's the <u>fourteenth</u> <u><u>Winter</u></u> (Olympics.)

2. The U.S. team is playing the Soviet team in the men's semifinal ice hockey match.

3. The supposedly unbeatable Soviet squad, winners of the last four gold medals in hockey, is so good that it has already beaten a team of National Hockey League all-stars.

4. Your film-buff friends have seen the Academy Award–winning *The Lord of the Rings*.

5. They love its strange-looking creatures and awesome special effects.

6. They admire its serious, profound, and heartwarming treatment of the age-old conflict between good and evil.

7. Children often do not meet their parents' career expectations of them.

8. I asked Robert Stevens whether there is an actual scientific basis for the negativity of expectations.

9. There's a medical condition called "focal dystonia," which is an abnormal muscle function caused by extreme concentration.

10. I stand at the top of a steep, icy slope, plotting my every move down the course.

2 | PARTY EXPECTATIONS

Grammar Notes 4–5

Bill and Nancy are going to attend a party at the home of Nancy's new boss. They are trying to dress for the occasion and aren't sure what is expected. Nancy is very worried about making a good impression. Unscramble the modifiers in their conversation. Place commas where they are needed.

BILL: This is a _____*formal office*_____ party, isn't it? What if I wear my
  1. (office / formal)

_____ tie?
  2. (silk / new)

NANCY: That's fine, but don't wear that _____ shirt with it. People will
  3. (purple / ugly / denim)

think you don't have any _____ clothes.
  4. (suitable / dress-up)

BILL: So what? Why should I pretend I like to dress up when I don't?

NANCY: Because there are going to be a lot of _____ businesspeople
5. (interesting / important)

there, and I want to make a _____ impression. It's my job,
6. (memorable / good)

remember? I don't want people to think I have a _____
7. (unstylish / sloppy)

dresser for a husband, which of course you're not. Humor me just this once, OK

sweetie? Hmmm . . . I wonder if I should wear my _____
8. (round / sapphire / blue)

earrings or the _____ ones.
9. (green / oval / emerald)

[*Later, at the party.*]

NANCY: Hi, Paul. This is Bill, my husband.

PAUL: Welcome. Bill, I'm glad to know you. You two are our first guests to arrive. Help

yourselves to snacks. There are some _____ sandwiches.
10. (excellent / tomato-and-cheese)

Please make yourselves at home. You know, Nancy, I'm sorry I didn't make it clear this

isn't a _____ party. You two look great, but I hope you won't
11. (dress-up / fancy)

feel out of place.

BILL: Thanks. We'll be fine. By the way, Paul, I really like that _____
12. (beautiful / denim / purple)

shirt you're wearing. Where did you get it?

---

3 | READING ALOUD

Grammar Note 6

Complete the sentences in this narrative with compound modifiers.

Pam and Allen Murray took their son Joshua to a reading specialist because Joshua could not

read aloud in class. Dr. Tanaka, the specialist, asked Joshua a number of questions about his

problems with reading. Joshua said that he got frustrated in his reading class, that even though it

was only a _____*50-minute*_____ period, it seemed to him like a year. During this
1. (lasting 50 minutes)

particular semester, the teacher was giving the students oral reading assignments every day. At first

the teacher had called on Joshua to read aloud, and Joshua would panic every time, even if it was

only a _____ assignment. Now she was no longer calling on him.
2. (one paragraph in length)

(continued)

Dr. Tanaka asked Joshua if he had any problem with silent reading. Joshua said he didn't, adding that he loved to read to himself and could finish a _____ book in
3. (300 pages in length)
a day or two. Pam, Joshua's mother, noted that his reading comprehension was excellent.

Dr. Tanaka asked Pam and Allen how long this problem had been going on. Allen said it had begun when Joshua was in the first grade. Since Joshua was now 12, the situation had been a _____ ordeal. Dr. Tanaka wondered how the problem had started. Pam
4. (lasting six years)
replied that she felt it was definitely a _____ problem, for Joshua had
5. (related to stress)
lisped when he started school. Joshua added that he had felt bad when the other children would laugh at him when he pronounced his "s" sounds as "th" sounds. The problem simply got worse until Joshua was no longer able to read orally at all.

Dr. Tanaka agreed that teasing might have caused Joshua's problem but suggested another possibility—that Joshua's inability to read aloud could be an _____
6. (related to eyesight)
problem. He asked if it would be all right to test Joshua's vision. When the Murrays agreed, Dr. Tanaka asked Joshua to read two eye charts, which he was able to read perfectly. He then asked Joshua to read a short passage that he held at a distance. The passage went like this: "Night was falling in Dodge City. The gunfighter walked down the street wearing a _____ hat."
7. (holding 10 gallons)
Joshua read the passage with no difficulty at all, and Dr. Tanaka said he felt he now understood Joshua's problem well: He had _____ anxiety. He told the
8. (induced by performance)
Murrays he had distracted Joshua by referring to his vision. He then said he had a _____ program that would have Joshua reading aloud proficiently if he
9. (lasting two months)
was willing to try it. Joshua was more than willing, so the Murrays made arrangements to start the program soon.

4 | CREATIVE SENTENCES

Write a sentence for each of the following, changing the phrase so that the modifier appears before the head noun. Use correct punctuation.

1. a flight that takes 10 hours

Last month I was on a 10-hour flight from Rio to Bogotá.

2. a cat that has long hair

3. a jacket that is old and comfortable

4. an experience that amuses and interests you

5. a child who is 11 years old

6. a movie that wins an award

7. a table that has three legs

8. people who look unusual

9. a skirt that is made of cotton, is short, and is blue

10. a bowl originating in China and made of jade

11. a building that has 60 stories

12. a bag that weighs 40 kilos

5 | EDITING

Read this entry from medical student Jennifer Yu's computer journal. There are 11 mistakes in the use of modifiers. The first mistake is already corrected. Find and correct 10 more.

> FRIDAY: It's midnight, the end of a long day. My first week of ~~school medical~~ *medical school* is over, and I'm exhausted but happy! I'm so glad I decided to go to the university. It was definitely a good decision. I'm not completely sure yet, but I think I want to go into child psychiatry because I love working with children—especially nine- and ten-years-old kids.
>
> Yesterday our psychiatry class visited a new large hospital where many middle-class troubled children go for treatment. I expected to see a lot of boys and girls behaving badly, but most of them were pretty quiet and relaxed. They just looked like they needed some personal warm attention.
>
> Today in our surgery class we had a bright hardworking teacher, a Brazilian young doctor who was substituting for our usual professor. We got a foreign helpful viewpoint on things.
>
> The only thing I don't like about medical school is the cafeteria disgusting food. I'm going to have to start getting some hot tasty Chinese food from my local favorite place.
>
> Well, it's time for me to get some sleep. I hope this computer new program works correctly.

Communication Practice

6 | LISTENING

🎧 **A** *Joshua Murray is working on his reading program with Dr. Tanaka. Read these questions. Then listen to their conversation. Check **True** or **False**.*

	True	False
1. The first session will last only 30 minutes.	☑	☐
2. Joshua likes his own voice.	☐	☐
3. A rapid growth period occurs during adolescence.	☐	☐

4. Joshua is 13 years old. ☐ ☐

5. Joshua is afraid of reading aloud. ☐ ☐

6. The phrase that Joshua will say to distract himself will not be difficult to remember. ☐ ☐

7. The people in the story have three dogs. ☐ ☐

8. Large, warm, and furry dogs can keep you warm on a cold night. ☐ ☐

🎧 **B** *Now listen again and fill in the blanks. Place commas between adjectives when the speaker pauses, and be sure to hyphenate compound modifiers.*

1. Our first meeting is only going to be a _____ *30-minute session* _____ .

2. We don't want to make this a _____ .

3. I feel like a _____ .

4. And I feel like I have an _____ .

5. You're just going through a _____ .

6. It happens to a lot of _____ .

7. Now, the key to getting you over this _____ _____ is to distract you from thinking about how well you're doing.

8. Let's think of a _____ that you can keep in the back of your mind.

9. "It was an _____ ."

10. "It promised to be one of those _____ ."

11. What's a _____ ?

12. It's a night that's so cold that you need _____ to sleep with to keep you warm.

7 | GROUP DISCUSSION

Discuss these questions in small groups.

1. How does Joshua feel at the end of the session with Dr. Tanaka?

2. How can developmental problems like Joshua's affect a person's life? Do you know any examples you can share with the class?

3. If you had a friend with a similar problem, what advice would you give?

Example: **A:** Do you know anyone with stress-related problems like Joshua's?
B: Yes. My younger sister stuttered when she was a girl. It was definitely a stress-related problem. She . . .

8 | A STORY

A *Read a famous story.*

DEATH SPEAKS

There was a merchant in Baghdad who sent his servant to market to buy supplies. In a little while the servant came back, white and shaking, and said, "Master, just now when I was in the market I was bumped by a woman in the crowd, and when I turned I saw it was Death who had bumped me. She looked at me and made a threatening gesture. Now please lend me your horse, and I will ride away from this city and avoid my fate. I will go to Samarra, and there Death will not find me."

The merchant lent the servant his horse, and the servant mounted it. He rode away as fast as he could make the horse run. Then the merchant went down to the marketplace, and he saw me standing in the crowd. He came to me and said, "Why did you make a threatening gesture to my servant when you saw him this morning?"

"That was not a threatening gesture," I said. "It was only a gesture of surprise. I was amazed to see him in Baghdad, for I had an appointment with him tonight in Samarra."

B *Answer the questions. Then discuss your answers with a partner. Share your answers with the class. As a class, decide what the story shows about expectations.*

1. In the story, Death is _____.
   a. male
   b. female

2. In the last two paragraphs of the story, "I" and "me" refer to _____.
   a. the merchant
   b. Death

3. The servant expects to _____.
   a. escape from Death
   b. be captured by Death

4. The story suggests that _____.
   a. it's possible to escape fate
   b. it's not possible to escape fate

9 | PICTURE DISCUSSION

Form small groups. Look at this picture of the sinking of the Titanic *in April 1912.*

Describe what you see, using as many modifiers as possible. Share your sentences with other groups.

Example: The ship was sinking into the dark, icy ocean waters.

Then discuss what this painting suggests about expectations with the other groups.

Example: The builders of the *Titanic* didn't expect it to sink.

10 | WRITING

Have you ever expected something to happen that didn't turn out as you expected? For example, you didn't win a game, get an A, or win an election. Write two or three paragraphs telling what happened. Did it have anything to do with the expectation syndrome?

Example: A year ago our school basketball team was having a great year. In the regular season, we had a 19-1 record: 19 wins and one loss, and that one loss was in our first game. It seemed like we couldn't lose. When we got to the playoffs, however, things didn't turn out as we expected they would. In our first playoff game . . .

11 | ON THE INTERNET

Use the Internet to find out what was unexpected about one of the following topics. Share your findings with the class.

- the *Spruce Goose* of Howard Hughes

- the U.S. presidential election in 1948

- the reign of King Edward VIII of England

From **Grammar** to **Writing**
Agreement

There are two types of agreement: **subject-verb agreement** and **pronoun-antecedent agreement.**

Every sentence in English can be divided into two parts: the **subject** and the **predicate.** The subject is a person, place, or thing about which something is said. The predicate is what is said about the subject, and it always contains the principal verb. Subjects and verbs of English sentences must agree in person and number. In the following sentences, the complete subject is underlined once and the complete predicate twice.

<u>Birds</u> <u>chirp</u>.

<u>Koalas</u> <u>live in Australia</u>.

<u>The men at Ron's office</u> <u>like to play volleyball</u>.

<u>Nadia and Phil Lopez</u> <u>are trying to save money</u>.

<u>The danger of credit cards</u> <u>is that they encourage us to live beyond our means</u>.

To determine the **complete subject** of a sentence, ask a *who* or *what* question. The answer to that question will be the complete subject.

The man on the train reminded Penny of her father.

Who reminded Penny of her father? The man on the train. (complete subject)

The increasing extinction of plant and animal species is alarming.

What is alarming? The increasing extinction of plant and animal species. (complete subject)

1 | *Underline the complete subject in each of the sentences.*

1. <u>Five of my best friends</u> are coming over tonight to play cards.

2. The Siberian tiger and the blue whale are endangered species.

3. That man who is sitting at the mahogany desk is our loan officer.

4. Relatively few adults or teenagers are able to handle credit cards wisely.

5. The expectation that we will like well-known works of art, literature, or music can detract from our appreciation of them.

There is normally one word in the complete subject that controls the verb in the sentence. To determine this **main** (or **simple**) **subject**, find the word that the other words modify. In the following sentences, the main subject is underlined.

My blue silk <u>necktie</u> is gorgeous.

Our first three <u>attempts</u> were unsuccessful.

Notice that the main (simple) subject of a sentence is never located in a prepositional phrase (a phrase beginning with a preposition and ending with a noun or pronoun, for example, *on the table*). In the following sentences, the prepositional phrases are underlined, the main subject is circled, and an arrow is drawn between the main subject and the verb.

(One) <u>of my best friends</u> has nine credit cards.

(Both) <u>of my brothers</u> are behind on their car payments.

The (list) <u>on the bulletin board</u> is out of date.

(Either) <u>of the plans</u> is worthwhile.

The (man) <u>in the gray flannel suit</u> is a salesman.

(Neither) <u>of the skaters</u> is expected to win a gold medal.

2 | *Circle the main subject in each of the sentences, and draw an arrow between it and the verb.*

1. A (list) of available jobs was posted on the office bulletin board.

2. Much of what you were told was inaccurate.

3. Neither of those two politicians is in favor of cutting taxes.

4. None of the work has been completed successfully.

5. Very little of this work can be done by one person working alone.

6. The singing of that famous Australian opera star is uplifting.

Be careful with the word *there*. Even though *there* is often the grammatical subject of a sentence, it is linked to a word later in the sentence that controls the verb. In the following sentences, an arrow connects the word *there* and the noun it is linked to. Note the underlined verb.

There <u>are</u> numerous animals on the Endangered Species List.

There <u>have</u> been many environmental disasters in the last 20 years.

There <u>is</u> a large, fierce dog guarding the house.

BE CAREFUL! You will sometimes hear *there* used with a singular verb even though the noun that follows is plural. This occurs in conversation but is not correct in standard formal English.

Conversational:	**There's** some papers on my desk.
Standard:	**There are** some papers on my desk.

3 | *Choose the correct verb to complete each sentence.*

1. There _____*has*_____ never been an environmental disaster of this magnitude.
   (has / have)

2. There _____ many reasons why I am against the use of nuclear power.
   (is / are)

3. There _____ always a rational explanation for his behavior.
   (isn't / aren't)

4. There _____ been fewer business mergers this year than last.
   (has / have)

5. There _____ numerous demonstrators present at the environmental rally.
   (was / were)

6. There _____ any elegantly dressed people at the party. Everyone was
   (wasn't / weren't)
   wearing blue jeans.

Compound subjects are those in which the subject is composed of more than one item. The items are often connected by *and*.

Ron and Laurie are going to join a health club. (two subjects: *Ron, Laurie*)

The blue whale, the timber wolf, and **the whooping crane** need our protection. (three subjects: *whale, wolf, crane*)

Sometimes words appear to be compound subjects, but they really constitute a single phrase made up of two or more items acting as a unit. These take a **singular verb.**

Bacon and eggs is a high-cholesterol but nourishing meal. (*Bacon and eggs* is a single dish.)

The owner and manager of the bank is Mr. Bates. (*Mr. Bates* is one person who has two roles.)

4 | *Choose the correct verb to complete each sentence.*

1. Both the whale and the grizzly bear _____*need*_____ federal protection.
   (needs / need)

2. Bipolar disorder and schizophrenia _____ two serious mental disorders.
   (is / are)

3. The director and star of the film _____ Robert Redford.
   (was / were)

4. Liver and onions _____ a meal detested by many children.
   (is / are)

5. Mathematics and physics _____ often considered difficult subjects.
   (is / are)

Pronoun-antecedent agreement is similar to subject-verb agreement. In formal English, pronouns agree in person, number, and gender with their antecedents (words to which they refer).

All the **students** brought **their** books to class on the first day. (*Their* agrees with *students*.)

Jack ate **his** lunch quickly. (*His* agrees with *Jack*.)

Martha stopped by to see **her** mother after class. (*Her* agrees with *Martha*.)

Each of **us** needs to bring **our** own ideas to the meeting. (*Our* agrees with *us*.)

The pronouns *everyone / everybody, anyone / anybody, someone / somebody,* and *no one / nobody* are often treated differently in conversational and standard formal English. Look at these examples.

Formal	**Informal**
Everyone drove **his or her** own car to the picnic.	**Everyone** drove **their** own car to the picnic.
If you see **anyone** from our office, tell **him or her** to see me.	If you see **anyone** from our office, tell **them** to see me.
Everybody may leave when **he or she** wishes.	**Everybody** may leave when **they** wish.

BE CAREFUL! Use the forms on the right above only in informal (conversational) English. Use the correct singular forms in writing and formal speech.

Sometimes it is possible to make a sentence correct for formal English by changing the subject to a plural.

Informal: **Everyone** brought **their** own lunch.
Formal: **All the employees** brought **their** own lunch.

5 | *Complete each of these sentences with forms for formal and informal English.*

Formal

1. Does everyone have _____*his or her*_____ book with him or her?
   a.

2. No one knows _____ own destiny.
   a.

3. If anyone shows up, send

   _____ to my office.
   a.

4. Everybody needs to have

   _____ priorities straight.
   a.

Informal

Does everyone have _____ book with them?
b.

No one knows _____ own destiny.
b.

If anyone shows up, send

_____ to my office.
b.

Everybody needs to have

_____ priorities straight.
b.

In formal English, subjects connected by **either / or** and **neither / nor** behave differently from compound subjects. The subject that is closer to the verb determines the agreement.

> Either the **president** or his cabinet **members are** responsible for this environmental policy. (two subjects: *president, members; members* is closer to the verb and requires the plural verb *are*)

> Neither the **members** of the city council nor the **mayor supports** more real estate development. (two subjects: *members, mayor; mayor* is closer to the verb and requires the singular verb *supports*)

Note that if we reverse the order of the subjects in the above sentences, the verb changes:

> Either the cabinet **members** or the **president is** responsible for this environmental policy.

> Neither the **mayor** nor the **members** of the city council **support** more real estate development.

Pronouns whose antecedents are nouns connected by *either / or* and *neither / nor* behave in the same way. The noun closer to the pronoun determines the correct pronoun.

> Neither **Susan** nor **the Johnsons** enrolled **their** children in that school. (*The Johnsons* is closer to the pronoun and requires *their*.)

6 | Choose the correct verb or pronoun to complete the sentences.

1. Either Bob Ashcroft or the Mendozas ____*are*____ going to host this year's party.
   (is / are)

2. Neither pollution nor other atmospheric factors _____ thought to be related to the
   (is / are)

   unusual weather we've been having.

3. Neither the local environmentalists nor the mayor _____ a plan that will satisfy everyone.
   (has / have)

4. Either major credit cards or a check _____ an acceptable means of payment.
   (is / are)

5. Neither Venus nor the outer planets _____ a breathable atmosphere.
   (has / have)

6. Neither my daughters nor my son owns _____ own car.
   (their / his)

7 Read the letter to the editor of a newspaper. There are 12 mistakes in subject-verb agreement and pronoun-antecedent agreement. The first mistake is already corrected. Find and correct 11 more. Use forms that are correct for formal English.

Editor, The Times:

    Many parts of our once-beautiful city ~~is~~ *are* starting to look like mini garbage dumps. You will recall that legislation requiring recycling within the city limits were passed last year, and the mayor and other local politicians encourages us to recycle, but in my apartment complex there's no bins for recycling. The result is that people take no responsibility for his own actions, and everyone tosses their trash and recyclables (glass, plastic bottles, cans, etc.) right in with the food that is being thrown away. Neither the manager of the complex nor the owners of the building has bought any new containers for items that are supposed to be recycled. So what else can everybody do but mix his trash together? Either the manager or the owners is responsible for breaking the law here. Not us! Meanwhile, trash cans in the downtown area is overflowing with garbage, and vacant lots all around the city is littered with soda cans, broken glass, and paper. The owner and publisher of your newspaper, Stanford Black, have always been a supporter of a clean environment. I urge your paper to take leadership in solving this problem.

8 Interview someone about his or her family or close friends. Ask about brothers, sisters, children, activities, and so on. Then write a paragraph of five or six sentences summarizing what you learned. Make sure that you have correct subject-verb and pronoun-antecedent agreement. Write the paragraph using the forms used in informal English. Exchange papers with a partner. Edit each other's paragraph. Then rewrite your paragraphs, if necessary, and submit them to your teacher.

Review Test

I   *Fill in the blanks with **a / an** or **the**, or leave a blank if no article is needed.*

According to ___the___ National Weather Service, _____ cyclones are _____ areas of
            1.   **2.**   **3.**

circulating winds that rotate counterclockwise in _____ Northern Hemisphere and clockwise
                                          4.

in _____ Southern Hemisphere. They are generally accompanied by some kind of _____
     5.   **6.**

precipitation and by _____ stormy weather. _____ tornadoes and _____ hurricanes
              7.   **8.**   **9.**

are _____ types of cyclones, as are _____ typhoons, which are _____ storms that
    10.   **11.**   **12.**

occur in _____ western Pacific Ocean.
       13.

_____ hurricane is _____ cyclone that forms over _____ tropical oceans and seas
  14.   **15.**   **16.**

and has _____ winds of at least 74 miles _____ hour. _____ hurricane rotates in
       17.   **18.**   **19.**

_____ shape of _____ oval or _____ circle. _____ hurricanes can cause
 20.   **21.**   **22.**   **23.**

_____ great environmental damage. _____ Hurricane Charley, which hit Jamaica, Cuba,
 24.   **25.**

_____ west coast of Florida, and the Carolinas in August 2004, caused _____ extreme
 26.   **27.**

devastation. In terms of _____ environmental damage, _____ Hurricane Charley is one of
               28.   **29.**

_____ most destructive hurricanes ever to hit _____ United States. More than 20 people
 30.   **31.**

died because of _____ Charley's effects.
         32.

II *Each of the following sentences contains one mistake in the use of articles. Correct each sentence by rewriting the incorrect phrase.*

1. One of the best things we can do to help the environment is to encourage the recycling.

   to encourage recycling

2. Bats are mammals, not the birds.

   _____

3. An orangutan is humanlike ape living in the jungles of Borneo and Sumatra.

   _____

4. The Mesozoic era was third of the four major eras of geologic time.

   _____

5. Jurassic period was the period of the Mesozoic era when dinosaurs were present and birds first appeared.

   _____

6. The euro is official currency of the European Union.

   _____

7. The meltdown is an unplanned melting of a nuclear reactor's core.

   _____

8. Statues on Easter Island were apparently carved and erected by the Easter Islanders themselves.

   _____

9. Rain forests in South America are being cleared to make fields for raising the cattle.

   _____

10. Telephone was invented in 1876 by Alexander Graham Bell.

   _____

III *Look at the pictures here and on page 176. Write a sentence under each picture in which the noun in parentheses is used in a countable sense, either with **a / an** or in the plural.*

1. (soda)

She's drinking a soda.

2. (furniture)

3. (work)

4. (advice)

5. (people)

6. (spices)

(continued)

7. (lightning)   8. (cheese)

_____   _____

_____   _____

IV | *Complete the conversations by putting the modifiers in the correct order.*

1. A: It feels like a _____*sweltering summer*_____ day here, even though it's spring.

                             a. (summer / sweltering)

What's it like where you are?

   B: Here it feels like a _____ day. I envy you.

                                        b. (chilly / winter)

2. A: What do you think of my _____ tie?

                                        a. (silk / pink / new)

   B: It makes you look like a _____ businessman.

                                     b. (European / young / handsome)

3. A: We were finally able to build a _____ house. It's just

                                      a. (brick / new / beautiful)

what we've always wanted.

   B: It sounds great. Maybe we could do the same. We feel like we're living in a

_____ cabin.

                b. (little / dirty / old)

V | *Complete the conversations with the correct quantifiers, choosing from the words in parentheses.*

1. A: Let's get off this freeway. There's just too _____*much*_____ traffic.

                                       a. (much / many)

   B: Yeah, let's. The _____*number*_____ of people driving is incredible. I've never seen this

                    b. (amount / number)

_____*many*_____ cars.

      c. (much / many)

2. A: Can you bring soda to the picnic? I don't have _____.

                                    a. (some / any)

   B: Yes, I think I've got _____ left over from the party.

                      b. (some / any)

3. **A:** How do you feel about your new job? Do you have as _____ responsibilities
   a. (much / many)

   as you used to?

   B: The job is great. I have about the same _____ of work as before, but I have
   b. (amount / number)

   _____ stress and _____ problems.
   c. (less / fewer)   d. (less / fewer)

4. **A:** How do you think you did on the test? I think I only missed _____
   a. (a few / a little)

   questions. In fact, I hope I didn't miss _____ questions at all.
   b. (some / any)

   B: Well, I think I probably made _____ mistakes, but I have the feeling I did
   c. (few / a few)

   well overall.

5. **A:** Mr. President, do you believe _____ of your proposed legislation will be
   a. (much / many)

   passed by Congress during this session?

   B: Yes, I think _____ of our proposals will be approved. We're not making
   b. (a great deal / a great many)

   _____ assumptions, though. We still have _____ work to
   c. (no / any)   d. (a great deal of / a great many)

   do.

   A: The polls say there's _____ support nationwide for your military program.
   e. (little / a little)

   Isn't that going to hurt you?

   B: Not in the long run, no. _____ of the voters actually support the military
   f. (Few / A few)

   system the way it is now. I think we'll be successful.

VI *Circle the letter of the one underlined word or phrase in each sentence that is not correct.*

1. The journey from Los Angeles to San Diego is a three-hours   **A B (C) D**
   A   B   C

   trip if the traffic isn't heavy.
                   D

2. The chief executive officer of the company I work for lives in   **A B C D**
   A   B

   beautiful condominium in a 10-story building.
   C   D

3. Plan to build an extensive monorail system is a citizen-initiated proposal.   **A B C D**
   A   B   C   D

4. One of the most famous inventions in the history of humankind is a wheel.   **A B C D**
              A   B   C   D

(continued)

5. The <u>two first</u> films shown in last weekend's film series were   **A B C D**
_A   _B

<u>the most popular ones</u> in <u>the series</u>.
_C   _D

6. <u>The extinction</u> of <u>the dinosaurs</u> is still <u>a matter</u> of debate   **A B C D**
_A   _B   _C

in <u>scientific community</u>.
_D

7. Vancouver, <u>the largest city</u> in <u>Canadian Southwest</u>, is   **A B C D**
_A   _B

<u>the closest major Canadian port</u> to <u>the Far East</u>.
_C   _D

8. When Sarah was a child, she disliked <u>cauliflower</u>, <u>carrots</u>, <u>bean</u>,   **A B C D**
_A   _B   _C

and <u>most other vegetables</u>.
_D

9. <u>The Wheelers'</u> <u>10-years-old</u> daughter, Melanie, was born in   **A B C D**
_A   _B

<u>the city of Rotterdam</u> in <u>the Netherlands</u>.
_C   _D

10. Ralph is in <u>the intensive care ward</u> of <u>the city hospital</u> after   **A B C D**
_A   _B

being struck by <u>a lightning</u> on <u>a camping trip</u>.
_C   _D

VII *Go back to your answers to Exercise VI. Write the correct form for each item that you believe is incorrect.*

1. _____ *three-hour* _____   6. _____

2. _____   7. _____

3. _____   8. _____

4. _____   9. _____

5. _____   10. _____

▶ *To check your answers, go to the Answer Key on page RT-2.*

PART IV

Adjective Clauses

Grammar in Context

BEFORE YOU READ

1 *Complete this sentence with the one adjective that best describes your personality: "I am a person who is _____."*

2 *Is it helpful to classify people into personality types or to place yourself in a personality category? Why or why not?*

🎧 *Read this article about personality types.*

WHAT TYPE ARE YOU ?

Sunflowers

Four o'clocks

Suppose you attend a party where there are several people you know well. The hosts have a new party game that involves asking everyone to compare each person to a flower. Which flower would you choose for each person and which flower for yourself? Are you the kind of person who resembles a sunflower, open to the world most of the time? Or are you more like a four o'clock, someone who opens up only at special moments?

This may sound like just an amusing activity, but there is a science of personality identification that grew out of the work of Swiss psychologist Carl Jung and that of two American women, Katharine Briggs and her daughter, Isabel Briggs Myers. After studying Jung's work, Briggs and her daughter developed a system of 4 personality dimensions and 16 different personality types. Based on this system, they developed a test, which has been refined many times over the decades and has been taken by millions of people. Take a look at the following descriptions based on the Myers-Briggs test. Try to place people you know into one or more of the categories.* You may learn something about your co-workers, friends, loved ones, and yourself.

* To learn more about personality type and to determine your type, visit <u>www.personality.type.com</u>.

WHAT TYPE ARE YOU?

Category 1: extrovert or introvert. This category has to do with the way that people direct their energy. An extrovert is basically a person whose energies are activated by being with others. An introvert is essentially a person whose energies are activated by being alone. Mary is a good example of an extrovert. She's the kind of person whom others consider shy, but there's no correlation between shyness and either introversion or extroversion. At a party, Mary starts to open up and get energized once she meets some people who make her feel comfortable. Her friend Bill is the opposite. He isn't shy at all, but after he's been at a party for a while, he's tired and ready to go home. He finds the conversation interesting enough but is just as likely to be imagining a time when he was hiking alone in the mountains.

Category 2: sensor or intuitive. This category has to do with the kind of information we notice and remember easily. Sensors are practical people who notice what is going on around them and rely on past experiences to make conclusions. Intuitives are more interested in relationships between things or people, tending to focus on what *might* be. Consider Jack and Barbara, who have been married for years. At a party, Jack, whose parents own a sofa company, notices that their hosts have bought a new sofa and asks where they bought it. Barbara is less interested in the sofa and more interested in the tense way the hosts are talking with each other. Did they have a fight? Jack is the sensor and Barbara the intuitive.

Category 3: thinker or feeler. This category is about the way that we make conclusions. Thinkers are those who tend to make decisions objectively, on the basis of logic. Feelers make decisions based on their personal values and how they feel about choices. Helen and Gary are at a bank applying for a loan. The loan officer tells them they owe too much on their credit cards and will have to pay off their debt before they can borrow money. This makes perfect sense to Helen, which classifies her as a thinker. Gary's reaction is quite different. The loan officer, who makes Gary feel criticized, is only trying to do his job. However, Gary takes the loan officer's comments personally, which classifies him as a feeler.

Category 4: judger or perceiver. This dimension is about the kind of environment that makes us feel most comfortable. Judgers are people who prefer a predictable environment. They like to make decisions and have things settled. Perceivers are more interested in keeping their options open, preferring to experience as much of the world as possible. Consider Tim and Samantha. Tim, who always has a plan for everything, gets impatient with Samantha when he calls her to plan a time when they can get together. Tim wants things to be definite; Samantha wants to keep her options flexible.

So we're left with this question: What good is classifying people? It certainly doesn't give us any magic powers or tools for relationships. But it can give us insight. It can help us understand others better, and perhaps minimize or reduce conflict. Best of all, it can help us understand ourselves.

AFTER YOU READ

What does each sentence mean? Circle the correct answer.

1. An extrovert is basically a person whose energies are activated by being with others.
   a. Extroverts get energy from others.
   b. Others get energy from extroverts.

2. She's the kind of person whom others consider shy.
   a. She thinks others are shy.
   b. Others think she's shy.

3. Gary takes the loan officer's comments personally, which classifies him as a feeler.
   a. We classify Gary as a feeler.
   b. We classify the loan officer as a feeler.

Grammar Presentation

ADJECTIVE CLAUSES: REVIEW AND EXPANSION

ADJECTIVE CLAUSES: PLACEMENT

Main Clause		Adjective Clause	
	Noun / Pronoun	Relative Pronoun	
They met	a woman	**who**	**teaches psychology.**
I've read	everything	**that**	**discusses her work.**

Main . . .		Adjective Clause		. . . Clause
Noun / Pronoun	Relative Pronoun		
The woman	**who**	**teaches psychology**	is also a writer.
Everything	**that**	**discusses her work**	is very positive.

RELATIVE PRONOUNS: *WHO, WHOM, WHICH, THAT*

Subjects: *Who, Which, That*					
People			Things		
I have a friend	**who**	loves to talk.	This is a book	**which**	is useful.
I have friends	**that**	love to talk.	These are books	**that**	are useful.

Objects: *Who(m), Which, That, Ø**					
People			**Things**		
This is the doctor	who(m) **that** Ø	we consulted.	This is the test	which **that** Ø	he gave us.

*Ø = no pronoun

WHOSE TO INDICATE POSSESSION

Whose + **Noun**	
People	**Things**
She is the woman **whose son** is so famous.	It's the book **whose reviews** were so good.
She is the woman **whose son** I am tutoring.	It's the book **whose reviews** I have just read.

WHERE AND *WHEN* IN ADJECTIVE CLAUSES

Where		
Place		
I remember the café	**where**	we met.

When		
Time		
I remember the day	(when) **(that)** Ø	we parted.

ADJECTIVE CLAUSES: IDENTIFYING OR NONIDENTIFYING

Identifying Clause
No Commas
The woman **who / that created the test** studied psychology. The test **which / that / Ø she created** describes personality types.

Nonidentifying Clause
Commas
Katharine Briggs, **who created the test**, studied psychology. The Myers-Briggs test, **which she created**, describes personality types.

GRAMMAR NOTES	EXAMPLES
1. A sentence with an **adjective clause** can be seen as a combination of two sentences.	*John is a man. + He works hard. =* • John is a man **who works hard**. *Mary is interesting. + I like her a lot. =* • Mary, **whom I like a lot**, is interesting.
2. An adjective clause is a **dependent clause**. It modifies a noun or a pronoun in a main clause. An adjective clause often begins with a **relative pronoun**: *who*, *whom*, *which*, or *that*. It can also begin with *whose*, *when*, or *where*. The word that begins an adjective clause usually comes directly after the noun or pronoun that the clause modifies. An adjective clause can occur after a main clause or inside a main clause.	• Frank, **who is an introvert**, spends a lot of time alone. • Let's do something **that is fun**. • Toronto, **which is the largest city in Canada**, is a beautiful place. • Harriet is a woman **whom I respect**. • The house **that we bought** is in the suburbs.
3. To refer to people, use *who* and *that* as the subjects of verbs in adjective clauses. To refer to things, use *which* and *that* as the subjects of verbs in adjective clauses. **USAGE NOTE:** *That* is less formal than *who* or *which*. The verb in an adjective clause agrees with the noun or pronoun that the clause modifies. ▶ **BE CAREFUL!** Do not use a double subject in an adjective clause.	• The Ings are the **people who** bought the house. • Sam is the **man that** lives next door to me. • Math is the **subject which** is the easiest for me. • This is the **car that** is the nicest. • There are many **people who have taken** this personality test. • This test is the **one that is** the best known. • Extroverts are people **who like to be with others**. NOT Extroverts are people who ~~they~~ like to be with others.

4. To refer to people, use **whom**, **who**, and **that** as the **objects** of verbs in adjective clauses. *Whom* is very formal. *Who* and *that* are less formal and used in conversation and informal writing. *That* is the least formal.

- **Mr. Pitkin**, **whom** I mentioned yesterday, is my boss.
- Mr. Pitkin was the **person who** I mentioned.
- Mr. Pitkin was the **person that** I mentioned.

To refer to things, use **which** and **that** as the **objects** of verbs in adjective clauses. *Which* is a bit more formal.

- The **test which** I took was difficult.
- The **test that** I took was difficult.

In conversation and informal writing, you can sometimes omit the relative pronoun if it is an object. This is the most common spoken form. *(See note 8 for more information on omitting relative pronouns.)*

- Mr. Pitkin is the man **I mentioned.**
- The test **I took** was difficult.

The verb in an adjective clause agrees with the subject of the clause, not with the object.

- The Mendozas are the people **that Sally sees frequently**.

  NOT The Mendozas are the people that Sally ~~see~~ frequently.

5. Use **whose** to introduce an adjective clause that indicates **possession**. We use *whose* to replace *his / her / its / their* + noun. An adjective clause with *whose* can modify people or things.

Ken is the man + We met his wife. =
- Ken is the man **whose wife we met**.

  It's a theory. + Its origins go back many years. =
- It's a theory **whose origins go back many years**.

▶ **BE CAREFUL!** *Whose* cannot be omitted.

- Harvey, **whose house we're renting**, is a lawyer.

  NOT Harvey, ~~house we're renting,~~ is a lawyer.

(continued)

6. You can use **where** to introduce an adjective clause that modifies a noun of **place**. *Where* replaces the word *there*.

► **BE CAREFUL!** Use an adjective clause with **where** only if you can restate the location with the word *there*. Do not use an adjective clause with *where* if the location cannot be stated in this way.

NOTE: *Where* can be replaced by *which* or *that* + a preposition, such as *in*, *at*, or *for*. In this type of adjective clause, *which / that* can be omitted.

This is the restaurant. + We ate there. =

- This is the restaurant **where we ate**.
- Chihuahua is the town **where I was born**. = Chihuahua is the town. I was born **there**.

  NOT Rio de Janeiro is a city ~~where has beautiful scenery~~.
- Rio de Janeiro is a city **that has beautiful scenery**.
- This is the building **where** she works.
- This is the building (**that**) she works **in**.

---

7. You can use **when** or **that** to begin an adjective clause that modifies a noun of **time**. You can omit *when* and *that* in this type of adjective clause. The sentence without *when* or *that* is informal.

- I can't think of a time **when / that I wasn't happy**.
- I can't think of a time **I wasn't happy**.

---

8. An adjective clause that distinguishes one person or thing from another is called **identifying** or essential. The clause is not enclosed in commas.

An adjective clause that adds extra information but does not distinguish one person or thing from another is called **nonidentifying** or nonessential. The clause is enclosed in commas.

► **BE CAREFUL!**

a. You can omit relative pronouns only in identifying adjective clauses. You cannot omit the relative pronoun in a nonidentifying adjective clause.

b. Don't use **that** as a relative pronoun in a nonidentifying clause.

You can use **which** informally to refer to an entire previous idea.

In formal writing and speech, use a noun at the beginning of a **which** clause.

- The man **who delivers the mail** is friendly.

- The man, **who delivers the mail**, is friendly.

- The man **you met on Friday** is Tarik.
- That's Tarik, **who you met on Friday**.
  NOT That's Tarik, ~~you met on Friday~~.

- The Myers-Briggs test, **which I took a long time ago**, has proved to be accurate.
  NOT The Myers-Briggs test, ~~that I took a long time ago~~, has proved to be accurate.

- **Helen is hardworking, which** impresses me.

- **Helen is hardworking, a characteristic which** impresses me.

Focused Practice

1 | DISCOVER THE GRAMMAR

A *Look at these sentences based on the opening reading. Could the relative pronoun be replaced by the relative pronoun in parentheses without creating a different meaning or making an incorrect sentence?*

__yes__ 1. Are you the kind of person **who** resembles a sunflower? (that)

_____ 2. There is a science of personality identification **that** grew out of the work of Swiss psychologist Carl Jung. (which)

_____ 3. Based on this system, they developed a test, **which** has been refined many times over the decades. (that)

_____ 4. She's the kind of person **whom** others consider shy. (that)

_____ 5. He is just as likely to be imagining a time **when** he was hiking alone in the mountains. (that)

_____ 6. Jack and Barbara, **who** have been married for years, are good examples. (whom)

_____ 7. The loan officer, **who** makes Gary feel criticized, is only trying to do his job. (that)

_____ 8. Judgers are people **who** prefer a predictable environment. (which)

B *Find three sentences in the reading in which the relative pronoun has been omitted. Add a correct relative pronoun to each sentence.*

1. _____

   _____

2. _____

   _____

3. _____

   _____

C *Look at these sentences based on the opening reading. Underline the adjective clause in each sentence. Then say whether the clause is identifying (I) or nonidentifying (NI).*

_____*I*_____ 1. Suppose you attend a party <u>where there are a lot of people</u>.

_____ 2. Are you the kind of person who resembles a sunflower?

_____ 3. They developed a test, which has been refined many times over the decades.

_____ 4. An introvert is a person whose energies are activated by being alone.

_____ 5. Mary starts to open up once she meets some people who make her feel comfortable.

_____ 6. He is imagining a time when he was hiking alone in the mountains.

_____ 7. Good examples are Jack and Barbara, who have been married for years.

_____ 8. Jack, whose parents own a sofa company, notices that their hosts have bought a new sofa.

_____ 9. The loan officer, who makes Gary feel criticized, is only trying to do his job.

_____ 10. However, Gary takes his comments personally, which classifies him a feeler.

2 | ABOUT MY FAMILY
Grammar Notes 3, 5–6, 8

Circle the correct relative pronoun in each sentence.

1. I come from a family (that / whom) has eight members.

2. I have three sisters and two brothers, (that / which) made things pretty crowded when we were growing up.

3. Our house, (which / that) is four stories high, has eight bedrooms.

4. The members of my family, (who / whom) are all interesting, fit nicely into the Meyers-Briggs personality categories.

5. My mother and father, (who / whom) both like to be with people a great deal, are extroverts.

6. My favorite brother, with (who / whom) I still spend a lot of time, is a perceiver and an introvert.

7. My other brother, (who / which) is a judger, is a great guy but always has to be right.

8. My favorite sister, (who / whose) fiancé is the same age as I am, is an intuitive.

9. Of my other two sisters, the one (no pronoun / which) I am closer to is a feeler.

10. I'm less close to the sister (who / no pronoun) is much older than I am. She's a thinker.

3 | PEOPLE IN THE WORKPLACE

Grammar Notes 6–8

Dolores Atwood, a personnel officer for a publishing company, is writing an evaluation of the employees in her department who are being considered for promotion. Complete her sentences using one of the pronouns in parentheses. Put the verbs in the correct form.

KIRBY, BROWN, AND EAGER

Confidential

Personnel Evaluation

Elaine Correa has only been with us for a year but is definitely ready for promotion,

_____which is not surprising_____ given the excellent recommendations
   1. (that / which) / not / be surprising

from the business _____ before.
   2. (which / where) / she / work

Burt Drysdale has proven himself to be a team player, amazingly. He had some prob-

lems at the company _____ previously, and
   3. (where / that) / he / work for

during the first month _____ here, he irritated
   4. (which / no pronoun) / he / work

everyone. I do recommend him for promotion.

Alice Anderdoff is not performing up to expectations, _____
   5. (that / which) / bother

_____me because I was the one who recruited her. There was an early period

_____ excellent, but I don't believe she should
   6. (when / which) / her performance / be

be promoted at this time.

Mel Tualapa is an employee _____ because
   7. (which / no pronoun) / everyone / like

he's congenial and hardworking, but he can't be promoted yet because he's only been with us

for six months.

Tom Curran is an employee _____ often
   8. (that / no pronoun) / have

been ill and is consistently late to work. This is mystifying because at the time

_____ he seemed to be a model employee. I
   9. (when / which) / he / be hired

don't recommend him at this time.

4. We sometimes **shorten adjective clauses** to **adjective phrases** with the same meaning.

Remember that a clause is a group of words that has a subject and a verb. A phrase is a group of words that doesn't have both a subject and a verb.

- Anyone **who is interested in drama** should see this play. *(adjective clause)*
- Anyone **interested in drama** should see this play. *(adjective phrase)*

---

5. To shorten an adjective clause with a **be** verb, **reduce** the clause to an adjective phrase by deleting the relative pronoun and the *be* verb.

▶ **BE CAREFUL!** Adjective clauses with *be* verbs can be reduced only when *who*, *which*, or *that* is the subject pronoun of the clause

If an adjective clause needs commas, the corresponding phrase also needs commas.

- *Titanic*, **which was directed by James Cameron**, won many awards.
- *Titanic*, **directed by James Cameron**, won many awards.
- I met Chris Rock, **whose latest film is a hit**.
  NOT I met Chris Rock, ~~latest film is a hit~~.
- Cher starred in *Moonstruck*, **which was released in 1987**.
- Cher starred in *Moonstruck*, **released in 1987**.

---

6. If there is no *be* verb in the adjective clause, it is often possible to **change** the clause to an adjective phrase. Do this by deleting the relative pronoun and changing the verb to its *-ing* form. You can do this only when *who*, *which*, or *that* is the subject pronoun of the clause.

- *Titanic*, **which stars Leonardo DiCaprio**, is the top-earning film.
- *Titanic*, **starring Leonardo DiCaprio**, is the top-earning film.
- I like any movie **that features Helen Hunt**.
- I like any movie **featuring Helen Hunt**.

Focused Practice

1 | DISCOVER THE GRAMMAR

A *Look again at the opening reading. Find four adjective clauses containing prepositions plus* **which** *and two containing prepositions plus* **whom.** *Underline them. Then circle the head noun referred to by each relative pronoun and draw a line between it and the clause.*

films . . . most of which bored me silly

B *Look at eight adjective phrases that have been reduced from clauses. Make each adjective phrase a clause by adding a relative pronoun and a verb.*

1. which causes anyone <u>putting it on</u> to become invisible

   who / that puts it on

2. which eventually corrupts anyone <u>continuing to wear it</u>

   _____

3. small people who live in a tiny country <u>called the Shire</u>

   _____

4. the forces of evil, <u>represented by</u> the Dark Lord, orcs, and a bad wizard

   _____

5. if you're the type of person <u>inclined to ask</u>

   _____

6. anyone <u>interested in cinema</u>

   _____

7. many prominent actors, <u>including</u> Elijah Wood playing Frodo

   _____

8. a computer-generated character <u>based on</u> Serkis's prototype

   _____

2 | FILM TRIVIA
Grammar Note 2

Complete the following statements about movies using adjective clauses in the form of quantifier + preposition + relative pronoun.

1. Walt Disney's animated productions, ____*most of which are loved by children*____, are
   (most / be loved by children)

   known all over the world.

2. *Saving Private Ryan* and *Schindler's List*, _____,
   (both / be directed by Steven Spielberg)

   are critical and commercial successes.

3. Roberto Benigni, Wim Wenders, and Lina Wertmüller, _____
   (all / be / highly regarded European directors)

   _____, are not too well known in the United States.

(continued)

4. *Star Wars*, *The Empire Strikes Back*, and *Return of the Jedi*, _____

                               (all / have / earn a great deal of money)

_____, are the middle three films in a nine-part series.

5. Sean Connery and Roger Moore, _____, are from

                               (both / have / play the role of James Bond)

Britain, while Pierce Brosnan, a more recent Bond, is from Ireland.

6. Richard Gere, Catherine Zeta-Jones, and Renée Zellweger, _____

                               (none / be known as singers)

_____, surprised everyone with their singing in *Chicago*.

---

3 | POPULAR MOVIES   *Grammar Notes 5–6*

Combine each pair of sentences into one sentence with an adjective phrase. Note that in sentence 4, the adjective phrase will come from the second sentence; in all other cases, the adjective phrase will come from the first sentence.

1. *E.T.* was directed by Steven Spielberg. It was the top-earning film until it was passed by *Titanic* and the reissued *Star Wars*.

   E.T., directed by Steven Spielberg, was the top-earning film until it was passed by Titanic and the reissued Star Wars.

2. *Spider-Man* is based on the popular comic book. It is the fifth-highest-earning movie of all time.

   _____

   _____

3. *The Matrix* and *The Matrix: Reloaded* star Keanu Reeves. They are both very popular.

   _____

   _____

4. James Cameron has directed many big movies. These include *Titanic*, *True Lies*, and the *Terminator* films.

   _____

   _____

5. The Harry Potter novels were written by J. K. Rowling. They have translated well to the screen.

   _____

   _____

6. *Star Wars*, *The Empire Strikes Back*, and *Return of the Jedi* feature Harrison Ford, Carrie Fisher, and Mark Hamill. They were conceived, written, and directed by George Lucas.

   _____

   _____

4 | MOVIE TYPES

Each of these sentences about types of films contains an adjective clause or phrase. Imagine that each sentence was formed from an original pair of sentences. Write the original pairs.

1. Comedies, examples of which are *Legally Blonde*, *Barbershop*, and *Johnny English*, have continued to be popular and successful.

   Comedies have continued to be popular and successful. Examples of these are Legally Blonde,

   Barbershop, and Johnny English.

2. Many recent science fiction films have been financially successful, including *The Phantom Menace*, *Independence Day*, and *Spider-Man I* and *II*.

   _____

   _____

3. The top-earning animated films, both of which I've seen, are *The Lion King* and *Shrek*.

   _____

   _____

4. *Chicago*, featuring three well-known actors, was the best picture of 2002.

   _____

   _____

5. Sequels to big movie hits may lose their appeal, causing filmmakers to become more creative.

   _____

   _____

5 | MY MOVIES

Use the items in the box to describe movies you have seen or that you know about. Write a sentence for each item.

directed by	examples of which	featuring
including	quantifier + *of which*	starring

Examples: I've seen a lot of Arnold Schwarzenegger's movies, **including** *Terminator I, II,* and *III* and *True Lies*.

Dances with Wolves and *Unforgiven*, **both of which I've seen**, made westerns more popular.

6 | EDITING

Read this letter. There are ten mistakes in the use of adjective clauses and phrases. The first mistake is already corrected. Find and correct nine more. Delete verbs or change pronouns where necessary, but do not change punctuation or add relative pronouns.

Venice Beach Rialto

July 28

Dear Brent,

Sarah and I are having a great time in Los Angeles. We spent the first day at the beach in Venice and saw where *The Sting* was filmed—you know, that famous movie
~~starring~~ Paul Newman and Robert Redford? Yesterday we went to Universal Studios and learned about all the cinematic tricks, most of that I wasn't aware of. Amazing! The funny thing is that even though you know the illusion presenting on the screen is just an illusion, you still believe it's real when you see the movie. Then we took the tram tour around the premises and saw several actors working, some which I recognized. I felt like jumping off the tram and shouting, "Would everyone is famous please give me your autograph?" In the evening we went to a party at the home of one of Diana's friends, many of them are connected with the movie business. I had a really interesting conversation with a fellow works in the industry who claims that a lot of movies making these days are modeled conceptually after amusement park rides. Just like the rides, the movies start slowly and easily, then they have a lot of twists and turns are calculated to scare you to death, and they end happily. Maybe *Pirates of the Caribbean* is an example. Pretty fascinating, huh? What next?

Sorry to spend so much time talking about movies, but you know what an addict I am. Anyway, I'll let you know my arrival time, that I'm not sure of yet, so that you can pick me up at the airport.

Love you lots,

Amanda

Communication Practice

7 | LISTENING

🎧 *Listen to the TV film reviewer give her weekly review. Then listen again to certain of the reviewer's sentences. Write **T** (true) or **F** (false) to indicate if each item correctly restates the sentence that you hear.*

___T___ 1. The film festival can be seen this holiday weekend.

_____ 2. None of these great movies has been shown in more than a decade.

_____ 3. *A Beautiful Mind* is about a character created by director Ron Howard.

_____ 4. Jennifer Connelly won an Oscar for her portrayal of Nash's wife.

_____ 5. *Saving Private Ryan* is about an army captain who is rescued by a soldier in World War II.

_____ 6. *Saving Private Ryan* makes the reviewer cry.

_____ 7. *Chicago* has only one main star.

_____ 8. Michael J. Fox was responsible for launching *Back to the Future.*

_____ 9. All who regard themselves as serious movie buffs must see *Casablanca.*

_____ 10. The reviewer says black-and-white movies are not pretty.

8 | INFORMATION GAP: A MOVIE REVIEW

Work with a partner. Each of you will read a version of a review of the film A Beautiful Mind. *Each version is missing some information. Take turns asking your partner questions to get the missing information.*

Student A, read the review of A Beautiful Mind. *Ask questions and fill in the missing information. Then answer Student B's questions.*

Student B, turn to the Information Gap on page 209 and follow the instructions there.

Example: **A:** What is the movie inspired by?
B: It is inspired by incidents in the life of John Nash. What was Nash's occupation?
A: Nash was . . .

(continued)

A Beautiful Mind

(2002) C-135 m.

Rating: ***   **Director:** Ron Howard

Starring: Russell Crowe, Jennifer Connelly, Ed Harris, Paul Bettany, Christopher Plummer, Adam Goldberg, Judd Hirsch, Josh Lucas, Anthony Rapp, Austin Pendleton

An unusual story inspired by _____ in the life of John Nash, a brilliant West Virginia mathematician who flowers at Princeton in the late 1940s and goes to work at _____. But his marriage and sanity are put to a painful test. _____ is amazing—and completely unexpected. Crowe is excellent as usual, and the film offers an overdue showcase for _____, as the student who becomes his wife. Oscar winner for Best Picture, Director, Supporting Actress (Connelly), and Adapted Screenplay (Akiva Goldsman). PG-13.

9 | GROUP DISCUSSION: MOVIE RATINGS

*Look at the chart describing the current movie rating system. Then complete the following questionnaire for yourself; circle **yes** or **no**. Discuss your answers with a partner. Then discuss your answers with the class as a whole.*

> **Example:** **A:** I think many movies are too violent today.
> **B:** I disagree. Sometimes violence is necessary for the director to make the point.

Movie Ratings	Description
G	Suitable for general audiences, all ages.
PG	Parental guidance is suggested; some material may not be appropriate for children.
PG-13	Parents strongly cautioned; some material may not be appropriate for children under 13.
R	Restricted; anyone under 17 must be accompanied by a parent or adult guardian.
NC-17	No one under 17 is admitted.

Movies and Rating Systems		
Movie rating systems are a good idea.	yes	no
Rating systems are enforced in my area.	yes	no
If I want to see a movie, I don't pay attention to the rating.	yes	no
Many movies today are too violent.	yes	no
Movie rating systems should be made stronger.	yes	no

10 | PICTURE DISCUSSION

A *Discuss the picture with a partner, using adjective clauses or phrases whenever possible.*

> **Example:** **A:** In the theater there are a lot of people trying to concentrate on the movie.
> **B:** One woman is talking on her cell phone, annoying the people near her.

B *What is proper behavior at movie theaters? Discuss these points with the class as a whole.*

- Should cell phones be allowed in movie theaters?

- Should moviegoers have to pick up their own trash?

- Should small children be allowed at movies?

- Should people be allowed to talk during showings of movies?

> **Example:** **A:** I don't think cell phones should be allowed in movie theaters.
> **B:** Why not?
> **A:** It's inconsiderate to other people because . . .

11 | WRITING

Write your own movie review in three or more paragraphs. Choose a film that you liked or disliked, but try to be objective in your review. Read your review to the class, and answer any questions your classmates might ask about the movie. Use adjective clauses and phrases as appropriate.

Example: One of the best movies I've seen recently is *Super Size Me*, directed by Morgan Spurlock. Spurlock, fascinated by the recent court case in which two American women sued McDonald's for serving food that was less than healthy, decided to find out whether or not fast food is really unhealthy. His plan was simple: eat nothing but McDonald's food for a month. The film is about his month-long adventure. It's humorous and interesting, and . . .

12 | ON THE INTERNET

Use the Internet to find out the answers to these questions. Report your findings to the class.

- Who has won the most Academy Awards for best actor?
- Who has won the most Academy Awards for best actress?
- What is the all-time top moneymaking film?
- What are the three most expensive movies ever made?
- What male director has made the most films?
- What female director has made the most films?

INFORMATION GAP FOR STUDENT B

Student B, read the review of A Beautiful Mind. *Answer Student A's questions. Then ask your own questions and fill in the missing information.*

Example: **A:** What is the movie inspired by?
           B: It is inspired by incidents in the life of John Nash. What was Nash's occupation?
           A: Nash was . . .

A Beautiful Mind
(2002) C-135 m.

Rating: ***   **Director:** Ron Howard
Starring: Russell Crowe, Jennifer Connelly, Ed Harris, Paul Bettany, Christopher Plummer, Adam Goldberg, Judd Hirsch, Josh Lucas, Anthony Rapp, Austin Pendleton

An unusual story inspired by incidents in the life of John Nash, a brilliant West Virginia _____ who flowers at Princeton in the late 1940s and goes to work at M. I. T. But his _____ are put to a painful test. The central story twist is amazing—and completely unexpected. _____ is excellent as usual, and the film offers an overdue showcase for Connelly, as the student who becomes _____. Oscar winner for Best Picture, Director, Supporting Actress (Connelly), and Adapted Screenplay (Akiva Goldsman). PG-13.

IV From **Grammar** to **Writing**
Punctuation of Adjective Clauses and Phrases

Remember that the two types of adjective clauses are **identifying** and **nonidentifying**. Identifying adjective clauses give information essential for distinguishing one person or thing from another. Nonidentifying clauses give additional (= nonessential) information that doesn't identify.

> **Example:** I saw three movies last week. The movie **that I liked best** was *Vanity Fair*.

The adjective clause *that I liked best* is identifying because it says which movie I am talking about. If the clause were removed, the sentence would not make complete sense:

> The movie was *Vanity Fair*.

Therefore, the clause is essential for the sentence's meaning.

> *Casablanca*, **which contains the famous song "As Time Goes By,"** is considered a film classic.

The nonidentifying clause *which contains the famous song "As Time Goes By"* adds information about *Casablanca*; however, it is not used to identify. If it were removed, the sentence would still make sense:

> *Casablanca* is considered a film classic.

In speech, identifying clauses have no pauses before or after them and are not enclosed in commas when written. Nonidentifying clauses, on the other hand, do have pauses before and after them when spoken and are enclosed in commas when written.

> **Examples:** A person who needs others to become energized is an extrovert. (identifying; no commas)
>
> James, who comes alive in the presence of friends, is an extrovert. (nonidentifying; commas)

1 | *Punctuate the following sentences containing adjective clauses. They form a narration.*

1. Tom and Sandra, who have been married for more than 30 years, are both outgoing people.^

2. Tom who is clearly an extrovert loves meeting new people.

3. Sandra who is very quick to make friends loves to have friends over for dinner.

4. Tom and Sandra have two married sons both of whom live abroad.

5. The son who is older lives with his family in Britain.

6. The son who is younger lives with his family in southern Italy.

7. Tom and Sandra own a house in the city and one in the country. The one where they spend most of their time is in the city.

8. The house that they spend summers in is located in New Hampshire.

One way to decide whether a clause is identifying or nonidentifying is to ask whether (1) it refers to a unique person or thing or (2) it refers to all the members of a group. If it is either type, it is a nonidentifying clause and needs commas.

My eldest brother, **whose name is Jim,** is a businessman. (refers to my eldest brother, a unique individual; needs commas)

Bats, **which are actually mammals,** are active mostly at night. (refers to all the members of the group—all bats; needs commas)

In contrast, a clause that refers to one or more but not all the members of a group is identifying.

The bats **that live in Carlsbad Caverns** are seen nightly by visiting tourists. (refers to some of the members of the group—a particular group of bats; identifying)

2 | *Punctuate the following pairs of sentences containing adjective clauses. One sentence in each pair is identifying, and one is nonidentifying.*

1. **a.** College students who live close to campuses spend less money on gas.
   b. College students who are expected to study hard have to become responsible for themselves.

2. **a.** People who are the only animals with a capacity for creative language have highly developed brains.
   b. People who live in glass houses shouldn't throw stones.

3. **a.** The car which was invented in the late 19th century has revolutionized modern life.
   b. The car which I would really like to buy is the one in the far corner of the lot.

4. **a.** Science fiction movies which have become extremely popular in the last two decades often earn hundreds of millions of dollars for their studios.
   b. The science fiction movies which have earned the most money collectively are the *Star Wars* films.

5. **a.** The panda that was given to the National Zoo died recently.
   b. The panda which is native only to China is on the Endangered Species List.

Like adjective clauses, adjective phrases are also identifying or nonidentifying, depending on whether they add essential or extra information.

Examples: The postwar director **most responsible for putting Italian cinema on the map** is Federico Fellini. (identifying; no commas)

Federico Fellini, **the director of such classics as 8½,** died in 1993. (nonidentifying; commas)

3 | *Punctuate these sentences containing adjective phrases.*

1. A film produced by George Lucas is almost a guaranteed success.
2. A film directed by Steven Spielberg is likely to be a blockbuster.
3. *A Beautiful Mind* directed by Ron Howard won the Academy Award for best picture.
4. Many Canadians including Donald Sutherland and Michael J. Fox are major international film stars.
5. The Universal Studios facility located in California was established decades ago.
6. The Cineplex theater complex near our neighborhood has 12 separate theaters.

4 | *Complete the punctuation of this letter containing adjective phrases and clauses.*

September 30

Dear Mom and Dad,

Thanks again for bringing me down here to the university last weekend. Classes didn't start until Wednesday, so I had a few days to get adjusted. I'm signed up for five classes: zoology, calculus, English, and two history sections. It's a heavy load, but they're all courses that will count for my degree. The zoology class, which meets at 8:00 every morning is going to be my hardest subject. The history class that I have in the morning is on Western civilization; the one that I have in the afternoon is on early U.S. history. Calculus which I have at noon every day looks like it's going to be relatively easy. Besides zoology, the other class that's going to be hard is English which we have to write a composition a week for.

I like all of my roommates but one. There are four of us in our suite including two girls from Texas and a girl from Manitoba. Sally who is from San Antonio is great; I feel like I've known her all my life. I also really like Anne the girl from Manitoba. But Heather the other girl from Texas is kind of a pain. She's one of those types of people who never tell you what's bothering them and then get hostile. All in all, though, it looks like it's going to be a great year. I'll write again in a week or so.

Love,
Vicky

5 *Bring to class a detailed photograph from a magazine, a newspaper, or your own collection. In class, write a paragraph of eight to ten sentences describing the picture. Include a number of adjective clauses in your paragraph, making sure to use at least one identifying and one nonidentifying adjective clause. Exchange your paper with a partner. Read each other's paragraph and make suggestions or corrections if necessary. Check for correct punctuation.*

I *Read the composition and underline all of the adjective clauses. Write **I** (identifying) or **NI** (nonidentifying) above each clause.*

We've all heard it said that "Things may not be what they seem." Recently at work I had an experience <u>that proved to me the truth of that saying</u>. The experience involved two people I work with in my secretarial job. The first, whom I'll call "Jennifer," is one of those sunny types who always greet you in a friendly manner and never have an unkind word to say. The second, whom I'll call "Myrtle," is the type who rarely gives compliments and can sometimes be critical. Between the two of them, I thought Jennifer was the one who was my friend. Myrtle never seemed to care much for me, which is why I didn't seek out her friendship. I learned, though, that I had been reading them wrong.

About two months ago, some money was stolen from someone's purse in the office. It happened on an afternoon when all three of us, Jennifer, Myrtle, and I, were working together. Our boss, who tends to jump to conclusions, questioned the three of us and said that someone whose name he wouldn't reveal had implicated me in the theft. Jennifer, whom I expected to stand up for me, said she didn't know where I'd been at the time of the theft, which was a lie. Myrtle, however, spoke up and said she knew I couldn't have been the one who had stolen the money because she and I had been working together all afternoon. The boss accepted her statement, and that ended the unpleasantness and my friendship with Jennifer as well. I found out later that she wanted my job. I don't know whether or not she was the one who took the money, but I do know that the old proverb that tells us not to judge a book by its cover has some truth in it. Myrtle and I have been friends ever since.

II *Read the sentences, which form a narration. Circle the correct relative pronoun for each sentence.*

1. Jerry and Sue Carter, (that / who) got married about a year ago, recently bought a new house.

2. The neighborhood (where / which) they had been living is a somewhat dangerous one.

3. The neighborhood (that / whose) they are moving into is much safer.

4. Their new house, (that / which) they bought quite cheaply, does need some fixing up.

5. However, they will be receiving some help from their neighbors, most of (who / whom) they like.

6. The Ingrams, (who / whom) live next door to them, have volunteered to lend their tools.

7. The Thomases, (which / whose) house is across the street from Jerry and Sue's, have promised to help them put in a new lawn.

8. The Ingrams, (who / whose) daughter is the same age as Laura, Jerry and Sue's daughter, are helping Laura make new friends.

9. Sue, (that / who) works for a county hospital, will still have to commute to work.

10. Jerry, (whom / whose) company is nearby, will be able to walk to work.

III *Read the sentences, which form a narration. Put parentheses around each relative pronoun that can be omitted. Do not put relative pronouns in parentheses if they are subjects.*

1. On our trip to Europe last summer, we met a lot of people (whom) we liked.

2. One of the most interesting was Cosimo, a young Italian man who picked us up when we were hitchhiking outside Florence.

3. Cosimo, who was on his way home to Pisa, was driving so slowly that it was easy for him to stop.

4. The car that he was driving was a 1986 Volkswagen.

5. We were afraid that the car, which looked like a lemon, wouldn't make it to Pisa, but it did.

6. Cosimo took us to the house that he and his family lived in and invited us to stay for a few days.

7. The house, which was not far from downtown Pisa, was charming.

8. He also introduced us to a group of people that we felt very comfortable with.

9. We were scheduled to go to Switzerland next, so Cosimo gave us the address of a cousin of his who lived in Bern.

10. We had such a wonderful time in Italy and Switzerland that we decided to go back next year, which will cost money but will be worth it.

IV *Rewrite these sentences, reducing or changing the adjective clauses to adjective phrases.*

1. A movie that is directed by Peter Jackson is likely to be successful.

   A movie directed by Peter Jackson is likely to be successful.

2. A film that stars Jamie Foxx will probably be a blockbuster.

_____

3. *Seabiscuit*, which features Chris Cooper in a supporting role, is a heartwarming movie.

_____

4. *Cats*, which was written by Andrew Lloyd Webber and Tim Rice, was a long-running Broadway musical.

_____

5. Several James Cameron films, which include the *Terminator* movies and *Titanic*, have earned a great deal of money.

_____

V Write sentences containing an adjective clause describing the people or things indicated. Punctuate the clauses correctly, paying attention to whether the clauses are identifying or nonidentifying. Use **who**, **whom**, **whose**, **that**, or **which**.

1. The man *who is talking with the receptionist has brought his daughter to the dentist.*

2. The man _____

3. The girl _____

4. The boy _____

5. The poster _____

6. The poster _____

7. The woman _____

8. The woman _____

VI *Circle the letter of the one underlined word or phrase in each sentence that is not correct.*

1. George Lucas, <u>whose</u> work <u>including</u> *Star Wars*, *The Empire Strikes*
   A   B
   Back, and *Return of the Jedi* and <u>who</u> <u>has become</u> a world-famous
          C   D
   movie director and producer, has been directing more *Star Wars* films.

   A   Ⓑ   C   D

2. Previously married couple Kenneth Branagh and Emma Thompson,
   <u>both</u> <u>of which</u> are well known internationally, appeared together
   A   B
   while still married in films <u>directed</u> by Branagh, <u>including</u> *Henry V*
             C   D
   and *Peter's Friends*.

   A   B   C   D

3. Police <u>in Charleston</u> are investigating a crime <u>that</u> was <u>committing</u>
        A   B   C
   yesterday evening between 11:00 P.M. and midnight at the city art
   museum, <u>which</u> is located on Fifth Avenue.
          D

   A   B   C   D

4. Detective Amanda Reynolds, <u>who</u> is the chief investigating officer
                    A
   in the case, says <u>that</u> the police have no suspects yet but are focusing
             B
   on tips <u>suggest</u> <u>that</u> the theft may have been an inside job.
         C   D

   A   B   C   D

5. Al, <u>whom</u> is a freshman at the university, is pleased with his college
      A
   living situation because he likes <u>the people</u> <u>he</u> is rooming <u>with</u>.
                           B   C   D

   A   B   C   D

6. His courses, <u>none</u> of <u>which</u> are easy, are all classes <u>requiring</u> a
           A   B   C
   considerable amount of study, <u>that</u> is why he has joined a study group.
                         D

   A   B   C   D

7. Textrix, <u>the company</u> for <u>that</u> Alex works part-time, tends to employ
           A   B
   people <u>who are</u> highly motivated and <u>who have</u> at least 10 years
          C   D
   of experience in the field.

   A   B   C   D

8. Alicia, <u>an extrovert loves</u> working with people and <u>who can</u> also work
          A   B
   independently, accomplished a great deal in her last job, <u>which</u> is why
                                             C
   I think she's <u>the person we should hire</u>.
               D

   A   B   C   D

(continued)

9. The lines <u>to get into</u> the remake of *King Kong*, <u>a movie</u> <u>directed</u>
   A   B   C
   by Peter Jackson, may be long, <u>in that case</u> I would recommend
                                       D
   going to a matinee screening.

   A B C D

10. Jaime, <u>who</u> has been employed for ten years at a company <u>that</u>
    A   B
    stresses team-building and cooperative effort, is a person <u>who</u> has
                                                                C
    learned to value <u>the people with he works</u>.
                          D

    A B C D

VII *Go back to your answers to Exercise VI. Write the correct form for each item that you believe is incorrect.*

1. _____ *includes* _____   6. _____

2. _____   7. _____

3. _____   8. _____

4. _____   9. _____

5. _____   10. _____

▶ *To check your answers, go to the Answer Key on page RT-3.*

PART V

Passive Voice

Grammar in Context

BEFORE YOU READ

1 *Many people find unsolved mysteries fascinating. Do you enjoy hearing about them? If so, why? Do you know of any unsolved mysteries?*

2 *Some people think there is a need for mystery in life, for things to remain unexplained. Do you agree or disagree?*

3 *Why do people sometimes sympathize with criminals and want them to get away with their crimes?*

🎧 *Read this news article about an unsolved mystery.*

Did He Get Away With It? ✈

A lot of crimes never get solved. The case of Dan Cooper is one that hasn't been. It was an evening in late November in 1971. On a short flight between Portland and Seattle, the flight attendant was handed a note by a mysterious middle-aged man dressed in a dark suit. The flight attendant thought he was making a romantic advance, so she slipped the unread note into her pocket. The man leaned closer to her, saying, "Miss, you'd better look at that note. I have a bomb." He then opened his briefcase so that she could see several red cylinders and a lot of wires. The man, who used the alias "Dan Cooper," was demanding $200,000, four parachutes, and a plane that would fly him to Mexico.

The plane proceeded to Seattle with none of the other passengers even aware that it was being hijacked. The other passengers got off the plane, and "Cooper" got what he was demanding. He received the $200,000, all in $20 bills that had been photocopied by FBI agents so that they could easily be identified. Then the plane was refueled and took off for Mexico.

A few minutes later, Cooper ordered the flight attendant to go to the cockpit and stay there. As she was leaving, she noticed him trying to tie something around his waist—presumably the bag of money. Then he opened the plane's rear stairway and jumped out of the plane. The crew felt pressure bumps that were probably caused

Did He Get Away With It?

by Cooper's jumping off the stairway. When Cooper jumped, the air temperature was seven degrees below zero. He was wearing no survival gear and only light, casual shoes on his feet.

Cooper has not been seen or heard from since that night. Who was Cooper? Did he get away with his plan? Or was he killed trying to commit the perfect crime?

The authorities speculate that Cooper landed near Ariel, a small town near the Columbia River north of Portland. Only one real clue has been discovered. Eight and a half years later, an eight-year-old boy who was digging in a sandbank found $5,800 of Cooper's money. It was only a few inches below the surface of the earth, but it had decayed so much that only the picture and the serial numbers on the bills were visible.

Decaying rubber bands were found along with the money, indicating that the cash must have been deposited there before the bands fell apart. Since then, the area has been searched thoroughly, but no trace of Cooper has been found.

So what really happened? Many investigators believe that Cooper had to have been killed by the combination of the weather conditions and the impact of his fall. If this is true, though, why have none of the man's remains ever been discovered? Is more information known about this case than has been released? Is Cooper's body in some remote part of the wilderness area into which he jumped, or is he living a luxurious life under an alias somewhere and driving a Rolls-Royce? Did he have the $5,800 buried by an associate in order to throw the authorities off the track? Or did he bury it himself?

Cooper has become a legend. His story has been told in books and articles and even a movie. In Ariel, the small town near where he might have landed, patrons of a tavern still celebrate the anniversary of the hijacking every year. The bar's owner, Dona Elliot, says, "He did get away with it . . . so far." Others don't think so. Jerry Thomas, a retired soldier who has been working independently on the case, thinks that Cooper didn't survive the fall and that his body will eventually be found. "I know there is something out here," he says. "There has to be."

The mystery goes on.

AFTER YOU READ

What does each sentence mean? Circle the letter of the correct answer.

1. Cooper has not been seen or heard from since that night.
   a. No one has seen or heard from Cooper since then.
   b. Cooper has not seen or heard from anyone since then.

2. Or was he killed trying to commit the perfect crime?
   a. Did he die trying to commit the crime?
   b. Did he kill someone trying to commit the crime?

3. Did he have the $5,800 buried by an associate in order to throw the authorities off the track?
   a. Did Cooper bury it himself?
   b. Did Cooper arrange for another person to bury it?

Grammar Presentation

THE PASSIVE: REVIEW AND EXPANSION

Active Sentences				Passive Sentences		
Subject	**Verb**	**Object**		**Subject**	***Be* + Past Participle**	**(*By* + Agent)**
Cooper	**hijacked**	the plane.		The plane	**was hijacked**	**by** Cooper.
Someone	**found**	the bills.		The bills	**were found**.	

Passive Verb Forms				
		Be (not)	**Past Participle**	
SIMPLE PRESENT		**is (not)**		
PRESENT PROGRESSIVE		**is (not) being**		
SIMPLE PAST		**was (not)**		
PAST PROGRESSIVE		**was (not) being**		
FUTURE	The crime	**will (not) be** **is (not) going to be**	**investigated**	(by the new team).
PRESENT PERFECT		**has (not) been**		
PAST PERFECT		**had (not) been**		
FUTURE PERFECT		**will (not) have been**		

The Passive with Modals				
	Modals	*Be / have been*	**Past Participle**	
The case	**can (not)** **may (not)** **might (not)** **should (not)** **ought (not) to** **must (not)** **had better (not)**	**be**	**reopened**	in the future.
The case	**could (not)** **might (not)** **must (not)** **should (not)** **ought (not) to**	**have been**	**reopened**	years ago.

The Passive Causative				
Subject	*Have / Get*	**Object**	**Past Participle**	(*By* + Agent)
We	**had**	the evidence	**checked**	by experts.
She	**has had**	the note	**analyzed.**	
They	**got**	the report	**printed**	by professionals.
He	**is going to get**	a copy	**made.**	

GRAMMAR NOTES

1. A sentence in the **passive voice** has a corresponding sentence in the **active voice**. The object in the active sentence becomes the subject in the passive sentence. We can say that the subject of a passive sentence is acted upon.

The subject of the active sentence becomes the agent (preceded by the preposition **by**) in the passive sentence, or disappears.

▶ **BE CAREFUL!** Only transitive verbs, those that can be followed by an object, can be made passive. Intransitive verbs (those that cannot be followed by an object) cannot be made passive.

EXAMPLES

- The police never **catch**

object

some criminals.

subject
- **Some criminals are** never **caught**.

subject
- **Someone took** the money.
- The money **was taken**

agent

(by someone).

- No one **has seen** Cooper since 1971.
- Cooper **has not been seen** since 1971.
- Several people **died** in the accident.

NOT Several people ~~were~~ died in the accident.

(continued)

2. Passive sentences are formed with *be* + past participle. They occur in present, past, and future forms.

- Police officers **are** well **trained**.
- The suspect **was arrested** yesterday.
- He **will be held** in the local jail.
- Cooper **has not been caught**.

To make a negative passive sentence, place *not* after the first verb.

Use the present progressive and past progressive passives to describe actions in progress (= not finished) at a certain time.

- The suspect **is being held** in prison.
- The robbery occurred while the money **was being taken** to a bank.

3. Use the passive voice:

a. when we don't know who performed the action or when it is not important to say who performed it

- The money **was stolen**.
- The plane **was refueled**.

b. when we want to avoid mentioning the agent

- A criminal **is** sometimes **regarded** as a hero.
  (We don't want to say who regards him as a hero.)

       receiver   result   agent

c. when we want to focus on the receiver or the result of an action instead of the agent

- The thief **was caught** by the detective.

4. Use the passive with a *by* phrase:

a. to introduce new information about the agent

- The money was stolen **by a person who has a criminal record**.

b. to credit someone who did something

- The bills were photocopied **by FBI agents**.

c. when the agent is surprising

- The money was found **by a little boy**.

You can omit the *by* phrase in passive sentences if you feel it is unnecessary or undesirable to mention the agent.

- Why **hasn't** this crime **been solved**?

5. Most commonly, the direct object of an active sentence is the subject of the corresponding passive sentence.

direct object
- The police **arrested** the suspect.

subject
- The suspect **was arrested** by the police.

However, an indirect object is sometimes the subject of a passive sentence.

indirect object
- The F.B.I. **gave** Cooper the money.

subject
- Cooper **was given** the money by the F.B.I.

6. We often use **modals** and modal-like auxiliaries in the passive. To form the present passive with a modal, use the modal + *be* + past participle. To form the past passive with a modal, use the modal + *have been* + past participle.

- The criminal **should be arrested**.
- He **could have been arrested** before this.

Use *have (got) to*, *had better*, *had to*, *must*, *ought to*, and *should* in passive sentences to express advisability, obligation, and necessity.

- The charges **had to be dropped**.
- Criminal suspects **must be charged**.

Use *can* and *could* to express present and past ability.

- Suspects **can't be kept** in jail.
- The thief **could have been caught**.

Use *will* and *be going to* to talk about future events.

- This prisoner **will be tried**.
- The suspects **are going to be released**.

Use *can't*, *could*, *may*, and *might* to talk about future possibility and impossibility.

- The mystery **may** never **be solved**.
- He **can't be released** from jail.

7. The **passive** can also be formed **with *get***. The passive with *get* is more informal than the passive with *be*. It is conversational and characteristic of informal writing.

- Will that criminal ever **get caught**?
- Our team **got beaten** in the soccer game.

▶ **BE CAREFUL!** Although the *be* passive is used both with action and non-action verbs, the *get* passive is used only with action verbs.

- More research **is needed** about the causes of crime.

NOT More research ~~gets needed~~ about the causes of crime.

(continued)

8. *Have* or *get* + object + past participle are used to form the **passive causative**. There is usually little difference in meaning between the causative with *have* and with *get*.

- You should **have** your car **serviced**.
- I just **got** my best suit **dry-cleaned**.

The passive causative is used in the past, present, and future and with modals.

- We **had** the windows **washed**.
- I **get** my car **tuned up** twice a year.
- She**'s going to get** her hair **cut**.

---

9. Use the **passive causative** to talk about services or activities that people arrange for someone else to do.

- The detective **had** the evidence **analyzed**.
- Sometimes criminals **get** their hair **dyed** or **shaved**.

The passive causative can occur with a *by* phrase, but this phrase is often omitted. Use the *by* phrase only when it is necessary to mention the agent.

- I **got** my photos **developed** at the drugstore.
- We **had** our house **inspected by Jim.**

▶ **BE CAREFUL!** Don't confuse the simple past causative with the past perfect.

- They **had** the grass **cut**. *(simple past causative—someone else cut the grass)*
- They **had cut** the grass. *(past perfect—they had done this before a specific time in the past)*

▶ **BE CAREFUL!** Don't confuse the passive causative with the expression *to get something done* meaning *to finish something*.

- I **got** the work **done** by a mechanic. *(passive causative)*
- I **got** the work **done** by noon. *(I finished the work by 12 P.M.)*

Reference Note
For use of **modals,** see Units 5 and 6.

Focused Practice

1 | DISCOVER THE GRAMMAR

A *Look again at the last half of the opening reading, starting with paragraph 5. Find and underline 12 passive constructions.*

B *Now look at Grammar Note 3 on page 224. Write **a**, **b**, or **c** above each passive construction you underlined to show why the passive is used.*

2 | THE SCENE OF THE CRIME
Grammar Notes 1–2

*Examine the verbs in these sentences. Write **T** (transitive) or **I** (intransitive). Then complete the sentences with active and passive verb forms, as appropriate.*

___I___ 1. Criminals often _____*return*_____ to the scene of a crime. (return)

_____ 2. If they are not careful, they _____ (catch) by the authorities.

_____ 3. Smart criminals _____ (disappear) entirely from the scene.

_____ 4. They never _____ (go) back to the locale.

_____ 5. Usually a smart criminal _____ (help) by one or more accomplices.

_____ 6. The accomplices _____ (reward) by the intelligent criminal.

_____ 7. Most criminals, however, aren't smart. They _____ (not realize) how resourceful the police are.

_____ 8. Crime scenes _____ (watch) very closely by the police, but most criminals don't believe this.

3 | A TV NEWS BULLETIN
Grammar Note 2

Complete the TV news bulletin with present progressive and past progressive passives.

Here is breaking news from KKBO News Channel 6. Two suspects _____*are being held*_____
1. (hold)
in the county jail, where they _____ about their role in a bank robbery
2. (question)
that took place this morning at the downtown branch of First International Bank. As the bank's

vault _____, the suspects, wearing masks and carrying guns, burst in and
3. (open)
demanded that an undisclosed amount of money be placed in a paper bag. They escaped with the

funds but were later caught after a customer who _____ noticed the
4. (help)
license plate number of the vehicle the suspects were driving and notified bank authorities. The

identities of the two suspects _____ until the initial investigation is
5. (withhold)
completed. Other bank customers _____ for additional information. This
6. (currently / interview)
is Ron Mason for KKBO News Channel 6. Stay tuned for further updates.

4 | TWO FAMOUS MYSTERIES

Grammar Notes 2, 6

Fill in the blanks in this article with passive constructions with **be** *and the correct forms of the verbs in parentheses.*

Two Unsolved Mysteries Continue to Fascinate

So you think there are no more mysteries, that all mysteries _____*are solved*_____ in

1. (solve)

time? Think again. The pages of history are full of mysteries that _____.

2. (not crack)

Consider, for example, the case of the ship *Mary Celeste*. The ship had left New York for Italy in

1872. Later it _____ floating east of the Azores. No one

3. (sight)

_____ on board, though everything else on the ship

4. (find)

_____ to be in order, and there was no indication why the *Mary Celeste*

5. (determine)

_____. Apparently, in fact, tables _____ for

6. (abandon)   **7. (set)**

afternoon tea. One theory speculates that the ship _____ by an explosion

8. (might / threaten)

that _____ by fumes from its cargo of alcohol. That theory, however,

9. (cause)

_____.

10. (not prove)

   A second perplexing mystery is that of Amelia Earhart, the famous aviator who in the 1920s

and 1930s _____ the best example of a strong woman. Earhart flew

11. (consider)

across the Atlantic with two men in 1928 and set a record for a cross-Atlantic flight in 1932. In

1937 she embarked on her most ambitious plan, a flight around the world. Earhart began her

flight in Miami in June and _____ only by Fred Noonan, her navigator.

12. (accompany)

They reached New Guinea and left for Howland Island in the South Pacific on July 1. After that,

no radio reports or messages of any kind _____. No remains of her plane

13. (receive)

_____ by naval investigators in the years since then. Did she simply

14. (discover)

attempt the impossible? _____ when her plane ran out of fuel and

15. (Could / she and Noonan / kill)

crashed? Or could something else have happened? No one really knows.

   For the time being, at least, the riddle of the *Mary Celeste* and the fate of Amelia Earhart will

have to remain mysterious. Maybe they _____ at all.

16. (should / not solve)

5 | THE WORK OF A DETECTIVE

A *Read the sentences. Then circle the letter of the choice that explains the meaning of each sentence.*

Last week Detective Harry Sadler had an extremely busy schedule.

1. On Monday morning, he had a tooth pulled before going to work.

   a. He pulled the tooth himself.   **b.** He arranged for someone to pull the tooth.

2. When he got to work, he had some crime notes typed up.

   a. He typed them himself.   **b.** Someone else typed them.

3. In the afternoon, he had to review the report of another officer. He had finished it by 6:00 P.M.

   a. He finished it himself.   **b.** Someone else finished it.

4. On Tuesday and Wednesday, he had to write his own report on a case he had been working on. He got it done by the end of the day.

   a. He did it himself.   **b.** Someone else did it.

5. On Thursday, Harry got some crime pictures microfilmed.

   a. He microfilmed them himself.   **b.** Someone else microfilmed them.

6. On Friday, he worked until 5:30 P.M. and then went to an appointment. He'd had his income taxes done and needed to go over them.

   a. He did the taxes himself.   **b.** Someone else did the taxes.

B *Complete the paragraph using the passive causative or active past perfect forms of the verbs in parentheses.*

Yesterday was a typically unpredictable day in the life of detective Harry Sadler. Since Harry

hadn't been able to eat at home, he _____ *got some breakfast brought* _____ up to his

               1. (get / some breakfast / bring)

office from the cafeteria as soon as he arrived at work. After breakfast he e-mailed some digital

photos of a crime scene to the lab to _____. He spent

               2. (have / them / enlarge)

a couple of hours going over files and then left the office for the garage where he was

_____. Harry's mechanic said that he should also

     3. (get / his car / tune up)

_____. Harry agreed and arranged to pick the car up

     4. (have / the windshield / replace)

at the end of the day. At lunchtime he met with the members of his investigative team. Time was

short, so they _____ from a nearby restaurant. They

     5. (get / lunch / deliver)

studied the evidence they had _____ by the police

     6. (get / analyze)

crime lab. They _____ by 2:00. After the meeting

     7. (have / complete / the work)

(continued)

Harry spent a couple of hours writing a report by hand. He _____

8. (have / finish / the report)

by 4:00, so he then _____ by his secretary. At 5:30 he

9. (have / it / type)

left the office, picked up his car, and then met his wife for dinner and a movie. They were

_____ and couldn't do any cooking. At 11:00 P.M.

10. (have / their kitchen / remodel)

they arrived home. It's a good thing Harry loves his work because it was another long, tiring, but

interesting day.

6 | AN ACCIDENT
Grammar Notes 1–4

*Complete the script for a radio bulletin about a hit-and-run accident using active or passive forms as appropriate. Use **by** phrases only if necessary. Change nouns to pronouns to avoid unnecessary repetition.*

1. a hit-and-run accident / occur / this evening at 8:45 P.M.

   A hit-and-run accident occurred this evening at 8:45 P.M.

2. an eight-year-old boy / crossing / the intersection of 4th and Madison

   _____

3. a blue late-model Toyota Corolla / hit / the boy

   _____

4. the Toyota / disappear / from the scene / immediately

   _____

5. the boy / sustain / massive injuries

   _____

6. paramedics / take / the boy / to / Downtown Medical Center

   _____

7. at present / medical personnel / caring for / the boy / in the Intensive Care Unit

   _____

8. they / describe / his condition / as critical

   _____

9. the authorities / ask / anyone with information / to call 444-6968

   _____

10. they / offering / a reward

    _____

7 | EDITING

Read this student essay about the crop circles in Britain and elsewhere. There are 15 mistakes in the use of the passive. The first one is already corrected. Find and correct 14 more.

The Crop Circles

believe
In our day we are believed in science and have the feeling that every question can be explain and every problem can be solved. But some of us want the opposite. We don't want everything to be explained. We like puzzles. We feel that mystery is needing in our lives.

The mysterious crop circles that have been appeared around the world in the last 25 years or so are an example of this. These formations have reported in more than 20 countries, including the United States, Canada, and Australia. But most of them have been finding in grain fields in southern England. These circles, which are large and flat, are caused by a force that flattens the grain but does not destroy it. They are still been made.

How have these circles produced? By whom have they been made? Since the first discovery of the circles, many explanations have been proposed. According to some people, the circles has been made by spirit creatures like fairies. Others say they have been causing by "Star Wars" experiments or are messages that been left by extraterrestrials visiting our planet. Two British painters, David Chorley and Douglas Bower, say they were made the crop circles over a period of years as a joke. If this is true, however, how can we explain the crop circles in Australia and Canada and other places? They couldn't all have being made by Chorley and Bower, could they?

In 2002, director M. Night Shyamalan released his movie *Signs*, which is about the crop circle question. The movie shows clearly that the crop circles made by invading aliens from beyond our solar system. This is one interesting and enjoyable theory. More explanations like it get needed. What's fun is speculation. The mystery doesn't need to be solved.

Communication Practice

8 | LISTENING

⌒ *Some animals have been stolen from the city zoo. Listen to the conversation between police detective Harry Sadler and zoo administrator Lane Akimura. Then listen again. Circle the letter of the sentence in each pair that gives correct information about what happened.*

1. **a.** The janitor found the keeper.
   b. The keeper found the janitor.

2. **a.** Akimura examined the keeper.
   b. A physician examined the keeper.

3. **a.** The keeper had apparently been drugged.
   b. The keeper had apparently taken drugs.

4. **a.** It takes two weeks to see turtles.
   b. Two sea turtles were taken two weeks ago.

5. **a.** The police were notified quickly about the first robbery.
   b. The police were not notified quickly about the first robbery.

6. **a.** The zoo expansion has been completed.
   b. The zoo expansion has not been completed.

7. **a.** Voters have not yet approved the zoo expansion.
   b. Voters have already approved the zoo expansion.

8. **a.** First the animals eat. Then the food preparation area is cleaned.
   b. First the food preparation area is cleaned. Then the animals eat.

9. **a.** Detective Sadler will check the janitor's references himself.
   b. Detective Sadler will arrange for someone to check the janitor's references.

9 | INFORMATION GAP: A MYSTERY OBJECT

Work in pairs (A and B). Student A, read clues 1–4 to Student B. Student B will complete the clues. Switch roles after item 4. Then put the clues in the correct order and decide what the mystery object is.

Student B, turn to page 234 and follow the instructions there.

Student A's Clues

1. I was born, or maybe I should say I was created . . .

2. An all-night card game . . .

3. I was created by . . .

4. The "hero" type of me gets its name . . .

Student A's Completions

5. . . . have been known by my name since then.

6. . . . some slices of meat between two slices of bread.

7. . . . is shaped like a submarine.

8. . . . so he ordered a snack to be delivered to the gaming table.

9. . . . that I'm being eaten somewhere in the world this very minute.

10 | PICTURE DISCUSSION

These are photos of a UFO and of one of the aliens supposedly taken from a UFO crash near Roswell, New Mexico, in 1947. In small groups, discuss the pictures. What do you think they represent? Do you think there really was a UFO crash in 1947? Was the incident covered up by the government, as some people say? How can UFOs be explained?

Example: A: Do you think the Roswell alien story was covered up by the government?
B: No, I don't.
A: How else can it be explained?
B: I think . . .

11 | WRITING

Write three or four paragraphs describing an unsolved mystery in the area where you live or another mystery that you know about. It could involve a crime, someone's disappearance, or some strange natural phenomenon. Describe what the mystery is and how it might have been caused. Offer some possible solutions to the mystery.

Example: We've all heard about the Bermuda Triangle, an area in the Caribbean Sea where planes and ships supposedly get captured by unknown forces. One of the most famous mysteries of the Bermuda Triangle is the case of Flight 19, a U.S. military expedition that took off on December 5, 1945, to do navigational research. There were five planes, and all of them were piloted by skilled fliers . . .

12 | ON THE INTERNET

Use the Internet to do research about a mystery you would like to know about. Choose from these topics or create your own topic. Share your findings with the class.

- disappearances in the Bermuda Triangle
- the death of Billy the Kid
- the Tunguska Event
- the existence of the city of Troy

INFORMATION GAP FOR STUDENT B

Choose one of phrases 1–4 to complete each clue that Student A reads. Switch roles after item 4. Then put the clues in the correct order and decide what the mystery object is.

Student B's Completions

1. . . . because of the hero-sized appetite that's needed to eat one.

2. . . . at 5:00 in the morning on August 6, 1762.

3. . . . was being played at a gaming table.

4. . . . an Englishman named John Montagu, the fourth earl of the place I was named after.

Student B's Clues

5. The snack ordered by my creator was composed of . . .

6. It's almost certain . . .

7. My creator was hungry but too busy to leave the game, . . .

8. Two slices of bread with a filling between them . . .

9. And the "submarine" type of me . . .

The Passive to Describe Situations and to Report Opinions

Grammar in Context

BEFORE YOU READ

1 *Think of an aspect of your culture that might be hard for people of other cultures to understand. How would you explain it? Discuss this with a partner.*

2 *Look at the picture. What are the sacred creatures?*

⌒ *Read this article about an unusual group of people and their favorite animals.*

SACRED BEASTS

For decades anthropologists have been studying strange and unusual peoples all over the world. One of the strangest peoples of all is a group called the Asu, a prominent tribe living in North America.

The territory of the Asu is located roughly between that of the Tarahumara of Mexico and that of the Ojibwa of Canada. On the southeast, their territory is bordered by the Caribbean. Relatively little is known of the origin of this people, though they are said to be from somewhere in the East. Actually, the Asu may be related to certain European peoples.

Anthropologists have noted a number of similarities in cultural practices between the

(continued)

Sacred Creatures

Sacred Creatures

SACRED BEASTS

Asu and other ethnic groups. One particularly striking similarity is the Asu's fondness for its sacred animal. Just as in India the cow is regarded as a sacred animal and is treated with great respect, in Asu culture the rac is considered sacred. The Asu expend great effort and expense in maintaining their racs, which they love greatly.

What exactly is this unusual creature? The rac is very common in Asu society and is possessed by the vast majority of Asu families. In fact, it is felt that the more racs a family has, the higher its social status is. Those not possessing at least one rac are considered to be of low social status. Some wealthy Asu people even possess small herds of these creatures.

Though almost every Asu family owns at least one rac, these beasts have some rather serious drawbacks, most notably their relatively poor health. With a life span averaging only five to seven years, racs need frequent visits to special doctors, of which there are a great many in Asu culture. The most common ailment of the rac involves the tendency for its shoes to deteriorate rapidly—far more quickly than, for example, the shoes of horses. Rac doctors must be given rather valuable charms in return for providing new foot apparel. Another drawback of the rac is the uselessness of its excrement for fertilizer or for fuel. While in many cultures the excrement of animals is regarded as a valuable commodity, rac excrement is considered foul smelling and is thought to be quite dangerous to the environment.

A further problem associated with this animal is overpopulation. Racs are ridden a great deal and are often used as beasts of burden. With more and more racs every year, however, the pathways on which they move are increasingly subject to deterioration. In fact, racs multiply so often that there is an ongoing need for Asu citizens to construct more and more rac pathways, at ever-increasing expense. In some large Asu cities citizens are surrounded by their racs to such an extent that they can hardly move. Some Asu citizens even like to race their racs, so it is necessary to construct perfectly formed pathways that prevent individual racs from harming each other. In addition, merchants that provide rac food are sometimes alleged to be profiting excessively at the expense of Asu society.

Clearly, the Asu are a curious tribe. Much more research is needed in order to understand this strange people and their particular fondness for the rac. It is especially hoped that anthropologists and other specialists will focus their research on discovering ways of stopping the rac population explosion.

AFTER YOU READ

What does each sentence mean? Circle the letter of the correct answer.

1. Relatively little is known of the origin of this people, though they are said to be from somewhere in the East.

   a. This is true.

   b. People say this is true.

2. In fact, it is felt that the more racs a family has, the higher its social status is.

    a. The Asu believe this idea is accurate.

    b. The Asu feel good about this idea.

3. Merchants that provide rac food are sometimes alleged to be profiting excessively at the expense of Asu society.

    a. These merchants profit excessively.

    b. Some Asu people think these merchants profit excessively.

Grammar Presentation

THE PASSIVE TO DESCRIBE SITUATIONS AND TO REPORT OPINIONS

DESCRIBING SITUATIONS OR STATES (STATIVE PASSIVE)

Active Sentences	Passive Sentences			
	Subject	***Be* + Past Participle**	**Prepositional Phrase**	**(*By* + Agent)**
Ø*	The people	**are related**	(**to** each other).	Ø*
	The country	**is composed**	**of** two regions.	
	The island	**is connected**	**to** the mainland.	
	The capital	**was located**	**in** the south.	

*Ø = These forms do not occur.

REPORTING OPINIONS OR IDEAS

Active Sentences		
Subject	**Verb**	***That* Clause**
Some anthropologists	**say** **think** **believe** **allege**	**(that)** the people came from the East.

Passive Sentences with *It* + *That* Clause			
It	***Be* + Past Participle**	**(*By* + Agent)**	***That* Clause**
It	**is said** **is thought** **is believed** **is alleged**	(by some anthropologists)	**(that)** the people came from the East.

(continued)

Passive Sentences with *To* Phrase			
Subject	*Be* + Past Participle	(*By* + Agent)	*To* Phrase
The people	**are said** **are thought** **are believed** **are alleged**	(by some anthropologists)	**to** have come from the East.

GRAMMAR NOTES

EXAMPLES

1. Remember that the passive is used to describe situations in which the subject is acted upon. The passive is also used to describe situations or states. This use is called the **stative passive**.

   In addition, the passive is used to report opinions, ideas, and beliefs.

   - These peoples **are related** to each other.
   - St. Louis **is located** on the Missouri River.
   - Steven Spielberg **is considered** an excellent director.
   - Bigfoot **is thought** to live in the Pacific Northwest.

2. The **stative passive** is formed with *be* + past participle. Stative passive sentences do not normally have a corresponding active sentence, and they do not contain a *by* phrase.

   - Our two families **are related**.

     NOT ~~Genealogists relate~~ our two families.

     NOT Our two families are related ~~by genealogists~~.

3. We use the **stative passive** to describe situations or states. In stative passive sentences there is normally no action taking place.

   In stative passive constructions, the past participle functions as an adjective. It is often followed by a prepositional phrase.

   Stative passive sentences are often used in everyday English. Examples of stative passives: *be bordered by, be composed of, be connected to / with / by, be divided into / by, be found in, be located in / on, be made up of, be related to, be surrounded by.*

   - The United States **is composed** of 50 states.
   - Cuba **is located** in the Caribbean.
   - Curitiba **is found** in southern Brazil.
   - A peninsula **is surrounded** by water on three sides.

4. Passives used to report ideas, beliefs, and opinions often occur in the form *it* + *be* + past participle + *that* clause. Common examples of verbs used to form this type of passive: *allege, assume, believe, claim, say,* and *think.*

- **It is assumed that** this culture is very old.
- **It is said that** present-day Basques are descendants of Atlanteans.

Passive sentences of this type have corresponding active sentences.

- Scholars **assume that** this culture is very old.

▶ **BE CAREFUL!** We use this structure only with verbs that can be followed by a *that* clause. *That* is optional and is frequently omitted in informal English.

- It **is said** (**that**) these people came from Asia.

  NOT ~~It is regarded (that) these people came from Asia.~~

These passive structures may take an optional *by* phrase.

- It **is claimed** (**by some scholars**) **that** Shakespeare didn't write all his plays.

---

5. Passives that report ideas, beliefs, and opinions also commonly occur in the form subject + *be* + past participle + *to* phrase. This type of sentence can be converted from an equivalent active sentence with a *that* clause. A *by* phrase is optional.

- **The culture is thought** (by scholars) **to date** from 5000 B.C.
- Scholars **think that the culture dates** from 5000 B.C.

The verb in the *to* phrase can be present or past.

- He is said **to be** the author.
- The Japanese are thought **to have visited** the New World before Columbus.

NOTE: *Consider* can take an infinitive but is often followed by just a noun phrase or an adjective. *Regard* is followed by *as* + a noun phrase.

- Native Americans **are considered (to be) the real discoverers**.
- Columbus **is regarded as the discoverer of America**.

---

6. Passive sentences with *that* clauses or infinitive phrases are often used in academic discourse and in reporting the news. They create an objective impression by distancing the author from the idea.

- It **is believed that** the abominable snowman actually **exists**.
- The defendant **is alleged to have committed** the crime.

Authors can create the greatest distance between themselves and an idea by starting a passive sentence with *It* + *be* + past participle + *that* clause. This type of sentence is formal.

- **It is thought that** the Vikings explored the New World long ago.

▶ **BE CAREFUL!** This construction with *it* occurs only with verbs that can be followed by a clause beginning with *that*.

Reference Notes

For use of ***that* clauses**, see Unit 21.

For use of **infinitive phrases**, see Unit 16.

For a list of **verbs used in the passive followed by a *that* clause**, see Appendix 10 on page A-6.

For a list of **common stative passive verbs + prepositions**, see Appendix 11 on page A-6.

Focused Practice

1 | DISCOVER THE GRAMMAR

A *Read these sentences. Are the underlined passive structures stative passives* **(S)** *or opinion passives* **(O)***?*

___S___ 1. The territory of the Asu <u>is located</u> roughly between that of the Tarahumara of Mexico and that of the Ojibwa of Canada.

_____ 2. On the southeast, their territory <u>is bordered</u> by the Caribbean.

_____ 3. They <u>are said</u> to be from somewhere in the East.

_____ 4. Actually, the Asu may <u>be related</u> to certain European peoples.

_____ 5. In Asu culture the rac <u>is considered</u> sacred.

_____ 6. It <u>is felt</u> that the more racs a family has, the higher its social status is.

_____ 7. Rac excrement <u>is considered</u> foul smelling.

_____ 8. It <u>is thought</u> to be quite dangerous to the environment.

_____ 9. In some large Asu cities citizens <u>are surrounded</u> by their racs to such an extent that they can hardly move.

_____ 10. Merchants that provide rac food <u>are</u> sometimes <u>alleged</u> to be profiting excessively at the expense of Asu society.

B *Read these sentences from the opening reading. For each sentence, answer these questions* **yes** *or* **no***:*

a. *Could the sentence be rewritten with a* by *phrase?*

b. *Could the sentence be rewritten in the active voice?*

1. The territory of the Asu is located roughly between that of the Tarahumara of Mexico and that of the Ojibwa of Canada.

   a. _____   b. _____

2. Actually, the Asu may be related to certain European peoples.

   a. _____   b. _____

3. The cow is regarded as a sacred animal.

   a. _____   b. _____

4. It is felt that the more racs a family has, the higher its social status is.

   a. _____   b. _____

2 | THE CARIBBEAN

Look at the map. Complete the sentences by writing the stative passive forms of the verbs in the box. Some of the choices may be used more than once.

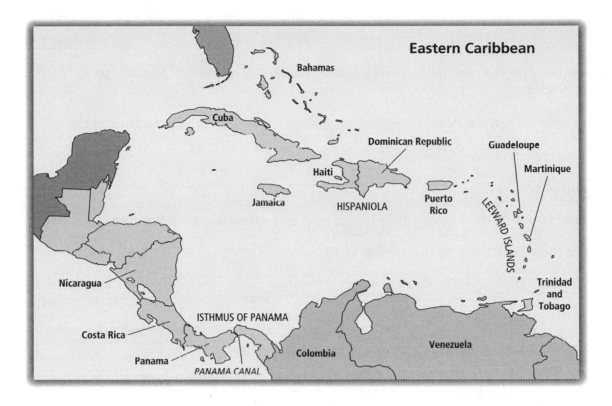

| border by | compose of | connect by | divide into |
| find (in) | locate (in) | make up of | surround by |

1. North and South America _____*are connected by*_____ the Isthmus of Panama.

2. The island nations of the region, of course, _____ the waters of the Caribbean.

3. The island of Hispaniola _____ two nations: Haiti and the Dominican Republic.

4. Cuba _____ about 90 miles south of Florida.

5. The nation of Trinidad and Tobago _____ two separate islands: Trinidad and Tobago.

6. On the north, Costa Rica _____ Nicaragua and on the south by Panama.

7. The nation of The Bahamas _____ many islands, some large and some small.

8. The nation of Panama _____ two parts by the Panama Canal.

(continued)

9. Jamaica and Puerto Rico _____ west and east, respectively, of Hispaniola.

10. The French-speaking islands of Guadeloupe and Martinique _____ the eastern Caribbean, north of South America.

3 | BELIEFS, THOUGHTS, AND OPINIONS   *Grammar Notes 5–6*

A *Complete the sentences with a passive form of the verbs in parentheses. Add **as** or **to** as needed.*

1. In some circles, the Basques _____*are considered to be*_____ the descendants of the Atlanteans.
   (consider / be)

2. For centuries before Copernicus, the Earth _____ the center of the
   (think / be)

   universe.

3. Lee Harvey Oswald _____ the assassin of President John Kennedy,
   (claim / be)

   but there are some who don't believe this.

4. Mother Teresa and Albert Schweitzer _____ great humanitarians.
   (regard)

5. In the Middle Ages, fairies and other spirit creatures _____ real.
   (believe / be)

6. Since the 19th century, George Washington and Abraham Lincoln

   _____ the greatest American presidents by many.
   (consider)

7. Bigfoot, a large, mysterious forest creature, _____ in the Pacific
   (say / live)

   Northwest.

8. In the 15th century and afterwards, King Richard III of England

   _____ a monster king. Today he has a better reputation.
   (regard)

9. Today William Shakespeare _____ the author of the plays credited to
   (assume / be)

   him, but some have suggested he couldn't have written them all.

10. From time to time, certain people _____ criminals, but they are later
    (allege / be)

    proved innocent by DNA evidence.

B *Rewrite sentences 2, 3, 5, 7, 9, and 10 using a passive sentence with* **it** + **be** + *past participle +* **that** *clause.*

2. *For centuries before Copernicus, it was thought that the Earth was the center of the universe.*

3. _____

5. _____

7. _____

9. _____

10. _____

4 | IN MY CULTURE
Grammar Note 5

Use each of the items in the box to write passive sentences showing beliefs, opinions, or facts about people or things in your country.

allege to be	assume to be	believe to be	claim to be
consider	regard as	say to be	think to be

Example: Jorge Amado **is considered** one of the greatest Brazilian writers.

1. _____

2. _____

3. _____

4. _____

5. _____

6. _____

7. _____

8. _____

5 | EDITING

Read this student essay about a creature that may or may not be real. There are nine mistakes in passive constructions. The first one is already corrected. Find and correct eight more.

The Snowman

Every area of the world has its own legends, and Asia is no different. One of the most famous Asian legends is about the Abominable Snowman, also called the yeti, of the Himalayas. Is the yeti just a legend that is ~~believe~~ *believed* because people want things to be real, or does he really exist?

The yeti thought to be a huge creature—perhaps as tall as eight feet. His body is supposed to be covered with long, brown hair. He says to have a pointed head and a hairless face that looks something like a man's. It is claiming that he lives near Mount Everest, the highest mountain in the world, which locates on the border of Nepal and Tibet.

Sightings of the yeti have been reported for centuries, but the yeti was make known to the rest of the world only in 1921. In that year, members of an expedition to climb Mt. Everest saw very large tracks in the snow that looked like prints of human feet. No conclusive evidence of the yeti's existence was found during that expedition, but interest was stimulated. Other expeditions were made. In 1951, explorer Eric Shipton led a search in which some gigantic, human-appearing tracks were found. Once again, the yeti himself was not seen. In 1969, Sir Edmund Hillary, who is regarded one of the greatest climbers ever, arranged another expedition, this time with the intention of not only seeing the yeti but of capturing him. Once again, tracks were discovered, but that was all. Hillary eventually decided the footprints might simply considered normal animal tracks enlarged by the daytime melting of the snow. In 1964, Boris F. Porshev, a Russian scientist, said that he believed that the yeti actually existed. He theorized that the yeti is a surviving descendant of Neanderthal man, a creature who is believed to live from 200,000 to 25,000 years ago and is thought by some to be an ancestor of modern humans. Porshev has never actually been able to spot the yeti, however.

The mystery continues. Does the yeti really exist, or do people just want to believe he exists? It seems to me that there must be more to this mystery than just melted tracks. Centuries of reports by Himalayan trail guides must mean something. Besides, other yeti-type creatures have been reported—most notably, Bigfoot in North America. Time will tell, but maybe we shouldn't be so quick to dismiss the Abominable Snowman as nothing more than an entertaining story.

Communication Practice

6 | LISTENING 1

🎧 *Listen to the news bulletin. Then listen again and mark the statements* **True** *or* **False** *based on what you heard.*

	True	False
1. The earthquakes are said to have registered a nine on the Richter scale.	☑	☐
2. The epicenter of the quakes was located in the Pacific Ocean.	☐	☐
3. The exact number of drowned people is known.	☐	☐
4. It is thought that severe flooding has occurred inland.	☐	☐
5. The president was vacationing at his seaside retreat.	☐	☐
6. So far, no looting has been reported.	☐	☐
7. The citizens of this country are expected to stay calm, gentle, and law-abiding.	☐	☐
8. The citizens of the country should go to low areas.	☐	☐

7 | MORE ABOUT THE ASU

Go back and reread the opening reading of the unit. Then read more about the Asu.

Racs play an important role in coming-of-age rituals among the Asu. At the approximate age of 16, the average young Asu undergoes sometimes difficult initiation rites into adult society. Young persons who pass the ritual tests are granted the right to use a rac in public and often even to own one. Their acceptance into adult culture is formally symbolized by their achievement of this right.

Now work in small groups. Answer these questions and report your answers to the class.

1. Who are the Asu? Where does their name come from?
2. Is this article completely serious, or is it supposed to be funny?
3. What is the sacred animal of the Asu?
4. What is referred to in the description of the tendency of the rac's footwear to deteriorate?
5. Why can the rac's excrement not be used for fertilizer or fuel?
6. Who are the merchants who allegedly charge too much for rac food?
7. What do you think the author was trying to show in this article?

8 | LISTENING 2

🎧 *Listen to part of a TV quiz show. Then listen again. Match the statements on the right to the names on the left.*

_____ **1.** Homer

_____ **2.** Siddhartha Gautama

_____ **3.** Simón Bolívar

_____ **4.** Anastasia Romanova

_____ **5.** Plato

_____ **6.** Anne Boleyn

a. It is thought that she was murdered in the 1917 Russian revolution.

b. It is believed that he was the author of the myth of Atlantis.

c. Her daughter is regarded as one of the greatest of the English monarchs.

d. He is considered the father of South American democracy.

e. He is assumed to be the author of the *Iliad* and the *Odyssey*.

f. He is known as the founder of Buddhism.

9 | PICTURE DISCUSSION

A *Look at the pictures here and on page 247. In small groups, talk about each of these people, using passive constructions.*

Example: Albert Einstein is considered one of the greatest scientists of all time.

Albert Einstein

Mahatma Gandhi

Nelson Mandela   *Vincent Van Gogh*

B *Discuss the quality of these individuals' contributions to culture. Who has made the most significant contributions? Share your conclusions with the class.*

> **Example:** A: We believe the most significant contribution to world culture has been made by _____.
>
> B: Why do you think so?

10 | WRITING

Write a three- or four-paragraph summary of a legend or myth from your culture or another you are familiar with.

> **Example:** My favorite American myth is the story of Paul Bunyan. Paul was a giant of a man who lived in the North Woods of Minnesota. He was a lumberjack who had great strength, and he also had a gigantic blue ox named Babe. The story of Paul and Babe is probably considered the most famous American myth. Here's how Paul got his start in life . . .

11 | ON THE INTERNET

© *Do some research on the Internet to create a group guessing game. Form groups of four to six. Using passive constructions, prepare five or more statements about any famous figure you choose: a political or religious leader, an author, an explorer, an inventor, and so on. Students in other groups will try to guess who the figure is. Make the first statements less obvious than the later ones.*

Example
1. In the world today, he is considered one of the greatest religious leaders of all time.
2. He was called "great soul" by his followers and admirers.
3. In his time, he was revered for, among other things, his efforts in favor of the untouchables.
4. He is known today as the father of the nonviolent movement called passive resistance.
5. He is regarded as the principal force behind the achievement of India's independence.
   Answer: Mohandas (Mahatma) Gandhi.

From **Grammar** to **Writing**
Parallelism

Parallelism (also called **parallel structure**) is an important feature of English that makes our speaking, and especially our writing, easier to understand. To make structures in speech or writing parallel, put all items in a series in the same grammatical form.

> **Examples:** Over the weekend I **bought a new car, painted the living room**, and **planted a garden.** (All the verbs in the predicate are in the simple past and in the active voice.)
>
> The prisoner was **arrested, taken** to the police station, **booked**, and **fingerprinted.** (All four verbs are in the simple past and in the passive voice.)
>
> My favorite hobbies are **snorkeling, reading**, and **playing** the guitar. (All three subject complements are gerunds or gerund phrases.)
>
> Children in this school are not allowed **to watch television** or **to eat junk food.** (The two complements are infinitive phrases.)

We will concentrate in this Part on parallelism with nouns and articles and with active or passive voice. See Part VI From Grammar to Writing, pages 287–289, for a discussion of parallelism with gerunds and infinitives.

A. Parallelism of Nouns and Articles

In writing sentences that contain a series of nouns and articles, you can place the article before each noun or before the first noun only. However, it is more common to place the article before each noun.

> **Examples:** On her shopping trip, Mrs. Figucroa bought a book, a dress, and a CD. OR
>
> On her shopping trip, Mrs. Figueroa bought a book, dress, and CD.
>
> NOT On her shopping trip, Mrs. Figueroa bought a book, ~~dress,~~ and a CD.

1 | *Read the following paragraph and correct the four mistakes in parallel structure with nouns and articles.*

    Rolleen Laing poured herself a second cup of coffee as she ate her breakfast, which consisted of a fried egg, *an* orange, and a piece of dry toast. She was 62 years old and had been successful as a university professor, writer of detective fiction, and an amateur detective. Just then, the telephone rang. It was Harry Sadler, a local police detective. Ever since Rolleen had helped Harry crack a murder case several years previously, she had been called in as an unofficial consultant on several cases. She had helped Harry solve cases involving a hit-and-run victim, a murdered television executive, and, most recently, koala stolen from the city zoo.

"Hi, Rolleen. This is Harry. You're needed on another case. It's a robbery this time. Some thieves broke into the art museum and stole a Van Gogh, a Picasso, Gauguin, and a Matisse. Meet me at the museum at 10:00, OK?"

B. Parallelism with the Active or Passive Voice

In sentences with the passive voice, the auxiliary may be repeated each time or before the first item only. If the parallel items are short, the auxiliary is generally not repeated.

The prisoner **was arrested, tried**, and **found** innocent.

If the parallel items are long, the auxiliary is generally repeated for clarity.

The mythical nation of Atlantis **is said** to have existed about 12,000 years ago, **is thought** to have been located in the Atlantic Ocean west of the Strait of Gibraltar, and **is well known** as a source of many present-day legends of lost peoples.

Note the following nonparallel sentence with two items in the passive voice and one in the active.

The evidence was taken to the crime lab, a team of biochemists analyzed it, and used in a criminal trial.

To put this sentence in parallel structure, we change the second item to the passive voice, eliminating the word *it*.

The evidence **was taken** to the crime lab, **analyzed** by a team of biochemists, and **used** in a criminal trial.

2 Each of the following sentences contains a mistake in parallelism in the use of the active or passive voice. In each case, one item is nonparallel to the others. Correct the nonparallel item.

1. The yeti is described as a huge creature, ᴵˢ said to have long brown hair, and is thought to live in the Himalayas.

2. According to historical records, the American outlaw Billy the Kid was known as a fearless gunfighter, was hunted by the law, and killed in a gunfight.

3. Anthropologists speculate that the Anasazi might have been attacked by unfriendly tribes, decimated by crop failures, or drought might have driven them away.

(continued)

4. After Amelia Earhart's airplane was lost, naval investigators searched for debris, interviewed residents of various South Pacific islands, but no trace of Earhart and her navigator was found.

5. According to legend, the continent of Atlantis was struck by devastating earthquakes, inundated by floods, and the ocean swallowed it up.

3 | *Read this paragraph about the Judge Crater mystery. There are five mistakes in parallelism with the active or passive voice. The first mistake is already corrected. Find and correct four more.*

On the evening of August 6, 1930, Judge Joseph Force Crater, a wealthy, successful, and good-looking New Yorker, disappeared without a trace. Earlier in the evening he had been seen with friends at a Manhattan restaurant and ~~they observed him~~ *observed* departing. At 9:10 P.M. he walked out the door of the restaurant and hailed a taxi. He was soon driven away. No one ever saw or heard from him again. It was 10 days before he was even reported missing. On August 16, his wife called his courthouse, the secretary was asked of his whereabouts, and learned that he was probably off on political business. This news reassured Mrs. Crater somewhat, but when he still hadn't turned up by August 26, a group of his fellow judges started an investigation. A grand jury was convened, but its members could not come to any conclusion as to what had happened to Judge Crater. They theorized that the judge might have developed amnesia, might have run away voluntarily, or been a crime victim. His wife disagreed with the first two possibilities, holding that he had been murdered by someone in the Tammany Hall organization, the political machine that controlled New York City at the time. The mystery remains unsolved to this day. Crater could have been killed by a Tammany Hall agent, a girlfriend could have murdered him, or kidnapped by an organized crime group. He might in fact have suffered from amnesia, or his own disappearance might have been planned by him. Reports of Judge Crater sightings have continued to surface over the last 70 years.

4 | *Write a paragraph of six to ten sentences on one of the following topics. Use the passive voice where appropriate.*

- An accident or natural disaster that you have witnessed or heard about

- An unsolved mystery that you are aware of

- An unusual or mysterious experience that you have had

In your paragraph, include at least one sentence containing verbs in the passive voice in parallel structure. Also include at least one sentence containing a series of nouns in parallel structure. Exchange papers with a partner. Discuss each other's paper and then rewrite your paragraph if necessary. Submit your paragraph to your teacher.

Review Test

I *Complete the conversations with passive forms of the verbs in parentheses. Use* **be** *unless* **get** *or* **have** *is specified.*

1. A: Where _____*was the missing child found*_____?
   a. (the missing child / find)

   B: She _____ walking barefoot along Stinson Beach.
   b. (discover)

2. A: How do you think the team is going to do this year?

   B: Pretty well, except that I predict they _____ by Central
   (will / get / beat)

   University.

3. A: What happened to your car?

   B: It _____ by a truck—a small one, fortunately.
   (get / hit)

4. A: Sally, _____ for six months now.
   a. (we / getting / overcharge)

   B: I think we ought to _____. I've heard the same
   b. (have / the company / investigate)

   complaint from the neighbors.

5. A: Why are these floors so dirty? _____ every day?
   a. (not / they / clean)

   B: Normally, yes, but somehow the cleaning _____ this
   b. (not / get / do)

   morning.

6. A: Please don't give food to the animals. They _____ a
   a. (feed)

   special diet.

   B: _____ in the next couple of hours? We're staying
   b. (they / being / feed)

   until 3:00.

   C: Sorry. They _____ until 4:30.
   c. (not / will / feed)

II *Complete the newspaper article. Circle the correct choices in parentheses.*

(Local citizen Ronald Mason says) / It is said by local citizen Ronald Mason) that (he has
1.
learned his lesson / his lesson has been learned by him). On Tuesday, Mason was in a hurry
2.
to get to a job interview. (He parked his motorcycle / His motorcycle was parked by him) in a
3.
handicapped parking space. When Mason came out of the interview, (he discovered / it was
4.
discovered by him) that (a person had removed his motorcycle / his motorcycle had been
5.
removed) from the handicapped spot. (Someone had placed it / It had been placed) upside
6.
down in the pool of the adjacent fountain. (People had noticed no one / No one had been
7.
noticed) in the area. After recovering his motorcycle, (Mason commented / it was
8.
commented by Mason), "I'll never do that again. I deserved what I got."

III *Fill in the blanks in the paragraph with passive forms of the verbs in parentheses.*

Consider the situation of the mysterious "lost colony" established by Sir Walter Raleigh

in 1585 on the Outer Banks of what is now North Carolina. It _____*is felt*_____
1. (feel)
today that the plan for the settlement, which _____ on Roanoke
2. (locate)
Island, was ill conceived from the start. Geographical conditions were not favorable, and the

local tribes were not friendly. In 1590, all of the colonists _____ by
3. (find)
explorers to have vanished, leaving behind only some refuse and the word "Croatoan," the

name of a nearby island, written on a tree. What happened to the colonists? No one knows

for sure, but today they _____ to have been killed or carried away
4. (assume)
by neighboring peoples.

Today it _____ in some circles that at least a few of the colonists
5. (believe)
were absorbed into local tribes. In fact, descendants of the original native inhabitants of the

area claim Raleigh's colonists as their ancestors. If this is true, the people of the lost colony

_____ lost at all, for their genes live on in those descendants.
6. (not / should / consider)

IV *Look at the pictures. For each picture, write a passive sentence using the words in parentheses. Use* **be** *unless* **get** *is specified.*

1.

Mrs. O'Reilly (get / catch)

Mrs. O'Reilly is going to get

caught for speeding.

_____

2.

Mrs. O'Reilly (just / get / stop)

_____

_____

_____

3.

Two months ago (tear down)

_____

_____

_____

4.

Now (build)

_____

_____

_____

(continued)

5.

Mrs. Platt (have / repair)

_____

_____

_____

6.

Once a month / Mr. Platt
(get / cut and trim)

_____

_____

_____

7.

The yeti (think / live) in the
Himalayas

_____

_____

_____

8.

The lost continent of Atlantis
(say / be located) in the Atlantic Ocean

_____

_____

_____

V *Circle the letter of the one underlined word or phrase in each sentence that is not correct.*

1. The Hawaiian island of Kahoolawe <u>has</u> just <u>being</u> <u>hit</u> <u>by</u> a tsunami.
                                  A   B   C D

         A (B) C D

2. The tsunami <u>got</u> <u>caused</u> <u>by</u> an earthquake <u>centered</u> in the Pacific
             A   B   C   D
Ocean southeast of Midway Island.

         A   B   C   D

3. Damage on Kahoolawe <u>is</u> <u>say</u> <u>to</u> <u>be</u> extensive.
                              A B C D

                       A B C D

A B C D

4. In Central Africa, a breakthrough <u>is</u> <u>being</u> <u>report</u> <u>involving</u>
                               A   B   C   D
    resumption of the stalled peace talks.

A B C D

5. These talks <u>were</u> <u>been</u> <u>held</u> last week <u>between</u> the leaders
                  A   B   C   D
    of Tintoria and Illyria.

A B C D

6. They <u>were</u> <u>suspending</u> <u>when</u> the president of Illyria <u>stormed</u>
         A   B   C   D
    out during the second face-to-face meeting.

A B C D

7. The secretary-general of the United Nations <u>said</u>, "We <u>must</u> <u>get</u>
                                       A   B C
    these talks <u>start</u> again."
              D

A B C D

8. In fact, it <u>is</u> <u>rumored</u> that the talks <u>are</u> <u>be</u> <u>resumed</u> next week in Switzerland.
           A   B   C   D

A B C D

9. The new space station that <u>is being</u> <u>sponsored</u> by the seven-nation
                              A   B
    consortium <u>will</u> <u>launch</u> next week from Woomera Field in Australia.
               C   D

A B C D

10. The station <u>will</u> <u>be</u> <u>staff</u> by astronauts from each of the seven
               A   B   C
    <u>participating</u> nations.
      D

A B C D

VI *Go back to your answers to Exercise V. Write the correct answer for each item that you believe is incorrect.*

1. _____ *been* _____   6. _____

2. _____   7. _____

3. _____   8. _____

4. _____   9. _____

5. _____   10. _____

▶ *To check your answers, go to the Answer Key on page RT-3.*

PART VI

Gerunds and Infinitives

15 Gerunds

Grammar in Context

BEFORE YOU READ

1 *What do you value in friendships? Discuss this question with a partner.*

2 *Make a short list of some of the friends you have and have had. Are they all the same type of friend?*

Read this article about types of friends.

FRIENDS

by Jim Garcia

I was having difficulty finding a subject for this month's column until I remembered that this is National Friendship Week. I also remembered learning, as a child, a rhyme that went like this: "True friends are diamonds, precious and rare; false friends are oak leaves that fall anywhere." Are friendships really that black and white? This was my childhood concept, but I now see that my perceiving friendship in this way was pretty simplistic. I've long since stopped thinking of friendship in these terms. It's clear that some friends are true and others are false, but there are many different types of "true" friends. In fact, I can recognize at least six types:

Type 1: Convenience friends

These are the friends we make when our schedules and activities coincide. For example, years ago I played on a soccer team. I didn't have a way of getting to the practices and tried taking the bus, but it always got me there late. Then I learned that Andres, a team member, lived three streets away from me. He had a car and agreed to pick me up because it was convenient for him. We became friends by riding with each other and developed a good relationship. We didn't see each other outside of the soccer context, though.

Type 2: Special-interest friends

My brother's passion is kayaking, and he belongs to a kayaking club. He's been going

FRIENDS

to meetings for years and tells me he's made several good friends on river trips. They have great times, and living through dangerous experiences has made them close. Once the trips are over, though, they don't socialize with each other. Their special interest, kayaking, is the only thing that holds them together.

Type 3: Long-time friends

I have several of these, but my best long-time friend is a guy named Al. We've known each other since we were 12 years old, and our friendship links our past to our present. We can go months or years without contacting each other, but whenever we do make contact it seems like we were just together yesterday. We enjoy just catching up on each other's activities. We would like to spend more time together, but it doesn't seem to matter if we don't.

Type 4: Cross-generational friends

When we seek friends, we often look for people in our own age group, but cross-generational friendships are worth pursuing. My friend Bill is an example. He's about 25 years older than I am, and I suppose he's a kind of father figure. He's more than that, however. Actually, Bill was my teacher in a writing class when I was at the university. I was having trouble figuring out my career, but Bill supported my becoming a writer, and that's what I did. After the class was over, we became friends.

Type 5: Part-of-a-couple friends

My wife Amanda and Bill's wife Gretta are good examples of this very common type of friendship. When our partner has a friend in another couple, we have to go through the process of getting to know the "other person" in that couple. Sometimes this is difficult; people may feel they have little or nothing in common with their counterpart and may even resent being forced to socialize with a "friend" they didn't choose. Fortunately, Amanda and Gretta have become good friends on their own through their common interest in collecting rare books.

Type 6: "Best" friends

What is a "best" friend? In my view it's a person we can share just about everything with—someone with whom we don't have a problem being honest or vulnerable. It's someone who doesn't spare your feelings or avoid telling you what you need to hear when you need to hear it. I have two best friends. One is my friend Ken, whom I met when I was in the military. Our having gone through difficult experiences has bonded us for life. The other is my wife, Amanda. I love talking with both Amanda and Ken and having long conversations that can go everywhere and nowhere. Sometimes we talk for hours. Other times we just like being together without saying much of anything.

I would have a hard time living without my two "best" friends, but it's awfully important to have the others, too.

AFTER YOU READ

*Look at the pairs of sentences. According to the first sentence in each pair, is the second sentence true (**T**) or false (**F**)? Circle the correct answer.*

1. I've long since stopped thinking of friendship in these terms

    T F   I don't think of friendship in this way anymore.

2. Cross-generational friendships are worth pursuing.

    T F   We can gain financially by having friendships in different generations.

3. People may feel they have little or nothing in common with their counterpart and may even resent being forced to socialize with a "friend" they didn't choose.

    T F   People may not like required friendships.

4. A "best" friend is someone with whom we don't have a problem being honest or vulnerable.

    T F   It's difficult to be honest or vulnerable with a best friend.

Grammar Presentation

GERUNDS

Gerund as Subject		
Gerund (Subject)	**Verb**	**Object**
Kayaking	involves	some risks.
Swimming	builds	endurance.
Not inviting him	will cause	resentment.

Gerund as Object		
Subject	**Verb**	**Gerund (Object)**
They	enjoy	**kayaking**.
I	went	**swimming**.
We	don't advise	**not inviting** him.

Gerund as Subject Complement		
Subject	**Verb**	**Gerund (Subject Complement)**
My sport	is	**skiing**.
His problem	is	**not exercising**.

Gerund as Object Complement			
Subject	**Verb**	**Object**	**Gerund (Object Complement)**
He	spends	time	**reading**.
She	found	him	**not working**.

Gerund as Object of a Preposition			
	Preposition	**Gerund**	
She insists	**on**	**going out**	every weekend.
He's accustomed	**to**	**giving**	parties.
They have a reason	**for**	**not inviting**	Michael.

Possessive + Gerund			
	Possessive	**Gerund**	
Bob and Helen worry about	**Emily's**	**having**	so few friends.
	her		
	the children's		
	their		

Active and Passive Gerunds		
	Active Gerunds	**Passive Gerunds**
SIMPLE	**Inviting** them to her wedding was a nice gesture on her part.	**Being invited** to her wedding was a great surprise to them.
PAST	**Having invited** them to her wedding made her feel good.	**Having been invited** to her wedding is a fond memory for them.

GRAMMAR NOTES

EXAMPLES

1. A **gerund** is a noun made from a verb. To form a gerund, add *-ing* to the base form of the verb.

Gerunds and gerund phrases perform the same functions as nouns:

a. They act as subjects.

b. They act as objects.

c. They act as complements (phrases that describe or explain the subject or object of the sentence).

Add *not* before a gerund to make a negative statement.

- **Cooking** is my hobby. I like **eating**, too.

- **Talking** with friends is enjoyable.
- I love **getting** together with friends.
- Our favorite activity is **playing** cards. *(subject complement)*
- She has trouble **making** friends. *(object complement)*
- **Not calling** her was a big mistake.

(continued)

2. Many verbs and verb phrases in English have **gerunds as objects**. Common examples: *avoid, consider, enjoy, keep, mind.*	• I **enjoy meeting** new people. • You should **avoid working** late.
We often use *go* + **gerund** to talk about recreational activities: *go skiing, go swimming, go hiking,* etc.	• We **go skiing** every weekend in the winter.

3. Gerunds act as **objects of prepositions**.	• I made friends **by joining** a club.
Many preposition combinations are followed by gerunds:	
a. verb + preposition	• They **insisted on giving** us a present.
b. adjective + preposition	• She's **good at making** friends.
c. expressions	• I'll **look forward to seeing** you tonight. • I **am used to having** a lot of friends.
▶ **BE CAREFUL!** The word *to* can be a preposition or part of an infinitive.	• He will adjust **to working** hard. *(To is a preposition.)* • He tries **to work** hard. *(To is part of the infinitive.)*

4. In writing and formal speaking, use a **possessive** noun or pronoun **before a gerund** to show possession.	• **Pete's dominating** every conversation bothers me. • **His dominating** every conversation bothers me.
USAGE NOTE: In conversation, native speakers often use a name or an object pronoun before a gerund.	• I don't like **Pete dominating** every conversation. • I don't like **him dominating** every conversation.

5. Gerunds can occur in simple or past form. We can use a **simple gerund** (without a past participle) to make a generalization.

- **Making** friends is a natural thing to do.

We can use a **past gerund** (*having* + past participle) to show an action that occurred before the action of the main verb in the sentence.

- **Having met** Jane in my first week of college **helped** me throughout my college career.

NOTE: We use a past gerund to emphasize the difference in time between two actions. The simple gerund is also correct in many situations.

- **Having gone** to college is one of the best things **I've ever done**.

  OR

- **Going** to college is one of the best things **I've ever done**.

Gerunds can occur in **passive** form. In the present, use *being* + past participle. In the past, use *having been* + past participle.

- She hates **being ignored**.
- She's still angry at **having been ignored**.

▶ **BE CAREFUL!** Many words in English end in *-ing*. Do not confuse gerunds with verbs in the progressive form, or with present participles used as adjectives or in adverb phrases.

- I've been **making** friends at work.
- Mary is enrolled in a **cooking** class.
- **Walking** on the beach, I wondered why she was angry at me.

Reference Notes
For a list of common **verbs followed by gerunds**, see Appendix 12 on page A-7.
For a list of common **adjective + preposition combinations followed by gerunds**, see Appendix 13 on page A-7.
For **general statements with gerunds or infinitives**, see Unit 16.

Focused Practice

1 | DISCOVER THE GRAMMAR

A *Read these sentences. Indicate whether each gerund is used as a subject (**S**), an object (**O**), an object of a preposition (**OP**), or a subject or object complement (**C**).*

__C__ **1.** I was having difficulty finding a subject.

_____ **2.** I remembered learning a rhyme.

_____ **3.** My perceiving friendship in this way was pretty simplistic.

_____ **4.** I didn't have a way of getting to the practices.

(continued)

_____ 5. My brother's passion is kayaking.

_____ 6. We can go months or years without contacting each other.

_____ 7. I was having trouble figuring out my career.

_____ 8. Bill supported my becoming a writer.

_____ 9. I would have a hard time living without my two "best" friends.

B _Are the_ -ing _words in each of the following sentences gerunds? Write_ **Y** _(yes) or_ **N** _(no)._

__Y__ 1. I've long since stopped thinking of friendship in these terms.

_____ 2. These are the friends we make by engaging in some specific activity.

_____ 3. He belongs to a kayaking club.

_____ 4. We enjoy just catching up on each other's activities.

_____ 5. Cross-generational friendships are worth pursuing.

_____ 6. He was my teacher in a writing class.

_____ 7. They have become good friends on their own through their common interest in collecting rare books.

_____ 8. I would have a hard time being single again.

2 | ALL WORK AND NO PLAY
Grammar Notes 1–3

Brian Hansen is constantly tired and dissatisfied. He has gone to a doctor to see if there is anything physically wrong with him. Complete the conversation with gerunds. Make the gerunds negative if necessary.

DOCTOR: Well, Brian, what seems to be the problem?

BRIAN: I'm tired all the time. Some nights when I come home from work I'm so exhausted I

don't feel like _____doing_____ anything but collapsing on the sofa and
            1. (do)

_____ in front of the TV. Is there anything physically wrong with me?
2. (vegetate)

DOCTOR: No, I've looked at the test results, and you're healthy. How long have you been feeling

like this?

BRIAN: Oh, two or three months, I guess. Long enough so that I've begun _____
                                                                    3. (worry)

about _____ any energy. Basically I'm not doing anything besides
      4. (have)

punching a time clock.

DOCTOR: How much are you working?

BRIAN: Well, I'm putting in a lot of overtime—all in all, at least 60 hours a week, I'd say.

DOCTOR: Why are you doing this? Are you trying to kill yourself?

BRIAN: Well, at this point, _____ overtime is out of the question. I've got a lot of
5. (work)

bills to pay off. The other thing is that I only recently moved here, and I know hardly

anyone, so my focus is on _____ money for a while. I like
6. (make)

_____, and I really miss _____ any close friends, but I
7 (socialize) 8. (have)

don't know quite how to go about _____ new people.
9. (meet)

DOCTOR: You're not married, then?

BRIAN: No, not yet.

DOCTOR: Well, I think you need to stop _____ so much and start
10. (work)

_____ a little—to put things in balance. I'd say you need a hobby—and
11. (play)

some friends.

BRIAN: A hobby? You mean some boring thing like stamp _____?
12. (collect)

DOCTOR: No. That's an OK hobby if you like it, but there are more interesting ones.

BRIAN: Like what?

DOCTOR: Oh, maybe like karaoke. Do you like _____?
13. (sing)

BRIAN: I love music, but I don't have much of a voice. In my case, _____ is better
14. (sing)

than _____ off key.
15. (sing)

DOCTOR: Well, have you ever gone _____?
16. (orienteer)

BRIAN: What's that?

DOCTOR: People use a map and a compass and try to be the first person to find locations of

hidden clues.

BRIAN: Sounds great. Where can I find out more about it?

DOCTOR: I've got a friend who belongs to an orienteering club. I'll give you her number.

BRIAN: Super. Thanks.

3 | MY TWO BEST FRIENDS

Grammar Note 4

Complete the sentences with a possessive noun or pronoun and a gerund.

1. I have two best friends, Bob and Mary. Bob is my co-worker. I'm grateful for

   _____*his giving*_____ me a ride to work every day.
   <u>(he / give)</u>

2. I'm new to the firm, so I also appreciate _____ me learn my job.
   <u>(Bob / help)</u>

3. _____ my work is hard to deal with, so Bob's encouragement is vital.
   <u>(My boss / criticize)</u>

4. Mary is my neighbor. _____ so close is wonderful.
   <u>(She / live)</u>

5. I especially appreciate _____ me on tough issues.
   <u>(Mary / advise)</u>

6. She knows how to deal with _____ discouraged.
   <u>(I / become)</u>

7. I couldn't ask for two better friends than Bob and Mary. I'm thankful for _____
   <u>(they / be)</u>

   there for me when I need them.

8. _____ together frequently helps us stay close.
   <u>(We / get)</u>

4 | MY CROSS-GENERATIONAL FRIEND

Grammar Note 5

Complete the sentences with simple gerunds or past gerunds with **having** + past
participle. Use a past gerund if it is possible to do so.

Martha, who is 20 years older than I am, is my best cross-generational friend. _____*Having met*_____
                                                                                    1. (meet)

her when I was an unhappy college sophomore is one of the best things that has ever happened to

me. Martha and I have stayed friends. I look forward to _____ her
                                                          2. (see)

whenever our schedules permit. Our relationship hasn't always been smooth, though.

Martha and I were both in the same calculus class. I was having a lot of difficulty and was

angry at myself for _____ in a class that I didn't need for my degree. It
                      3. (enroll)

was too late to drop the class, however, and since I was frustrated, I frequently got irritated with

the teacher for _____ so much difficult homework every day.
                 4. (assign)

Martha stopped me one day after class. She said she was tired of my continual

_____ with the teacher. "You need to grow up," she said. I was offended
5. (argue)

at first, but the older I get the clearer it is to me that her _____ that
6. (say)

amounts to one of the major events in my life. I had to change my negative attitude. I did need to

grow up.

A few days later I asked Martha if she would mind _____ with me
7. (study)

and _____ me with the homework. She agreed. With a lot of patient
8. (help)

work, I succeeded in _____ the course. Eventually we became great
9. (pass)

friends.

I suspect that most of us know someone whose _____ us what we
10. (tell)

needed to hear when we needed to hear it has made a difference in our life. Martha has certainly

made a difference in mine.

5 | PREFERENCES

Grammar Notes 2, 4

A *Write a question using a passive gerund and an active gerund.*

Example: (like / awaken / by an alarm clock) (wake up / on your own)

Do you like **being awakened** by an alarm clock or **waking up** on your own?

1. (prefer / ask out on a date) (ask / someone / yourself)

_____

2. (more interested in / entertain / yourself) (in / entertain / by others)

_____

3. (prefer / prepare dinner / yourself) (invite / to dinner / by friends)

_____

4. (like / tell / what to do) (give / orders)

_____

5. (like / figure things out / yourself) (show / how to do things)

_____

6. (prefer / give / advice by friends) (give / your friends / advice)

_____

(continued)

B *Now work with a partner. Take turns asking and answering the questions.*

Example: A: Do you like being awakened by an alarm clock or waking up on your own?
B: I like waking up on my own. I hate being awakened by an alarm clock. What about you?

6 | A PERSONAL INVENTORY   *Grammar Notes 1–4*

Using events in your own life, complete these sentences with gerunds or gerund phrases.

Example: I especially enjoy **playing** board games with friends.

1. I especially enjoy _____

2. I have stopped _____

3. I remember _____

4. I've always avoided _____

5. _____ worth_____

6. I have trouble _____

7. I spend a lot of time_____

8. I'm looking forward to _____

9. I'm good at _____

10. My_____

11. I'm still not used to _____

12. I strongly dislike _____

13. On weekends I don't feel like _____

14. If you visit my country, I recommend _____

_____

7 | EDITING

This letter has 14 mistakes in the use of gerunds. The first mistake is already corrected. Find and correct 13 more.

ENCHANTED DESERT RANCH

Dear Adam,

    I've been here for three days and am having a great time, but I can't help

wishing

~~wish~~ you were here too. Tell your boss I'm really angry at him. Not let you take

any vacation time qualifies him for the Jerk-of-the-Year Award. (Just kidding.

Don't say that!)

    Believe it or not, the first night I missed to hear all the city noises, but I

haven't really had any trouble to get used to the peace and quiet since then.

Everything's all so relaxed here—there's no rush around or write things down in

your Daily Planner. Get out of New York City was definitely what I needed, even

if it's only for two weeks. The ranch has lots of activities—horseback ride, river

raft on the Rio Grande, to hike in the wilderness—you name it. The ranch

employees do everything for you—being taken care of is nice, for a change, and I

love be chauffeured around Santa Fe in the ranch limousine. Tonight a group of

us are going out to a country western dance place called Rodeo Nites in Santa Fe,

so having taken those two-step dance lessons last summer will come in handy. It's

just too bad you couldn't come along so we could both have a good time. Tomorrow

we're all going to Taos Pueblo to watch some weave being done and to see some

Native American dancing, which is great because I'm really interested in learn

more about Native American culture. And I'm looking forward to see *Carmen* at

the Santa Fe Opera on Saturday.

    I'll write again in a day or two. Miss you lots.

        Love,

        Louise

Communication Practice

8 | LISTENING

🎧 *Brian Hansen and Jane Travanti are having a telephone conversation about the orienteering club Jane belongs to. Listen to the conversation. Then listen again and mark these statements* **True** *or* **False**, *based on what you heard.*

	True	False
1. Brian has tried orienteering before.	☐	☑
2. Dr. Stevens wants Brian to stop working.	☐	☐
3. Being experienced in orienteering is necessary to join Jane's club.	☐	☐
4. Jane's club tries to go orienteering at least twice a month.	☐	☐
5. In the summer, they get around by biking.	☐	☐
6. In the winter, they get around by cross-country skiing.	☐	☐
7. Brian has done cross-country skiing before.	☐	☐
8. Being married is a requirement for joining the club.	☐	☐
9. The club collects dues to pay for organizing their activities.	☐	☐
10. On the 15th, they'll get to the forest by carpooling.	☐	☐

9 | GROUP DISCUSSION

What do you value in friendships? Add your own item to the chart. Then complete the chart for yourself by ranking each item:

  3: Very Important in a Friendship

  2: Somewhat Important in a Friendship

  1: Not Important in a Friendship

Discuss your answers with three classmates. Report your overall results to the class.

	Rank
Giving each other presents	
Always being honest with one another	
Not hurting each other's feelings	
Giving help whenever it is asked for	
Lending money if it is asked for	

10 | WRITING

Look again at the categories of friendship in the opening reading. Choose one of the categories and write three or four paragraphs about a friend of yours who fits into it.

Example: I have a friend named Sarah who perfectly fits the category of long-time friend. Sarah and I met when we were in the fifth grade, when I had just moved to a new town and didn't know anyone. Ever since Sarah and I became friends, we've enjoyed sharing all kinds of experiences and can't go more than a month or so without contacting each other. Making friends wasn't that easy at first, however . . .

11 | ON THE INTERNET

Do a search to learn about the relationship between the people in one of these pairs, or choose another pair of your own. Report your results to the class.

- Dean Martin and Jerry Lewis (the United States)
- Queen Victoria and Benjamin Disraeli (Great Britain)
- Diego Rivera and Frida Kahlo (Mexico)

Grammar in Context

BEFORE YOU READ

1 *What is procrastination?*

2 *What are the dangers of procrastination?*

3 *Do you ever procrastinate? In what situations?*

◯ *Read this article about procrastination.*

SEIZE THE DAY

by Jessica Taylor

Picture this scenario: It's Sunday evening at 7 P.M. Your sister Alice comes to you with her term paper, which is due tomorrow. It's written in longhand, but it has to be typed. Alice doesn't type well. Here is the conversation that takes place:

Alice: Steve, can you type my paper? It's due tomorrow.

Steve: No, Alice, I can't. My friends will be here in half an hour, and I'm very busy. I can't stop to type your paper now.

Alice: But, Steve, I need you to. I can't do it myself. It'll take me all night.

Steve: Why didn't you ask me before this?

Alice: I forgot to. I really did plan to ask. Steve, you have to do it. I'll fail if I don't turn it in tomorrow. Please?

Steve: No, Alice, I don't have to. Now you go and sit down and start typing.

Welcome to Procrasination Theater brought to you by ... whoa, we don't have a sponsor again this week because the sales staff forgot to sell ads!

This is a great show!

London's Times
© 2002 Rick London and Rich Diesslin

SEIZE THE DAY

Does this situation sound familiar? It illustrates the problem of procrastination, which I asked psychiatrist Robert Stevens to talk about.

Taylor: Thank you for joining us. Today I want to ask you if there's such a thing as a procrastination syndrome.

Stevens: Well, I don't know if we could go so far as to call it a syndrome, but for many people procrastination is a very serious problem.

Taylor: Can we start with a definition of procrastination?

Stevens: Of course. To procrastinate is literally to put things off until tomorrow. It's a postponing of events until a later time. But unlike the word "postpone," which has a neutral sense, the word "procrastinate" definitely has a negative sense to it. There are occasionally good reasons to postpone things, but never to procrastinate. Procrastinating has the sense of avoidance.

Taylor: All right. Now what causes people to procrastinate? Laziness?

Stevens: That's a popular idea, but I'd have to say that laziness is a relatively minor cause. No, I think that fear is really the most important force that motivates people to put off doing something until later.

Taylor: Fear? Not laziness? You'll have to explain that to me a bit.

Stevens: Well, it's actually somewhat related to the expectation syndrome. A lot of people do what others expect in order to live up to their expectations. Procrastinators are afraid to fail. They're afraid to make mistakes, or maybe they don't want to be rejected. They let fear take control of them, and they put off any action.

Taylor: What would be an example of that?

Stevens: Well, let's see . . . Suppose someone—a young woman we'll call Blanche—has been planning a party. She's mentioned the party to people she knows but has put off making any actual invitations. Either consciously or subconsciously, she expects to fail, so she delays calling people until the very last moment. Her friends no doubt expected her to have called them, and when she didn't, they forgot about the event and made other plans. It's too short notice for most of them to be able to come. Blanche's fear has caused things to turn out like this.

Taylor: Uh-huh. Well, what if someone is a procrastinator and wants to change? What would you advise that person to do?

Stevens: Well, there are three principles I recommend for my clients. The first is never to put off until tomorrow what needs to be done today. Not to avoid painful or difficult things is the second. Some experiences in life are difficult or painful, and we need to accept that. The third is contained in the Latin phrase *carpe diem*—"seize the day." I try to consider everything that comes before me as an opportunity. I don't advise people to take unnecessary or foolish risks, but I do advise them not to put off living. They may not get another chance.

Taylor: Well, Dr. Stevens, thanks for another stimulating discussion.

AFTER YOU READ

What does each sentence mean? Circle the letter of the correct answer.

1. I can't stop to type your paper now.
   a. I can't stop the activity of typing.
   b. I can't stop another activity in order to type your paper.

2. There are occasionally good reasons to postpone things, but never to procrastinate.
   a. It's never acceptable to postpone things.
   b. It's sometimes acceptable to postpone things.

3. It's too short notice for most of them to be able to come.
   a. Most will not be able to come.
   b. Most will be able to come.

Grammar Presentation

INFINITIVES

Infinitive as Subject		
Infinitive (Subject)	**Verb**	**Object**
To procrastinate	causes	a lot of problems.
Not to go ahead	proved	a mistake.

Infinitive as Object		
Subject	**Verb**	**Infinitive (Object)**
Not everyone	wants	**to procrastinate.**
He	decided	**not to go ahead.**

Infinitive as Subject Complement			
Subject	**Verb**	**Infinitive (Subject Complement)**	
His job	is	**to motivate**	people.
Their real intention	is	**not to succeed.**	

It + Infinitive				
It	*Be*	**Adjective**	(*For / Of* + Noun / Pronoun)	**Infinitive**
It	is	foolish	(for Alice / her)	**to procrastinate.**
It	was	wrong	(of Hal / him)	**not to go ahead.**

Verbs Followed by Infinitives

	Verb	(Noun / Pronoun)	Infinitive
They	**decided / hoped / neglected**, etc.	Ø*	
	convinced / told / urged, etc.	Steve / him	**to call**.
	expected / needed / wanted, etc.	(Steve / him)	

* Ø = not used

Adjectives Followed by Infinitives

	Adjective	Infinitive	
Hal is	**reluctant**	**to complete**	his work on time.
He's	**careful**	**not to make**	mistakes.
They're	**happy**	**to hear**	the test has been postponed.

Nouns Followed by Infinitives

	Noun	Infinitive	
He can always think of	**reasons**	**to put off**	studying.
It seems like	**the thing**	**to do**.	
She always shows	**reluctance**	**to finish**	a job.

Too / Enough with Infinitives

	Too + Adjective / Adverb	Infinitive	
The project is	**too** complicated	**to finish**	on time.
Alice types	**too** slowly	**to meet**	the deadline.
	Adjective / Adverb + *Enough*	Infinitive	
Steve is	intelligent **enough**	**to understand**	the situation.
He didn't call	quickly **enough**	**to get**	the job.
	Enough + Noun	Infinitive	
They have	**enough** intelligence	**to pass**	the test.
	intelligence **enough**		

Active and Passive Infinitives

	Active Infinitives	Passive Infinitives
SIMPLE	She plans **to invite** them.	They expect **to be invited**.
PAST	She was glad **to have invited** them.	They were happy **to have been invited**.

GRAMMAR NOTES	**EXAMPLES**
1. An **infinitive** is *to* plus the base form of a verb.	• **To graduate** from college is important. I want **to do** that.
Infinitives and infinitive phrases often perform the same functions as nouns.	
a. They act as subjects.	• **To finish** what you started is advisable.
NOTE: Using an infinitive as a subject is formal. *It* + an infinitive phrase is more common. We often add *for* + a noun or pronoun to say who or what does the action.	• **It's** advisable **to finish** what you started. • **It's** important **for a student to take** good notes in class.
b. They act as objects.	• I'd like **to invite** you to dinner.
c. They act as subject complements (phrases that describe or explain the subject of a sentence).	• A teacher's job is **to create** a desire to learn.
To make an infinitive negative, place *not* before *to*.	• I warned you **not to** put this off.
▶ **BE CAREFUL!** Don't confuse *to* in an infinitive with *to* as a preposition. *To* in an infinitive is followed by the base form of the verb. *To* as a preposition is followed by a gerund, regular noun, or pronoun.	• **I plan to work** hard. • **I'm used to working** hard.

2. Certain **verbs** are followed only by **infinitives**.	• She **offered to help** me. • He **learned to be** efficient.
Other verbs are followed by a required noun or pronoun + an infinitive.	• I **warned Stan to make** the payments. NOT ~~I warned to make the payments.~~
Still other verbs are followed by an optional noun or pronoun + an infinitive, depending on the meaning of the verb.	• We **expected to finish** on time. • We **expected Jim to finish** on time.

3. Certain **adjectives** can be followed by **infinitives**. These adjectives usually describe people, not things. They often express feelings about the action described in the infinitive.	• George is **afraid to make** mistakes. • Mary is **not willing to help** us.
Common adjectives followed by infinitives: *afraid, amazed, excited, fortunate, glad, happy, important, likely, proud, reluctant, sorry,* and *willing.*	

4. A **noun** is often followed by an **infinitive**. When this occurs, the infinitive gives information about the noun.

A noun + infinitive often expresses advisability or necessity.

- Cozumel is a good **place to spend** a vacation.
- Generosity is a good **trait to have**.
- Starting immediately is the **thing to do**.

5. **BE CAREFUL!** Remember that some verbs can be followed only by infinitives, others only by gerunds, and others by either infinitives or gerunds. These verbs fall into four patterns:

   a. Examples of verbs and verb phrases followed only by infinitives: *appear, decide, expect, hope, manage, need, pretend, seem, want, would like.*

- They **managed to find** new jobs.
- She **pretended to be** busy.

   b. Examples of verbs and verb phrases followed only by gerunds: *avoid, be worth, can't help, consider, enjoy, feel like, have trouble, keep, mind, miss, spend* (time).

- We **considered hiring** him.
- I don't **feel like working** today.

   c. Examples of verbs followed by infinitives or gerunds with no change in meaning: *begin, can't stand, continue, hate, like, love, prefer, start.*

- They **began to encourage** her.
- They **began encouraging** her.

   d. Examples of verbs followed by infinitives or gerunds with a significant change in meaning: *forget, go on, quit, regret, remember, stop, try.*

- I **stopped / quit to go** to the store. (= *I stopped / quit another activity in order to go to the store.*)
- I **stopped / quit going** to the store. (= *I stopped / quit the activity of shopping at the store.*)

6. The words *too* and *enough* are often used before infinitives. *Too* is used in this pattern: *too* + adjective / adverb + infinitive. It implies a negative result.

Enough* + infinitive is used after an adjective / adverb.

Enough* can be used before a noun + infinitive.

Enough* can also be used after a noun. This usage is formal.

NOTE: Add *for* + a noun or pronoun to show who performs the action of the infinitive.

- We're **too tired to do** any work today.
- Sam started **too late to finish** on time.
- Ken is **strong enough to lift** 80 kilos.
- Mia runs **fast enough to be** first.
- There's not **enough money to pay** for the repairs.
- There is not **money enough to pay** for the repairs.
- There's not **enough money for Jane to pay** for the repairs.

(continued)

7. Infinitives can occur in simple or past forms. We use a **simple infinitive** (without a past participle) to indicate an action in the same general time frame as the action in the main verb.

- I **expected** you **to call**.

We use a **past infinitive** (*to* + *have* + past participle) to show an action that occurred before the action of the main verb in the sentence.

- You **seem to have forgotten** the report that was due today.

Infinitives can occur in **passive** form. In the present, use *to* + *be* or *get* + past participle. In the past, use *to* + *have* + *been* + past participle. Use the past form to indicate an action that occurred before the action of the main verb.

- The work is supposed **to be finished** by tomorrow.
- The work was **to have been done** before now.

8. USAGE NOTE: In formal English, it is sometimes considered incorrect to split an infinitive—i.e., to place a word between *to* and the base form of the verb. Place the word before or after the infinitive. In conversation, it is acceptable to split an infinitive.

- NOT *Star Trek* explorers are told ~~to boldly go~~ where no one has gone before.
- *Star Trek* explorers are told **to go boldly** where no one has gone before.

OR

- *Star Trek* explorers are told **boldly to go** where no one has gone before.

To avoid repeating an infinitive just mentioned, simply use *to*. This is called **ellipsis**.

- Steve knew he had to go to work, but he didn't want **to**.

Reference Notes

For a list of **verbs followed directly by infinitives**, see Appendix 14 on page A-7.
For **verbs followed by gerunds or infinitives**, see Unit 15 and Appendices 15 and 16 on page A-8.
For a list of **verbs followed by noun / pronoun + infinitives**, see Appendix 17 on page A-8.
For a list of **adjectives followed by infinitives**, see Appendix 18 on page A-9.

Focused Practice

1 | DISCOVER THE GRAMMAR

A *Read these sentences. Is each underlined infinitive or infinitive phrase used as a subject* **(S),** *an object* **(O),** *or a subject complement* **(SC)?**

_*O*_ 1. I really did plan <u>to ask</u>.

_____ 2. I want <u>to ask</u> you if there's such a thing as . . .

_____ 3. <u>To procrastinate</u> is literally to put things off until tomorrow.

_____ 4. To procrastinate is literally <u>to put</u> things <u>off</u> until tomorrow.

_____ 5. Maybe they don't want <u>to be rejected</u>.

_____ 6. She expects <u>to fail</u>.

_____ 7. The first is never <u>to put off</u> until tomorrow what needs to be done today.

_____ 8. <u>Not to avoid</u> painful or difficult things is the second.

_____ 9. I try <u>to consider</u> everything that comes before me as an opportunity.

B *Look at the pairs of sentences. According to the first sentence in each pair, is the second sentence true* **(T)** *or false* **(F)?** *Circle the correct answer.*

1. I can't stop to type your paper now.
   Ⓣ F   The speaker is not able to stop what he is doing for the purpose of typing the paper.

2. I forgot to, Steve, but I really did plan to ask.
   T F   The speaker doesn't remember asking Steve.

3. Maybe they don't want to be rejected.
   T F   Maybe they're worried about rejecting someone.

4. Maybe they just don't want to be told no.
   T F   Maybe they always want to have yes answers.

5. Her friends no doubt expected her to have called them.
   T F   Her friends probably thought she was going to call them before now.

6. The second piece of advice is not to avoid painful or difficult things.
   T F   The advice is to stay away from painful or difficult things.

2 | MY STRUGGLE WITH PROCRASTINATION *Grammar Notes 2–3*

Complete these sentences with a verb + infinitive or verb + noun / pronoun + infinitive.
Three constructions will contain adjectives as well. If necessary, refer to Appendices 14, 17,
and 18 on pages A-7–A-9 for help in completing this exercise.

I'm basically a procrastinator. I've always _____ *wanted to stop* _____ procrastinating but

1. (want / stop)

never knew how. It started when I was a teenager and I had trouble getting my schoolwork done.

My parents always _____ doing my assignments, but they

2. (warn / not / put off)

_____ my own decisions. I guess they thought it

3. (be willing / allow / make)

_____ the consequences of one's actions, and they never

4. (be important / experience)

_____ at any particular time, so I didn't. I guess I

5. (force / study)

_____ from high school. When I got to college, I

6. (be fortunate / graduate)

_____ my courses by doing things at the last minute, or not doing

7. (expect / pass)

them at all. However, things were different there. There were a hundred students in my history

class, and the professor _____ a term paper. I put it off, of course,

8. (require / write)

and didn't even start it until the day it was due. When I tried to turn it in a week late, the

professor _____ it. That action _____

9. (refuse / accept)   10. (cause / fail)

the course. I asked my counselor what to do, and she _____ the

11. (advise / retake)

course and change my whole attitude toward finishing necessary tasks. She

_____ my assignments without worrying about whether they were

12. (encourage / start)

perfect. I took her advice and, many painful months later, conquered the procrastination demon.

3 | LEAVE IT TO THE KIDS *Grammar Note 7*

Complete the following account with past infinitives. One sentence will be in the passive.

My husband and I took a five-day trip out of town and left the kids in charge. On the morning we

were returning, we called our son and daughter. We expected them _____ *to have cleaned* _____

1. (clean)

the house because we were having dinner guests that evening. When I asked Jennifer about this,

she at first seemed _____ me and quickly changed the subject. I persisted

2. (not / hear)

in the question, and this time Jennifer pretended _____ what I'd said.

3. (not / understand)

"You mean the house needs to be clean tonight?" she said. "Yes," I said. "Did you clean it?"

"Well, sort of. Josh was supposed _____ some cleaning supplies, but I
4. (get)

can't find them anywhere. I did what I could, Mom." "Well, this is important, Jen. We expect you

_____ the cleaning by the time we get home," I said in my firmest voice.
5. (finish)

When we got home, the house appeared _____ by a tornado. The kids
6. (hit)

were nowhere to be found. Dirty dishes were everywhere. Jennifer and Josh appeared

_____ the animals, but they seemed _____
7. (feed)   **8. (not / do)**

anything else. Next time we won't leave things to the kids.

4 | WHAT WOULD YOU EXPECT? *Grammar Note 8*

A *For each item, complete the question with a passive infinitive.*

1. On your second day of a new job, you are an hour late to work. (fire)

   Would you expect _to be fired_ _____?

2. You have a flat tire on a busy freeway. (help / by a passing motorist)

   Would you expect _____?

3. You have put off paying your phone bill for more than two months. (phone service / disconnect)

   Would you expect _____?

4. Your son or daughter has been stopped for speeding. (notify / by the police)

   Would you expect _____?

5. You are going 10 miles over the speed limit. (stop / by a police officer)

   Would you expect _____?

6. Your English term paper was due three days ago. (question / by your teacher)

   Would you expect _____?

B *Now work with a partner. Take turns asking and answering the questions.*

Example: **A:** On your second day of a new job, you are an hour late to work. Would you expect to be fired?

              B: No, I wouldn't expect to be fired. How about you?

5 | TOO MUCH? NOT ENOUGH?
Grammar Note 6

For each situation, write a sentence with **too** *or* **enough** *and an infinitive.*

1. It's 5:15. Jill's flight leaves at 5:45, and it takes 45 minutes to get to the airport. (enough)

  Jill doesn't have enough time to get to the airport.

2. Jack's 10-page report is due in an hour. He types only 25 words a minute. (too)

_____

3. Marcy wants to buy her friend's used car, which costs $5,000. She has $4,000 in the bank and is able to save $400 a month. Her friend must sell the car within three months. (enough)

_____

4. Eve invited guests to dinner. She waited until 6:15 to start preparing the meal. The guests are expected by 7:00. (too)

_____

5. Sally's doctor advised her to eat three meals a day to stay healthy. To lose weight, Sally ate only one small meal a day. She became quite sick. (enough)

_____

6. Carlos is enrolled in an extremely difficult calculus class, but he is a very intelligent man and can pass the course if he applies himself. (enough)

_____

6 | A PERSONAL INVENTORY
Grammar Notes 3–5, 7

Write sentences on these topics, based on your own experience. Use infinitive or gerund structures.

1. _____
(something you stopped doing)

2. _____
(an activity you stopped in order to do something else)

3. _____
(something you remember doing)

4. _____
(something you didn't remember to do)

5. _____
(something you are reluctant to do)

6. _____
(something you have always been afraid to do)

7. _____
(something you feel is wrong for people to do)

8. _____
(something you expected to have happened before now)

9. _____
(a quality that you feel is important to have)

10. _____
(something that you are happy to have experienced [use the past passive])

7 | EDITING

Read this entry from Alice's diary. There are 11 mistakes in the use of infinitives. The first mistake is already corrected. Find and correct 10 more.

I just had to write tonight. Until now I've never had the courage ^to^ do this, but now I do. I've decided to have confronted Sarah about her irresponsibility. This is something that has been bothering me for some time now, but somehow I've always been reluctant force the issue. So here's the situation: Sarah invites people for to do things, but she doesn't follow through. Last week she asked my fiancé, Al, and me have dinner, and she also invited our friends Mark and Debbie. The four of us made plans for go to her house on Friday evening. Something told me I should call Sarah asking what we should bring, and it's a good thing I did. Sarah said, "Dinner? I'm not having dinner tonight. I know I mentioned it as a possibility, but I never settled it with you guys. You misunderstood me." Well, that's just silly. She said planning on it for Friday evening at 7 P.M. When I told the others, they were furious. Al said, "I don't expect being treated like royalty. I do expect to have been treated with consideration." So tomorrow I'm going to call Sarah up and make my point. I'm not going to allow Sarah make my life miserable.

Enough for now. Time for bed.

Communication Practice

8 | LISTENING

🎧 *Listen to the news bulletin. Read the questions. Then listen again. Answer each question in a complete sentence.*

1. How many prisoners are reported to have escaped?

Three prisoners are reported to have escaped.

2. How are they believed to have escaped?

_____

3. By whom are they believed to have been helped?

_____

4. When was the new security system supposed to have been installed?

_____

5. What are the prisoners thought to have?

_____

6. In what direction are they believed to be heading?

_____

7. What are listeners warned not to do?

_____

8. What are they asked to do if they have any information?

_____

9 | GROUP DISCUSSION: PHILOSOPHICAL INFINITIVES

A *Work in small groups. Put each saying in your own words.*

Example: "It is better to light one candle than to curse the darkness."
—*The motto of the Christophers*
It's better to do one small, positive thing than to complain about a problem and do nothing.

1. "To be or not to be, that is the question."—*William Shakespeare*

2. "It is better to die on your feet than to live on your knees."—*attributed to Emiliano Zapata*

3. "To err is human, to forgive divine."—*Alexander Pope*

4. "It is better to seek than to find."—*source unknown*

5. "It is better to have loved and lost than never to have loved at all."—*Alfred, Lord Tennyson*

6. "It is better to arrive late than never to arrive at all."—*source unknown*

B *In your group, discuss the extent to which you believe these sayings are true.*

Example: I basically agree that it is better to light one candle than to curse the darkness. Complaining about a difficult situation doesn't help to solve it.

10 | PICTURE DISCUSSION

Discuss this photo in small groups. What does it show about procrastination? Does it seem to say that procrastination is a bad thing, or perhaps partially a good thing? What would you advise the owner of this desk to do?

Example: **A:** I would advise the owner of this desk to put the desk in order.
              B: I disagree. I'd advise the owner to . . .

11 | WRITING

Most of us have procrastinated at one time or another. Write two or three paragraphs about a time when you put off doing something that needed to be done. Tell about the results. Speculate about the reasons for your procrastination and discuss the consequences.

Example: I've had lots of experiences with putting off things that needed to be done, but one that sticks in my mind is about getting my car tuned up. I was scheduled to go on a cross-country trip, and I knew I needed to take my car in for a tune-up. One thing led to another, though, and I continued to procrastinate. Finally, the day of my departure arrived, and I hadn't had the tune-up done. I said to myself . . .

12 | ON THE INTERNET

*How would you advise someone who wants to conquer procrastination? Do a search on **defeating** or **overcoming** and **procrastination**. Read an article and prepare some advice. Report your suggestions to the class.*

From **Grammar** to **Writing**
Parallelism of Gerunds and Infinitives

Remember that in parallel structure, all items in a series are in the same grammatical form: singulars with singulars, plurals with plurals, actives with actives, passives with passives, and so forth. Parallelism makes our speaking and writing more communicative. Mixing gerunds and infinitives in the same series is a common parallelism error.

Examples

gerund   gerund   gerund

My summer hobbies are **hiking, boating,** and **swimming**.

NOT My summer hobbies are hiking, boating, and ~~to swim~~.

infinitive

When my friend Pam started college, her goals were **to make** new friends and

infinitive
to become well educated.

NOT When my friend Pam started college, her goals were to make new friends and ~~becoming~~ well educated.

A series of infinitive phrases may be presented with the word *to* before each item or before the first item only.

Helen loves **to read, to write,** and **to attend** the opera.

OR Helen loves **to read, write,** and **attend** the opera.

If a sentence is long, it is often best to include the word *to* before each infinitive phrase.

In his sensitivity training at work, Dan learned **to listen** carefully to other people, **to consider** their feelings, and **to imagine** himself in their situations.

Gerunds or gerund phrases containing a possessive and / or *having* + past participle should also be presented in parallel structure.

I want to thank everyone for making this party a success. I especially appreciate **Sarah's having invited** the guests, **Jack's having cooked** the food, and **Jennifer's having organized** the whole thing.

Similarly, long infinitive phrases should be presented in parallel structure.

Applicants to the university are expected **to have completed** a college preparatory program, **to have graduated** in the upper third of their high school class, and **to have participated** in extracurricular activities.

1 | *Each of the following sentences contains an error involving parallelism with gerunds or gerund phrases. Correct the nonparallel items.*

1. Kenneth loves camping, ~~to collect~~ *collecting* stamps, and surfing the Internet.

2. Lately I've been trying to stop speeding in traffic, to schedule too many activities, and rushing through each day like a crazy person.

3. To have a happier family life, we should all focus on eating meals together, on airing our problems and concerns, and on take time to talk to one another.

4. Mr. Mason's planning the agenda, Ms. Bono renting the hall, and Mrs. Tanaka's arranging for the guest speakers made the conference a success.

5. Ken's life is vastly changed because of his having stopped working all the time, joined a singles group, and having met some interesting new friends.

2 | *Each of the following sentences contains an error in parallelism with infinitives or infinitive phrases. Correct the nonparallel items.*

1. On our vacation this year we want to see the Butchart Gardens in Victoria, British Columbia, *to* ^ camp near Great Slave Lake, and to drive up the Alaska Highway to the Yukon.

2. I'm advising you not to sell your property, take out a loan, and not to buy a new house right now.

3. Most presidents want to be reelected to a second term, taken seriously by other world leaders, and to be remembered fondly after they leave office.

4. To be hired in this firm, you are expected to have earned a bachelor's degree and having worked in a bank for at least two years.

3 | *Read the following paragraph about speech anxiety. There are ten mistakes in parallelism with gerunds and infinitives. The first one is already corrected. Find and correct nine more.*

What are you most afraid of? Are you worried about being cheated, ~~to lose~~ *losing* your job, or contracting a deadly disease? Well, if you're like the vast majority of Americans, you fear standing up, to face an audience, and to deliver a speech more than anything else. Surveys have found that anxiety about public speaking terrifies Americans more than dying does. Somehow, people expect to be laughed at, ridiculed, or to be scorned by an audience. Many college students fear public speaking so much that they put off taking a speech class or even to think about it until their last term before graduation. Speech instructors and others familiar with the principles of public speaking stress that the technique of desensitization works best for overcoming speech anxiety. This idea holds that people can get over their fear of speaking in public by enrolling in a course, to attend the class faithfully, and to force themselves to perform the speech activities. Once they have discovered that it is rare for people to die, making fools of themselves, or to be laughed at while making a speech, they're on their way to success. Consequently, their anxiety becomes a little less each time they get up and talk in public. It may take a while, but eventually they find themselves able to stand up willingly, speaking comfortably, and expressing themselves clearly.

4 *Write a paragraph of six or seven sentences on one of these topics:*

- Ways you enjoy spending your leisure time

- Things you like to do

- Things you have difficulty doing

In your paragraph, include examples of parallelism of gerunds, of infinitives, or of both. Then work with a partner. Edit each other's paragraph. Pay particular attention to parallel structures.

VI Review Test

I *Complete the conversations with a gerund or infinitive form of the verb in parentheses. Include both forms if either a gerund or infinitive can be used without a significant change in meaning.*

1. **A:** What do you want _____*to do*_____ tonight?
   a. (do)

   B: I feel like _____ to a movie.
   b. (go)

2. **A:** It's not so bad _____ a white lie, is it?
   a. (tell)

   B: I don't think _____ is ever right.
   b. (lie)

3. **A:** It isn't wrong _____ yourself, is it?
   a. (defend)

   B: I think _____ yourself is the right thing to do if you have a good reason.
   b. (defend)

4. **A:** Why did you decide _____ in forestry?
   a. (major)

   B: I've always loved _____ outdoors. And I've always had trouble
   b. (be)

   _____ desk jobs.
   c. (do)

II *Read the following article about the role of timing in historical events. Fill in the blanks with gerund phrases containing a possessive + past participle. Include* **having** *if necessary.*

Timing Is Everything

Is there such a thing as good or bad timing—an exact moment when events combine, luckily or unluckily, to cause major changes? Apparently there are such moments, though of course the labels *good* and *bad* depend heavily on one's viewpoint.

On August 3, 1492, for example, Christopher Columbus set sail for what would later become known as the New World. _____*His having persuaded*_____ the Spanish monarchs, King
1. (He / persuade)

Ferdinand and Queen Isabella, to sponsor his voyage at a moment when they were willing to help him is a classic example of historical good timing—from the European viewpoint, that is.

Another example of good timing occurred on March 30, 1867, when the United States

purchased Alaska from Russia for $7.2 million as a result of the efforts of Secretary of State

William H. Seward. _____ the potential worth of Alaska
2. (Seward / perceive)

eventually disproved the criticism of his detractors, who called the territory "Seward's Icebox"

and the purchase "Seward's Folly."

A momentous example of good timing occurred on December 5, 1955, in Montgomery,

Alabama, when Rosa Parks, an African-American woman, refused to give up her seat in the

section reserved for white people and to move to the back of a city bus. The U.S. Supreme

_____ school segregation a year and a half previously had set
3. (Court / outlaw)

the stage for the event. _____ not to give up her seat and
4. (Parks / decide)

_____ to back down set in motion the Montgomery Bus
5. (she / refuse)

Boycott, a movement that brought to prominence the pastor of Parks's church, Martin Luther

King, Jr., and immeasurably affected the U.S. civil rights movement.

_____ to make a political trip to Dallas, Texas, on
6. (John F. Kennedy / agree)

November 22, 1963, which turned out to be the day of his assassination, is a tragic example of

bad timing, especially in light of _____ by several advisors not
7. (he / be / warn)

to go to Dallas at that time.

Another example of bad timing occurred in 1968 in Prague, when the brief experiment with

the democratization of the communist regime in Czechoslovakia ended with Warsaw Pact forces

invading the country and dooming the hopes of the reformers.

_____ the determination of the Soviets apparently paved the
8. (The reformers / misjudge)

way for the invasion. In November 1989, however, amid the tide of revolt that was sweeping

Eastern Europe, _____ new elections led to the
9. (protesters / seize the moment / and / demand)

resignation of the communist leadership and to the end of communism in Czechoslovakia—today

the Czech and Slovak Republics. Their timing was certainly right the second time around.

III *Complete the traffic report with gerund or infinitive forms of the verbs in parentheses. Put the verbs in the past, present, or future, as appropriate. Some verb forms need to be in the passive voice.*

You'll have trouble _____*commuting*_____ this afternoon, folks. Interstate 5 is blocked for two
　　　　　　　　　　1.(commute)

miles north and south of 80th Street, so I suggest _____ an alternate route if
　　　　　　　　　　　　　　　　　　　　　　　　2.(use)

possible. Construction on the Factoria interchange has caused _____ on I-405, so
　　　　　　　　　　　　　　　　　　　　　　　　　　　　3.(slow)

use caution there. Repairs on the Evergreen Point Bridge were expected _____ by
　　　　　　　　　　　　　　　　　　　　　　　　　　　　　　　　　4.(complete)

6:00 A.M. today, but the bridge is still closed. The Highway Department issued a statement

apologizing for _____ further inconvenience to motorists, but the fix is taking
　　　　　　　　5.(cause)

longer than planned. Repairs are expected _____ by 5:00 A.M. Tuesday. Meanwhile,
　　　　　　　　　　　　　　　　　　　　　6.(finish)

an accident involving an overturned van in the left lane on the westbound 509 freeway isn't

expected _____ for at least half an hour, so avoid _____ the 509. You
　　　　　7.(clear)　　　　　　　　　　　　　　　　　　　　　　　**8.(take)**

can improve your commute by _____ to Highway 99, where traffic is smooth and
　　　　　　　　　　　　　　9.(switch)

relatively light. This is Hank Simmons for KQRS Traffic Watch.

IV *Complete the conversations, using ellipsis. Make the verbs negative if necessary.*

1. A: Why didn't Alex and Anna come to the party?

　B: They _____*were going to*_____, but they got called to the hospital.
　　　　　　　　　(be going)

2. A: Wasn't Gabe going to bring hot dogs to the picnic?

　B: He _____, but I don't see any. I don't think he did.
　　　　　　(be supposed)

3. A: Are you going to attend the university?

　B: I'm _____, but I have to earn some money first.
　　　　　　　(plan)

4. A: Doesn't Amanda know how to cook?

　B: She _____. She's worked in a restaurant for more than a year.
　　　　　　　(ought)

5. A: Why didn't you type my paper? It's due tomorrow!

　B: I _____. I had my own work to do.
　　　　(have time)

6. A: Aren't you going to buy that house?

　B: No, I _____, after all. It doesn't have a view.
　　　　　　(want)

V *Describe a day in the life of Alice Matthews. Fill in the blanks with an appropriate gerund or infinitive. Include both forms if either a gerund or infinitive can be used.*

1. Alice Matthews enjoys

_____*taking*_____ the bus to work. It

gives her the chance _____.

2. She avoids _____ because

of the heavy traffic. This also keeps her

from _____ too stressed.

3. Alice starts _____ at

9:00 A.M.

4. Unfortunately, she has trouble

_____ awake in meetings.

5. Alice stops _____ at

5:00 P.M.

6. She usually spends her evenings

_____.

VI *Circle the letter of the choice that correctly completes each sentence.*

1. We are in favor of _____ the bridge.   A Ⓑ C D
   (**A**) build   (**C**) to build
   (**B**) building   (**D**) having built

2. I asked Juanita _____ the proposal.   A B C D
   (**A**) review   (**C**) to review
   (**B**) reviewing   (**D**) having reviewed

3. "Bob, can you type my paper?" "I don't have time _____ right now."   A B C D
   (**A**) to   (**C**) to doing
   (**B**) to do   (**D**) to have done

4. _____ my lifestyle is the best thing I ever did.   A B C D
   (**A**) My having changed   (**C**) Me having changed
   (**B**) Having changing   (**D**) My change

5. You're expected _____ well prepared for a job interview.   A B C D
   (**A**) be   (**C**) being
   (**B**) to be   (**D**) having been

6. "The report was supposed _____ completed by March 1. What happened?"   A B C D
   (**A**) being   (**C**) have been
   (**B**) be   (**D**) to have been

7. The sign warned pedestrians _____ on the grass.   A B C D
   (**A**) not walking   (**C**) not walk
   (**B**) not to walk   (**D**) not to have walked

8. Ms. Francis is said _____ the article.   A B C D
   (**A**) to write   (**C**) to have written
   (**B**) writing   (**D**) write

9. When the teacher asked the students _____, they kept making noise.   A B C D
   (**A**) stop talking   (**C**) stopped to talk
   (**B**) to stop to talk   (**D**) to stop talking

10. Harriet remembered _____ the door earlier that morning, but she couldn't find her key.   A B C D
    (**A**) to have locked   (**C**) locking
    (**B**) lock   (**D**) having been locked

▶ *To check your answers, go to the Answer Key on page RT-4.*

PART VII

Adverbs

17 Adverbs: Functions, Types, Placement, and Meaning

Grammar in Context

BEFORE YOU READ

1 *How do you feel about military service? Should it be required, or should it be voluntary?*

2 *What is your opinion of women in military service? Should women participate in combat?*

Read or listen to this transcript of a radio call-in show.

Time to Sound Off
Show #267

McGAFFEY: Good evening, and welcome to *Sound Off*, the international talk show where you express your unrestricted opinions on today's controversial issues. I'm Mike McGaffey. Tonight's topic is military service. Should military service be required or voluntary? A related issue that has recently become controversial is whether women should join the military, and if they do, should they fight alongside men in combat? Let's see if we can shed some light on these issues. Give me a call and we'll talk. All right, here we go with our first caller, Jerry Burns, from Kingston, Jamaica. Go ahead, Jerry. Where do you stand?

BURNS: Hi, Mike. Basically, I think service should be voluntary. And I'm definitely not in favor of women being in combat.

McGAFFEY: OK. Let's take those one at a time. Why do you think military service ought to be voluntary? Why shouldn't it be required of everyone?

Time to Sound Off

BURNS: Mainly because young people are not all made the same. Some people have a military orientation. For them, military service is fine. But others aren't oriented that way. Compulsory military service interferes with their freedom, essentially.

McGAFFEY: But many people argue that we all owe our country something. The country protects us and provides us benefits. Shouldn't we give something in return?

BURNS: We should if we're motivated to do so. But it shouldn't be an obligation. And I'd go even further: A lot of evil things have been done by military forces. Maybe we shouldn't even have them.

McGAFFEY: Hmmm. I don't know, Jerry—I'm a pretty accepting guy, but even I find that suggestion extreme. But let's go to your second point. Why do you believe women shouldn't be in combat?

BURNS: Well, men and women are clearly different. Women just aren't suited for combat. I want to keep men as men and women as women. If women are serving in combat, they're just like men. There goes the difference between the sexes.

McGAFFEY: Are you saying that women are too weak, that only men are strong enough? That's an old stereotype, isn't it?

BURNS: No, I'm not saying that at all. I don't think fighting is feminine.

McGAFFEY: Wow. All right, Jerry, very interesting. I expect we'll hear some pretty spirited responses to what you've said. Our next caller is Sarah Lopez from Toronto, Canada. Go ahead, Sarah. What do you think about Jerry's comments? Is he on target, or is this just fuzzy thinking?

LOPEZ: Thanks, Mike. Actually, I couldn't disagree more with what your first caller said. It's not a question of fuzzy thinking at all. He made his point clearly, but I just don't agree with him.

McGAFFEY: OK. So you disagree with his statement about military service being voluntary?

LOPEZ: Yes, I do. If we're going to have military service, I think it needs to be required.

McGAFFEY: Why?

LOPEZ: Because that's the only way to ensure fair treatment for all. People in the military make major sacrifices—sometimes they have to risk their lives. That kind of risk should be spread out more evenly. Actually, I'd go further: I'd support required national service. It wouldn't have to be only military.

McGAFFEY: Expand a bit on that.

LOPEZ: Well, there are lots of worthwhile things that all citizens can do for their country. At the top of the list are service jobs like working in day-care centers or hospitals. Some could work in agencies like the U.S. Peace Corps and similar groups in other countries. National service has been started in a few countries, and it will hopefully be adopted in a lot more.

(continued)

Time to Sound Off

McGAFFEY: All right. Let's go to Jerry's other point. He's against women in combat. What's your position? Should it be allowed?

LOPEZ: Not only should it be allowed, but it should also be promoted. And I should know: I'm in the military now and have been for a year and a half.

McGAFFEY: You have?

LOPEZ: Yes, and I totally disagree with the way Jerry characterizes women. No way is combat nonfeminine!

McGAFFEY: Have you ever been in combat?

LOPEZ: I haven't been, but I know women who have. And if I'm ever called to combat, I'll go willingly. Most women wouldn't agree with Jerry's statement about maintaining the difference between the sexes. Neither do I. Women can be in combat and still be feminine.

McGAFFEY: OK, Sarah. Thanks for your comments. Let's see where we can go with this. Our next caller is from Singapore. Here's Lu Adijojo. Lu, what's your view?

AFTER YOU READ

*Look at the pairs of sentences. According to the first sentence in each pair, is the second sentence true (**T**) or false (**F**)? Circle the correct answer.*

1. I'm a pretty accepting guy, but even I find that suggestion extreme.

   T F   The speaker accepts most suggestions, but probably not this one.

2. He made his point clearly, but I just don't agree with him.

   T F   The speaker not only agrees with him but supports his idea.

3. National service has been started in a few countries, and it will hopefully be adopted in a lot more.

   T F   The speaker doesn't want national service to be adopted in other countries.

Grammar Presentation

ADVERBS: FUNCTIONS, TYPES, PLACEMENT, AND MEANING

Adverb Functions	
TO MODIFY VERBS	The topic **often** causes controversy.
TO MODIFY ADJECTIVES	The topic is **extremely** controversial.
TO MODIFY OTHER ADVERBS	He treated the topic **very** fairly.
TO MODIFY ENTIRE SENTENCES	**Unfortunately**, the topic is controversial.

Adverb Types	
MANNER	Some think he presents issues **dishonestly**.
TIME	Miliary service for women has become controversial **recently**.
PLACE	The director found a new position **there**.
FREQUENCY	The program's subjects are **often** unpopular.

Sentence Adverbs: Placement	
BEGINNING	**Clearly**, these are bitter controversies.
MIDDLE	These are **clearly** bitter controversies.
END	These are bitter controversies, **clearly**.

Focus Adverbs: Placement and Meaning				
They	**just** don't	support what he says.		They think he's wrong.
	don't **just**			They agree with him 100%.
Even	she	can do	that.	Anyone can do that task.
She	can do	**even**	that.	It's amazing how many things she can do.
Only	men	can	participate.	Women can't.
Men	can	**only**		They can't do anything else.

Negative Adverbs: Placement and Inversion			
We	**rarely**	agree	on such things.
Rarely	do we		
I have	**seldom**	heard	that idea.
Seldom	have I		
They	**never**	disagreed	with him.
Never	did they	disagree	

Adverbs and Adverbials		
	Adverbs	Adverbials
The participants came	**here**.	
		downtown.
The debate was broadcast	**recently**.	
		this morning.
Everyone talked	**excitedly**.	
		with enthusiasm.

GRAMMAR NOTES	**EXAMPLES**

---

1. Adverbs modify verbs, adjectives, and other adverbs.

- He learns **quickly**.
- Jenny has a **really** challenging job.
- She does **very** well at her job.

Adverbs indicate how, when, where, or how often things happen.

Adverbs of

a. manner indicate how

b. time indicate when

c. place indicate where

d. frequency indicate how often

- He speaks **clearly**.
- We arrived **yesterday**.
- They are staying **here**.
- She **usually** works late.

---

2. Adverbs of manner usually follow the verb and any object present. Common adverbs of manner are *angrily, carefully, carelessly, cautiously, clearly, happily,* and *thoughtfully*.

- He **replied cautiously**.
- She **answered the question thoughtfully**.

Adverbs of time normally follow the verb and any object or complement. Common adverbs of time are *later, next, now, soon, then, today, tomorrow,* and *yesterday*.

- We'll **call soon**.
- Jack **bought the gift today**.

Adverbs of place usually follow the verb and any object. Common adverbs of place are *along, away, back, down, here, there,* and *up*.

- They **live there**.
- I **sent the package back**.

Adverbs of frequency normally occur after *be* and before other verbs. Common adverbs of frequency are *always, never, normally, occasionally, often, rarely, seldom, sometimes,* and *usually*.

- She **is usually** on time.
- He **occasionally arrives** early.

Occasionally, often, sometimes, and *usually* can also occur at the beginning, middle, or end of a sentence with no change in meaning.

- **Sometimes** she disagrees with me.
- She **sometimes** disagrees with me.
- She disagrees with me **sometimes**.

---

3. Some adverbs modify entire sentences. These are called **sentence adverbs** (also called viewpoint adverbs) because they express an opinion about an entire sentence. Common sentence adverbs are *actually, basically, certainly, clearly, fortunately, hopefully, mainly, obviously, maybe, perhaps,* and *surely*.

- He is **clearly** a very good speaker. (*a sentence adverb that modifies the entire idea; = it is clear that he is a very good speaker*)
- He speaks **clearly**. (*not a sentence adverb—a manner adverb that modifies* speaks)

You can use sentence adverbs in various places in a sentence. If the adverb comes first or last in a sentence, it is separated from the rest of the sentence by a comma.

- **Basically**, I'm in favor of that.
- I'm **basically** in favor of that.
- I'm in favor of that, **basically**.

4. Focus adverbs* focus attention on a word or phrase. These adverbs usually precede the word or phrase focused on. Common focus adverbs are *almost*, *even*, *just*, and *only*.

NOTE: Changing the position of a focus adverb often changes the meaning of the sentence.

NOTE: In spoken English, the word you are focusing on is stressed.

- **Even I** believe that. (*focuses on* I)
- I believe **even that**. (*focuses on* that)

- **Only teenagers** can attend. (*focuses on* teenagers—*they are the only ones allowed to attend.*)
- Teenagers can **only attend**. (*focuses on* attend—*they're not allowed to participate.*)
- **Only** TEENAGERS can attend.
- Teenagers can **only** ATTEND.

---

5. Negative adverbs include *hardly*, *in no way* (informal, *no way*), *little*, *neither*, *never*, *not only*, *only*, *rarely*, and *seldom*. When negative adverbs come at the beginning of a sentence, they force inversion. In sentences or clauses beginning with a negative adverb, put the verb or auxiliary before the subject to emphasize the negative meaning.

If the verb is in the simple present or simple past (except for the verb *be*), use *do*, *does*, or *did* after an initial negative adverb.

If the verb is in perfect form, place the auxiliary before the subject.

NOTE: Sentences beginning with *neither* are common in both formal and informal English. Sentences beginning with other negative adverbs are usually formal.

- **Women are** required to serve in the military **only in Israel**.
- **Only in Israel are women** required to serve in the military.
- **He is seldom** on time.
- **Seldom is he** on time.

- **Rarely do** people **make** a career of the military.

- **Never had I heard** such a strange idea.

- My grandfather didn't join the military. **Neither** did my father.
- **Seldom** have women served in combat. (*formal*)

---

6. Other adverbs that force inversion when they come at the beginning of a sentence are *here* and *there*.

▶ BE CAREFUL! Invert the subject and verb only if the subject is a noun. Don't invert them if it's a pronoun.

- **Here is your money**.
- **There goes the bus**.

- **Here is my report**.
- **Here it is**.
  NOT ~~Here is it.~~

(continued)

---

*The author wishes to acknowledge L. G. Alexander regarding the term *focus adverb* (*Longman Advanced Grammar, Reference and Practice*, New York: Longman Publishing, 1993).

> **7. Adverbials** are words and phrases that modify verbs, adjectives, or other adverbs in the same way that single adverbs do. These include nouns, noun phrases, and prepositional phrases. They normally come at the end of a clause.
>
> - They went **downtown** and then **home**. *(adverbial use of nouns showing place)*
> - I called **this afternoon**. *(noun phrase showing time)*
> - They arrived **by bus**. *(prepositional phrase showing manner)*

Reference Note
For a list of **sentence adverbs**, see Appendix 19 on page A-9.

Focused Practice

1 | DISCOVER THE GRAMMAR

A *Look at the underlined adverbs in these sentences. Classify them as sentence adverbs (**S**), negative adverbs (**N**), focus adverbs (**F**), adverbs of manner (**M**), or adverbs of time (**T**).*

___T___ **1.** A related issue that has <u>recently</u> become controversial is whether women should join the military.

_____ **2.** <u>Basically</u>, I think service should be voluntary.

_____ **3.** <u>Mainly</u> because young people are not all made the same.

_____ **4.** I'm a pretty accepting guy, but <u>even</u> I find that suggestion extreme.

_____ **5.** Men and women are <u>clearly</u> different.

_____ **6.** He made his point <u>clearly</u>.

_____ **7.** I <u>just</u> don't agree with him.

_____ **8.** That kind of risk should be spread out more <u>evenly</u>.

_____ **9.** <u>Not only</u> should it be allowed, but it should also be promoted.

_____ **10.** Have you <u>ever</u> been in combat?

B *Read the following sentences. Could they be rewritten as shown without changing the meaning or creating an incorrect sentence? Write* **Y** *(yes) or* **N** *(no).*

__Y__ **1.** Basically, I think service should be voluntary. (I think service should be voluntary, basically.)

_____ **2.** I'm a pretty accepting guy, but even I find that suggestion extreme. (. . . but I even find that suggestion extreme).

_____ **3.** Men and women are clearly different. (Clearly, men and women are different.)

_____ **4.** He made his point clearly. (Clearly, he made his point.)

_____ **5.** But I just don't agree with him. (But I don't just agree with him.)

_____ **6.** It will hopefully be adopted in a lot more. (It will be adopted in a lot more, hopefully.)

_____ **7.** No way is combat nonfeminine for women. (No way combat is nonfeminine for women.)

_____ **8.** And if I'm ever called to combat. I'll go willingly. (Willingly, if I'm ever called to combat, I'll go.)

C *Look again at the reading. Find and underline the six sentences where adverbs force inversion of the subject and the verb or auxiliary.*

---

2 | THINGS YOU MIGHT HEAR ON A TALK SHOW   *Grammar Note 3*

Read these pairs of sentences that you might hear on a radio talk show. Combine each pair into one sentence with a sentence adverb. Make sure that the sentence adverbs appear at least once in each position: beginning, middle, and end.

1. National service is beneficial. This is obvious.

Obviously, national service is beneficial. / National service is obviously beneficial. / National service is beneficial, obviously.

2. Military service can be dangerous. That's unfortunate.

3. I'm against the death penalty. The essential reason for this is that I consider it cruel and unusual punishment.

4. There's a lot more violence in movies than in the past. This is certain.

5. Nuclear weapons can be eliminated. I hope this is the case.

6. A vaccine against AIDS can be found. This is possible.

7. The prime minister's position is wrong. It's clear.

8. There's increasing opposition to people's owning SUVs. This is the actual situation.

3 | OPINIONS ABOUT CONTROVERSIAL ISSUES

Grammar Note 4

Complete each sentence with the choice containing the correctly used focus adverb. Circle the letter of the correct answer.

1. Bill supports women in the military, but he feels _____ in noncombat roles.

   (a.) they should only serve   b. only they should serve

2. Carrie supports required military service for both sexes, but she feels _____ in combat.

   a. men should serve only   b. only men should serve

3. Samantha is against gambling, but _____ the benefits of lotteries.

   a. even she can recognize   b. she can even recognize

4. I'm in favor of higher taxes. _____ taxing food and medicine.

   a. Even I'm in favor of   b. I'm even in favor of

5. Charles _____ every environmental cause—except for removing dams.

   a. is in favor of almost   b. is almost in favor of

6. You _____ that idea, but I still have two questions.

   a. have persuaded me to almost support   b. have almost persuaded me to support

7. My husband has some good reasons for supporting nuclear power. However, I _____ with his reasoning.

   a. don't just agree   b. just don't agree

8. My father _____ the military draft; he's a military recruiter.

   a. doesn't just support   b. just doesn't support

4 | CURRENT ISSUES

Grammar Note 5

Read the statements about current issues. Modify one sentence in each pair by adding a negative adverb from the box to the beginning of the sentence. Some of the adverbs may be used more than once. In all but one case, the second sentence will be modified. Make all necessary changes.

in no way	neither	never	not only	rarely

1. I don't support the government's policy on taxation. My friends don't support the government's policy.

   I don't support the government's policy on taxation. Neither do my friends.

2. There are many women in the military. Women fight alongside men in combat.

   _____

3. Some uninformed people oppose the military. Military service is useless.

   _____

4. Violence won't ever be completely eliminated. Poverty won't be completely eliminated.

_____

5. We need to stop global warming. We also need to find new energy sources.

_____

6. I bought an SUV. It had occurred to me that SUVs could harm the environment, but I learned they could.

_____

5 | ARGUMENTATIVE STATEMENTS   *Grammar Notes 3–6*

Complete each sentence by arranging the words in the correct order. Use correct punctuation.

1. brother / conservative / support / Even / my / doesn't / power / nuclear

   Even my conservative brother doesn't support nuclear power.

2. people / are / Seldom / treated / homeless / kindly

   _____

3. soon / service / will / Hopefully / national / established / be

   _____

4. arguments / cloning / humans / Here / my / of / are / against / the

   _____

5. can't / think / reason / one / even / I / him / support / to / of

   _____

6. cloning / basically / I'm / favor / in / not / of

   _____

7. policies / like / just / her / I / don't / support / I / strongly/ them

   _____;_____

8. way / hunting / do / In / support / I / no

   _____

6 | AROUND THE WORLD

Grammar Notes 3–5

Study the chart. Complete the sentences with the adverbs **even**, **just**, **only in**, *or* **not only . . . but also**, *and a form of the verbs in parentheses.*

Country	Has a military	Military service required	Allows women to serve in the military	Requires women to serve in the military	Allows women to serve in combat
BRAZIL	X		X		X
CANADA	X		X		X
COSTA RICA					
ISRAEL	X	X	X	X	
SWITZERLAND	X	X			
THE UNITED STATES	X		X		X
VENEZUELA	X		X		X

Here are some facts about military service worldwide.

1. _____Only in_____ Costa Rica _____is there_____ no military.
   (there / be)

2. Though it is officially a neutral country, _____ Switzerland _____
   (have)

   a military.

3. _____ Israel and Switzerland _____.
   (military service / require)

4. _____ do Brazil, Canada, the United States, and Venezuela allow women to

   serve in the military, _____ them to serve in combat.
   (they / allow)

5. Women _____ to serve in combat in these four countries.
   (not / require)

6. _____ Israel _____ to do military service.
   (women / require)

7 | EDITING

There are ten mistakes in the use of adverbs in the following letter. The first mistake is already corrected. Find and correct nine more.

Dear Dad,

    I'm sitting in the train station, waiting for the 5:25 to get here, so ~~just I~~ *I just* thought I'd drop you a quick note. I've been attending the conference on reducing global warming. Actually, I almost didn't get to go to the conference because almost we didn't get our taxes done on time. Vicky and I stayed up until midnight last night, though, and I mailed the forms this morning.

    I hate income taxes! Only once in the last ten years we have gotten a refund, and this time the tax return was so complicated that Vicky got even upset, and you know how calm she is. Maybe we should move to Antarctica or something. No taxes there.

    Besides that, we've been having a few problems with Donna. It's probably nothing more serious than teenage rebellion, but whenever we try to lay down the law, she gets defensive. Rarely if ever she takes criticism well. The other night she and her friend stayed out until 1 A.M.—this was the second time in two weeks—and when we asked her what they'd been doing she said, "Just we were talking and listening to dance music at the Teen Club. Why can't you leave me alone?" Then she stomped out of the room. Fortunately, Sam and Toby have been behaving like angels—but they're not teenagers!

    Meanwhile, Donna's school has started a new open-campus policy. Students can leave the campus whenever they don't have a class. Even they don't have to tell the school office where they're going and when they'll be back. No way Vicky and I do approve of that policy. School time, in our view, is for studying and learning, not for socializing. Little those school officials realize how much trouble teenagers can get into whenever they're roaming around unsupervised.

    Well, Dad, here the train comes. I'll sign off now. Write soon.

                Love,

                Ken

Communication Practice

8 | LISTENING

🎧 *Read these questions. Listen to the next part of the radio call-in show. Then listen again and circle the letter of the correct answer.*

1. The caller listens to the radio show _____.

   ⓐ only once a week   **b.** only twice a week

2. The caller likes the program _____.

   a. a lot   **b.** somewhat

3. The caller is basically closer to the viewpoint of _____.

   a. the man from Jamaica   **b.** the woman from Canada

4. The caller doesn't totally disagree with _____.

   a. the man   **b.** the woman

5. The caller thinks it _____ right for women to go into combat.

   a. is   **b.** isn't

6. The caller thinks combat _____ advisable for mothers.

   a. is   **b.** isn't

7. The caller thinks pro-military people _____ support the idea of women in combat.

   a. do   **b.** don't

8. The caller thinks national service _____ basically a great idea.

   a. is   **b.** isn't

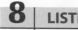

9 | WRITING

A *Work in small groups. Choose a controversial topic that might be discussed on a TV or radio call-in show. Brainstorm and write down points supporting both sides of the issue. Choose from the topics in the box or select your own topic.*

capital punishment	electric vs. gas-powered cars	helping the homeless
higher / lower taxes	universal health care	women in combat

Examples: Nuclear power should be phased out.
Nuclear power should be expanded.
Nuclear power should be allowed on a limited basis.

B *Write three or four paragraphs on a controversial topic. Do research on your topic outside of class or on the Internet. You can use one of the topics in Part A or select a topic of your own. Be objective: Support your view with specifics, but also touch on points opposite to your view. Try to use at least two viewpoint adverbs, two focus adverbs, and two negative adverbs in your essay.*

Example: Nuclear power has been used for at least the past 40 years, and there are certainly some advantages to it. Some countries, for example, have few natural resources that can be used for power. Also, there have been no nuclear disasters in most of the countries where nuclear power is used. However, I feel that nuclear power should be phased out all over the world. It's just too dangerous . . .

10 | ON THE INTERNET

C *Write down two questions about controversial topics to which you would like answers. Then do a search to find answers to these questions. Report your findings to the class.*

Examples: In what countries in the world is capital punishment legal?
How many countries in the world participate in whaling?

Grammar in Context

BEFORE YOU READ

1 *What is your view of sports? Is it basically positive, negative, or somewhere in between?*

2 *What are some benefits of sports? What are some negative aspects of them?*

🎧 *Read this editorial about sports.*

EDITORIAL
ARE SPORTS STILL SPORTING?
by Buck Jacobs

As I was watching the Olympics the other night, a commentator mentioned several new "sports." I couldn't believe my ears when he said bowling, roller skating, tug-of-war, ballroom dancing, and chess have been proposed for future Olympic games. Chess? Ballroom dancing? We've already reached depths of silliness with badminton and synchronized swimming. Where will it stop? Will video gaming and skateboarding be recognized by the time the 2008 Beijing Olympics start? Now don't get me wrong. I'm one of the original sports fans; the first thing I read after I get up in the morning is the sports page. But the

Roller Skating

commentator's remarks made me think about the whole sports arena. Are we on the wrong track? Has our approach to sports become excessive? I've concluded that the whole sports scene is in need of repair.

When the Olympic games started about 2,700 years ago in Greece, the contests held were basically those related to war. For example, the javelin throw paralleled the throwing of a spear in a battle; running paralleled the physical exertion you might have to make if an enemy was chasing you. When the modern Olympic games started in 1896, the philosophy had moved 180

EDITORIAL: **ARE SPORTS STILL SPORTING?**

degrees. The modern Olympics were designed to promote peace. Emphasis was placed on demonstrating physical stamina and excellence in challenging contests.

How things have changed in recent years. Although athletes still try to achieve their personal best, the emphasis has shifted away from the individual pursuit of excellence to the breaking of records and the achievement of fame. Can we really say that someone who finishes the 400-meter swim one-tenth of a second ahead of his or her nearest rival is a champion, while that rival is an also-ran? And since there are ever-increasing possibilities for product endorsement, I can't help thinking that money is playing a major role.

The excesses of the Olympics started me thinking about some of the other excesses in sports. Consider the cost of attending a major athletic competition, for example. In the United States, the average cost of a ticket to a National Football League game in 2004 was about $53. If you added to that the cost of parking and eating, the cost was up to at least $75. A ticket to an NBA basketball game is similar in price. Baseball is cheaper, though it's not really a bargain at an average ticket cost of $25. For a moment I wondered why tickets have gotten so expensive until I remembered the key factor in the equation: players' salaries. Basketball star Shaquille O'Neal earns between $27 and $31 million a year. Baseball player Alex Rodriguez makes at least $25 million yearly. Is anyone worth that much money? The president of the

Tug-of-War

United States, in contrast, earns only $400,000 a year. Schoolteachers in the United States make an average of about $45,000 a year. Who is more valuable to society, a basketball player or a schoolteacher? What we pay people says a lot about what we value in society.

This led me to ponder another excess—violence. We see it wherever we look, and it's certainly not decreasing. Fights occur frequently in professional sports, with ice hockey one of the worst offenders. In the 2003–2004 season, for instance, player Steve Moore had to be hospitalized because another player hit him in the head and seriously injured him. However, there seems to be increasing acceptance of violence as "just part of the game." Once we accept violence as inevitable, it will be almost impossible to stop. This sort of thing doesn't just happen in North America, either. We've all heard about the well-publicized violence surrounding soccer games in Europe.

No, somehow sports have gone off course. They have become big business entertainment, with money the underlying governing principle. What can we do about this? One thing is to pay more attention to local, small-time athletics and events like the Special Olympics, in which disabled people get a chance to show what they can do. We need to refuse to pay ridiculously high ticket costs. We need to demand an end to violence. And above all we need to get back to this idea: It's not whether you win or lose; it's how you play the game.

AFTER YOU READ

*Look at each pair of sentences. Does the second sentence mean about the same as the first? Circle yes (**Y**) or no (**N**).*

1. Will video gaming be recognized by the time the 2008 Beijing Olympics start?

    Y   N   Will this sport be recognized before the start of the 2008 Olympics?

2. Although athletes still try to achieve their personal best, the emphasis has shifted to the breaking of records.

    Y   N   Because athletes are trying to achieve their personal best, the emphasis is now on the breaking of records.

3. Once we accept violence as inevitable, it will be almost impossible to stop.

    Y   N   We won't be able to stop violence as soon as we think it's inevitable.

Grammar Presentation

ADVERB CLAUSES

PLACEMENT AND PUNCTUATION

Main Clause	Adverb Clause
We watched TV a lot	**when the Olympics were on.**
Tickets cost more	**because athletes earn so much.**

Adverb Clause	Main Clause
When the Olympics were on,	we watched TV a lot.
Because athletes earn so much,	tickets cost more.

TYPES

Adverb Clauses of Time	
Before I played basketball,	I was a soccer player.
The coach met with her players	**after the game was over.**
While the team was on the field,	the fans cheered continuously.

Adverb Clauses of Place	
I've seen children playing soccer	**everywhere I've been outside the U.S.**
Anywhere you go,	sports stars are national heroes.
I work out at a gym	**wherever I travel.**

Adverb Clauses of Reason	
Since she plays well,	I want her on our team.
He was unable to play in the final game	**as he had hurt his ankle.**
Now that television covers the games,	billions of people can see the Olympics.

Adverb Clauses of Condition	
Unless the tickets cost too much,	we'll go to the game next Saturday.
You'll be comfortable inside the dome	**even if it's cold and raining outside.**
Only if she wins the gold medal	will she get a professional contract.

Adverb Clauses of Contrast	
They won the game,	**though they didn't really deserve the victory.**
Although their team is talented,	they just didn't win.
Swimmers are rarely injured,	**whereas hockey players are often hurt.**

GRAMMAR NOTES

EXAMPLES

1. A **clause** is a group of words that contains at least one subject and a verb showing past, present, or future time. Clauses are either independent or dependent.

   Independent clauses (also called main clauses) can stand alone as complete sentences.

   Dependent clauses (also called subordinate clauses) cannot stand alone. They *do* need another clause to be fully understood.

   Sentences containing both an independent clause and a dependent clause are called **complex sentences**. In a complex sentence, the main idea is in the independent clause.

   NOTE: In a complex sentence, the clauses can come in either order. If the dependent clause comes first, we place a comma after it.

   - **You could win a medal.**
   - **We'll go to the game.**

        independent clause   dependent clause
   - You could win a medal **if you practice enough**.

        dep. clause   indep. clause (main idea)
   - **If we can get tickets**, we'll go to the game.

   - **Whenever I exercise**, I feel good.
   - I feel good **whenever I exercise**.

(continued)

2. Adverb clauses are dependent clauses that indicate how, when, where, why, or under what conditions things happen; or they introduce a contrast.

Adverb clauses begin with **subordinating conjunctions** (also called subordinating adverbs), which can be either single words or phrases.

NOTE: Adverb clauses sometimes come inside independent clauses.

- I went home **when the game was over**.
- She dropped out of the race **because she was injured**.
- We won't win **unless we try harder**.
- It began to rain **while we were playing**.
- I have to practice a lot **now that I'm on the team**.
- Her ability **when she got to high school** was remarkable.

---

3. Adverb clauses of time indicate when something happens. They are introduced by *after, as, as soon as, before, by the time, once, since, until / till, when, whenever, while,* etc.

NOTE: *Until* and *till* have the same meaning. *Till* is informal and used more in conversation.

▶ **BE CAREFUL!** In complex sentences, do not use *will* and *be going to* in the dependent clause to show future time.

- The race will start **as soon as everyone is in place**.
- We always drink water **before we start a game**.
- I'll wait here **until / till they arrive**.
- We'll leave **when they get here**.
  NOT We'll leave when they ~~will~~ get here.

---

4. Adverb clauses of place indicate where something happens. They are introduced by *anywhere, everywhere, where, wherever,* etc.

- Professional sports are played **where there are big stadiums**.
- Major athletes are popular **wherever they go**.

---

5. Adverb clauses of reason indicate why something happens. They are introduced by *as, because, now that* (= because now), *since,* etc.

NOTE: *Since* is used both in adverb clauses of reason and of time.

NOTE: *As* is used both in adverb clauses of time and of reason.

- She won the medal **because she had practiced tirelessly**.
- **Since he didn't register in time**, he can't play.
- **Since Nan doesn't like sports**, she refused to go to the game. (*reason*—since = because)
- Barry has played sports **since he entered high school**. (*time*—since = starting from that point)
- He set a world record **as we were watching**. (*time*—as = while)
- **As he was badly hurt**, he had to drop out of the game. (*reason*—as = because)

6. Adverb clauses of condition indicate under what conditions something happens. They are introduced by *even if, if, only if, unless,* etc.

Even if means that the condition does not matter; the result will be the same.

Only if means that only one condition will produce the result.

Unless means *if . . . not . . .*

NOTE: If the sentence begins with *only if,* the subject and verb of the main clause are inverted, and no comma is used.

▶ **BE CAREFUL!** Don't confuse *even if* or *even though* and *even*.

- You'll improve **if you practice daily**.

- **Even if he practices constantly**, he won't make the team.

- Betty will make the team **only if another athlete drops out**.

- **Unless you train a great deal**, you won't be a champion.

- **Only if** another athlete drops out **will Betty** make the team.

- **Even if** they win this game, they won't be the champions.

- **Even** my mother understands the rules of baseball.

---

7. Adverb clauses of contrast make a contrast with the idea expressed in the independent clause. They are introduced by *although, even though, though, whereas, while,* etc.

We usually use *although, even though,* and *though* when we want to show an unexpected result.

To make a direct contrast, we use *while* or *whereas*.

USAGE NOTE: *Whereas* is used in formal written English and careful speech.

NOTE: *While* is used to introduce both a clause of contrast and a clause of time.

- He lost the race **although he was favored**.
- **Even though she is tall**, she doesn't score much.
- **Although / Even though / Though he is quite young**, he was selected for the team.
- **While / Whereas downhill skiing is very expensive**, cross-country skiing is cheap.

- **While they lost the game**, they played their best. *(contrast)*
- We ate **while we were watching the game**. *(time)*

Reference Notes
For a list of **subordinating conjunctions**, see Appendix 20 on page A-9.
For more practice on **future time clauses**, see Unit 1.

Focused Practice

1 | DISCOVER THE GRAMMAR

A *Look at paragraph 1 of the opening reading. Underline the four adverb clauses in the paragraph.*

B *Look at paragraph 3. Underline the three adverb clauses in the paragraph.*

C *In each of the following sentences, underline the dependent clause once and the independent clause twice. Then write* **contrast, where, when,** *or* **under what conditions** *above the dependent clauses.*

1. <u><u>Will video gaming and skateboarding be recognized</u></u> <u>by the time the 2008 Beijing Olympics</u> *when*
   <u>start</u>?

2. When the Olympic games started about 2,700 years ago in Greece, the contests held were basically those related to war.

3. Although athletes still try to achieve their personal best, the emphasis has shifted away from the individual pursuit of excellence.

4. If you added to that the cost of parking and eating, the cost was up to at least $75.

5. We see it wherever we look.

2 | THE NAME OF THE GAME
Grammar Notes 3, 5–7

Rearrange the words to make sentences, each containing an adverb clause. Add necessary punctuation. Then match the sentences with the names of the sports in the box.

American football	baseball	basketball	ice hockey
the marathon	~~skiing~~	soccer	tennis

1. ticket / can / to / Before / lift / buy / a / you / you / have / start

   Before you can start, you have to buy a lift ticket. (skiing)

2. player's / love / zero / If / score / the / one / forty / is / is / score

   _____

3. puck / unless / can't / You / you / ice / have / game / skates / a / and / this / play

   _____

4. free-throw / line / You / after / you've / go / the / to / fouled / been

   _____

5. use / head / hands / Though / may / you / you / your / your / use / can't

_____

6. kilometers / You've / you've / 42.2 / course / finished / run / the / when

_____

7. bat / until / Your / team / team / can't / outs / three / makes / the / other

_____

8. touchdown / scores / If / team / your / earns / points / a / it / six

_____

3 | SOME FACTS ABOUT THE OLYMPICS   Grammar Notes 3, 5–6

Combine each pair of sentences into one sentence containing an adverb clause and a main clause. Keep the clauses in the same order. Add necessary punctuation.

1. There are some similarities between the ancient and modern Olympics. There are also many differences.

   Though / Although / While / Even though there are some similarities between the ancient and

   modern Olympics, there are also many differences.

2. Greek city-states were often at war with one another. Olympic contestants stopped fighting during the games.

   _____

   _____

3. The ancient Olympic games were outlawed by the Roman Emperor Theodosius I. They had been held for over 1,000 years.

   _____

   _____

4. He outlawed them in A.D. 393. Romans thought the Greeks wore too few clothes.

   _____

   _____

5. French educator Pierre de Coubertin revived the Olympics. He thought they would promote international peace.

   _____

   _____

6. Tug-of-war was dropped from the Olympics in 1920. American and British athletes disagreed about how it should be played.

   _____

   _____

(continued)

7. New Olympic sports often first appear as demonstration events. They are adopted as medal sports.

_____

_____

8. Any sport can potentially become a medal event. It can be scored and fulfills certain criteria.

_____

_____

4 | EXTREME SPORTS *Grammar Notes 3–7*

Read this excerpt from an article about extreme sports. Then answer the questions.

When Sports Become Too Extreme
by Alex Salkever

While some of the best professional big-wave surfers in the world looked out over 40-foot waves crashing onto the shore of Oahu's Waimea Bay, the decision seemed disappointingly clear. The Quiksilver Invitation surfing competition had to be canceled. The waves were just too big.

But on that same late-January day, relatively unknown big-wave rider Greg Russ had to be physically restrained by lifeguards from launching out into the biggest surf in more than a decade. The guards were interfering with his right to make money, he said.

The incentive: $50,000 from the surf-equipment manufacturer K2 to anyone who can ride the biggest wave of the year and get it on film.

From ice climbing to mountain biking to big-wave surfing, more people are becoming extreme athletes, putting their lives in danger for the ultimate thrill. But the K2 contest, and the growing popularity of extreme sports worldwide, has raised questions about the financial and human consequences for athletes and the rescuers who watch over them. For many, the incident at Waimea perfectly illustrates the dangers unleashed when big money, big egos, and big challenges are mixed.

Although exact figures on how many extreme athletes exist are hard to come by, isolated statistical evidence points to a rapid increase. For example, the number of climbers attempting to climb Alaska's 20,300-foot Mt. McKinley—the tallest peak in North America—increased from 695 in 1984 to 1,110 in 1997.

"It's a numbers deal, and clearly there are more people getting hurt than there were when I started doing rescues 20 years ago," says Dan Burnett, a mission coordinator with the all-volunteer Summit County Search and Rescue Group in Colorado. "We're responding in areas now that even four years ago I would have thought we didn't need to check because nobody goes there."

Some strides have been made toward creating a safer extreme-sports world. Three years ago, Denali National Park in Alaska, for instance, instituted a mandatory $150 fee for climbers seeking to ascend Mt. McKinley. The fee pays for an educational program that park rangers credit with dramatically reducing the number of search-and-rescue missions and fatalities.

1. Find the adverb clause in paragraph 1. What subordinating conjunction could replace the conjunction that begins the clause while keeping the basic meaning?

   As some of the best professional big-wave surfers in the world looked out over 40-foot waves

   crashing onto the shore of Oahu's Waimea Bay (while)

2. Combine the last two sentences in paragraph 1 into one sentence containing an adverb clause and an independent clause. _____

   _____

3. Read paragraph 2. Complete this sentence in your own words: Big-wave rider Greg Russ had to be physically restrained by lifeguards because_____

   _____

4. Read paragraph 3. Complete this sentence with an adverb clause showing under what conditions: You'll get $50,000 from the surf-equipment manufacturer if _____

   _____

5. Look at the first sentence in paragraph 4. Complete this sentence in your own words: More people are becoming extreme athletes and putting their lives in danger because_____

   _____

6. Underline the adverb clause in paragraph 5. What three subordinating conjunctions could replace the conjunction that begins that clause? _____

   _____

7. Read paragraph 6. Underline the first adverb clause. If you replace the subordinating conjunction with *whenever,* will the sentence still make sense? _____

   _____

8. Underline the second adverb clause in paragraph 6. What two subordinating conjunctions could replace the conjunction that begins this clause? _____

   _____

9. Read paragraph 7. Complete this sentence: Because _____

   _____,

   the number of search-and-rescue missions and fatalities has been reduced.

5 | MOMENTS IN SPORTS

Look at the pictures. Complete the sentence describing each picture with an adverb clause.
Use a different subordinating conjunction in each clause.

1. The Sharks will win the game _____
(condition)

_____

_____

2. The other team can't win _____
(condition)

_____

_____

3. _____
(contrast)

_____

_____, their fans still love them.

4. The players are doing their best _____
(contrast)

_____

_____

5. _____
(reason)

_____

_____, the competition was postponed.

6. The competition won't be held _____
(time)

_____

_____ improve.

6 | A PERSONAL INVENTORY: MY FUTURE

Write sentences with adverb clauses about your possible future, using the subordinating conjunctions in parentheses. Place the dependent clause first in half of the sentences.

Example: When I'm rich, I'll sleep on a soft pillow.

1. (when) _____

_____

2. (if) _____

_____

3. (unless) _____

_____

4. (in case) _____

_____

5. (because) _____

_____

6. (after) _____

_____

7. (as soon as) _____

_____

8. (once) _____

_____

9. (before) _____

_____

10. (although) _____

_____

7 | EDITING

Read this student essay. There are ten mistakes in the use of adverb clauses, including incorrect subordinating conjunctions. The first mistake is already corrected. Find and correct nine more.

Why Sports?

by Jamal Jefferson

A lot of people are criticizing school sports these days. Some say there's too much emphasis on football and basketball, ~~if~~ *while* there's not enough emphasis on education. Others say the idea of the scholar-athlete is a joke. Still others say sports provide a way of encouraging violence. I think they're all wrong. If anything, school sports help prevent violence, not encourage it. Why do I think sports are a positive force?

For one thing, sports are positive even though they give students opportunities to be involved in something. Every day on TV we hear that violence is increasing. I think a lot of people get involved in crime when they won't have enough to do to keep themselves busy. After you'll play two or three hours of basketball, baseball, or any other kind of sport, it's hard to commit a violent act even you want to.

Second, sports teach people a lot of worthwhile things, especially at the high school level. If they play on a team, students learn to get along and work with others. Wherever their team wins, they learn how to be good winners; when their team will lose, they find out they have to struggle to improve. They discover that winning a few and losing a few are part of the normal ups and downs of life. Also, there's no doubt that students improve their physical condition by participating in sports.

Finally, sports are positive although they allow students who do not have enough money to go to college to get sports scholarships and improve their chances for a successful life. Whereas a young basketball player from a small village in Nigeria can get a scholarship to play for say, UCLA, he will have a chance to get an education and probably make his life better. Wherever a young woman with little money is accepted on the University of Toronto swim team and gets a scholarship, she'll have the chance to earn a college degree and go on to a high-paying job. Because school sports programs have some deficiencies that need to be corrected, their benefits outweigh their disadvantages. I should know because I'm one of those students. School sports must stay.

Communication Practice

8 | LISTENING

🎧 *Read these questions. Listen to the interview with a sports star. Then listen again and answer each question in a complete sentence with an adverb clause.*

1. Why did Lillian Swanson become successful?

   Lillian Swanson became successful because her parents loved and supported her.

2. When did Lillian learn to swim?

   _____

3. Why does Lillian think she became a good swimmer?

   _____

4. Why did Lillian and her family spend a lot of time at the beach?

   _____

5. What did Lillian decide when she was 12?

   _____

6. Under what conditions did Lillian's parents agree to pay for lessons?

   _____

7. When did Lillian get discouraged?

   _____

8. Why can't Lillian imagine herself doing anything else?

   _____

9. What happened once Lillian started her lessons?

   _____

9 | GROUP DISCUSSION

Reread the article "When Sports Become Too Extreme" on page 318. Form small groups and discuss these questions. Report your conclusions to the entire class. Then discuss the questions as a class.

- Should there be laws preventing extreme athletes from putting their own lives in danger?
- Should companies be prevented from offering athletes money to do things that endanger their lives?
- Who should pay for the costs of rescuing extreme athletes who get into trouble?

10 | PICTURE DISCUSSION

Work in pairs. Discuss what is happening here. In your view, how does this picture reflect sports in the world today? Have sports everywhere become too violent, or is this sort of behavior just "part of the game"?

11 | WRITING

Choose one of the following topics and write three or four paragraphs about it. If possible, support your ideas with examples from your personal experience.

- Sports are valuable to society because they provide entertainment.

- Sports have become too violent.

- Sports provide opportunities to people who have few other opportunities.

- Sports stars earn ridiculously large salaries.

Example: Many people say that sports are overemphasized in our culture. My opinion, however, is that the advantages of sports outweigh their disadvantages. In particular, I strongly believe that sports provide opportunities to people who don't have many other opportunities. Consider the inner-city boy, for example, whose parents can't afford to send him to college, even though he's a good student. One of my best friends falls into this category. He . . .

12 | ON THE INTERNET

Form small groups. Use the Internet outside of class to develop a sports knowledge game to be played in class. Each team writes five sports-based questions. Play in teams and score points.

Example: **A:** When David Beckham moved to this team, he probably disappointed Manchester United fans. What team was it?
B: Real Madrid.

Grammar in Context

BEFORE YOU READ

1 *What is your definition of compassion?*

2 *How important a value is compassion in society?*

🎧 *Read this article about compassion.*

Compassion

*I*t was the evening of September 29, 1994. Having spent a wonderful day exploring the ruins at Paestum in southern Italy, Reg and Maggie Green were driving south in the area of Italy known as the boot, their children Nicholas and Eleanor sleeping peacefully in the back seat. Suddenly an old, broken-down car pulled up alongside them, and an Italian with a bandanna over his face screamed at them, signaling them to stop. Not knowing what to do, Reg carefully weighed the options. If they stopped, they risked a potentially deadly confrontation with criminals; if they sped away, they might escape. Guessing that their newer-model car could probably get away from the old car the criminals were driving, Reg floored the gas pedal. Shots rang out, shattering both windows on the driver's side of the car. The Greens' car took off, easily outdistancing the bandits' car. Checking the children, Reg and Maggie found them still sleeping peacefully in the back seat.

Compassion

A bit farther down the road, Reg saw a police car parked on the shoulder and pulled over to alert the authorities. Upon opening the door, he saw blood oozing from the back of Nicholas's head. After being rushed to a hospital, Nicholas lay in a coma for two days. Then doctors declared him brain-dead.

This was not the end of the story, however. As Nicholas lay on his deathbed, Reg and Maggie decided that something good ought to come out of the situation. Realizing that it would be far better to return good for evil than to seek revenge, they offered Nicholas's organs for transplant. "Someone should have the future he lost," Reg said. Profoundly moved by the gesture, Italians poured out their emotions. Maurizio Costanzo, the host of a talk show, summed up the common feeling by saying, "You have given us a lesson in civility . . . shown us how to react in the face of pain and sorrow."

The great irony of this tragedy was that it was a mistake. Investigators later determined that Nicholas was killed by two small-time criminals who thought the Greens were jewelers carrying precious stones. They were placed on trial after being turned over to the police.

People all over Europe and North America reacted in sorrow. Headlines in Italian newspapers spoke of *La Nostra Vergogna* ("Our Shame"). Wherever the Greens went, they met Italians who begged their forgiveness. The Greens were given a medal, Italy's highest honor, by the prime minister.

Some good has indeed come out of Nicholas's death. Seven Italians received Nicholas's heart, liver, kidneys, islet cells (cells related to diabetes), and corneas. Perhaps more importantly, a blow was struck for organ donation. Having heard Reg and Maggie speak on French television, 40,000 French people pledged to donate their organs when they died. After returning to the United States, the Greens began to receive requests to tell their son's story and speak about organ donation. "It gradually dawned on us," said Reg, "that we'd been given a life's work."

Nicholas Green is gone, but others live on because of his parents' compassionate act. How many of us would do the same thing, given the chance?

AFTER YOU READ

*Read the pairs of sentences. According to the first sentence in each pair, is the second sentence (true) **T** or (false) **F**?*

1. Reg and Maggie Green were driving south, their children Nicholas and Eleanor sleeping peacefully in the back seat.

   T F   The children were sleeping while their parents were driving.

2. An Italian with a bandanna over his face screamed at them, signaling them to stop.

   T F   The screaming and the signaling took place at the same general time.

3. Having heard Reg and Maggie speak on television, 40,000 French people pledged to donate their organs when they died.

   T F   Many French people decided to donate their organs before they heard Reg and Maggie speak on television.

Grammar Presentation

ADVERB AND ADVERBIAL PHRASES

REDUCING ADVERB CLAUSES OF TIME TO ADVERB PHRASES

Adverb Clause		Adverb Phrase	
While they were in Italy,	they had trouble.	**While in Italy,**	they had trouble.
While I was in Italy,		Ø*	
When I am traveling,	I keep a journal.	**When traveling,**	I keep a journal.
When Sue is traveling,		Ø	

*Ø = no change possible

CHANGING ADVERB CLAUSES OF TIME TO ADVERB PHRASES

Adverb Clause		Adverb Phrase	
Before we left,	we visited Rome.	**Before leaving,**	we visited Rome.
Before Ann left,		Ø	
After they (had) investigated,	the police identified the killers.	**After investigating,**	the police identified the killers.
		After having investigated,	
When they saw Reg speak,	many Italians were moved.	**On / Upon seeing Reg speak,**	many Italians were moved.

CHANGING ADVERB CLAUSES OF TIME TO ADVERBIAL PHRASES

Adverb Clause		Adverbial Phrase	
While they waited at the hospital,	they were deeply troubled.	**Waiting at the hospital,**	they were deeply troubled.
After they heard the news,	they decided what to do.	**Hearing the news,**	they decided what to do.

CHANGING ADVERB CLAUSES OF REASON TO ADVERBIAL PHRASES

Adverb Clause		Adverbial Phrase	
As he saw the guns,	he chose to flee.	**Seeing the guns,**	he chose to flee.
Because they were unable to catch him,	the pursuers fired several shots.	**Being unable to catch him,**	the pursuers fired several shots.
Because I've been to Bari,	I hope to return.	**Having been to Bari,**	I hope to return.
Because I'd been to Bari,	I hoped to return.		I hoped to return.
Since they were accused by the police,	they had to appear in court.	**Accused by the police,**	they had to appear in court.

GRAMMAR NOTES

EXAMPLES

1. Remember that a **clause** is a group of words with a subject and a verb that shows time. A **phrase** does not have the subject and verb that a clause has but commonly has a present or past participle.

> clause
- **After he sped away**, he heard a shot.

> phrase
- **After speeding away**, he heard a shot.

Some **adverb clauses** can be shortened to **adverb phrases** in ways similar to the ways adjective clauses can be shortened: by **reducing** the clauses or by **changing** them.

> adverb clause
- We had a flat tire **while we were touring**.

> adverb phrase (reduced)
- We had a flat tire **while touring**.

> adverb clause
- **After we fixed the flat tire**, we were on our way again.

> adverb phrase (changed)
- **After fixing the flat tire**, we were on our way again.

Negative adverb phrases contain the word *not* or *never* before the participle.

- After **not eating** all day, we were very hungry.

---

2. Some **adverb clauses** can be **reduced to adverb phrases** when the clause has a form of *be*. To reduce an adverb clause to a phrase, omit the subject pronoun and the form of *be*. If the original sentence has commas, keep the commas in the reduced sentence.

> adverb clause
- **While they were driving**, they were attacked by bandits.

> adverb phrase
- **While driving**, they were attacked by bandits.

▶ **BE CAREFUL!** You can reduce an adverb clause to an adverb phrase only if the subjects in both clauses of the sentence refer to the same person or thing.

- **Reg and Maggie** drove while **the children** were sleeping.

  NOT ~~Reg and Maggie drove while sleeping.~~

NOTE: An adverb phrase can come first or second in the sentence. When it comes first, we usually place a comma after it.

- **While driving**, they were attacked by bandits.

---

3. **Adverb clauses of time** beginning with *after*, *before*, *since*, and *while* can be **changed to adverb phrases** when the clause has no form of *be*. To change an adverb clause to a phrase, omit the subject pronoun and change the verb to its *-ing* form. Keep the subordinating conjunction and the original punctuation.

> adverb clause
- **After they visited Paestum**, the Greens drove south.

> adverb phrase
- **After visiting Paestum**, the Greens drove south.

▶ **BE CAREFUL!** You can change an adverb clause to a phrase only if the subjects in the two clauses of the sentence refer to the same person or thing.

- After **the bandits** saw the Greens' car, **the Greens** sped away.

  NOT ~~After seeing the Greens' car, the Greens sped away.~~

(continued)

4. A simple past or past perfect verb in an adverb clause changes to the *-ing* form or to *having* + past participle in an adverb phrase.	• After they **(had) opened** the door, they saw the blood. • After **opening** the door, they saw the blood. OR • After **having opened** the door, they saw the blood.

5. *Upon* or *on* + *-ing* in an adverb phrase usually has the same meaning as *when* in an adverb clause.	adverb phrase • **Upon / On realizing** what had happened, they pulled to the side of the road. adverb clause • **When they realized** what had happened, they pulled to the side of the road.

6. The **subordinating conjunction** is sometimes omitted in a phrase. A phrase without a subordinating conjunction is called an **adverbial phrase**.	adverb phrase • **While sitting on the porch**, I thought about my future. adverbial phrase • **Sitting on the porch**, I thought about my future.

7. Adverb clauses of reason can be **changed to adverbial phrases.** The subordinating conjunctions *because*, *since*, or *as* at the beginning of the clause are omitted in the phrase.	adverb clause • **Because / Since / As the children were sleeping in the car**, they were not aware of what was happening. adverbial phrase • **Sleeping in the car**, the children were not aware of what was happening.
Because / Since / As + a form of *be* can be changed to *being* in an adverbial phrase.	• **Because / Since / As** they **were** not satisfied, they decided to do something about the problem. • Not **being** satisfied, they decided to do something about the problem.
A present perfect or past perfect verb in an adverb clause can be changed to *having* + past participle in an adverbial phrase.	• Because they **had been** moved by the situation, people became organ donors. • **Having been** moved by the situation, people became organ donors.

8. **A clause containing a passive verb** can be **changed to an adverbial phrase with just a past participle**. If the subordinating conjunction can be omitted without changing the meaning, delete the subject and any auxiliaries in the passive sentence.

▶ **BE CAREFUL!** If the subordinating conjunction cannot be omitted without changing the meaning, as in some clauses of time, form an adverb phrase by deleting the subject and changing the form of *be* to *being*.

- **Since I was given two options**, I chose the harder of the two.
- **Given two options**, I chose the harder of the two.

- **Before I was told** the nature of the problem, I had no idea what to do.
- **Before being told** the nature of the problem, I had no idea what to do.

  NOT ~~Told the nature of the problem, I had no idea what to do~~.

Reference Notes

For more information and practice on **shortening adverb clauses** and on **sentence combining**, see From Grammar to Writing for Part VII.

For **shortening adjective clauses to adjective phrases**, see Unit 12.

Focused Practice

1 | DISCOVER THE GRAMMAR

A *In the opening reading, find the four adverb phrases with a subordinating conjunction and write them here.*

1. _____

2. _____

3. _____

4. _____

B *Find the two adverbial phrases with* **having** + *past participle and write them here.*

1. _____

2. _____

C *Read these sentences. Is the second sentence a correct rewriting of the first? Circle* **Y** *(yes) or* **N** *(no).*

1. Having spent a wonderful day exploring the ruins at Paestum, Reg and Maggie Green were driving south.

   Y (N) Spending a wonderful day exploring the ruins at Paestum, Reg and Maggie Green were driving south.

2. An Italian with a bandanna over his face screamed at them, signaling them to stop.

   Y   N   An Italian with a bandanna over his face screamed at them while signaling them to stop.

(continued)

3. Not knowing what to do, Reg carefully weighed the options.

    Y N   Because he didn't know what to do, Reg carefully weighed the options.

4. Shots rang out, shattering both windows on the driver's side of the car.

    Y N   Having shattered both windows on the driver's side of the car, shots rang out.

5. The Greens' car took off, easily outdistancing the bandits' car.

    Y N   Having outdistanced the bandits' car, the Green's car took off.

6. Upon opening the door, he saw blood oozing from the back of Nicholas's head.

    Y N   When he opened the door, he saw blood oozing from the back of Nicholas's head.

7. After being rushed to a hospital, Nicholas lay in a coma for two days.

    Y N   After he was rushed to a hospital, Nicholas lay in a coma for two days.

8. How many of us would do the same thing, given the chance?

    Y N   How many of us would do the same thing if we were given the chance?

2 | SHORTENING

Grammar Notes 1–3

*Read these sentences. For each item, circle the subjects and connect the circles. If the subjects refer to the same person or thing, make one sentence and then shorten the sentence by reducing or changing the adverb clause to a phrase. If the subjects are different, write **cannot be shortened**.*

1. When a broken-down car pulled alongside their car, an Italian with a bandanna over his face screamed at them.

    cannot be shortened

2. Reg carefully considered the options before he sped away.

    _____

3. Because the criminals were a deadly threat, Reg floored the gas pedal.

    _____

4. When Reg saw a police car parked on the shoulder, he pulled over to alert the authorities.

    _____

5. As Nicholas lay on his deathbed, Reg and Maggie decided that something good ought to come out of the situation.

    _____

6. Because the criminals thought the Greens had precious stones, they fired shots that killed Nicholas.

    _____

3 | **DO ANIMALS SHOW GRIEF?** *Grammar Notes 2–8*

A *Read this article about an apparently grieving animal.*

A Caring Elephant That Died of Grief

By Sutapa Mukerjee, The Associated Press

LUCKNOW, India. Distressed by a companion's death, Damini refused to move, to eat, to drink. For 24 days, zookeepers and veterinarians tried everything they could think of to save an elephant who seemed determined to die.

Despite all their efforts, Damini died yesterday in her enclosure. After she had suffered for so long, loose gray skin hung over her protruding bones, and bedsores covered much of her body.

Zoo officials said Damini was 72. She came to the zoo last year after she was taken from owners who were illegally transporting her. She was alone for five months until the arrival in September of a pregnant younger elephant named Champakali.

Champakali came from Dudhwa National Park, where she had worked carrying around tourists. When she became pregnant, park officials decided to send her to the zoo in Lucknow for a kind of maternity leave.

The two elephants "became inseparable in no time," said the zookeeper. Damini made herself available at all hours for Champakali, who seemed to love the attention.

"Elephants are very social animals. They can form very close bonds with others in their social group," said Pat Thomas, curator of mammals at the Bronx Zoo in New York City. "It's been pretty well documented that they do exhibit emotions that we would consider grieving" when a calf or other elephant dies.

However, he said, an age-related medical problem should not be discounted as well in the case of an elephant as old as Damini.

On April 11, giving birth to a stillborn calf, Champakali died. Damini seemed to shed tears, then showed little interest in food or anything else, according to zoo officials.

For days, Damini stood still in her enclosure, barely nibbling at the two tons of sugarcane, bananas, and grass heaped in front of her.

Her legs soon swelled up and eventually gave way. After that, Damini lay still on her side, head and ears drooping, trunk curled. Tears rolled down her eyes, and the four-ton elephant rapidly lost weight.

A week ago, Damini completely stopped eating or drinking her usual daily quota of 40 gallons of water, despite the 116-degree heat.

Alarmed, veterinarians pumped more than 25 gallons of glucose, saline, and vitamins through a vein in her ear.

Yesterday, Damini died.

"It will take me some time to get over the death of my two loved ones," her keeper said.

B *Refer to the article and follow the instructions.*

1. Rewrite the adverbial phrase in the first sentence of the article as an adverb clause.

   Because Damini was distressed by a companion's death,

2. Read the original and revised sentences. Is the revised sentence correct?

   Original: After she had suffered for so long, loose gray skin hung over her protruding bones, and bedsores covered much of her body.

   Revised: After suffering for so long, loose gray skin hung over her protruding bones, and bedsores covered much of her body.

   _____ yes _____ no

3. Rewrite this sentence; change the adverb clause to an adverb phrase.

   She came to the zoo last year after she was taken from owners.

   _____

4. Read the original and revised sentences. Is the revised sentence correct?

   Original: When she became pregnant, park officials decided to send her to the zoo in Lucknow.

   Revised: Becoming pregnant, park officials decided to send her to the zoo in Lucknow.

   _____ yes _____ no

5. Read the original and combined sentences. Is the combined sentence correct?

   Original: Elephants are very social animals. They can form very close bonds with others in their social group.

   Combined sentence: Being very social animals, elephants can form very close bonds with others in their social group.

   _____ yes _____ no

6. Rewrite the adverbial phrase as an adverb phrase by adding a subordinating conjunction.

   On April 11, giving birth to a stillborn calf, Champakali died.

   _____

7. Rewrite this sentence as two independent clauses.

   Damini stood still in her enclosure, barely nibbling at the two tons of food in front of her.

   _____

4 | **ENTERPRISE**

Look at the pictures. Write a sentence with an adverb or adverbial phrase and a main clause to describe each situation. Use the prompts.

1.

(present participle)

Coming out of the train station, the
tourists saw a boy selling guidebooks.

2.

(present participle)

_____

_____

3.

(*not* + present participle)

_____

_____

4.

(past participle)

_____

_____

(continued)

5.

(present participle)

_____

_____

6.

(_having_ + past participle)

_____

_____

7.

(_after_ + present participle)

_____

_____

8.

(_having_ + past participle)

_____

_____

5 | EDITING

The following magazine article has not been proofread. It contains ten mistakes involving the use of adverb and adverbial phrases. The first mistake is already corrected. Find and correct nine more.

A Helping Hand

by Jim Lamoureaux

If you're at all like me, you tire of requests to help others. ~~Hitting~~ *Hit* by seemingly constant appeals for money to support homeless shelters, the Special Olympics, or the like, I tend to tune out, my brain numbed. I don't think I'm selfish. But subjecting to so many requests, I only remember the flashy ones. By being argued that I don't have enough money to help others, I am able to ignore the requests. Or at least that was the way I saw the situation before sent by my magazine to South America to do a human interest story on homeless children. Having hearing many TV requests asking viewers to sponsor a child overseas, I always said to myself, "I'll bet the money is pocketed by some local politician." My opinion changed when I saw the reality of the life of a poor child.

While landing in Santa Simona, I took a taxi to my hotel in the center of town, where I met Elena, a girl of 10 or 11. Sat on a dirty blanket on the sidewalk in front of the hotel, she caught my eye. Elena was trying to earn a living by selling mangoes. Smiling at me, she asked, "Mangos, señor? –Mangoes, sir?" I bought some mangoes and some other fruit, and we talked together. Elena's life had been difficult. Her parents were both dead, and she lived with an elderly aunt. Having polio at the age of five, she now walked with a limp. She and her aunt often went hungry.

Investigated the question the next day, I talked to several different authorities. Having convinced that money from sponsors does in fact get to those who need it, I knew my attitude had to change. Learning that I could sponsor Elena for less than a dollar a day, I began to feel ashamed; after all, I spend more than that on my dogs. But what remains most vivid in my mind is my vision of Elena. She didn't beg or feel sorry for herself. Selling her mangoes, she earned a living, and her spirit shone through in the process. So I say to all of you reading this: The next time you hear an ad about sponsoring a child, pay attention.

Communication Practice

6 | LISTENING

 *Read the questions. Listen to the news broadcast. Then answer each question in a complete sentence.*

1. When asked whether he would attend next week's peace conference, did rebel leader Amalde commit himself?

   No, he declined to commit himself.
   _____

2. According to Mr. Amalde, how could Mr. Tintor demonstrate good faith?

   _____

3. Did the president's aide speak on or off the record?

   _____

4. What did researchers from the Global Health Foundation acknowledge?

   _____

5. How is the new nation to be known?

   _____

6. What will it need in order to become a viable state?

   _____

7. Why had Michaels almost given up hope of being rescued?

   _____

8. How did Hutchinson save him?

   _____

7 | GROUP DISCUSSION

Review the article "A Caring Elephant That Died of Grief" on page 333. In small groups, discuss these questions. Share your answers with the class.

1. Compare animals and humans in regard to showing emotion. Do you think animals are capable of grief or any other kind of emotion?

2. Give a personal example of an animal showing grief or another emotion.

   Example: A: I don't think animals show emotion.
   B: I disagree.
   A: Why?
   B: My aunt died last year. Her dog . . .

8 | WRITING

Write three or four paragraphs about an act you have witnessed that you believe qualifies as compassionate. Describe the situation fully. What made the act compassionate? Did the compassionate person have anything to gain from showing compassion?

Example: Perhaps the best example of compassion I have witnessed occurred about a year ago. Having attended an office party, I finally managed to leave about 10:00 P.M. Driving home on a major expressway, I suddenly felt the car slow down and heard a grinding noise. Realizing that I probably had a flat tire, I quickly pulled over to the side of the road. I looked for the jack to change the flat but couldn't find it. I thought about calling my brother but couldn't find my cell phone, either. Just then a group of teenagers slowed down and stopped . . .

9 | ON THE INTERNET

Do an Internet search. Find and read an article about another example of organ donation. Use the key words **transplantation and organ donation** *in your search. Report what you learn to the class.*

Grammar in Context

BEFORE YOU READ

1 *What is your earliest memory?*

2 *What are methods that help you to remember things?*

⌒ *Read this article about memory.*

TRY TO • • • • • • • • • • • •
REMEMBER
• • • • • • • • • • • • by Helen Giuliani

Have you ever had this experience? You're with a friend, and suddenly up walks somebody you've known for a long time. You want to introduce this person to your friend. However, just as you say, "Nancy, I'd like you to meet . . . ," your mind goes blank, and you can't remember the person's name. It's embarrassing and maybe a little worrisome. I wouldn't be too concerned, though, for it's also very common. As we get older, we tend to become more forgetful, especially of things we've experienced recently.

How does memory work, and what can we do to improve it? I was worried about memory loss on my part; therefore, I decided to do some research into the problem. Here's what I learned.

First, let's distinguish between two types of memory, long-term and short-term. Long-term memory refers to things that we experienced a considerable time ago and that form the core of our knowledge of ourselves. Short-term memory can be called "working" memory—the type we use in everyday activity. It is involved in processing such things as phone numbers, names of new people we meet, and e-mail addresses. As we grow older, our long-term memory holds up remarkably well. Thus, we are able to remember the vacation we took at the age of 10 to Everglades National Park and the alligators we saw there. Meanwhile, things have been happening to our short-term memory. It, in contrast, doesn't hold up as well as our long-term memory does.

TRY TO REMEMBER ··

Because of this, we may have difficulty remembering people's names right after we meet them or remembering someone's phone number we've heard only twice. Memory problems are generally short-term memory problems.

Second, let's look a little at the physical side of the memory process. The frontal lobes of the brain are the area where short-term memory operations occur. As we age, these lobes tend to lose mass, as much as 5 to 10 percent per decade. However, there are things we can do to slow memory decline. Maintaining a steady supply of glucose can lessen the problem of shrinking lobes. Consequently, elderly people would do well to eat several small meals each day rather than two or three big ones. There is evidence, moreover, that staying mentally active can help prevent memory deterioration.

Another interesting aspect of memory involves the many materials on the market designed to help us remember things better. Do they work? Well, yes and no. All memory courses, books, audiotapes, or whatever, depend on the creation of a peg, or mental picture, on which to hang something we want to recollect. Suppose, for example, that you have difficulty, as most of us do,

There are things we can do to slow memory decline.

remembering names. Let's say, for instance, that you're at a party and are introduced to a man named Terry Baer. You look at him. He has long, thick hair, rather like that of a bear. Baer = bear. Furthermore, the first syllable of "Terry" rhymes with "bear." Ter and Baer. It might work. The point is that you need to create a mental picture that you can relate to the person, place, or thing you want to recall. The more vivid the association is, the greater is the chance that you'll remember it.

There is one particularly important point in all this: Memory improvement takes work. If we think carefully about our own involvement in remembering things, we may realize that the real problem is usually not an inability to remember something we learned earlier but the fact that we weren't paying enough attention when we learned it. Think about the last time you were introduced to someone whose name you immediately forgot. Were you really paying attention to the person's name? Or were you, instead, focusing on yourself and the impression you might be making? Memory courses can work, of course, but they depend on techniques that we can create and perform for ourselves. The real trick lies in our willingness to tap what's within us and to work on using it.

AFTER YOU READ

What does each sentence mean? Circle the letter of the correct choice.

1. I wouldn't be too concerned, though, for it's also very common.

   a. But I wouldn't be too concerned about this, since it's common.

   b. And I wouldn't be too concerned about this, since it's common.

2. I was worried about memory loss; therefore, I decided to do some research.

   a. Because of this, I decided to do research.

   b. In spite of this, I decided to do research.

(continued)

3. Meanwhile, things have been happening to our short-term memory.

   a. Because of this, our short-term memory has been affected.

   b. During this time, our short-term memory has been affected.

Grammar Presentation

CONNECTORS

Connectors: Placement and Punctuation	
Type of Connector	**Examples**
Coordinating Conjunction	I was worried, **so** I did some research.
Subordinating Conjunction	**Because** I was worried, I did some research.
	I did some research **because** I was worried.
Transition	I was worried. **Therefore**, I did some research.
	I was worried. I, **therefore**, did some research.
	I was worried. I did some research, **therefore**.

Connectors: Functions			
Function	**Coordinating Conjunctions**	**Subordinating Conjunctions**	**Transitions**
Addition	and, nor, or		besides, furthermore, indeed, in addition, moreover
Condition	or	if, even if, only if, unless	otherwise
Contrast	but, or, yet	although, though, even though, whereas, while	however, nevertheless, nonetheless, on the contrary, on the other hand
Cause / Reason	for	as, because, since	
Effect / Result	so		consequently, otherwise, therefore, thus
Time		after, before, when, while	afterwards, meanwhile, next

Transitions: Connecting Sentences

Functions	Examples	
ADDITION	She couldn't remember names.	**Furthermore**, she forgot addresses.
	Human brains lose mass.	**Indeed**, they may lose 10 percent a year.
CONDITION	Older people should eat several small meals a day.	**Otherwise**, their memory might deteriorate.
CONTRAST	I often have trouble with names.	**However**, I always remember faces.
	We all forget things.	**Nevertheless**, we shouldn't worry.
EFFECT / RESULT	I wasn't concentrating when we met.	**Consequently**, I couldn't recall her name.
	He wanted to improve his memory.	**Therefore**, he took a memory course.
TIME	He studied for his course.	**Meanwhile**, his wife read a book.
	She completed the book.	**Next**, she bought a memory video.

Transitions: Connecting Blocks of Text

Functions	Examples
LISTING IDEAS IN ORDER OF TIME / IMPORTANCE	**First of all**, we need to distinguish between two types of memory.
GIVING EXAMPLES	**For example**, you need to stay mentally active.
SUMMARIZING	**To summarize**: Memory improvement requires work.
ADDING A CONCLUSION	**In conclusion**, we can prevent the deterioration of memory.

GRAMMAR NOTES	EXAMPLES

1. Connectors (often called discourse connectors) are words and phrases that connect ideas both within sentences and between sentences or larger blocks of text.

Three types of connectors are:

a. coordinating conjunctions

- I try hard, **but** I can never remember new people's names.

b. subordinating conjunctions

- I can't remember her name **although** I can remember her face.

c. transitions

- I spent a lot on a memory improvement course. **However**, it was a waste of money.

2. Coordinating conjunctions join two independent clauses. Coordinating conjunctions come between clauses and are preceded by a comma.

- I often forget things, **so** I write everything down.
- I heard what you said, **but** what did you really mean?

Subordinating conjunctions connect ideas within sentences. They come at the beginning of a subordinate clause. If the subordinate clause comes first in a sentence, it is followed by a comma. If the subordinate clause follows the independent clause, it is not usually preceded by a comma.

- **Because** I often forget things, I write everything down.
- I write everything down **because** I often forget things.

3. Transitions connect ideas between sentences or larger sections of text. Transitions that connect sentences can come at the beginning of a sentence, within it, or at the end. Common transitions include *besides*, *consequently*, *however*, *in addition*, *nevertheless*, *otherwise*, and *therefore*.

At the beginning of a sentence, a transition is preceded by a period or semicolon and followed by a comma; in the middle of a sentence, it is preceded and followed by a comma; and at the end of a sentence, it is preceded by a comma.

- He said he would support the idea. **However**, I wouldn't count on him.
- He said he would support the idea. I wouldn't, **however**, count on him.
- He said he would support the idea. I wouldn't count on him, **however**.

4. There are five principal types of **transitions that connect sentences**:

a. Some transitions show **addition**. These include *additionally*, *besides*, *furthermore*, *in addition*, *likewise*, *moreover*, and *plus*.

- I remember her telephone number. **In addition**, I remember what street she lives on.
- I live too far away to visit you. **Besides**, I can never remember your address.

b. One transition of **condition**, *otherwise*, indicates that a result opposite to what is expected will happen if a certain action isn't taken.

- I need to write down your e-mail address. **Otherwise**, I'll never remember it.

c. Some transitions show **contrast**. These include *however*, *in contrast*, *in spite of this*, *instead*, *nevertheless*, *nonetheless*, *still*, and *though*.

- Her speech was good; **nevertheless**, I can't support her ideas.
- Jim thinks I'm against his ideas. **On the contrary**, I'm one of his biggest supporters.

d. Some transitions show **effect / result**. These include *accordingly*, *as a result*, *because of this*, *consequently*, *on account of this*, *otherwise*, *therefore*, and *thus*.

- I was not paying attention when she was introduced. **Consequently**, her name escapes me.
- This new memory technique is helpful. **On account of this**, I recommend it to you.

e. Some transitions show **relationships** of actions, events, and ideas **in time**. These include *after that*, *afterwards*, *in the meantime*, *meanwhile*, *next*, and *then*.

- Barry spent three years in the military. **Meanwhile**, his brother was earning a college degree.
- I went to a memory workshop. **Afterwards**, I couldn't remember a single thing.

(continued)

5. Some **transitions connect blocks of text**. They usually come at the beginning of a sentence and are commonly followed by a comma.

Such transitions have these uses:

a. to **list ideas in order of time or importance**. These include *finally, first, most importantly, next, second,* and *third.*

- **First**, let's consider the question of short-term memory.
- **Most importantly**, let's consider the question of memory improvement courses.

b. to **give examples**. These include *for example* and *for instance.*

- I can remember lots of things about people. **For example**, I always remember what they're wearing.

c. to **summarize**. These include *all in all, in summary, to summarize.*

- **In summary**, these are the key points about memory loss.

d. to **add a conclusion**. These include *in conclusion* and *to conclude.*

- **To conclude**, let me just say that we can all improve our memory if we work at it.

Reference Notes
For **subordinating conjunctions**, see Unit 18.
For more complete lists of **transitions**, see Appendices 21 and 22 on page A-10.
For more practice on **connectors**, see From Grammar to Writing for Part IX.

Focused Practice

1 | DISCOVER THE GRAMMAR

A *Find the two transitions in the opening reading that show addition. Write the phrases in which they occur here.*

1. _____

2. _____

B *Find the five transitions that show contrast. Write the phrases in which they occur here.*

1. _____   4. _____

2. _____   5. _____

3. _____

C *Find the four transitions that show effect / result. Write the phrases in which they occur here.*

1. _____   3. _____

2. _____   4. _____

D *Find the four transitions that connect blocks of text. Write the phrases in which they occur here.*

1. _____   3. _____

2. _____   4. _____

2 | MAKING CONNECTIONS   *Grammar Notes 2–5*

Combine each of the following pairs of sentences into one sentence. Rewrite numbers 1 and 3 using a coordinating conjunction, a subordinating conjunction, and a transition. Rewrite numbers 2 and 4 with only a coordinating conjunction and a transition.

1. Jim is a wonderful man. I can't see myself married to him. (contrast)

   Jim is a wonderful man, but I can't see myself married to him.

   Although Jim is a wonderful man, I can't see myself married to him.

   Jim is a wonderful man; however, I can't see myself married to him.

2. He was having problems remembering his appointments. He bought a daily planner. (effect / result)

   _____

   _____

   _____

3. It's important for Nancy to take her medications. She forgot today. (contrast)

   _____

   _____

   _____

4. Jack remembers everyone's name. He never forgets a face. (addition)

   _____

   _____

3 | MY TRAFFIC PROBLEMS WILL SOON BE JUST A BAD MEMORY   *Grammar Notes 2–5*

Read a segment of a radio broadcast. Fill in the blanks with connectors from the box. Use each connector only once.

and	as a result	first	however	in addition
meanwhile	~~next~~	otherwise	second	therefore

_____Next_____, we focus on the aftermath of the earthquake. Investigators have
 1.

determined that it will cost approximately $8 billion to rebuild damaged highways. According to

the governor, two actions have to be taken: _____, the federal government will have
 2.

to approve disaster funds to pay for reconstruction; _____, insurance investigators
 3.

will need to determine how much their companies will have to pay in the rebuilding effort. With

luck, the governor says, some key highways could be rebuilt within six months. He cautioned,

_____, that the six-month figure is only an estimate. The process depends on timely
 4.

allocation of funds, and certain insurance companies have been slow to approve such funds in the

past. The rebuilding effort could, _____, drag on for at least a year.
 5.

_____, bad weather could prevent the speedy completion of the project.
 6.

_____, it is taking some people as long as four hours to commute to work, and
 7.

others haven't been able to get to work at all. Interviewed by our news team, one commuter who

works in an office downtown said, "This has been ridiculous. It took me three hours to drive to

work last Friday. I knew I'd have to find some other way of getting there; _____, I'd
 8.

never make it. Well, yesterday I took the train and got there in 50 minutes. _____
 9.

you know, the trip was really pleasant. I even had the chance to read the morning paper.

_____, I'm going to switch permanently to the train."
 10.

4 | **A STRING AROUND HIS FINGER?** *Grammar Notes 2–4*

Look at the pictures. Write two sentences describing what happened to Hank in each picture. Use the suggested prompts.

1. (and / in addition)

2. (but / however)

3. (so / consequently)

4. (and / besides that)

5. (while this was happening / meanwhile)

6. (or / otherwise)

5 | EDITING

There are 12 mistakes involving connectors in this student composition. The first mistake is already corrected. Find and correct 11 more. You may add or eliminate words, but do not change word order or punctuation.

My Car Is Moving to the Suburbs

by Ed Snyder

October 12

Yesterday I drove my car to the downtown campus of the college. I usually have trouble finding a parking place, ~~however~~ *but* this time it was almost impossible. There were simply no parking places anywhere near the campus, therefore I had to park in the downtown mall, which is about a mile away. When I finished class, I walked back to the mall. Therefore, I couldn't remember where I'd parked my car! Believe it or not, it took me 45 minutes to find it, and I was about ready to panic when I finally did. That was the last straw. I've decided that I'm going to send my car to a new home in the suburbs.

I used to think that a car was the most wonderful thing in the world. I loved the freedom of being able to come and go to my part-time job or to the college whenever I wanted. A year ago I was in a carpool with four other people, nevertheless I hated having to wait around even though my carpool members weren't ready to leave, so I started driving alone.

Although, I've changed my mind since then. Now it's clear to me that there are just too many disadvantages to having a car in town. Accordingly, sitting stalled in your car in a traffic jam is stressful, besides it's a phenomenal waste of time. In addition, it would cost me $200 a month to park my car in the city (which is why I don't do that), moreover there's always the chance it will be vandalized.

Nonetheless, I've decided to leave it at my cousin Brent's house in the suburbs. Otherwise, I'll end up going broke paying for parking or memory improvement. My car will have a good home, in addition I'll use it just for longer trips. When I'm in the city, although, I'll take the bus or the tram, otherwise I'll walk. Who knows? They say you can meet some interesting people on the bus. Maybe I'll find the love of my life. My only problem will be remembering which bus to take.

Communication Practice

6 | LISTENING

🎧 *Read these questions. Then listen to the excerpt from a memory training workshop.*
Listen again and answer the questions in complete sentences.

1. What is the first point the workshop leader makes?

   It's important to get people's names in your short-term memory.

2. According to her, why is it important to remember clients' names?

   _____

3. What is the second point the leader makes?

   _____

4. What did the visitor tell the people in the workshop to do?

   _____

5. What are the two reasons one of the men knows the visit was planned and not real?

   a. _____

   b. _____

6. Why were they all able to remember the last word the visitor said?

   _____

7. According to the workshop leader, what is the most important thing the participants in the workshop have to learn to do?

   _____

7 | THE MEMORY GAME

Form two teams. Each student on each team prepares one statement. The statements should test the other team's memory and may involve either personal or general knowledge. Each statement must contain a connector of some sort. Teams take turns making their statements while the other team listens and takes notes. When all the statements have been made, the teams attempt to reproduce the statements of the other team.

> **Examples:** **Team A:** Washington, D.C., is the capital of the United States. However, it's not the largest city.
>
> **Team B:** I have been to France three times, and I've been to Britain twice.

8 | WRITING

Write three or four paragraphs about a significant memory you have. Explain clearly why this memory is important to you, and speculate as to why you remember it well. Use specific details to support your ideas and statements. Include appropriate connectors in your composition.

> **Example:** One of my most significant, and most painful, memories is of my accordion recital when I was 13 years old. I had been taking accordion lessons for three years and was told by my teacher that I had made excellent progress. She scheduled me for a recital in which I was to play two easy songs and one difficult one. I looked forward to the recital and practiced hard. However, things didn't go at all as planned . . .

9 | PICTURE DISCUSSION

Pieter Bruegel the Elder, Return of the Hunters

Study this painting for two minutes. Then close your book. Working with a partner, write down as many details as you remember. Then open your book again and check your memory. Which details were you able to remember best? Why?

Example: I can remember _____. I also remember _____. However, I can't remember _____.

10 | ON THE INTERNET

Do a search to find out who said each of these statements. Speculate as to the meaning of each quotation, and discuss your ideas with the class as a whole.

- "The difference between false memories and true ones is the same as for jewels: It is always the false ones that look the most real, the most brilliant."

- "Memories are the key not to the past, but to the future."

- "Those who cannot remember the past are condemned to repeat it."

VII From **Grammar** to **Writing**
Sentences and Fragments

As you have learned, a sentence must have at least one independent, or main, clause. (See Part I From Grammar to Writing, pages 46–48, for a discussion of the sentence.) If a group of words does not have an independent clause, it is a **fragment**, not a sentence.

> **Examples:** We need to do something about violence.
> (sentence—independent clause)
>
> Because it's tearing apart the fabric of societies everywhere.
> (fragment—dependent clause).

In formal writing, sentence fragments should be avoided. To correct a fragment, we often attach it to an independent clause. We can do this with the fragment above.

> We need to do something about violence **because it's tearing apart the fabric of societies everywhere.**

If there is no independent clause to which a dependent clause can be attached, we can correct a fragment by adding a subject or a verb or both.

> Interviewed by our news team. (fragment—no independent clause)
>
> **One commuter was** interviewed by our news team. (sentence)

1 | *In the following sentences, underline dependent clauses once and independent clauses twice. Do not underline phrases. In the blank to the left of each item, write **S** for a sentence or **F** for a fragment.*

_S_ Though there are benefits to genetic engineering, there are also dangers.

_____ As soon as I've saved enough money.

_____ Although China is overpopulated, it is trying to correct the problem.

_____ We won't solve the problem of illiteracy until we provide enough teachers.

_____ If a young basketball player from Nigeria can get a scholarship.

_____ Because I was one of those students.

_____ The economy is perhaps too dependent on high-tech industries.

_____ Carried out right, this procedure would cause the economy to expand.

_____ By the time the train finally arrived in Boston.

_____ We need to make some personal sacrifices if we want to help the poor.

2 | Read the following paragraph. Correct the eight fragments by joining them to the independent clauses to which they are logically connected. Where necessary, add commas and change capitalization, but do not add words.

The life of Stella and Hank Wong has improved immeasurably, ~~S~~ince they both got new jobs. Stella got a position as a proofreader and editor at a publishing company. That is pioneering new workplace methods. Hank was hired as a full-time consultant for an engineering firm. The difference between their new jobs and their old ones can be summed up in one word: flextime. Until they secured these new positions. Stella and Hank had a very difficult time raising their two small children. Their life was extremely stressful. Because they were at the mercy a nine-to-five schedule and had to pay a lot for day care. In order to get to work on time. They had to have the children at the day care center by 7:30 every morning. Each of their new companies, however, offers a flextime schedule. As long as Stella and Hank put in their 40 hours a week. They are free to work. When it is convenient for them. Now they can take turns staying home with the children, and day care is just a memory. Best of all, the children are much happier. Because they are getting the attention they need.

If a sentence has only an independent clause, it is called a **simple** sentence.

Example: I bought a new car last month. (simple sentence—one independent clause)

If two independent clauses are connected by a coordinating conjunction (*and*, *but*, *for*, *nor*, *or*, *so*, *yet*), the larger sentence is called a **compound** sentence. We place a comma before the coordinating conjunction.

Example: The tea was virtually flavorless. The sandwich tasted like cardboard.

The tea was virtually flavorless, **and** the sandwich tasted like cardboard.

We don't normally place a comma before a coordinating conjunction if it does not connect two independent clauses.* That is, there must be a subject and a verb in both clauses.

Example: We can go out to a movie or stay home and watch a video. (There is no subject in the second half of the sentence.)

Note, though, that if we join two very short independent clauses with a coordinating conjunction, we can eliminate the comma before the coordinating conjunction.

Example: I love movies but I hate TV.

*Remember, however, that you can use a comma before a coordinating conjunction when it is being used before the last item in a series (I don't like pie, cake, or ice cream.)

If a sentence contains an independent clause and one or more dependent clauses, it is called a **complex** sentence. If the dependent clause comes first, we normally place a comma after it. If it comes second, we normally don't place a comma before it unless the dependent clause establishes a contrast.

Examples: Because they provide activity, school sports are worthwhile.

School sports are worthwhile **because they provide activity.**

Though they aren't everything, jobs are important.

Jobs are important, **though they aren't everything.**

(The subordinating conjunction *though* establishes a contrast, so there is a comma before it.)

3 | *Place commas where possible in the following sentences. In the blank to the left of each item, write **S** for a simple sentence, **C** for a compound sentence, or **X** for a complex sentence.*

_C_ 1. Violence exists nearly everywhere in the world, and it is spreading.

_____ 2. Since we usually watch TV at home in our living room a TV show doesn't seem like a special event.

_____ 3. The population will continue to increase but natural resources won't.

_____ 4. We must make trains fast and comfortable if we expect people to use them.

_____ 5. I listened politely for a while and then excused myself.

_____ 6. The governor isn't in favor of higher taxes nor does he encourage the development of mass transit.

_____ 7. We don't have to buy a lot of groceries all at once for we can always stop at the supermarket on the way home from work.

_____ 8. Tim passed his driving exam with flying colors though he could use some practice in parallel parking.

_____ 9. As I was entering the dining car a violent lurch of the train threw me to the left.

Coordinating conjunctions, subordinating conjunctions, and transitions often have similarities in meaning but are used with different sentence patterns and punctuation. Notice the use of *but, although,* and *however* in the following sentences.

Examples: Dams provide many benefits, **but** they also do considerable harm to wildlife.

Although dams provide many benefits, they also do considerable harm to wildlife.

Dams provide many benefits. **However,** they also do considerable harm to wildlife.

The meanings of these three examples are similar, but the emphasis is different. It is also correct to use a semicolon before *however* and a lowercase letter in the third example.

4 | *For each of the following sentences, write two other sentences that express a similar meaning. Use the connectors in parentheses.*

Drake tried to think of a justification for his actions. However, he was unable to come up with a single thing.

1. (but)_____

_____

2. (although)_____

_____

Dams provide a great many economic benefits, so I don't think they should be removed.

3. (because)_____

_____

4. (therefore)_____

_____

Besides being an excellent athlete, Bruce is a top student.

5. (and)_____

_____

6. (in addition)_____

_____

5 | *Write a paragraph of six to ten sentences on one of these topics or a similar topic that interests you:*

- One reason why sports are so popular today
- My earliest memory
- One danger of cloning
- A kind act I experienced

In your paragraph, include at least one transition (such as **however**, **therefore***), one coordinating conjunction (for example,* **and**, **but***), and one subordinating conjunction (such as* **because**, **as soon as***). Leave your paragraph unpunctuated. Exchange papers with a partner. Read and punctuate each other's paper, paying particular attention to avoiding fragments and using commas and semicolons correctly. Discuss your papers together. Then rewrite your paragraph and submit it to your teacher.*

Review Test

I *Read the conversations. Underline all of the adverb clauses.*

1. **A:** Sarah, we're going to be late for the play <u>if we don't leave right now</u>.

   B: OK. We can leave <u>as soon as you back the car out of the garage</u>.

2. **A:** Harry is a lot more responsible <u>since he's been class president</u>.

   B: Yes, I know. He never used to do his chores <u>unless I threatened him</u>.

3. **A:** I'll call you <u>when the plane gets in</u>.

   B: OK, but you'd better take down Harriet's number <u>in case I'm not home</u>.

4. **A:** Wasn't that a great dinner? It won't surprise me <u>if I'm five pounds heavier tomorrow</u>.

   B: Yeah. <u>Whenever I come home to visit</u>, I gain weight. Mom is such a great cook.

5. **A:** There were better TV shows <u>before there were so many channels</u>.

   B: I don't agree. <u>Now that cable is available</u>, we have access to some impressive programming.

6. **A:** Joe, <u>since you didn't turn in your term paper</u>, you didn't pass the course—<u>even though you did well on the tests</u>.

   B: Yes, I know. I didn't do the term paper <u>because I couldn't think of anything to write about</u>.

7. **A:** Is your new house going to be finished <u>by the time you leave on your big trip</u>?

   B: I think so. <u>Once they've laid the foundation</u>, they can start building.

II *Choose transitions from the box to complete the news item. Use each transition only once.*

| however | moreover | ~~next~~ | on the contrary | otherwise | therefore |

_____ *Next* _____, we focus on the mission of Ares, the manned space
       1.

mission of WASA, the World Aeronautics and Space Association. Ares was launched seven

months ago from Woomera Spaceport in Australia. _____, contact
               2.

had been lost with Ares for the past three weeks, and WASA officials had feared the worst.

Project officials were _____ elated when they received a radio
         3.

message today confirming that Ares has made a successful landing on Mars. Harald

Svendorf, chief of WASA, had this to say in today's news conference: "We needed a victory;

_____, we might have lost our United Nations funding. This
      4.

successful landing should silence our critics, who have been calling the Ares Project a

disastrous waste of time and money. The project will, _____, be one
                                  5.

of the most cost-effective missions in the history of space exploration.

_____, it will pave the way toward realization of other manned
      6.

missions to the moons of Jupiter and to Venus."

III   *Combine the two sentences into one sentence using a dependent clause and an
independent clause with the appropriate subordinating conjunction from the box.*

~~because~~	though	unless	when	while

1. Mel and Charlotte Figueroa were in a difficult situation. They both had jobs and didn't have
   day care for their two children.

   *Mel and Charlotte Figueroa were in a difficult situation because they both had jobs and didn't have
   day care for their two children.*

2. They had been leaving the children with Sarah's mother. This wasn't a satisfactory solution

   _____

   _____

3. One of them was going to have to quit working. They could find a solution to the problem.

   _____

   _____

4. One of their neighbors proposed the creation of a day-care co-op involving five families. Their
   problem was solved.

   _____

   _____

5. Each day, one of the parents in the co-op cares for all the children. The other parents are
   working.

   _____

   _____

IV *There are eight mistakes in the use of adverbs in this letter. The first one is already corrected. Find and correct seven more.*

Dear Samantha,

I wanted to thank you again for your hospitality while we were in Vancouver. Not only *did you and Michael show* ~~you and Michael showed~~ us a wonderful time, but we also got to reestablish the close ties we used to have. The even kids enjoyed the trip, and you know how kids are on vacations. Only I hope that Dan and I can reciprocate sometime.

The drive back to Edmonton was something else; almost we didn't make it back in one piece. About 4:30 on the day we left, there was an ice storm near Calgary that turned the highway into a sheet of ice. Little did we know that it would take us four hours to get through the city. Rarely I have been in such an awful traffic jam. By the time we got off the freeway, it was 11:30 at night, and the kids were crying. We stopped at a motel to try to get a room; they were full up, but when we asked the proprietors if just we could spend the night in their lobby, they took pity on us and made us up a bed in their living room. People can be so kind sometimes. Never again I will think twice about helping people when they need it. By the next morning, the roads had been cleared, and we made it safely back to Edmonton.

Well, here the kids come to get their afternoon snack. Please write soon. Thanks again.

Love,

Barb

V *Punctuate these sentences, which form a narration, with commas or semicolons. Do not add periods or capital letters.*

1. Tim and Zeya Donovan felt their children were watching too much television, but they didn't know what to do about the problem. ^

2. They tried combinations of threats, punishments, and rewards however, nothing seemed to work.

3. Tim and Zeya both got home about 5:30 P.M. and they needed to occupy the children's attention while they were fixing dinner.

4. Though they felt so much TV watching wasn't good they allowed it because they had no alternative.

5. Their children weren't getting enough exercise in addition, they weren't interacting with the other children in the neighborhood.

6. Since a lot of their neighbors were having similar problems with their children someone came up with the idea of starting a neighborhood activity club.

7. The club met every afternoon from 5:00 until 6:30 and two parents from different families supervised activities.

8. The club has been a big success none of the children have watched very much television lately.

VI *Circle the letter of the one underlined word or phrase in each sentence that is not correct.*

1. If pooling the world's food supply, we might conceivably avert   (**A**) **B** **C** **D**
   A$$B
   starvation —provided that the food were distributed evenly.
   C$$D

2. To feel that pleas to sponsor orphans in Third World nations were   **A** **B** **C** **D**
   A
   only money-making schemes, I refused until recently even to consider
   BCD
   giving money.

3. Drivers should be extremely careful when giving rides to hitchhikers,   **A** **B** **C** **D**
   A$$BC
   even they look completely respectable.
   D

4. Though his writing is not easy to understand, the columnist forcefully   **A** **B** **C** **D**
   A$$B
   makes the point that only rarely capital punishment is carried out equitably.
   CD

5. Automobiles certainly cause many problems, however they fortunately   **A** **B** **C** **D**
   ABC
   provide us with benefits also.
   D

6. Feeling that the subject was clear beneath me, I unfortunately learned   **A** **B** **C** **D**
   ABC
   nothing at all when I took calculus last semester.
   D

(continued)

7. <u>Fortunately</u>, the leaders of <u>almost</u> all world nations seem to have   **A B C D**
_A _B

    realized that something must <u>obvious</u> be done <u>to control</u> the problem
_C _D

    of toxic waste.

8. <u>My having landed</u> at Orly Airport, <u>I was taken</u> <u>speedily</u> to the hotel   **A B C D**
_A _B _C

    <u>where</u> the conference was to be held.
_D

9. Bruce does not <u>often</u> accept constructive criticism <u>well</u>; <u>in addition</u>   **A B C D**
_A _B _C

    there are times when <u>even he doesn't</u> listen.
_D

10. I <u>actually</u> thought Ben wasn't going to be able to come to the   **A B C D**
_A

    party <u>at all</u>, <u>but</u> here <u>comes he</u> now.
_B _C _D

VII   *Go back to your answers to Exercise VI. Write the correct form for each item that you believe is incorrect. You may change single words or expressions, but do not change punctuation.*

1. _____ *If we pool* _____   6. _____

2. _____   7. _____

3. _____   8. _____

4. _____   9. _____

5. _____   10. _____

▶ *To check your answers, go to the Answer Key on page RT-4.*

PART

VIII

Noun Clauses

21 Noun Clauses: Subjects, Objects, and Complements

Grammar in Context

BEFORE YOU READ

1 *What kinds of things make you laugh?*

2 *What benefits do humor and laughter provide us?*

🎧 *Read this story about brothers competing for their mother's love.*

THE THREE BROTHERS

There was once a lady who had three sons. In many ways the relationship between the woman and her boys was a positive one. The sons were good citizens, were all well-off financially, and were admirable persons overall. What wasn't so admirable was the rivalry among the three. A spirit of competition had characterized their relationship ever since they had been small boys. Each brother was constantly trying to figure out how he could outdo the other two. What the sons wanted was a secure place in their mother's affections. They didn't understand that their mother loved each boy for his own uniqueness. That the boys were intensely competitive had always bothered the lady, but she didn't know what to do about it.

The formula for the area of a circle is πr^2.

Time passed, and as the mother aged, she began to lose her sight. Before long, she was almost blind. The boys realized that their mother's final days were approaching, and, competitive to the end, each searched for a way to prove he was the best son. Each boy promised to buy her whatever she wanted. Their mother said that there was nothing she needed, but the boys didn't believe her.

THE THREE BROTHERS

Moe, son number one, bought his mother a 15-room mansion. It cost him a great deal, but of course money was no object where his mother was concerned. He was sure that the mansion would be the very best thing any of them could give her.

Joe, son number two, felt that he had to outdo his first brother, so he bought his mother a beautiful luxury car. As an afterthought, he hired a chauffeur to drive the car and to be on call 24 hours a day. Joe thought that he would certainly win his mother's approval with this gift.

Curly, son number three, was in a dilemma, wondering what he could do to top the gifts of the other two brothers. While strolling downtown one day, he happened to see a beautiful parrot in the window of a pet store. The store owner told him this was a specially trained parrot that had memorized the entire *Encyclopedia Britannica*. One could ask the parrot whatever one wanted to know, and the parrot would answer accurately. Curly was delighted and bought the parrot, convinced that this gift would make him number one in his mother's eyes.

After a few weeks, the mother invited the boys over to her mansion.

"Boys," she said, "I wanted to thank you all for your wonderful gifts. I don't know if you believed me, though, when I said I didn't need anything. Moe, this is a gorgeous house, and it would make someone a nice home, but it's much too big for me. I live in only two rooms and don't have the time or energy to clean or take care of the entire house. I'd suggest selling it."

Turning to Joe, she said, "And Joe, that car you bought me is beautiful. It has everything you could possibly want in it, but I don't drive anymore. Plus, the fact that the chauffeur doesn't speak English is a problem. I recommend selling it."

Then the elderly lady turned to Curly, saying, "But Curly, yours was the best gift of all. I just can't thank you enough."

Curly was pleased that he had finally risen to the number one spot in his mother's affections. "That's great, Mom. Have you learned a lot from him?"

Puzzled, his mother said, "I don't know what you mean, son. All I know is that the chicken you gave me was delicious."

AFTER YOU READ

*Read the pairs of sentences. According to the first sentence in each pair, is the second sentence true (**T**) or false (**F**)?*

1. What wasn't so admirable was the rivalry among the three.

   T   F   Their rivalry was basically a positive thing.

2. One could ask the parrot whatever one wanted to know, and the parrot would answer accurately.

   T   F   The parrot could answer any question.

3. The fact that the chauffeur doesn't speak English is a problem.

   T   F   The chauffeur knows English.

Grammar Presentation

NOUN CLAUSES: SUBJECTS, OBJECTS, AND COMPLEMENTS

NOUN CLAUSES BEGINNING WITH *THAT*

Subject	Object
That she loves them is obvious.	You can see **(that) she loves them**.
That they give gifts is unfortunate.	She knows **(that) they give gifts**.

Complement	
SUBJECT COMPLEMENT	The problem was **(that) the car was so expensive**.
ADJECTIVE COMPLEMENT	It is important **(that) people develop a sense of humor**.

NOUN CLAUSES BEGINNING WITH QUESTION WORDS

Subject	Object
What I should give her is obvious.	I wonder **what I should give her**.
Why he did that wasn't evident.	Can you explain **why he did that**?

Complement	
SUBJECT COMPLEMENT	The mystery is **how he could afford the car**.
ADJECTIVE COMPLEMENT	It's amusing **what she did with the bird**.

NOUN CLAUSES BEGINNING WITH *WHETHER* OR *IF*

Subject	Object	
Whether she'll like it is hard to tell.	I wonder **whether / if she'll like it**.	
Whether it's useful or not matters to me.	I care about	**whether / if it's useful (or not)**.
		whether (or not) it's useful.

Complement	
SUBJECT COMPLEMENT	The issue is **whether she needs such costly gifts**.
ADJECTIVE COMPLEMENT	He's uncertain **whether she'll like it**.

GRAMMAR NOTES	EXAMPLES
1. Noun clauses are dependent clauses that perform the same functions that regular nouns do. They can be: **a. subjects** **b. objects** **c. subject complements** **d. adjective complements** Noun clauses begin with *that*, question words, or *whether* or *if*.	• You can see **that I am easily amused**. • **What I like** is a good joke. • **What makes me laugh** is slapstick comedy. • I don't understand **why you find that funny**. • The question is **whether people will laugh**. • It's clear **that laughter involves an emotion**. • We realize **that she was joking**. • I don't understand **what it means**. • He doesn't know **if he should laugh or not**.
2. We use the word ***that*** to introduce certain noun clauses. In such cases, *that* is a grammatical word that simply introduces a clause. It has no clear meaning. *That* can be omitted when it introduces an object noun clause or a complement noun clause, especially in speaking. When *that* introduces a subject noun clause, it is never omitted. Subject noun clauses beginning with *that* are formal.	• **That she was a funny person** was apparent. • I believe **(that) humor is healthy**. • I told Sue **(that) she was a funny person**. • It's odd **(that) you laugh so little**. • **That Joe has a good sense of humor** is obvious. NOT ~~Joe has a good sense of humor is obvious.~~
3. ***The fact that*** is sometimes used in place of *that* in subject noun clauses. *The fact that* must be used in place of *that* in noun clauses that are objects of prepositions. *It* often functions as the subject of a sentence, with the noun clause coming at the end. Like the word *that*, *it*, when used with a noun clause, is a grammatical word with no clear meaning.	• **That you can laugh** is good. • **The fact that you can laugh** is good. • I'm impressed by **the fact that Bob is here**. NOT I'm impressed ~~by that Bob is here.~~ • It's funny **that you should say that**.

(continued)

4. A **question** that is **changed to a noun clause** is called an **embedded question**. We use statement word order in embedded questions, not question word order.

- I don't even know **if she's from around here**.
- I don't know **who she is**.
  NOT ~~I don't know who is she.~~

USAGE NOTE: An embedded question is more polite than a direct question.

- What time is it? (*direct*)
- Do you know **what time it is**? (*more polite*)

An embedded question can occur within a statement or within another question. An embedded question within a statement is followed by a period. An embedded question within another question is followed by a question mark.

- I'm not sure **what *incongruous* means**.
- Do you know **how far it is to the nearest town**?

5. *Wh-* question words introduce embedded *wh-* questions.

- Do you know **when she arrived**?
- I'm not sure **how many children she has**.

The subject of an embedded *wh-* question takes a singular verb.

- I'm not certain **who is going** with us.

▶ **BE CAREFUL!** Do not use *do*, *does*, or *did* in embedded questions.

- I have no idea **what she meant**.
  NOT I have no idea ~~what did she mean.~~

6. We use *if* and *whether (or not)* to introduce embedded *yes / no* questions.

- Do you know **if she came to work today**?
- Who knows **whether she's here**?
- I have no idea **whether she came or not**.

Note that *if* and *whether (or not)* are similar in meaning and can often be used interchangeably.

- We're not sure **if / whether (or not)** Bob is in town.

▶ **BE CAREFUL!** Do not use *if* to introduce a subject noun clause.

- **Whether (or not) she understood** is questionable.
  NOT ~~If she understood is questionable.~~

▶ **BE CAREFUL!** Do not omit *if* or *whether (or not)* in embedded *yes / no* questions.

- It is difficult to say **if / whether (or not)** his plan will work.
  NOT It is difficult to say ~~his plan will work.~~

7. ***Whether . . . or not*** can replace ***whether*** in all noun clauses.

- We don't know **whether** she got the job.

  OR

- We don't know **whether** she got the job **or not**.

If . . . or not can replace ***whether*** in all but subject noun clauses.

- No one has told me **whether / if** she received the letter **or not**.

- **Whether** she received it isn't known.

  NOT ~~If she received it or not isn't known.~~

Reference Notes

For work on **noun clauses used to report speech**, see Unit 22.
For work on **noun clauses in conditional sentences**, see Unit 23.
For work on **noun clauses using the subjunctive**, see Unit 24.

Focused Practice

1 | DISCOVER THE GRAMMAR

A *Look again at the opening reading. In the first three paragraphs, find one example each of a noun clause derived from a statement used as a subject, as an object, and as an adjective complement. Label them* **S**, **O**, *and* **C**, *respectively. Do not include clauses introduced with* **say** *or* **tell**.

1. _____

2. _____

3. _____

B *In the opening reading, find four noun clauses that are embedded questions. Underline the sentences in the text. For each embedded question, write the direct question it was derived from.*

1. _____

2. _____

3. _____

4. _____

2 | AT LEAST I KNOW WHERE I AM

Complete this humorous story with embedded yes / no *and* wh- *questions based on the direct questions below. Put the verbs in the simple past or the past perfect.*

Column A: My Questions	**Column B: His Answers**
1. Excuse me. How far is the nearest town?	I don't know.
2. Well, what's the name of the nearest town?	I'm not sure.
3. Is there a telephone booth nearby?	Not sure.
4. Well, are there any towing companies nearby?	I don't know that either.
5. Do you know the people in that house there?	No, I don't.
6. How long have you lived around here?	That's private information.
7. What's your name?	I'm not going to tell you.
8. Do you know anything at all?	Yes, I do. I'm smarter than you are. At least I know where I am, and you don't.

My wife and I had an irritating experience a year ago when we were traveling in the Midwest. Our car broke down, and I saw a farmer working in a field. I was sure he could help me, so I went up to him.

1. I asked him _____*how far the nearest town was*_____. He said he didn't know.

2. Then I asked him _____. He said he wasn't sure.

3. I asked him _____. He said he wasn't sure.

4. Then I asked him _____. He said he didn't know that, either.

5. I asked him _____ the people in a nearby house. He said he didn't.

6. I asked him _____ in the area. He said that was private information.

7. I asked him _____. He said he wasn't going to tell me.

8. I asked him _____. He said he did and that he was smarter than I was. He said he at least knew where he was, and I didn't.

3 | A THUMBNAIL SKETCH OF HUMOR   *Grammar Notes 4–5*

A *Work with a partner. Student A asks four direct questions. Student B answers with an embedded question inside a phrase, such as* **I don't know, I'm not entirely sure, I have no idea, I don't have a clue,** *and so on. Then switch roles.*

Example: what / happen / to our diaphragm / when we laugh
        A: What happens to our diaphragm when we laugh?
        B: I have no idea what happens to our diaphragm when we laugh.

1. what / a pun

_____

_____

2. what / *hyperbole* / mean

_____

_____

3. what / the humor of the unexpected happening

_____

_____

4. how / repetition / work in humor

_____

_____

5. what / the humor of the incongruous situation

_____

_____

6. how / sarcasm / differ from other humor

_____

_____

7. why / it / impossible to tickle yourself

_____

_____

8. what / endorphins

_____

_____

(continued)

B *Read "A Thumbnail Sketch of Humor." Then ask your partner questions from Part A again.*

A Thumbnail Sketch of Humor

Pun A pun is a kind of humor that depends on similarities in sound or meaning between two words. EXAMPLE: A woman saw a bear a week before her baby was born. Frightened, she asked the doctor, "Will seeing that *bear* affect my baby?" The doctor said, "Yes. Your baby will have two *bare* feet."

Hyperbole Hyperbole, much used in humor, is exaggeration. EXAMPLE: A: Why are you so tired? B: I got stuck in a traffic jam on the freeway. They've been working on that stupid freeway since about 1905.

Humor of the unexpected happening A great deal of humor depends on what is called the humor of the unexpected happening. EXAMPLE: In a movie, a woman in a restaurant opens her purse, and a bird flies out of it.

Repetition Many humorous stories are structured on the basis of repetition of an element, most often three times. EXAMPLE: A man can't find his car in a parking lot and tries to hitchhike. It is pouring rain. The first driver who drives along honks his horn and doesn't stop. The second car that comes by splashes water from a mud puddle all over him. Then another man comes out and unlocks the door of his parked car, next to the first man. Furious, the first man goes up to him, shakes him, and says, "I wouldn't accept a ride from you if you paid me."

Incongruous situation The humor of the incongruous situation depends on normal things happening in unusual places. No one thinks twice about seeing a dog in someone's yard, but if a dog enters an elevator in a downtown building, people will laugh.

Sarcasm Sarcasm is a kind of irony. It can be mild and gentle, but it is more often biting and hurtful. EXAMPLE: A: What do you think of Jones as a political candidate? B: Oh, he's sharp, all right. He's got a mind as good as any in the twelfth century.

Tickling Tickling is a not-completely-understood phenomenon. It is thought, however, that in order to experience tickling as a pleasant or laughter-producing experience, we must perceive it as a pretended, not real, attack. Therefore, it must be reasonably gentle. This explains why it is impossible for us to tickle ourselves. Our brain is aware of itself.

Physiological aspects of laughter When we laugh, our diaphragm moves quickly up and down. Endorphins, hormones that are created in the brain when we laugh or exercise, are instrumental in lessening pain and contributing to a sense of well-being.

4 | **BUMPER STICKERS**   *Grammar Notes 1–3*

With a partner, examine the bumper stickers and discuss the meaning of each one. Then write one or two sentences explaining the meaning of each, making sure to use a noun clause. Use phrases such as those in the box in your noun clauses.

the fact that	what the humor depends on	what this is about
what this is referring to	what this means	what's funny about this

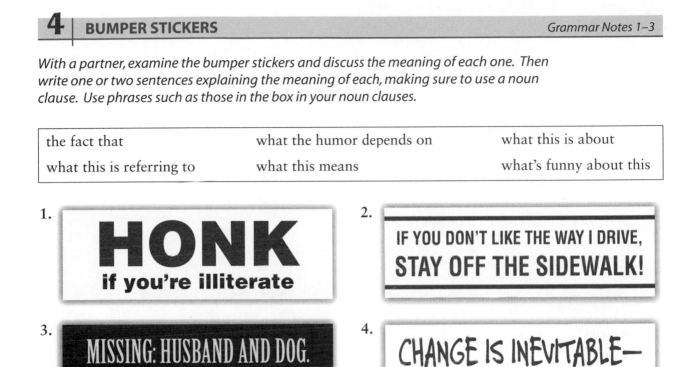

1. HONK
if you're illiterate

2. IF YOU DON'T LIKE THE WAY I DRIVE, **STAY OFF THE SIDEWALK!**

3. MISSING: HUSBAND AND DOG. ATTENTION: $100 Reward for Dog.

4. CHANGE IS INEVITABLE— EXCEPT FOR VENDING MACHINES.

5. I'm in no hurry. I'm on my way to work.

6. Everyone is entitled to my opinion.

7. FORGET ABOUT WORLD PEACE. VISUALIZE USING YOUR TURN SIGNAL.

8. ESCHEW OBFUSCATION.

Example: Is there life before coffee?
What this is referring to is the fact that many people cannot start the day without coffee. They act like they're dead.

5 | EDITING

Read the following statements about the proper way to tell a joke. There are nine mistakes in the use of noun clauses. The first mistake is already corrected. Find and correct eight more.

Nine Pieces of Advice About Telling a Joke

1. Make sure ~~is~~ the joke you're telling ^is^ funny.

2. The best jokes are broad enough so that everyone can enjoy them. Be certain that no one will be embarrassed by that you tell.

3. Also make certain that whichever you're saying won't embarrass anyone.

4. Ask yourself is the joke you want to tell vulgar. If it is, don't tell it.

5. Before you begin, be certain you remember what are the key details. Run through them in your mind before you start speaking.

6. Make sure what you have everybody's attention when you're ready to start.

7. Be certain whether you remember what the punch line of the joke is. Nothing is worse than listening to a joke when the teller can't remember the punch line.

8. The fact can you remember a joke doesn't guarantee success. You have to make the experience a performance. Be animated and dramatic.

9. If to laugh at your own jokes is always a question. Many comedians are criticized because they laugh at their own jokes. Don't laugh at what you're saying. Let others do the laughing.

Communication Practice

6 | LISTENING

🎧 *Read the questions. Listen to the conversation. Then listen again. Write answers to the questions, using a noun clause in each case.*

1. What bothers Greg about jokes?

   What bothers Greg about jokes is that they're too programmed.

2. According to Greg, what is the expectation when someone tells a joke?

3. According to Greg, what does everyone think if you don't laugh?

4. What is Greg's other problem about jokes?

5. What does he feel like in this situation?

6. What was the problem that some girls in a middle school were causing?

7. What did the principal of the school decide?

8. According to Jean, what did the principal want to show the girls?

7 | **GROUP DISCUSSION: WHAT'S FUNNY ABOUT THAT?**

A *Read this article about airline humor.*

They *Do* Have a Sense of Humor

by David Field, *USA Today*

Airline crews may not seem like a humorous group as they walk through the airport terminal with that look of determination and dedication on their faces. But behind the serious behavior, they are a funny lot. Here are some classic airline jokes selected from the collective memory of aviation writers.

Flight Attendant Remarks

Before the no-smoking announcement: "This is a nonsmoking flight. If you must smoke, please ring your attendant-call bell and one of us will escort you out to the wing."

After the no-smoking announcement: "Any passenger caught smoking in the lavatories will be asked to leave the plane immediately."

First-Time Fliers

Then there was the woman who, when asked if she wanted a window seat, responded, "No, not by the window. I've just had my hair done."

One passenger wanted to know how a plane could get from Chicago to Detroit, cities separated by a time zone, in just 15 minutes. Although the flight time was 75 minutes, the time zone made their airline's scheduled departure seem like the flight took only 15 minutes. He was finally satisfied with the explanation that it was a *very* fast airplane.

Pilot Humor

When controllers are uncertain what a pilot plans or wants to do, they usually say, "Please state your intentions."

Few pilots are daring enough to respond literally. But one was once overheard: "I intend to retire to a small farm in Georgia and raise peaches."

Pet Stories

Two airline cargo handlers were removing a pet carrier from a plane's cargo hold and discovered the cat inside was dead.

Fearful of the saddened owner's anger, the two went to the nearest cat pound and found an animal of the same breed, size, and color, and proudly delivered it to its destination.

As the animal leaped out of the cage, the owner gasped in shock, turned to the cargo handlers, and exclaimed, "This is not my cat! My cat was dead when I shipped him! He was stuffed!"

Plane Humor

Pilots and maintenance crews usually communicate in writing. A pilot typically writes up an item to be repaired such as a cockpit gauge or switch.

An overnight maintenance crew responds in writing that the work was done or wasn't needed or couldn't be done.

A pilot once left a note complaining, "Dead bugs are on the cockpit windshield." When the pilot came back in the morning, maintenance had replied: "Sorry, live bugs not available."

B *Now work with a partner. Tell your partner which jokes you find funny and which ones you don't. If you do find a particular joke humorous, explain what makes you laugh or smile about it. Explain to your partner what makes each joke a joke.*

Example: A: What I think is funny is the pilot's answer about retiring to Georgia to raise peaches.

B: Why?

8 | WRITING

Choose one of these activities.

1. Write three to five paragraphs about a situation that you witnessed or participated in that you found humorous. Describe the situation fully, using plenty of supporting details. Explain why the situation was funny for you.

2. If you know an extended joke (like the one in the opening reading for this unit), write it.

Example: One of the funniest situations I've ever been involved in happened in our office last year. It was April Fools' Day, and everyone in the office thought that we needed to play a practical joke on the secretary. She's always playing jokes on us, so we had to get back at her. Here's what we did . . .

9 | ON THE INTERNET

C *Do a search for a joke or a bumper sticker that amuses you. Narrow your search by restricting the joke or bumper sticker to a subject area. For example, use key words such as* **bumper sticker jokes driving.** *After you have found a joke you like, tell it to the class. As a class, discuss which jokes or bumper stickers you find most amusing, and why.*

22 Direct and Indirect Speech

Grammar in Context

BEFORE YOU READ

1 *In general, do you think news reporting is accurate?*

2 *How can one get an objective, accurate view of the news? Discuss this with a partner.*

Read this article about the accuracy of news reporting.

IS NEWS REPORTING ACCURATE?

Today most of us get our news from the media, particularly television. We're so busy that we don't have, or take, the time to research issues carefully, and depend instead on TV and radio broadcasters to keep us informed. A certain amount of news reporting is no doubt accurate and informative. But how much of it can be trusted, particularly when numbers are involved? Here is a list of five mistakes journalists commonly make with numbers:

Mistake #1: *Percent* **versus** *Percentage*

Report 1: "In other news, the profits of XYZ Corporation have dropped from 15 percent to 10 percent in the last six months. That's a 5 percent change and is less troubling than experts have been predicting."

Problem: *Percent* and *percentage* mean different things. The reporter was wrong when

he said that XYZ's profits had dropped 5 percent and that this was less troubling than experts had been predicting. It was a 5-*percentage-point drop*. A drop in profits from 15 to 10 percent is a drop of 33.3 percent—a lot more "troubling" than the reporter claimed.

IS NEWS REPORTING ACCURATE?

Mistake #2: Polls and the Margin of Error

Political polls are interesting, but they can be misleading because reporters often fail to emphasize the margin of error. Report 2: "In the latest GGG poll, Candidate A leads Candidate B by five points. This represents an increase of one point since a week ago, indicating there is a greater chance that Candidate A will win the election."

Problem: The reporter said Candidate A led Candidate B by five points, that this represented an increase of one point since the previous week, and that there was a greater chance that A would win. However, polls are merely a statistical survey, usually with about a three-point margin of error. Therefore, the two candidates are statistically tied. Candidate B could actually be ahead of Candidate A. Lest we think that poll predictions don't matter, we need only remember the United States presidential election of 1948, when polls indicated that Thomas Dewey was leading President Harry S. Truman and was likely to win. Truman won the election.

Mistake #3: Poll Momentum Swings

Report 3: "In political news, Candidate Q has gained two points on Candidate R. This suggests that Candidate Q is gaining momentum and that Candidate R is losing ground."

Problem: A gain of one or two points is statistically insignificant, so the reporter's claim that Q was gaining and that R was losing ground is unsupported. With such a small gain, there is no indication that either candidate has momentum.

Mistake #4: Addition and Subtraction

Report 4: "In the legislature, the Blues hold 40 seats and the Reds hold 46. That means that the Blues have to win 7 seats to take control. This is probably too many to hope for."

Problem: The reporter was misinterpreting the numbers when he stated that the Blues had to win 7 seats in order to take control and that this was too many to hope for. In reality, they had to win only 4, since each seat won by one party was a corresponding loss by the other party.

Mistake #5: Faulty Interpretation

Report 5: "Recent estimates by experts on pollution show that more than 100 million Americans breathe polluted air." The following night on another network, you hear Report 6, based on the same set of numbers: "On most days, the air in most American cities is healthy."

Problem: Both statements are true, but the same statistics can be used to support both sides of the issue. One reporter said that more than 100 million Americans breathed polluted air. The other said that the air in most American cities was healthy on most days. It is true that 100 million Americans breathe polluted air—occasionally. However, the statement makes it sound like a constant problem.

The bottom line: We need to take the time to listen carefully and ponder what reported statements actually mean, what context they occur in, and whether the source of the report is biased. At issue is this question: Are we thinking for ourselves or letting others tell us what to think?

AFTER YOU READ

What do these sentences mean? Circle the letter of the choice that correctly comments on the sentence.

1. The reporter was wrong when he said that XYZ's profits had dropped 5 percent and that this was less troubling than experts had been predicting.

   a. Things are actually better than experts had been predicting.

   b. Things are actually as bad as or worse than the experts had been predicting.

2. The reporter said Candidate A led Candidate B by five points, that this was an increase of one point since the previous week's poll, and that there was a greater chance that A would win.

   a. According to the reporter, A's chances of winning are improving.

   b. According to the reporter, A's chances of winning are decreasing.

3. A gain of one or two points is statistically insignificant, so the reporter's claim that Q was gaining and that R was losing ground is unsupported.

   a. The reporter's claim is reasonable.

   b. The reporter's claim is not reasonable.

Grammar Presentation

INDIRECT SPEECH

DIRECT AND INDIRECT SPEECH: STATEMENTS

Direct Speech		
Subject	**Reporting Verb**	**Direct Statement**
She	said,	"The report **is** wrong."
		"Candidate A **leads** in the polls."
		"The Blues **were** defeated."

Indirect Speech				
Subject	**Reporting Verb**	**Noun / Pronoun**	**Indirect Statement**	
She	said	Ø*	**(that)**	the report **was** wrong.
	told	Aaron / him		Candidate A **led** in the polls.
				the Blues **had been** defeated.

*Ø = not used.

DIRECT AND INDIRECT SPEECH: QUESTIONS

Direct Speech: *Yes / No* Questions		
Subject	**Reporting Verb**	**Direct Question**
The reporter	asked,	"**Have you read** the paper?"
		"**Do you think they are** going to win?"

Indirect Speech: *Yes / No* Questions				
Subject	**Reporting Verb**	**Noun / Pronoun**		**Indirect Question**
The reporter	asked	(Juana) (her)	**if** **whether** **(or not)**	**she had read** the paper.
				she thought they were going to win.

Direct Speech: *Wh-* Questions		
Subject	**Reporting Verb**	**Direct Question**
The mayor	asked,	"**Where do you vote**?"
		"**Who is ahead in the race**?"

Indirect Speech: *Wh-* Questions				
Subject	**Reporting Verb**	**Noun / Pronoun**		**Indirect Question**
The mayor	asked	(Mr. Andrews) (him)	**where**	**he voted.**
			who	**was ahead in the race.**

VERB CHANGES IN INDIRECT SPEECH

Direct Speech				Indirect Speech			
		Verb				**Verb**	
He said,	"I	**report**	the news."	He said	(that) he	**reported**	the news.
		am reporting				**was reporting**	
		reported **have reported** **had reported**				**had reported**	
		will report				**would report**	
		can report				**could report**	
		should report				**should report**	

(continued)

OTHER CHANGES IN INDIRECT SPEECH

	Direct Speech	**Indirect Speech**
PRONOUNS	"Andy, are **you** listening?" Mary asked.	Mary asked Andy if **he** was listening.
POSSESSIVES	The boss said, "Sue, bring **your** camera."	The boss told Sue to bring **her** camera.
THIS	"Can I have **this** film?" Sam asked.	Sam asked if he could have **that** film.
HERE	Mrs. Brown asked, "Will you be **here**?"	Mrs. Brown asked if I would be **there**.
AGO	"We came a year **ago**," Jim said.	Jim said (that) they had come one year **previously / before**.
NOW	Bob asked, "Are you leaving **now**?"	Bob asked if I was leaving **then**.
TODAY	"I need to work **today**," Jack said.	Jack said (that) he needed to work **that day**.
YESTERDAY	The reporter asked, "Did you call **yesterday**?"	The reporter asked if I had called **the previous day / the day before**.
TOMORROW	"Are you arriving **tomorrow**?" Sarah asked.	Sarah asked if we were arriving **the next day**.

GRAMMAR NOTES

EXAMPLES

1. We can **report speech** in two ways: direct speech and indirect speech. **Direct speech** (also called **quoted speech**) is the exact words (or thoughts) of someone speaking (or thinking). It is enclosed in quotation marks and is often introduced by a reporting verb such as *asked, claimed, said, stated, told,* and *wondered*.	• I said, **"I want Johnson to win the election."** • Mary asked, **"Do you think he'll win?"**
Indirect speech (also called **reported speech**) is someone's report of direct speech. It does not contain the exact words of a speaker and is not enclosed in quotation marks. Indirect speech reports what a speaker said in a **noun clause or phrase** introduced by a reporting verb.	noun clause • I said **(that) I wanted Johnson to win the election.** noun clause • Mary asked **if I thought he would win.**
If a statement is reported, the noun clause can be introduced by *that*. If a question is reported, the noun clause is introduced by *if, whether (or not),* or a *wh-* question word.	
▶ **BE CAREFUL!** Don't use quotation marks in indirect speech.	• John said **(that) he would be there.** NOT ~~John said "he would be there."~~

2. The verbs *say* and ***tell*** are the most common **reporting verbs**. We usually use the simple past form of these verbs in both direct and indirect speech.

- Hal **said**, "Martha, we have to leave."
- Hal **told** Martha they had to leave.

Be careful! *Say* and *tell* have similar meanings, but they are used differently. We *say* something but *tell* someone something.

- Andy **told Freda** (that) she shouldn't worry.

  Not <s>Andy said Freda that she shouldn't worry.</s>

Usage note: When the listener is mentioned, it is preferable to use *tell*.

- Frank **told us** to pay attention.
- Frank **said** to pay attention.

► **Be careful!** Don't use *tell* when the listener is not mentioned.

- Ms. Sasser **said** (that) she was going to watch the debate.

  Not <s>Ms. Sasser told (that) she was going to watch the debate.</s>

---

3. To **report indirect questions**, we normally use ***ask*** in its simple past form.

- Mrs. Mason **asked** Mary if she was going to vote.

► **Be careful!** Indirect questions end with a period, not a question mark. Do not use *do*, *does*, or *did* in an indirect question.

- Sue asked Helen **if she had heard the speech**.

  Not <s>Sue asked Helen did she hear the speech.</s>

Use *if* or ***whether (or not)***, not *that*, to introduce an **indirect** *yes / no* **question**. *If* and *whether (or not)* are similar in meaning and are often used interchangeably. We often use *whether (or not)* to emphasize alternatives or different possibilities.

- Bob asked, "Do you think she'll win the election?"
- Bob asked **if / whether (or not)** I thought she would win the election.

Use statement word order, not question word order, to report *yes / no* questions.

- I asked if **we would** know the results soon.

  Not <s>I asked will we know the results soon.</s>

---

4. We use **question words** to introduce **indirect** *wh-* **questions**.

- "When is the election?" my son asked.
- My son asked **when the election was**.
- "Which candidate do you prefer?" he asked.
- He asked **which candidate I preferred**.

Use statement word order to report indirect questions about the predicate.

- My daughter asked, "Why didn't more people vote?"
- My daughter asked why **more people hadn't voted**.

Use question word order to report indirect questions about the subject.

- "Who is going to win?" Mom asked.
- Mom asked **who was going to win**.

(continued)

5. If the reporting verb is in the simple past, the **verb in the noun clause** often changes:

- simple present → simple past

- Bill said, "I **invest** in the stock market."
- Bill said (that) he **invested** in the stock market.

- present progressive → past progressive

- Mary asked, "John, **are** you **studying** political science?"
- Mary asked John if he **was studying** political science.

- simple past → past perfect

- "I **voted** for Senator McLeod," Bob noted.
- Bob noted (that) he **had voted** for Senator McLeod.

- present perfect → past perfect

- "Sam, **have** you ever **voted** absentee?" Jack asked.
- Jack asked Sam if he **had** ever **voted** absentee.

6. In spoken English, we sometimes do not change verbs in a noun clause, especially if what we are reporting happened a short time ago.

- Yesterday Amy said, "Johnson **didn't win**."
- Yesterday Amy said Johnson **didn't win**.

OR

- Yesterday Amy said Johnson **hadn't won**.

Even in formal English, we often do not change verbs to past forms if general truths are reported.

- **Are** elections **held** often?" Kenny asked.
- Kenny asked if elections **are held** often.

OR

- Kenny asked if elections **were held** often.

When the reporting verb is in the simple present, present progressive, present perfect, or future, the verb in the noun clause does not change.

- Bruce says, "I'm going to vote."
- Bruce says he's going to vote.

7. Certain **modals** often change in indirect speech. *Can, may, must,* and *will* → *could, might, had to,* and *would,* respectively.

- "Sam, **can** you call me at 6:00 P.M.?" Ann asked.
- Ann asked Sam if he **could** call her at 6:00 P.M.
- "I **won't** be able to," replied Sam.
- Sam replied that he **wouldn't** be able to.

Could, might, ought to, should, and *would* do not change in indirect speech.

- I said, "Helen, I **might** attend the rally."
- I told Helen (that) I **might** attend the rally.
- "Sarah, you **should** be informed," Dad said.
- Dad told Sarah (that) she **should** be informed.

8. Note that, in addition to verbs, certain **other words** change in indirect speech. To keep the speaker's original meaning, make these changes as well:

- pronouns and possessive adjectives → other forms

  - Jeremy said, "**My** boss just promoted **me**."
  - Jeremy said **his** boss had just promoted **him**.

- *this* → *that* and *these* → *those*

  - Don asked, "Have you read **this** book?"
  - Don asked if I had read **that** book.

- *here* → *there*

  - "Please be **here** for the meeting," Sally asked.
  - Sally asked me to be **there** for the meeting.

- *now* → *then*

  - Mack said, "Alan's just arriving **now**."
  - Mack said Alan was just arriving **then**.

- *ago* → *before* or *previously*

  - Julie said, "I voted three years **ago**."
  - Julie said (that) she had voted three years **previously / before**.

- *yesterday, today,* and *tomorrow* → *the day before / the previous day, that day,* and *the next day / the day after,* respectively

  - "I can see you **tomorrow**," said Kayoko.
  - Kayoko said that she could see me **the next day**.

Reference Notes

For more information and practice on **reporting questions**, see Unit 21.

For information and practice on **reporting statements and questions in conditional sentences**, see Unit 23.

For a list of **reporting verbs for reported speech**, see Appendix 23 on page A-10.

Focused Practice

1 | DISCOVER THE GRAMMAR

A *Look again at the opening reading. Find an example of each of the following changes from direct to indirect speech. Write the examples on the lines provided.*

1. ___That . . . is less troubling / this was less troubling___
   (a present form of *be* changes to a past form of *be*)

2. _____
   (present progressive changes to past progressive)

3. _____
   (simple present changes to simple past)

4. _____
   (present perfect changes to past perfect)

5. _____
   (*will* changes to *would*)

6. _____
   (*ago* changes to another expression)

B *Read these statements in direct speech. Is the suggested change to indirect speech correct (**C**) or incorrect (**I**)?*

___C___ **1.** Direct: That's a 5 percent change.

Indirect: The reporter said that was a 5 percent change.

_____ **2.** Direct: In the latest GGG poll, Candidate A leads Candidate B by five points.

Indirect: The reporter said that in the latest GGG poll, Candidate A had led Candidate B by five points.

_____ **3.** Direct: Candidate Q has gained two points on Candidate R.

Indirect: The reporter said that Candidate Q gained two points on Candidate R.

_____ **4.** Direct: This suggests that Candidate Q is gaining momentum and that Candidate R is losing ground.

Indirect: The reporter said this suggested that Candidate Q was gaining momentum and that Candidate R was losing ground.

_____ **5.** Direct: That means that the Blues have to win 7 seats to take control.

Indirect: The reporter said that meant that the Blues must have won 7 seats to take control.

_____ **6.** Direct: Recent estimates by experts on pollution show that more than 100 million Americans breathe polluted air.

Indirect: The reporter said recent estimates by experts on pollution showed that more than 100 million Americans breathe polluted air.

2 | HEADLINES

Put these headlines into indirect speech. Be sure to include necessary auxiliaries.

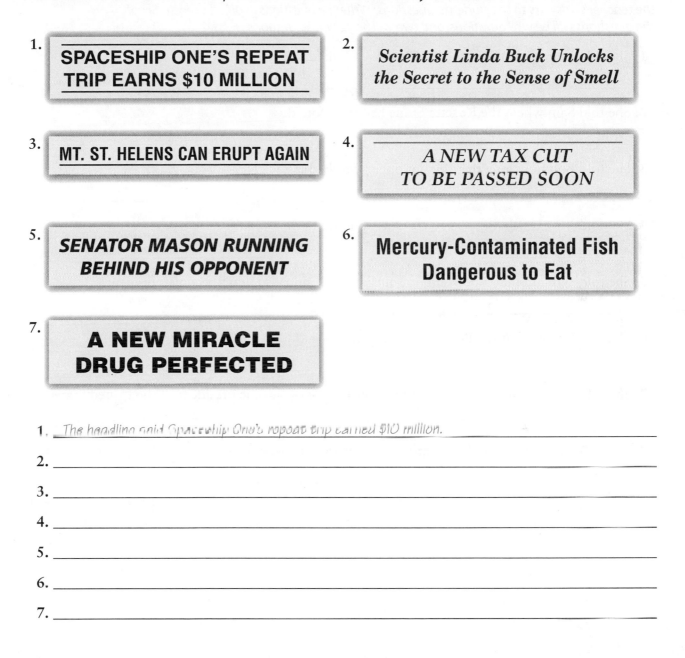

1.
> **SPACESHIP ONE'S REPEAT TRIP EARNS $10 MILLION**

2.
> *Scientist Linda Buck Unlocks the Secret to the Sense of Smell*

3.
> **MT. ST. HELENS CAN ERUPT AGAIN**

4.
> *A NEW TAX CUT TO BE PASSED SOON*

5.
> **SENATOR MASON RUNNING BEHIND HIS OPPONENT**

6.
> **Mercury-Contaminated Fish Dangerous to Eat**

7.
> **A NEW MIRACLE DRUG PERFECTED**

1. The headline said Spaceship One's repeat trip earned $10 million.

2. _____

3. _____

4. _____

5. _____

6. _____

7. _____

3 | A SUBSTITUTE TEACHER

Grammar Notes 3–4

A substitute teacher came to class and was asked many questions by the students. Read the teacher's answers to the students' questions. Write the questions in direct speech. Six of the questions will be wh- questions, and two will be yes / no questions.

1. She told Mary that Leonardo da Vinci had painted the Mona Lisa.

   Mary asked, "Who painted the Mona Lisa?"

2. She told Sam where the Rosetta Stone had been found.

   _____

3. She told Bob how long the Revolutionary War had lasted.

   _____

4. She told Minnie what the last two states to join the Union had been.

   _____

5. She told William that a person born outside the country couldn't become president.

   _____

6. She told Grant what the Boston Tea Party had been.

   _____

7. She told Amanda how many electoral votes it took to become president of the United States.

   _____

8. She told Zelda that population growth was increasing worldwide.

   _____

4 | MY DAUGHTER'S HOMEWORK

Grammar Notes 3–7

Read the conversation. Then complete the account with indirect speech forms.

SALLY: Dad, can you help me with my homework?

DAD: Yes, I can. What do you need to know?

SALLY: I have to write a report on political polls. How do they work?

DAD: Well, researchers call voters and ask them their positions on issues or candidates.

SALLY: Have there been times when they didn't predict correctly?

DAD: Yes, there have. One of the best examples was in the 1948 presidential election.

SALLY: What happened?

DAD: The polls were saying President Truman would lose. On election night some advisors said, "It looks like you're losing." Truman said, "Well, we'll see what happens. I'm going to bed." When he woke up in the morning, he discovered he had won. This means that polls aren't always accurate.

My daughter Sally asked me _____ *if I could help her with her* _____ homework. I told her
1.

_____ and asked _____ to
2.   **3.**

know. She said _____ to write a report on political polls. She
4.

asked _____. I told her that researchers _____
5.   **6.**

_____ voters and _____ them their positions on
7.

candidates and issues. Sally asked _____ times when they
8.

_____ correctly. I told Sally _____ _____
9.   **10.**

and that one of the best examples _____ in the 1948 presidential
11.

election. Sally asked what _____. I told her that the polls
12.

_____ that President Truman _____.
13.   **14.**

On election night some advisors told Truman that it _____.
15.

Truman said that _____ _____ and that he _____
16.   **17.**

_____ to bed. When he woke up in the morning, he discovered that he had won.

5 | STATEMENTS HEARD AT A TOWN MEETING
Grammar Notes 5, 7–8

Read the statements heard at a town meeting. Using the subjects in parentheses and choosing from the reporting verbs in the box, change each statement to indirect speech.

add	claim	comment	note	observe	point out	remark	say

1. The new budget will be submitted tomorrow. (the mayor)

   The mayor noted (that) the new budget would be submitted the next day.

2. Construction on the new subway system was started a year ago. (a member of the city council)

   _____

3. It probably won't be finished on schedule. (a reporter)

   _____

4. The assistant mayor resigned yesterday. (another member of the city council)

   _____

5. The voters don't want taxes raised now. (a townsperson)

   _____

6. We want tax relief this year. (another townsperson)

   _____

7. The citizens of this town are better off than they were four years ago. (the mayor)

   _____

8. Serious crime has increased since then. (the former mayor)

   _____

9. Life is better here than in most places. (the mayor)

   _____

10. You made this claim in the last election campaign. (another townsperson)

    _____

6 | EDITING

Read this letter from Charles to his sister. It has 14 mistakes in the use of direct and indirect speech. The first mistake is already corrected. Find and correct 13 more.

> January 20
>
> Dear Emily,
>
> I just wanted to fill you in on Tim's school adventures. About two months ago
> Melanie said she ~~feels~~ *felt* we should switch Tim to the public school. He'd been in a
> private school for several months, as you know. I asked her why you thought that,
> and she said, "He's miserable where he is, and the quality of education is poor." I
> couldn't help but agree. She said she thought we can move him to the local high
> school, which has a good academic reputation. I told that "I agreed but that we
> should ask Tim." The next morning we asked Tim if he wants to stay at the
> private school. I was surprised at how strong his response was. He said me that
> he hated this school and didn't want to go here any longer. So we changed him.
> He's been at the new school for a month now, and he's doing well. Whenever I ask
> him does he have his homework done., he says, Dad, I've already finished it. He's
> made several new friends. Every now and then he asks us why didn't we let him
> change sooner. I'm just glad we moved him when we did.
>
> Not much else is new. Oh, yes—I do need to ask are you coming for the
> holidays. Write soon and let us know. Or call.
>
> Love,
>
> Charles

Communication Practice

7 | LISTENING

⌒ *Read the questions. Listen to the news broadcast. Then answer the questions, using reported speech forms.*

1. What time did Mt. St. Andrea erupt?

   The reporter said that Mt. St. Andrea had erupted at 5:45 A.M.

2. What is covering the local area?

3. How many deaths have there been so far?

4. By how many points is Senator McLeod leading her challenger?

5. How far away is the election?

6. What is Marcine Miller confident of?

7. By what score did the Mariners win Game 7 of the World Series?

8. Which championship is this for the Mariners?

8 | GROUP REPORTING

Form two large groups, with each group sitting in a circle. Each group appoints a director. The director writes down a sentence about a general truth and whispers it in the ear of another student, who then whispers what was heard into the ear of the next student. The last student to hear the sentence writes it on the board. The director says whether the sentence is accurate. If it is not, the director locates where the message changed. Make the sentence long enough to be challenging but short enough to be easily remembered.

Example: **A:** Water freezes at 0 degrees Celsius.
B: She said (that) water freezes at 0 degrees Celsius.

9 | PICTURE DISCUSSION

A *In small groups, discuss what happened to cause the accident. Invent conversations for the police officers, the drivers, and the bystander. Report them in indirect speech.*

B *As a class, discuss who is most likely to give the most objective report of what happened and why.*

Example: The woman said that the driver of the other car had been speeding but she hadn't been.

10 | WRITING

Write a few paragraphs about a recent news story that interested you. The news story should contain examples of direct speech. Write a summary of the article, changing direct speech forms to indirect speech.

Example: The headline said, "He gave her his heart, then got a new one." Here's what the story was about:

A few hours after his wedding, Steven Dulka went to a hospital in Detroit, Michigan, to get a new heart. Dulka, who is 51 years old, was scheduled to marry Deidre Jacobsen on Saturday, October 2, 2004. Unfortunately, Dulka had a heart inflammation and needed a transplant. About two hours before the wedding was set to start, Dulka got a call from a hospital administrator telling him that a heart had become available. Dulka told the administrator that he was getting married at 2:00 P.M. that day . . .

11 | ON THE INTERNET

Who said each of following? Do a search to find out the author and the context in which it was said. Report your findings to the class.

- "I shall return."
- "I have not yet begun to fight."
- "I would rather be right than president."
- "Baseball is 90 percent mental; the other half is physical."

From **Grammar** to **Writing**
Writing Direct and Indirect Speech

Direct speech (also called quoted speech) states the exact words of a speaker. **Indirect speech** (also called reported speech) reports the words of a speaker but not all of the speaker's exact words.

In direct speech, quotation marks enclose the quotation. The reporting verb, such as *said*, *told*, or *responded*, is followed by a comma if it introduces the quotation. Quotation marks come after a final period, question mark, or exclamation point.

> **Examples:** Ben said, "Mom, I want to keep going to public school." (statement)
>
> Valerie asked Keith, "Can we afford to send Ben to a private school?" (question)
>
> Ben said to Keith and Valerie, "I won't go!" (exclamation)

If the reporting statement comes after the quotation, a comma follows the last word of the quotation, and the second set of quotation marks comes after the comma. A period ends the sentence.

> **Example:** "I don't want to go to private school," Ben said.

A quotation that is a question ends with a question mark; a quotation that is an exclamation ends with an exclamation point.

> **Examples:** "Ben, do you like school?" asked Aunt Emily.
>
> "I won't go to private school!" Ben yelled.

If the quotation is divided by the reporting statement, each part of the quotation is enclosed in quotation marks. The part of the quotation after the reporting statement does not begin with a capital letter if the remainder of the quotation is not part of a new sentence. Look at the punctuation and capitalization in this example:

"Ms. Baldwin," **the reporter asked,** "why are you all participating in this demonstration?"

In indirect speech there are no quotation marks. The first word of the indirect speech is not capitalized, and the reporting statement is not followed by a comma. An indirect question does not have a question mark at the end of the sentence. Note that since indirect speech is presented as a noun clause, it can be introduced by the word *that*. However, *that* is often omitted in conversation and informal writing.

Examples: Ben said (**that**) **he wanted to keep going to public school.**

Ben told his parents (**that**) **he wanted to keep going to public school.**

Valerie asked Keith **if they could afford to send Ben to a private school.**

Ben told his parents (**that**) **he wouldn't go.**

1 | *Punctuate these sentences in direct speech. Add capital letters if necessary.*

1. "Dad, I want to quit school and go to work," Jim murmured.

2. Sally, how would you evaluate your education the reporter queried

3. I absolutely love going to school Sally responded (exclamation)

4. Jim, Frank said, you're crazy if you think it's going to be easy to get a job

5. Frank said Jim, don't be a fool (exclamation)

6. The union spokesperson asked the management team when are you going to start taking our concerns seriously

2 | *Correct the capitalization and punctuation of the following examples of indirect speech.*

1. Union spokesperson Frances Baldwin said that the management had even refused to talk to them.

2. Company President Bates responded that "There was simply no money for salary raises."

3. TV reporter Joan Matthews asked Fumiko if, she agreed with Janice that cloning should be banned.

4. Frank asked Jim, What he would do if he couldn't find a job after he quit school?

5. Professor Martin asked Russell, if he intended to go to graduate school after earning his bachelor's degree

In conversation and informal writing, the most common reporting verbs in both direct and indirect speech are *say*, *tell*, and *ask*. In more formal writing, other verbs are also used: *add*, *claim*, *comment*, *confess*, *maintain*, *note*, *observe*, *point out*, *query*, *remark*, *report*, *respond*, *wonder*, and so on.

Chairman Bates **maintained** that the school district had no money to raise teachers' salaries. (= argued)

The union representative **claimed** that the company C.E.O. hadn't considered the union's demands. (= expressed the opinion)

3 | *In the following paragraph, change each instance of* **said** *to another reporting verb from the box.*

added	claimed	commented	maintained	noted	~~responded~~

Reporter Jennifer Goodenough asked Heidi Dennison what the single most enjoyable experience in her Peace Corps service had been. Dennison *said* that it had been the vacation she

responded
1.

had taken to Kenya, Tanzania, and Uganda at the end of her first year. Goodenough *said* that she

2.

was surprised at Dennison's answer because she had expected her to mention one of her accomplishments in Nigeria. She *said* that this was especially surprising given the fact that some

3.

people *said* that the Peace Corps existed simply for the purpose of giving Americans the chance to

4.

take vacations in exotic places. Dennison *said*, however, that the chance to learn about other

5.

countries was a valuable learning experience. She *said* that she thought such learning would

6.

contribute to international understanding in the long run.

4 Rewrite the following paragraph, changing all indirect speech to direct speech.
Refer to Unit 22 to review direct and indirect speech if necessary.

At dinner one night, Valerie told Keith that she thought it had been a mistake to pressure Ben to play football. Keith asked Valerie what had made her come to that conclusion. Valerie responded that Ben didn't have any real friends on the team. She added that his coach had said he'd seemed miserable for quite a long time. Keith said that he thought Valerie was probably right. He asked her if they should allow him to quit the team or encourage him to take up another sport.

1. _At dinner one night, Valerie said, "Keith, I think it was a mistake to pressure Ben to play football."_

_____

2. _____

_____

3. _____

_____

4. _____

_____

5. _____

_____

6. _____

_____

5 Interview a friend, classmate, or relative about a short, humorous incident that happened to the person. Write down the person's answers. Then write a one-paragraph record of the conversation in direct speech, paying particular attention to correct use of commas and quotation marks. Use the verbs **asked**, **said**, **told**, and any others that seem appropriate. Then rewrite the paragraph in indirect speech. Exchange papers with a partner. Proofread each other's paper and discuss the results. Then submit both of your paragraphs to your teacher.

Review Test

I *Read the conversations and underline each noun clause.*

1. **A:** I don't know <u>what we should do tonight.</u>

   B: Whatever you want to do is fine with me.

2. **A:** We haven't decided where we want to go on vacation.

   B: Don't you think Hawaii would be nice?

3. **A:** How do we decide who wins the prize?

   B: Give it to whoever gets the most points.

4. **A:** Do you think she's guilty?

   B: Well, the fact that she waited so long to contact the police doesn't help her case.

5. **A:** I can't believe what I'm seeing. The Bengals might even win this game.

   B: Yeah, I know. I'm amazed that they're doing this well.

6. **A:** Mr. Brown, I'm sorry to report that I need more time to complete the assignment.

   B: That's all right. Take whatever time you need. I want the job done well.

7. **A:** As for the problem of stopping violence in schools, I don't know what the answer is.

   B: I think that we need to ban weapons of all kinds.

8. **A:** Do you know what Samantha's problem is?

   B: No, but it's clear that she's very unhappy.

II *Read this letter. There are eight mistakes in the use of pronouns that introduce noun clauses. The first mistake is already corrected. Find and correct seven more.*

November 28

Dear Manny,

    Well, my first month as a literacy volunteer is over, and I feel exhilarated!

    ~~The fact that~~ *What* I like best is the chance to work with real people. In the mornings I

report to it's called "Open Classroom." I'm assigned to tutor whomever comes in

and asks for help. Most of the students are wonderful; sometimes I'm amazed

what they're so motivated to learn. In the afternoons I tutor my regular students.

I often work with a lady from Vietnam named Mrs. Tranh. When I started working

with her, she could hardly read at all. Now I'm really impressed by whichever

she's learned. At first I chose the assignments, but now we work on whomever

Mrs. Tranh chooses. If she wants to practice oral reading, that's which we do. If

she wants to work on comprehension, we do that for as long as she likes.

Sometimes we spend all afternoon on one thing, but that's OK; what she's so

motivated is very rewarding.

    Well, that's all for now. Write soon, and I'll do the same.

                Best,

                José

III *Complete the conversations with noun clauses, using the words in parentheses. Begin each noun clause with a word selected from the box. Some words will be used more than once.*

how far	that	the fact that	whatever	where	whoever

1. A: What shall we do when we get to Buenos Aires?

    B: _____ *Whatever you want to do* _____ is fine with me.
                  (you / want / do)

2. A: Where's Hattie?

B: I don't know _____. Maybe she's out in the backyard.
(she / be)

3. A: Do you think _____ an asset to our firm?
a. (Bill / be)

B: Well, _____ says something, I think.
b. (he / ill / a great deal)

4. A: What do you think we need to do about Bill's excessive absences?

B: I think _____ _____.
a. (we / need / do) b. (be / necessary)

5. A: Who do you think is behind this rumor?

B: I don't know, but _____ needs a talking to. It's obvious
a. (it / be)

_____ Ron. He has too much to lose.
b. (it / not / be)

6. A: Do you know _____ to San Andreas?
a. (it / be)

B: I think _____ about 90 miles from here.
b. (it / be)

IV *Study the pictures. Using the main verbs and clause introducers indicated, write a sentence containing a noun clause to explain each picture.*

1.

(clear / that / need)

It was clear that the Martins needed

a bigger house.

2.

(The Martins / wonder / if)

_____

_____

(continued)

3.

(Mrs. Martin's father / ask / where)

_____

_____

4.

(Mrs. Martin's mother / say / important / that)

_____

_____

5.

(Mrs. Martin's father / tell / that)

_____

_____

6.

(The Martins / thrilled / that)

_____

_____

V *Circle the letter of the choice that correctly completes each sentence.*

1. _____ students' test scores have not improved sufficiently in the last decade   A (B) C D

   suggests that the American education system is still in need of reform.
   - **(A)** The fact which
   - **(B)** That fact that
   - **(C)** Which
   - **(D)** What

2. Many educators seem convinced _____ students would respond   A B C D

   favorably to a change in the system.
   - **(A)** what
   - **(B)** the fact that
   - **(C)** that
   - **(D)** whatever

3. _____ America needs now is a two-track program in high schools.   A B C D
   - **(A)** What
   - **(B)** Whatever
   - **(C)** That
   - **(D)** Whichever

4. In the majority of high schools at present, many students are allowed   A B C D

   to take _____ courses they want.
   - **(A)** whoever
   - **(B)** however
   - **(C)** whichever
   - **(D)** whenever

5. In a two-track system, students would choose after the eighth grade   A B C D

   _____ educational track they wanted to study—academic or vocational.
   - **(A)** which
   - **(B)** who
   - **(C)** whom
   - **(D)** why

6. _____ was interested in a college education would study in the   A B C D

   academic track.
   - **(A)** Whatever
   - **(B)** Whoever
   - **(C)** Whomever
   - **(D)** Whichever

7. _____ students wanted to go right into the workplace after graduation   A B C D

   would choose the vocational track.
   - **(A)** Whatever
   - **(B)** However
   - **(C)** Whenever
   - **(D)** Whomever

8. _____ America is one of only two industrialized nations without a   A B C D

   two-track choice is a significant statistic.
   - **(A)** The fact which
   - **(B)** Which
   - **(C)** What
   - **(D)** The fact that

(continued)

9. It is obvious _____ the country needs this educational reform.   **A B C D**

   (**A**) what   (**C**) which

   (**B**) who   (**D**) that

10. It is important _____ that what they're learning is worthwhile.   **A B C D**

   (**A**) the fact that students believe   (**C**) whatever students believe

   (**B**) for students to believe   (**D**) however students believe

▶ *To check your answers, go to the Answer Key on page RT-6.*

PART IX

Conditionals and the Subjunctive

23 Conditionals; Other Ways to Express Unreality

Grammar in Context

BEFORE YOU READ

1 *What do you understand by "intuition"? Do you believe in intuition?*

2 *Have you had any experiences in which your or someone else's intuition proved correct?*

◯ *Read this story about trusting intuition.*

Intuition

I t was a sweltering day. Donna and Thain were driving down Maple Street, looking for a yard sale, when they spotted the old man. Waving at them with a halfhearted gesture, he looked as though he hadn't eaten for days.

"Nine-thirty in the morning, and it's already beastly hot. I wish I had an iced tea right now. Open your window, will you, Thain?"

"Wow! Look at that old man, Donna. Boy, I'd sure get out of this heat if I were him . . . Pull over, will you? Let's give him a ride. He's going to faint if he doesn't get out of the sun."

"Thain, I wish you would stop taking pity on every weirdo you see. He's probably an ax murderer. I bet he'll kill us and steal the car if we pick him up."

"I don't think so. He looks harmless to me—just a poor old guy. He's acting as if he's sick."

"But, Sweetie, we've got to get to that yard sale. There won't be anything worth buying if we don't get there soon. If only that chest of drawers would still be there!"

"My male intuition is telling me we'd better stop."

Intuition

"If I had a nickel for all the times we've done things because of your male intuition, I'd be a rich woman. Aren't females supposed to have the intuition, anyway? OK, but I just hope we don't end up in the newspaper headlines. I can see it all now: YOUNG MARRIED COUPLE MUTILATED BY SERIAL KILLER."

They pulled up to the curb in front of the old man. "Need some help, sir?" Thain asked.

The old man smiled. "Yes, thank you. Could you take me to a pharmacy? I'm diabetic, and I've run out of medicine. I'm on a trip around the country, but I keep forgetting to buy enough insulin. If I don't take my medicine regularly, I go into shock. If only I weren't so forgetful . . ."

They found a pharmacy and got the insulin. Back in the car, the old man said, "Now, if you can just take me to the bus station, I'll be on my way." Donna frowned, but Thain said, "Sure. We can do that." At the bus station, they helped the old man out of the car. "Can you tell me your names and your address? When I get back home, I'll send you a token of my appreciation." They gave him their names and address, said good-bye, and proceeded to the yard sale.

As Donna had predicted, all of the good merchandise had been sold. "We'd probably have that chest of drawers if we'd gotten here earlier," she said, "but I'm glad we stopped for the old guy. I'll be surprised if we ever hear from him, though. You don't really believe all that about his taking a trip around the country, do you, Thain?"

In a few days they had forgotten about the incident. Three months later they returned from a short vacation, and Donna was going through the pile of mail that had accumulated in their absence. She opened a long envelope with no return address.

"What in the world? Thain, come here and look at this!" There was a letter, neatly typed, which said,

> Dear Thain and Donna,
>
> I finished my trip around the country and had a marvelous time. I'm now back at home and won't be traveling anymore, I don't think. I met some wonderful people in my travels, the two of you among them.
>
> Thank you for your kindness to a forgetful old man. If you hadn't come along when you did and taken me to the pharmacy, I might have died. At the very least, I would have become quite ill if you hadn't been there to help. I wish there had been more time for us to get to know one another. If I had been fortunate enough to have any children of my own, I couldn't have had any nicer ones than you two. At any rate, I am enclosing a token of my gratitude.
>
> My warmest regards,
> Quentin Wilkerson

Something fluttered out of a second sheet of folded paper. It was a check for $50,000.

AFTER YOU READ

What do these sentences mean? Circle the letter of the sentence that correctly explains the meaning.

1. I wish I had an iced tea right now.

   a. She doesn't have an iced tea.　　b. She has an iced tea.

2. If only I weren't so forgetful.

   a. He remembers most things.　　b. He forgets a lot of things.

(continued)

3. At the very least, I would have become quite ill.

    a. He became ill.   **b.** He didn't become ill.

4. If I had been fortunate enough to have any children of my own, I couldn't have had any nicer ones than you two.

    a. He has children.   **b.** He doesn't have children.

Grammar Presentation

CONDITIONALS; OTHER WAYS TO EXPRESS UNREALITY

PRESENT AND FUTURE REAL CONDITIONALS

Present Conditionals		Future Conditionals	
If Clause	Result Clause	*If* Clause	Result Clause
If it **is** hot,	I **drink** iced tea.	If it **rains**,	we **will close** the windows.
If it **isn't** hot,	I **don't drink** iced tea.	If it **doesn't rain**,	we **won't close** the windows.

PRESENT UNREAL CONDITIONALS

Actual Situations	Conditionals	
	If Clause	Result Clause
It **is** rarely hot in Antarctica.	If it **were** hot in Antarctica,	it **would be** unusual.
It **is** usually hot in Egypt.	If it **weren't** hot in Egypt,	
It rarely **rains** in the Sahara.	If it **rained** in the Sahara,	
It usually **rains** in the jungle.	If it **didn't rain** in the jungle,	

PAST UNREAL CONDITIONALS

Actual Situations	Conditionals	
	If Clause	Result Clause
They **stopped**, so they **were** late.	If they **hadn't stopped**,	they **wouldn't have been** late.
They **didn't stop**, so they **weren't** late.	If they **had stopped**,	they **would have been** late.
They **helped** the man, so he **sent** a gift.	If they **hadn't helped** the man,	he **wouldn't have sent** a gift.
They **didn't help** the man, so he **didn't send** a gift.	If they **had helped** the man,	he **would have sent** a gift.

"MIXED" CONDITIONALS

Actual Situations	Conditionals	
	If Clause	Result Clause
He **didn't have** children, so he **is** alone.	past If he **had had** children,	present he **wouldn't be** alone.
His memory **is not** good, so he **didn't buy** his medicine.	present If his memory **were** good,	past he **would have bought** his medicine.

OTHER WAYS TO EXPRESS UNREALITY

Actual Situations	*Wish / If only* Statement
She **will miss** the sale.	She **wishes** (that) she **wouldn't miss** the sale.
	If only she **wouldn't miss** the sale.
They **can't buy** the chest of drawers.	They **wish** (that) they **could buy** the chest of drawers.
	If only they **could buy** the chest of drawers.
They **arrived** late.	They **wish** (that) they **hadn't arrived** late.
	If only they **hadn't arrived** late.

GRAMMAR NOTES

EXAMPLES

1. **Conditional sentences** describe situations that occur (or do not occur) because of certain conditions. They consist of two clauses, a **dependent condition clause** (also called the *if* **clause**) and an **independent result clause**. There are two types of conditional sentences: real and unreal.

   Real (or factual) **conditionals** are sentences that describe situations that

   a. occur regularly.

   - result   condition
   - Water **boils** if it **reaches** 100°C.

   b. are likely or possible in the future.

   - condition   result
   - If we **study**, we **will pass**.

   Unreal conditionals are sentences that describe situations that are untrue, unlikely, or impossible in the present or the past.

   - condition   result
   - If I **were** rich, I**'d buy** a car.

   - result   condition
   - I **would have helped** if you **had asked**.

   NOTE: In conditional sentences, the clauses can come in either order. The meaning is the same. We place a comma after the *if* clause if it comes first. We don't generally place a comma after the result clause if it comes first. Either or both clauses can be negative.

   - **If I don't finish my work early**, I won't be able to attend.

     OR
   - I won't be able to attend **if I don't finish my work early**.

(continued)

2. We use **present real conditional** sentences to talk about general truths, scientific facts, or habits and repeated events. We use the simple present in both clauses. We can also use the present progressive in the *if* clause.

In **future-time situations**, we use the simple present or the present progressive in the *if* clause and the future with *will* or *be going to, may, might, can,* or *could* in the result clause.

▶ **BE CAREFUL!** Use the simple present in the *if* clause, even though the time referred to is future.

- Plants **die** if they **don't get** enough water.
- People with diabetes **can control** their disease if they **take** insulin regularly.
- If **I'm flying**, I always feel nervous.
- If Barry **passes** the final exam, he **might pass** the course.
- Unless he **studies** hard, however, he **won't pass** the final exam.
- I'll contact you as soon as I **hear** from her.

  NOT I'll contact you ~~as soon as I'll hear from her.~~

---

3. Use the **present unreal conditional** to talk about unreal, untrue, imagined, or impossible conditions and their results. Use the simple past form of the verb in the *if* clause. If the verb is *be,* use *were* for all persons. Use *could, might,* or *would* + the base form of the verb in the result clause.

▶ **BE CAREFUL!** The simple past in the *if* clause is past in form only. It is not past in meaning.

▶ **BE CAREFUL!** Don't use *would* in the *if* clause in present unreal conditional sentences.

- If I **loved** you, **I'd ask** you to marry me.
- We **wouldn't stay up** so late if we **were** parents.
- I **might watch** videos if I **had** the day off.
- If I **were** you, I **wouldn't accept** the offer.

- I'd buy a new car if **I had** the money.

  NOT I'd buy a new car ~~if I would have the money.~~

---

4. Use the **past unreal conditional** to talk about past unreal, untrue, imagined, or impossible conditions and their unreal results. Use the past perfect in the *if* clause. Use *could, might,* or *would* + *have* + past participle in the result clause.

We often use the past unreal conditional to express regret about a situation that actually happened in the past.

- If I **had listened** to my inner voice, I **wouldn't have made** that mistake.
- Mary **would have accepted** your proposal if you**'d asked** in time.
- I **would have lent** you money if I **had known** you were in financial difficulty.

5. The times of the *if* clause and the result clause are sometimes different. Present unreal and past unreal conditional forms can be "**mixed**" in the same sentence.

past action
- If I **hadn't gone** to college, **I'd** still

present result
be working at the hardware store.
(*I went to college. I'm not working at the hardware store.*)

present action   past result
- If Sam **were coming**, he **would have arrived** by now.
(*Sam isn't coming. He hasn't arrived.*)

---

6. We often use **unreal conditionals** to express regret or sadness. In a similar way, we use *wish* + noun clause to express sadness or a desire for a different situation.

- I'd earn more **if I had a better job**.
- I **wish** (that) **I had a better job**.

a. Use *wish + could / would* + base form to express a wish about the future.

- I **wish** (that) you **would change** your mind about buying that house.

b. Use *wish* + the simple past to express a wish about the present.

- My wife **wishes** (that) I **helped** her with the housework more.

c. Use *wish* + the past perfect to express a wish about the past.

- My son **wishes** (that) he **hadn't taken** that job.

▶ **BE CAREFUL!** Don't confuse *wish* and *hope*. Use *wish* to express regrets about things that are unlikely or impossible to change. Use *hope* to express a desire about events that are possible or probable.

- I **wish** (that) she **would accept** my proposal
(*I don't think she will.*)
- I **hope** (that) she **accepts / will accept** my proposal.
(*It's possible or probable that she will.*)

(continued)

7. **If only** has a meaning similar to that of **wish**. *If only* is followed by a noun clause without *that*.

- I **wish** (that) I were good at sports.
- **If only** I were good at sports.

Use the simple past after *if only* to express a wish about something that is contrary to fact at present.

- **If only we weren't** so busy.

Use the past perfect after *if only* to express a wish that something had happened differently in the past.

- **If only I hadn't said** that.

▶ **BE CAREFUL!** Don't confuse *if only* with *only if*.

- **If only** Jerry studied more.
(= *I wish he would study more.*)
- **Only if** Jerry studied more would he have a chance of passing.
(= *This would be the only way for him to pass.*)

Focused Practice

1 | DISCOVER THE GRAMMAR

Look again at the opening reading and follow these instructions.

1. Find and circle the one present real conditional sentence that does not show future meaning.

2. Find and underline the five real conditional sentences that show future meaning.

3. Find the two sentences with *if only* and draw brackets ([ ]) around them.

4. Find and draw boxes around the two present unreal conditional sentences in the text.

5. Find and put dotted lines under the three past unreal conditional sentences.

6. Find and double underline the one mixed conditional sentence.

2 | SOME FACTS

Grammar Notes 1–2

Arrange the words in the correct order to create present real conditional sentences. Use correct punctuation.

1. sometimes / below / Farmers / temperature / drops / crops / zero / springtime / the / their / if / lose

   Farmers sometimes lose their crops if the springtime temperature drops below zero.

2. their / If / go / into / don't / shock / take / diabetics / sometimes / insulin / they

   _____

3. out / sources / if / energy / run / will / We / develop / alternate / of / don't / fuel / we

   _____

4. continues / warming / If / icecaps / the / global / could / polar / melt

_____

5. dies / Venus / it / A / doesn't / water / enough / flytrap / if / get

_____

6. by / population / world / trends / will / If / billion / the / reach / 2060 / continue / present / nine

_____

3 | WHAT WOULD YOU DO IF . . . ?   *Grammar Notes 2–3*

Use phrases in the box to complete the story with present and future conditional forms.

how would you feel	I will	I wouldn't be	I'd call
I'd keep	I'd take	I'd want	~~if I ask~~
if I were	if you really think	I'll do	it weren't
what would you do	will you give	you found	you were

JANE: Hello?

BILL: Hi, Jane. This is Bill. Got a couple of minutes for your little brother?

JANE: Always. What's up?

BILL: _____*If I ask*_____ you a question, _____ me an honest
                 1.   **2.**

answer? Tell me what you really think, not what you think I want to hear?

JANE: Of course _____. Shoot.
                        3.

BILL: _____ if _____ some money in a motel
             4.   **5.**

room?

JANE: _____ it to the front desk. Why?
             6.

BILL: Sally and I found $200 in our room at the motel we were staying at. She says we should keep

it, but a little voice told me I should call and ask you. If _____ so
                                                                    7.

much money, _____ concerned. _____ it.
                   8.   **9.**

But $200 is a quite a bit.

JANE: You mean you think this all depends on the amount of money?

BILL: Well, yes. Two hundred dollars is a significant amount, isn't it?

(continued)

JANE: I think it is. My take on this is that the previous occupants forgot it.

_____ if _____ the one who left it?
           10.   **11.**

BILL: I guess _____ someone to return it.
                              12.

JANE: Yeah. _____ you, _____ the front office
                              13.   **14.**

and ask if anyone has inquired about it.

BILL: OK, big sister. _____ it _____ it's the right
                              15.   **16.**

thing.

JANE: I do.

4 | WISHES

Grammar Notes 6–7

A *Look at the pictures. Write a sentence with* **wish** *for each.*

1.   *They wish the weather were better.* _____

2.   _____

3.   _____

4.   _____

5.   _____

6.   _____

1.

2.

3.

4.

5.

6.

B *Now rewrite each sentence with **if only**. Change subject pronouns and possessive adjectives where appropriate.*

1. *If only the weather were better.* _____

2. _____

3. _____

4. _____

5. _____

6. _____

5 | JUST THINK WHAT WOULD HAVE HAPPENED IF . . .

Complete the story with past unreal or mixed conditional sentences.

Stella and Hank were at the new racetrack one afternoon to meet their friends Kenny and

Allison and then go to dinner. Time passed, and Kenny and Allison didn't show up, so Stella and

Hank began to grow impatient. Hank said, "Let's go. They _____ *would have arrived* _____
                                                              1. (arrive)

by now if they _____." Now Stella and Hank had never bet on
                        2. (be coming)

a horse before and _____ so this time if Kenny and Allison
                            3. (not / do)

_____ there. There's a first time for everything, however, and
        4. (be)

Stella said, "OK, but we might as well bet on a horse as long as we're here." They studied the

racing form. Hank wanted to bet on Magic Dancer, a horse that had won many times. Stella's

intuition, however, was to go with Static, the horse that had won the fewest races. It's a good

thing they followed Stella's intuition, because things _____
                                                                    5. (turn out)

quite differently if _____. They went to the stands to watch the
                            6. (they / not)

race. At first it looked like Hank's original idea had been correct: Magic Dancer, the favored

horse, was running in the lead. In the final seconds, though, Static moved up suddenly and finally

passed Magic Dancer just before the finish line. Stella and Hank couldn't believe their eyes.

They'd won $10,000.

The next day they told Kenny and Allison about their adventure. "Sorry we didn't make it,"

Kenny said, "but we had a family emergency and couldn't call. I certainly _____
                                                                                    7. (not pick)

_____ Static if _____. Just think how much
                                    8. (I / be / betting)

money _____ if _____ $50
            9. (you / win)   **10. (you / bet)**

or $100 instead of $20! _____ rich now."
                                    11. (you / be)

Stella said, "It's too bad you had an emergency, but at least something good happened. We

_____ $10,000 richer right now if _____.
            12. (not / be)   **13. (you / make it)**

So we have you guys to thank."

6 | EDITING

There are nine mistakes in the use of conditionals and related forms in this diary entry. The first mistake is already corrected. Find and correct eight more.

June 4

                                        had

This has been one of those days when I wish I ~~would have~~ stayed in bed. It started at 7:30 this morning when Trudy called me up and asked me for "a little favor." She's always asking me to do things for her and never wants to take any responsibility for herself. She acts as if the world owes her a living. I wish she doesn't think like that. Today she wanted me to take her to the mall because she had to get her mother a birthday present. At first I said I couldn't because I had to be downtown at 11 A.M. for a job interview. Trudy said she'd do the same for me if I would ask her. Then she said it wouldn't take long to drive to the mall, and I'd have plenty of time to get downtown from there. I gave in and agreed to take her, but something told me I shouldn't. If I had listened to my inner voice, I might have had a job right now. When we were on the freeway, there was a major accident, and traffic was tied up for over an hour. By the time we got to the mall, it was 11:30, so I missed the appointment. I think I probably would get the job if I would have managed to make it to the interview, because my qualifications are strong. If only I wouldn't have listened to Trudy! I just wish she doesn't ask me to do things like this. If she asks me again, I wish I don't agree.

Communication Practice

7 | LISTENING

🎧 *Read the questions. Listen to the conversation. Then listen again and answer the questions in complete sentences.*

1. What does April wish?

   April wishes she and Bob weren't going together.

2. What does Sally wish April hadn't done?

   _____

3. What did April think Bob would do if she refused?

   _____

4. What would Sally have done?

   _____

5. What will the teacher do if she finds out?

   _____

6. What would Sally do if she were April?

   _____

7. What does Sally think April should tell Bob?

   _____

8. What should April do if Bob gets mad and says he wants to break up?

   _____

8 | THE CONDITIONAL GAME

Form two teams. Each team uses the prompts to construct eight conditional questions, four in the present and four in the past. Then each team creates two questions of its own, for a total of ten questions. The other team guesses what person or thing is being referred to.

Example: What / doing / if / spelunking
        A: What would you be doing if you were spelunking?
        B: We'd be exploring a cave.

Team A's Prompts

1. Where / be / if / in the capital of Honduras

2. How old / have to / be / if / the president of the United States.

3. Where / traveling / if / the monetary unit / the won

4. Where / be / if / visiting Angkor Wat

5. Who / been / if / the emperor of France in 1802

6. Who / been / if / the first prime minister of India

7. What country / been from / if / Marco Polo

8. What mountain / climbed / if / with Edmund Hillary and Tenzing Norgay

Team B's Prompts

1. How old / be / if / an octogenarian

2. Where / be traveling / if / in Machu Picchu

3. What / be / if / the largest mammal

4. What country / be in / if / standing and looking at Angel Falls

5. Who / been / if / the inventor of the telephone

6. What kind of creature / been / if / a stegosaurus

7. What / been your occupation / if / Genghis Khan

8. Who / been / if / Siddartha Gautama

9 | SMALL-GROUP DISCUSSION

Form small groups. Look again at the opening reading. How do you think the story ended? Would it have been ethical for Thain and Donna to cash the check Mr. Wilkerson sent them? Would it have been proper to keep the money? What would you have done if you had been in the situation? Tell the class about what your group has decided. Discuss the issue further as a class.

Example: **A:** If I'd been in their situation, I wouldn't have cashed the check.
        B: Why not?

10 | WRITING

*Write about a time when you ignored your intuition and inner voice and instead made a seemingly logical decision that turned out badly. Describe your original intuitive feelings, explain why you ignored them, and speculate on what would or might have happened if you had acted intuitively. Use conditional sentences and clauses with **wish** where appropriate.*

Example: A year ago I had an experience that taught me the advisability of going with my intuition. Looking back on the situation now, I wish I had paid attention to what my inner voice was telling me. Unfortunately, I didn't do that, and I had to suffer the consequences. I had saved up enough money for the down payment on a new car and was ready to close the deal. When a cousin heard of my plans, however, he offered to sell me his two-year-old car for half the price of the down payment. Something told me this was the wrong thing to do, but . . .

11 | ON THE INTERNET

Do a search to discover what happened on each of the following dates. What would or might have happened if these events hadn't occurred? How would the world be different?

- October 12, 1492
- November 22, 1963
- November 9, 1989

More Conditions;
The Subjunctive

Grammar in Context

BEFORE YOU READ

1 *What problems are you aware of regarding how we treat elderly people?*

2 *In your opinion, what is the best living situation for an elderly person?*

⌒ *Read this article about aging.*

THOSE HAPPY GOLDEN YEARS ?

An American woman in her forties visits her elderly mother's doctor for advice about dealing with her mother's problems and demands. Here is their conversation:

Woman: I'm at my wits' end. Mom is driving me crazy. She insists I come over and help her at a moment's notice. She says she's not getting enough exercise, but when I suggest she go out with me and take a walk, she gets angry. She's been living in her own house since Dad died, and it's gotten to be too much for her. Actually, I think she should sell that house. Had I known how things were going to turn out, I would have recommended she sell it a long time ago. I don't know what to do. It almost seems as if she's become the child and I've become the parent. You've known her for a long time. What would you recommend?

Doctor: Well, what if she moved in with you and your husband? Would that work?

Woman: I don't think so. I love her dearly, but my husband and I have our life too. She's always said it's important for her to keep her independence. But what other options are there? What would be best for her? I'd rather she not go into a nursing home. I've heard some pretty bad things about them.

Doctor: Well, there are good nursing homes and bad ones, but she's still quite healthy and doesn't need to go into one. My impression is that she's pretty social. If so, I'd say she needs a situation where she can have contact with people her own age.

(continued)

THOSE HAPPY GOLDEN YEARS?

Woman: Yes. She's always complaining about how lonely she is. I know it's important that she have friends, but she can't get out and make them on her own, and I can't do it for her.

Doctor: Then I'd propose you find a retirement center or an assisted living center. Otherwise, the problem will just get worse.

Woman: What's the difference between the two?

Doctor: Retirement centers are for people who are still active and can basically take care of themselves. They provide a lot of social activities, along with meals and other benefits. Assisted living is for people who can still function to some degree but need assistance with movement, taking medications, and the like. Actually, some facilities are both retirement center and assisted living center. I know of several good ones. I'd recommend you look into them.

Woman: Aren't those places pretty expensive?

Doctor: Yes, they are. But sometimes they're the best alternative.

The conversation illustrates how remarkably things have changed in the United States and elsewhere in the world. There are far more people, and they are living much longer than they used to. Average life expectancy has been increasing steadily for decades and is now greater than 77 years in the United States. In some countries it is higher: 79+ in France, about 80 in Switzerland, and about 81 in Japan. In fact, the worldwide trend is toward longer and longer lives. In the past, people lived much shorter lives. When they grew older, they depended on their children's support. Without it, they would have been in trouble. Increasingly, however, living with one's children is seen as an option less and less.

Another significant factor in the situation is the revolution of rising expectations, coupled with the rise in the overall standard of living. In today's world, people take for granted things that would have been unheard of 100 years ago. Older people go on European vacations. They take expensive ocean cruises. They participate in unusual and often costly hobbies. All of these things are expected. The question is how they will be paid for.

Today we're faced with a whole new set of challenges. We love our senior citizens and want the best for them. But expectations are higher, and there are more people living longer. We may run out of financial resources. Should that happen, we will need to come up with entirely new ways of caring for our seniors. Every one of us will one day be old, so it's essential that we understand the value of the elderly in society and how we can best provide for them.

AFTER YOU READ

*Look at each pair of sentences. Does the second sentence mean about the same as the first? Circle **Y** (yes) or **N** (no).*

1. When I suggest she go out with me and take a walk, she gets angry.

   Y N   When I suggest that we go out and take a walk, she gets angry.

2. What if she moved in with you and your husband?

   Y N   What happened when she moved in with you and your husband?

3. I know it's important that she have friends.

   Y N   I know it's important for her to have friends.

4. Then I'd propose you find a retirement center or an assisted living center; otherwise, the problem will just get worse.

   Y N   If you do, the problem will just get worse.

Grammar Presentation

MORE CONDITIONS; THE SUBJUNCTIVE

IMPLIED CONDITIONS

Nonstandard Condition	(= Implied Condition)	Result Clause
With a bit of luck,	(If we have a bit of luck,)	we'll find a place for her.
Without your help,	(If you hadn't helped,)	I wouldn't have succeeded.
But for his pension,	(If he didn't have a pension,)	he'd have no income.
She might be lucky; **if so**,	(If she is lucky,)	she'll meet some new friends.
He might get the chance; **if not**,	(If he doesn't get the chance,)	he won't retire.
She is lonely; **otherwise**,	(If she weren't lonely,)	she wouldn't need company.

INVERTED CONDITIONS

Inverted Condition	(= Standard Condition)	Result Clause
Were he in love,	(If he **were** in love,)	he would get married.
Were he **not** in love,	(If he **weren't** in love,)	he wouldn't get married.
Had I **seen** her,	(If I **had seen** her,)	I would have called you.
Should we **do** it,	(If we **should do** it,)	we will celebrate.

(continued)

The Subjunctive in Noun Clauses

Verbs of Advice, Necessity, and Urgency + Subjunctive	
Main Clause	Noun Clause
The doctor **suggested**	(that) Frank **switch** medications.
The boss **demanded**	(that) Rosa **arrive** at work by 9:00.
The fireman **insisted**	(that) she **leave** the burning building immediately.

Adjectives of Advice, Necessity, and Urgency + Subjunctive	
Main Clause	Noun Clause
It is **advisable**	(that) he **arrive** one-half hour before the appointment.
It is **mandatory**	(that) no one **enter** the building without a permit.
It is **urgent**	(that) she **get** to the hospital at once.

GRAMMAR NOTES

EXAMPLES

1. **Conditions in conditional sentences** are sometimes implied rather than stated directly in an *if* clause.

   Conditions may be implied by using *but for, if not, if so, otherwise, with, without,* etc.

   - Your mother may be lonely. **If so,** you should look into a retirement center.
     (= *If she is lonely . . .*)

   In a sentence with an implied condition, there is no change in the result clause.

   - She needs to be part of the decision. Otherwise, **she'll never be happy.**
     (= *If she isn't part of the decision, she'll never be happy*)

   As with other conditional sentences, the condition may precede or follow the result clause.

   - **But for her daughter's support,** she would live in poverty.

   - She would live in poverty **but for her daughter's support.**

2. Unreal conditions with *had* (past perfect), *should*, and *were* are sometimes expressed by deleting *if* and **inverting** the subject and the verb.

- **If I had known** she was ill, I would have done something.
- **Had I known** she was ill, I would have done something.

If there is an inverted condition, there is no change in the result clause.

- If I were to accept the job, **I would insist on benefits**.
- Were I to accept the job, **I would insist on benefits**.

As with other conditional sentences, the inverted condition clause can precede or follow the result clause.

▶ **BE CAREFUL!** Negative inversion is formed by adding *not* after the inverted verb and the subject. Don't contract *not* and the verb.

- **Had I not received** the phone call, I would not have been able to help.

  NOT ~~Hadn't I received the phone call, I wouldn't have been able to help.~~

USAGE NOTE: Sentences with inverted condition clauses have the same meaning as conditionals with *if* but are more formal.

---

3. The **subjunctive** is rather uncommon in English. However, one common example is the use of *were* in unreal conditions.

- If I **were** you, I'd visit my parents more often.
- We could take Mom for a walk if it **weren't** raining.

▶ **BE CAREFUL!** This use of *were* occurs only in present unreal conditions. It is not used for past situations.

- If I **had been** there, I would have helped her.

  NOT ~~If I were there~~, I would have helped her.

---

4. Another form of the **subjunctive** uses the **base form** of a verb in noun clauses.

    main clause   noun clause
- We recommend (that) he **see** a doctor.

▶ **BE CAREFUL!** The main verb in a noun clause can be past, present, or future. However, the subjunctive verb is the base form.

- We recommended (that) he **sell** his house.

  NOT ~~We recommended that he sold his house.~~

Form the negative of a subjunctive verb by placing *not* before the base form.

- My aunt and uncle insisted (that) we **not come** to visit them today.

To form a passive subjunctive, use *be* + the past participle.

- The doctor recommends (that) Uncle John **be hospitalized**.

NOTE: In noun clauses with subjunctive constructions, we can usually omit the word *that*.

(continued)

5. The **subjunctive** is used in noun clauses following **verbs of advice**, **necessity**, and **urgency**, such as *demand*, *insist*, *propose*, *recommend*, and *suggest*.

▶ **BE CAREFUL!** We do not use infinitives after these verbs.

Note that *insist (on)*, *propose*, *recommend*, and *suggest* can also be followed by a gerund phrase. The meaning of this structure is similar to the meaning of a sentence with a subjunctive in a noun clause.

Note that the verbs *ask*, *order*, *require*, *urge*, etc., may also occur in the pattern verb + object + infinitive. When they are used in subjunctive constructions, the word *that* is usually not omitted.

- I **propose** (that) we **ask** Mom and Dad about their wishes.

- My parents **insisted** (that) I **come** to visit them often.

- He **suggested** (that) we **talk**.
  NOT ~~He suggested us to talk.~~

- We **insist on / propose / recommend / suggest getting** a second opinion.

- I **asked** that my brothers and sisters **be** present.
  OR
- I **asked** my brothers and sisters **to be** present.

---

6. The **subjunctive** is also used after **adjectives of advice**, **necessity**, and **urgency**, such as *advisable*, *crucial*, *desirable*, *essential*, *important*, *mandatory*, *necessary*, and *urgent*. Subjunctive verbs after adjectives of urgency, necessity, and advice occur in the pattern *It + be +* adjective *+ that* clause. We do not usually omit the word *that* in this type of clause.

NOTE: The pattern shown above can be replaced with *It + be +* **adjective** *+ for +* **noun or object pronoun** *+* **infinitive**, which is more informal.

- It is **essential** that elderly people **be treated** with dignity.
- It's **important** that she **understand** her options.
- It was **necessary** that my father **get** medical treatment.

- It's **important for her to understand** her options.
- It was **necessary for my father to get** medical treatment.

Reference Note
For a list of **expressions followed by the subjunctive in a noun clause,** see Appendix 24 on page A-11.

Focused Practice

1 | DISCOVER THE GRAMMAR

A *Look again at the opening reading. Find the three examples of implied conditions and write the nonstandard conditions here.*

1. _____

2. _____

3. _____

B *Find the two sentences with inverted conditions and write the inverted conditions here.*

1. _____

2. _____

C *Circle the eight subjunctive verb forms in the opening reading.*

D *Read the following sentences. Is the second sentence a correct rewriting of the first? Circle* **Y** *(yes) or* **N** *(no).*

1. I would have recommended she sell it a long time ago.

   Y   N   I would have recommended her selling it a long time ago.

2. She's always said it's important for her to keep her independence.

   Y   N   She's always said it's important that she keep her independence.

3. I propose you find a retirement center or an assisted living center.

   Y   N   I propose you to find a retirement center or an assisted living center.

4. I'd recommend you look into them.

   Y   N   I'd recommend you to look into them.

5. So it's essential that we understand the value of the elderly in society.

   Y   N   So it's essential for us to understand the value of the elderly in society.

2 | PATIENT AND DOCTOR

Grammar Note 1

Read this conversation between a patient and his doctor. Rewrite the six conditional sentences. Replace the if *clauses with nonstandard conditions.*

DOCTOR: Bob, you've got to take your medications regularly. If you don't, you're going to get sick.

BOB: I just can't remember to take them.

DOCTOR: Maybe there's a friend at your center who can remind you. If there is, that would solve your problem.

BOB: And if there isn't, what can I do? My memory just isn't what it used to be.

DOCTOR: We can arrange for a nurse to monitor your medications. But now here's another thing. You need to stop smoking.

BOB: Impossible. If I don't have cigarettes, I can't make it through the day.

DOCTOR: There must be a way. You can do it if you find a buddy who has the same problem. You have friends there, don't you?

BOB: I sure do. I'd be lonely if it weren't for my friends. Maybe there's someone.

DOCTOR: Promise me you'll try to quit.

BOB: OK.

1. *Otherwise, you're going to get sick.* _____

2. _____

3. _____

4. _____

5. _____

6. _____

3 | A NEW LIFE

Grammar Notes 1–2

A *Fill in the blanks in the story with items from the box.*

had she known	if not	if so
otherwise	~~were she to stay~~	with

Doris Allen had just moved to St. Louis from Russellville, the small town where she had lived until her husband had died a year previously. For some time, Doris had felt it was necessary for her to leave Russellville. _____*Were she to stay*_____ in Russellville, she felt, she would just fall
                                        1.
into a rut she would never escape from, so she decided to leave and start a new life. At the age of 60 she still needed to work, however. _____ how difficult it would be to
                                                              2.

find employment, she might have stayed in her hometown. She loved the big city, though, and she had been looking hard for work. The only problem was that Doris needed to find a job fairly soon; _____ _{3.}, she wouldn't be able to afford her apartment. A lot of her savings were already gone.

There was another problem: Doris hadn't worked for years and was unaccustomed to job hunting. One day she was wandering around downtown, feeling that _____ _{4.} a bit of luck she might find something. She saw a pleasant-looking florist's shop. Maybe they were hiring. _____ _{5.}, she might get a job. _____ _{6.}, she wouldn't lose anything by going in and asking. Without even thinking further, she walked in.

"I'm Doris Allen, and I was wondering whether you were doing any hiring. I have a lot of experience with flowers and gardening."

The manager said, "Actually, we do need someone to work part-time. I was just going to put up a sign in the window. Tell me more about your experience."

Doris got the job.

B *Rewrite the word or phrase in each blank above with an if clause that restates the condition.*

1. *If she were to stay* _____

2. _____

3. _____

4. _____

5. _____

6. _____

4 | DECISIONS

Match the questions on the left with the correct responses on the right. Then complete the responses using the subjunctive forms of the verbs in the box.

do	go	spend	stay

1. What did the doctor say about Mom?

2. Where does he think she should go?

3. How long does he think she should stay?

4. What's his recommendation about Dad?

5. How do you think Dad will react?

6. Do you think I should try to persuade him?

a. Yes, if you insist _____ it, he'll go along with the plan.

b. He'll demand _____ all of his cooking and laundry—at his house.

c. He recommended _____ to Park West.

d. He suggested _____ three weeks in the home.

e. He proposed _____ some time in a nursing home.

f. He recommended _____ with us for the time Mom's away.

5 | INGREDIENTS FOR HAPPY GOLDEN YEARS

A *What do seniors need to enjoy their golden years? Complete each sentence with both an adjective and the correct form of a verb from the box. One verb will be used twice. The last sentence will be in the passive voice.*

advisable	crucial	~~desirable~~	essential	~~feel~~	important
make	necessary	stay	treat	visit	

1. It is ____*desirable that seniors feel*____ they are still independent.
   (seniors)

2. It is _____ at least some of their own decisions.
   (they)

3. It is _____ the doctor periodically.
   (an elderly person)

4. It is _____ them as often as possible.
   (their children)

5. It is _____ mentally active.
(a senior)

6. It is _____ with dignity.
(every elderly person)

B *Now rewrite each sentence in Exercise A using* **for** *+ noun or object pronoun + infinitive.*

1. _It is desirable for seniors to feel they are still independent._ _____

2. _____

3. _____

4. _____

5. _____

6. _____

6 | A PERSONAL INVENTORY
Grammar Notes 2–6

Complete each of the following sentences, drawing from your own experience or opinions. Use subjunctive verb forms where appropriate.

1. My parents suggested _____

2. My parents insisted _____

3. It's essential that I _____

4. It's important for me _____

5. It's essential that a person _____

6. Had I known _____

7. Were I _____

8. Should I _____

7 | EDITING

Read this letter. It has eight mistakes in verb constructions. The first mistake is already corrected. Find and correct seven more.

December 10

Dear Henrietta,

It's time I wrote and filled you in on what's been happening since I left Russellville. I finally got a job! Remember when you suggested I just ~~went~~ *go* walking around, getting a sense of what St. Louis was like? A few weeks ago I was getting rather worried since I had spent most of the money I had saved to get me through the job-hunting period. It's not easy for a 60-year-old woman to find a job, you know. I had gotten to the point where it was absolutely essential that I found something or came back to Russellville. So I decided to follow your advice. I had known how easy this would be, I would have tried it the first week I was here. I started walking around in the downtown area, and before I knew it, I saw a beautiful little florist's shop. I walked right in, unafraid, and asked if they needed anyone. Can you believe that they did?

I was really happy in my job until my boss hired a new assistant manager who has been making my life miserable. Among other things, he demands me to make coffee for him. He also insists that I'm doing other things that aren't in my job description. I took this job to work with plants, not to serve him coffee. I think I need to tell him where I stand. It's important that he stops treating me as his personal slave.

I have a few days off for the holidays. Do you have some time off? If so, how about coming down here for a visit? Wouldn't that be fun? I have a spare bedroom in my apartment. If you can come, I suggest you to drive, as it isn't far. Please write and let me know.

Love,

Doris

Communication Practice

8 | LISTENING

🎧 *Read the questions. Listen to the telephone conversation. Then listen again and answer the questions in complete sentences.*

1. What did the daughter ask that the mother do?

The daughter asked the mother to babysit.

2. What did the daughter almost do when the mother said no?

3. Had the mother known who was calling, what would she have done?

4. What did the mother have to do the last time this happened?

5. What is it important that the daughter do?

6. What does the mother's friend suggest she do?

9 | DISCUSSION

A *Read these statements. Then mark* **A** *(agree),* **D** *(disagree), or* **IB** *(in between), according to your personal beliefs.*

_____ **1.** It's desirable that elderly parents live with their children rather than being sent to nursing homes.

_____ **2.** Anyone over the age of 80 should not be allowed to drive.

_____ **3.** It is essential that national governments pay for the health care of the elderly.

_____ **4.** It is reasonable that national governments pay part of the costs of seniors' living in retirement centers or assisted living centers.

_____ **5.** People should work until they are 70 before receiving Social Security.

B *In small groups, discuss your answers. Share your group's opinions with the rest of the class.*

> **Example:** **A:** I think it is desirable that elderly parents live with their children.
> **B:** Why?
> **A:** The parents raised the children. Now the children owe them something.

10 | PICTURE DISCUSSION

In small groups, discuss this picture. What does it show about cross-generational relationships? What can older people teach the young?

Example:

A: What do you think the picture shows?

B: For one thing, it shows it's important that family members have close relationships . . .

Her First Book by Edward Gonzales © 1997 all rights reserved.

11 | WRITING

Write several paragraphs about an elderly person you know and respect. Describe some of your experiences with that person and explain why this person is important to you.

Example: One of the key persons in my life was my Aunt Harriet. She passed away a few years ago, but she helped me a great deal when I was younger. I had been considering college but had decided not to go since I didn't have the money. Aunt Harriet insisted that I go and told me that she would help me out by lending me the money . . .

12 | ON THE INTERNET

Choose a country (your own, if you wish) and do a search to find its standard of living and the life expectancy there of males and females. Use the key words **life expectancy** and **standard of living**, along with the country's name. Report the results of your search to the class.

From **Grammar** to **Writing**
Avoiding Run-On Sentences and Comma Splices

A sentence has at least one independent clause. A sentence containing more than one independent clause must be punctuated properly to avoid two kinds of errors: the **run-on sentence** and the **comma splice**.

A run-on sentence is a group of words containing at least two independent clauses without any punctuation separating them; the sentences are "run together."

independent clause   independent clause
Thain and Donna were on the way to a yard sale an old man waved to them.

Here are four ways to correct a run-on sentence:

1. Separate the two independent clauses with a period. Capitalize the first word of the second clause.

   Thain and Donna were on the way to a yard sale. **An** old man waved to them.

2. Separate the two independent clauses with a semicolon. Do not capitalize the first word of the second clause.

   Thain and Donna were on their way to a yard sale; an old man waved to them.

3. Join the two independent clauses with a comma and a coordinating conjunction.

   Thain and Donna were on their way to a yard sale, **and** an old man waved to them.

4. Make one of the independent clauses dependent by adding a subordinating conjunction, and separate the two clauses with a comma if the dependent clause comes first.

   When Thain and Donna were on their way to a yard sale, an old man waved to them.

1 | *Correct these run-on sentences by using the method in parentheses.*

1. The old man had forgotten to buy medicine. he went into diabetic shock. (period)

2. Thain asked Donna to pull over his intuition told him the old man needed their help.

   (semicolon)

3. Kate knew she had to change her relationship with her boss she didn't know how to do it.

   (coordinating conjunction and comma)

(continued)

4. Donna wished they had gotten to the yard sale on time she was glad they had stopped to help the old man. (subordinating conjunction and comma)

A **comma splice** is the joining of two independent clauses with only a comma. A comma, however, does not provide adequate punctuation.

independent clause   independent clause
Marsha read *The Assertive Individual's Handbook*, she learned a lot about expressing herself in the process.

A comma splice can be corrected by the same four methods used to correct a run-on sentence.

1. Use a period.

Marsha read *The Assertive Individual's Handbook*. **S**he learned a lot about expressing herself in the process.

2. Use a semicolon.

Marsha read *The Assertive Individual's Handbook*; she learned a lot about expressing herself in the process.

3. Use a comma and a coordinating conjunction.

Marsha read *The Assertive Individual's Handbook*, **and** she learned a lot about expressing herself in the process.

4. Make one of the clauses dependent by adding a subordinating conjunction.

When Marsha read *The Assertive Individual's Handbook*, she learned a lot about expressing herself in the process.

A fifth way of correcting a comma splice is to convert one of the clauses into an adverbial phrase if the subjects of the two clauses are the same.

Marsha read *The Assertive Individual's Handbook*, **learning** a lot about expressing herself in the process.

The period and the semicolon are similar punctuation marks in that they are both used between independent clauses. The period can be thought of as separating two clauses, and the semicolon can be thought of as joining two clauses. Remember not to capitalize the first word after a semicolon (unless it is *I* or a proper noun).

The teachers considered the Board of Education's offer; then they went on strike.

Use a semicolon instead of a period to join independent clauses if you feel that the two clauses have a close connection in meaning.

Kate's job situation deteriorated a great deal; she had to speak to her boss.

BE CAREFUL! Do not use a semicolon to connect an independent clause and a dependent clause.

While I was learning to be assertive, I learned many things about myself.

NOT While I was learning to be assertive; I learned many things about myself.

2 Correct each of these comma splices by using the method in parentheses.

1. The old man looked ill ⫻; he needed to get out of the sun quickly. (semicolon)

2. Thain and Donna drove to a pharmacy, they got the old man his insulin. (period)

3. Donna wanted to get to the yard sale, there was a chest of drawers for sale. (semicolon)

4. Donna didn't want to stop for the old man, Thain persuaded her it was necessary. (comma and coordinating conjunction)

5. Harold says he will seek professional help to overcome his anger, there is no assurance that he will carry out his promise. (subordinating conjunction / dependent clause and comma)

6. Nancy felt dominated by her mother-in-law, she needed to take assertive action. (Make the first clause an adverbial phrase.)

3 Correct the following run-on sentences, using the punctuation mark in parentheses. Capitalize where necessary.

1. A tiny voice inside Jeremy told him he would hate the job; therefore, he turned it down. (semicolon)

2. Nancy says she wants to do something worthwhile if so, she should consider volunteer work. (period)

3. I need to get a bank loan otherwise, I'll have to file for bankruptcy. (semicolon)

4. Ben and Carolyn would like to send Jim to a private school however, the school is expensive, and Jim doesn't want to go. (period)

5. Fred and Claudia love their new neighborhood in fact, they're going to buy a house there. (semicolon)

4 Carefully read and study this passage, which contains 13 independent clauses. There are 11 mistakes consisting of run-on sentences or comma splices. Correct the mistakes by adding periods or semicolons and capitalizing correctly. The first mistake is already corrected. Find and correct 10 more.

Call it either intuition or good vibrations. $\overset{W}{\text{w}}$hatever you want to call it, it works, last summer, I was one of four members of a committee to hire a new head nurse at the nursing home where I work, we interviewed two candidates as finalists, a man named Bob and a woman named Sarah on paper, Bob was better qualified he had a master's degree while Sarah had only a bachelor's degree, however, Sarah was the one who really impressed us she answered all of the questions straightforwardly and simply, Bob, on the other hand, evaded some of our questions while simultaneously trying to make us think he knew everything and could do everything all of us on the committee just liked Sarah better in fact, she got the job because she was the person we all felt we wanted to work with. Our intuition wasn't wrong, she's turned out to be a wonderful nurse.

5 | *Write a paragraph (six to ten sentences) on one of these topics or a similar topic that interests you.*

- A problem I overcame

- A problem I need to overcome

- A time when my intuition proved correct

Begin your first sentence with a capital letter, and end the last sentence with a period. However, do not include any other punctuation or capital letters at the beginnings of sentences. Exchange papers with a partner. Read your partner's paper and add punctuation and capitalization, making sure to avoid run-on sentences and comma splices. Discuss your papers. Then rewrite your paragraph and submit both copies to your teacher.

Review Test

PART IX

I   *Read the sentences. Do the underlined verb constructions indicate past (**P**), present (**PR**), or future (**F**) time?*

PR   **1.** If I <u>had</u> a million dollars, I'd give a lot of it to charity.

_____   **2.** We'll go to the movies if Mary and Pat <u>get</u> here on time.

_____   **3.** I wish you <u>would change</u> your mind about getting the car.

_____   **4.** If I <u>were</u> you, I'd apologize to him.

_____   **5.** <u>Had</u> I known you'd react like this, I never would have asked.

_____   **6.** She'<u>d be working</u> as a nurse if she'd finished college.

_____   **7.** If only we'<u>d taken</u> Jack's advice.

_____   **8.** Sheryl would help out if she <u>didn't have to work</u>.

_____   **9.** I'll leave a key out for you in case you <u>arrive</u> after we leave.

_____   **10.** Bill wishes he <u>owned</u> a house.

II   *Read the paragraph about Brandon's car problem. Then complete the sentences with conditional forms.*

     Recently I had an experience that taught me a lesson. My inner voice told me I needed to get the oil in my car changed, but I kept putting it off. Last Tuesday on the Appleton Expressway I was on my way to a job interview when the car just quit. The engine seized because it was out of oil. Before I could make it to the side of the road, another car rear-ended me. That did about $1,000 worth of damage to the car, and I had to have the car's engine completely replaced. I also had to pay a towing bill of $150, and I obviously didn't make it to the job interview. If only I'd listened to my inner voice. Hopefully, I've learned my lesson.

1. *Brandon wishes he had not put off changing the oil in his car.*
       (Brandon / wish / not put off / change / the oil in his car)

2. _____
       (If / he / change / the oil / the engine / not seize)

3. _____
       (If / the engine / not seize / the other car / not rear-end him)

4. _____
       (He / not / have to / pay a towing bill)

(continued)

439

5. _____
   (He / not / have to / replace the engine)

6. _____
   (He / could / make it to the job interview / if / all this / not happen)

7. _____
   (If / he / make it to the interview / he / might / have a job now)

8. _____
   (Brandon / wish / he / listen / to his inner voice)

III *Read the advice columnist's response to a letter from "Mary in Harrisburg." Then complete five subjunctive sentences that restate the columnist's suggestions.*

> **To Mary in Harrisburg:**
> No one should have to put up with a dog that barks all night. First, it's essential for you to talk with your next-door neighbor. At the same time, though, it's important not to lose your temper while you're explaining your side of the issue. Ask your neighbor to keep the dog in at night. Stay calm. If she refuses, insist on her getting rid of the animal. If she doesn't do something about the problem, I'd recommend calling the animal control bureau.

1. It is essential _____ *that Mary talk with her neighbor.* _____.

2. It is important _____ while she is explaining her side of the issue.

3. Mary should ask_____.

4. If she refuses, Mary should insist _____.

5. The columnist recommends _____ if her neighbor doesn't do something about the problem.

IV *Read this conversation. Complete the verb phrases that occur after* **wish**, **hope**, *and*
if only.

DONNA: I can't believe Mr. Wilkerson sent us a check for $50,000. I wish

_____*we'd been able to*_____ get better acquainted with him when he was here.
          1. (we / be able to)

THAIN: Yeah. If only _____ what was happening.
          2. (we / realize)

DONNA: I just hope _____ taking his insulin. I wish
       3. (he / keep)

_____ someone around to remind him in case he forgets.
     4. (there / be)

THAIN: You know, I really wish _____ him in some way. The trouble is,
        5. (we / can contact)

there's no return address on the envelope. Hey! What about the postmark? Where is that

envelope, anyway?

DONNA: Here it is. Oh no. Look at this! If only _____ so blurred. You
          6. (it / not / be)

can't see the city name.

THAIN: What I wish is that _____ a magnifying glass. Hey, wait; I can
        7. (we / have)

make out the zip code. It's . . . 93302. Honey, get the almanac, will you?

DONNA: Here it is. Zip codes that start with "9" are on the West Coast, aren't they? I hope

_____ like finding a needle in a haystack. Try California.
     8. (this / not / be)

THAIN: OK . . . Here it is! 93302—that's Bakersfield. If only _____
               9. (we / know)

someone in Bakersfield.

DONNA: I know! Let's get on the Internet and look up the Bakersfield phone directory. Maybe his

name will be listed. Let's hope _____, anyway.
          10. (it / be)

V *Look at the pictures. Using the words in parentheses, write a conditional or subjunctive sentence to describe each situation.*

1.

(suggested)

Sam suggested that they

stay just 15 minutes.

2.

(insisted)

_____

_____

3.

(not stay up late)

_____

_____

4.

(already get some gas)

_____

_____

5.

(take a taxi)

_____

_____

6.

(listen to Karen's advice)

_____

_____

VI *Circle the letter of the choice that correctly completes each sentence.*

1. You need to get some job retraining. _____ it, you risk being laid off.   A B C (D)

   (**A**) If so   (**C**) With

   (**B**) If not   (**D**) Without

2. I recommend that Miriam _____ a boarding school. She'd be much more challenged academically.   A B C D

   (**A**) attends   (**C**) is attending

   (**B**) attend   (**D**) were attending

3. Ambrose had to take a job at a fast-food restaurant; _____, he wouldn't have been able to make his car payment.   A B C D

   (**A**) otherwise   (**C**) had he done so

   (**B**) if so   (**D**) were that the case

4. I wish you _____ make it to the family reunion on the 15th. Everyone will be there.   A B C D

   (**A**) could   (**C**) can

   (**B**) were   (**D**) would

5. If Tim were planning to go, he _____ us by now.   A B C D

   (**A**) would contact   (**C**) might contact

   (**B**) would have contacted   (**D**) were contacting

6. At this point, Shannon wishes she _____ in mechanical drawing. She hates the course.   A B C D

   (**A**) didn't enroll   (**C**) hadn't enrolled

   (**B**) wouldn't enroll   (**D**) were to enroll

7. You were right when you suggested I _____ my intuition in this business deal. I did, and it worked.   A B C D

   (**A**) follow   (**C**) were to follow

   (**B**) followed   (**D**) had followed

8. If only we _____ to get to know one another in the time we had.   A B C D

   (**A**) will be able   (**C**) would have been able

   (**B**) were able   (**D**) had been able

9. My wife will be home by 7:00 P.M. on the 18th. _____ before she does, please water the lawn.   A B C D

   (**A**) Should arrive   (**C**) Should you arrive

   (**B**) You should arrive   (**D**) Should you have arrived

(continued)

10. It sounds like something is wrong with the car's engine. _____, we'd
    better take it to the garage immediately.

    (**A**) Otherwise   (**C**) If not

    (**B**) But for that   (**D**) If so

A B C D

▶ *To check your answers, go to the Answer Key on page RT-6.*

APPENDICES

1 | Irregular Verbs

BASE FORM	SIMPLE PAST	PAST PARTICIPLE
arise	arose	arisen
awake	awoke/awaked	awaked/awoken
be	was/were	been
bear	bore	borne/born
beat	beat	beaten/beat
become	became	become
begin	began	begun
bend	bent	bent
bet	bet	bet
bite	bit	bitten
bleed	bled	bled
blow	blew	blown
break	broke	broken
bring	brought	brought
broadcast	broadcast/broadcasted	broadcast/broadcasted
build	built	built
burn	burned/burnt	burned/burnt
burst	burst	burst
buy	bought	bought
cast	cast	cast
catch	caught	caught
choose	chose	chosen
cling	clung	clung
come	came	come
cost	cost	cost
creep	crept	crept
cut	cut	cut
deal	dealt	dealt
dig	dug	dug
dive	dived/dove	dived
do	did	done
draw	drew	drawn
dream	dreamed/dreamt	dreamed/dreamt
drink	drank	drunk
drive	drove	driven
eat	ate	eaten
fall	fell	fallen
feed	fed	fed
feel	felt	felt
fight	fought	fought
find	found	found
fit	fitted/fit	fitted/fit
flee	fled	fled
fling	flung	flung
fly	flew	flown
forbid	forbade/forbad	forbidden
forget	forgot	forgotten
forgive	forgave	forgiven

BASE FORM	SIMPLE PAST	PAST PARTICIPLE
forgo	forwent	forgone
freeze	froze	frozen
get	got	gotten/got
give	gave	given
go	went	gone
grind	ground	ground
grow	grew	grown
hang	hung/hanged*	hung/hanged*
have	had	had
hear	heard	heard
hide	hid	hidden
hit	hit	hit
hold	held	held
hurt	hurt	hurt
keep	kept	kept
kneel	knelt/kneeled	knelt/kneeled
knit	knit/knitted	knit/knitted
know	knew	known
lay	laid	laid
lead	led	led
leap	leaped/leapt	leaped/leapt
learn	learned/learnt	learned/learnt
leave	left	left
lend	lent	lent
let	let	let
lie (down)	lay	lain
light	lit/lighted	lit/lighted
lose	lost	lost
make	made	made
mean	meant	meant
meet	met	met
pay	paid	paid
prove	proved	proved/proven
put	put	put
quit	quit	quit
read	read	read
rid	rid	rid
ride	rode	ridden
ring	rang	rung
rise	rose	risen
run	ran	run
saw	sawed	sawed/sawn
say	said	said

*hung = hung an object
hanged = executed by hanging

(continued)

Base Form	Simple Past	Past Participle	Base Form	Simple Past	Past Participle
see	saw	seen	stick	stuck	stuck
seek	sought	sought	sting	stung	stung
sell	sold	sold	stink	stank/stunk	stunk
send	sent	sent	strew	strewed	strewn
set	set	set	stride	strode	stridden
sew	sewed	sewn/sewed	strike	struck	struck/stricken
shake	shook	shaken	swear	swore	sworn
shave	shaved	shaved/shaven	sweep	swept	swept
shear	sheared	sheared/shorn	swell	swelled	swelled/swollen
shine	shone/shined*	shone/shined*	swim	swam	swum
shoot	shot	shot	swing	swung	swung
show	showed	shown/showed	take	took	taken
shrink	shrank/shrunk	shrunk/shrunken	teach	taught	taught
shut	shut	shut	tear	tore	torn
sing	sang	sung	tell	told	told
sink	sank/sunk	sunk	think	thought	thought
sit	sat	sat	throw	threw	thrown
slay	slew/slayed	slain/slayed	undergo	underwent	undergone
sleep	slept	slept	understand	understood	understood
slide	slid	slid	upset	upset	upset
sneak	sneaked/snuck	sneaked/snuck	wake	woke/waked	woken/waked
speak	spoke	spoken	wear	wore	worn
speed	sped/speeded	sped/speeded	weave	wove/weaved	woven/weaved
spend	spent	spent	weep	wept	wept
spill	spilled/spilt	spilled/spilt	wet	wet/wetted	wet/wetted
spin	spun	spun	win	won	won
spit	spit/spat	spit/spat	wind	wound	wound
split	split	split	withdraw	withdrew	withdrawn
spread	spread	spread	wring	wrung	wrung
spring	sprang	sprung	write	wrote	written
stand	stood	stood			
steal	stole	stolen			

*shone = intransitive: *The sun shone brightly.*
 shined = transitive: *He shined his shoes.*

2 | Non-Action Verbs

EXAMPLES: She **seems** happy in her new job.
I **have** a terrible headache.
The food **smells** good.
Mary **owes** me money.

APPEARANCES	EMOTIONS	MENTAL STATES		PERCEPTION AND THE SENSES	POSSESSION	WANTS AND PREFERENCES
appear	abhor	agree	favor	ache	belong	desire
be	admire	amaze	feel (= believe)	feel	contain	need
concern	adore	amuse	figure (= assume)	hear	have	prefer
indicate	appreciate	annoy	find (= believe)	hurt	own	want
look	care	assume	guess	notice	pertain	wish
mean (= signify)	desire	astonish	hesitate	observe	possess	
parallel	detest	believe	hope	perceive		**OTHER**
represent	dislike	bore	imagine	see		cost
resemble	doubt	care	imply	sense		include
seem	empathize	consider	impress	smart		lack
signify (= mean)	envy	deem	infer	smell		matter
	fear	deny	know	sound		owe
	hate	disagree	mean	taste		refuse
	hope	disbelieve	mind			suffice
	like	entertain (= amuse)	presume			weigh
	love	estimate	realize			
	regret	expect	recognize			
	respect	fancy	recollect			

APPEARANCES	EMOTIONS	MENTAL STATES		PERCEPTION AND THE SENSES	POSSESSION	OTHER
	sympathize	remember	suspect			
	trust	revere	think (= believe)			
		see (= understand)	tire			
		suit	understand			
		suppose	wonder			

3 | Non-Action Verbs Sometimes Used in the Progressive

EXAMPLES: The students **are being** silly today.
We**'re having** dinner right now. Can I call you back?
Mary **is smelling** the roses.
The cook **is tasting** the soup.

ache	bore	expect	hear	include	perceive	sense
admire	consider	favor	hesitate	indicate	presume	smell
agree	deny	feel	hope	lack	realize	sympathize
amuse	disagree	figure	hurt	look	refuse	taste
annoy	doubt	find	imagine	notice	represent	think
assume	empathize	guess	imply	observe	see	wonder
be	entertain	have	impress			

4 | Irregular Noun Plurals

SINGULAR FORM	PLURAL FORM	SINGULAR FORM	PLURAL FORM	SINGULAR FORM	PLURAL FORM
alumna	alumnae	fish	fish/fishes*	paramecium	paramecia
alumnus	alumni	foot	feet	person	people
amoeba	amoebas/amoebae	genus	genera	people**	peoples
analysis	analyses	goose	geese	phenomenon	phenomena
antenna	antennae/antennas	half	halves	—	police
appendix	appendixes/appendices	index	indexes/indices	policeman	policemen
axis	axes	knife	knives	policewoman	policewomen
basis	bases	leaf	leaves	protozoan	protozoa/protozoans
businessman	businessmen	life	lives	radius	radii
businesswoman	businesswomen	loaf	loaves	series	series
calf	calves	louse	lice	sheaf	sheaves
—	cattle	man	men	sheep	sheep
child	children	millennium	millennia/millenniums	shelf	shelves
crisis	crises	money	monies/moneys	species	species
criterion	criteria	moose	moose	thesis	theses
datum	data	mouse	mice	tooth	teeth
deer	deer	octopus	octopuses/octopi	vertebra	vertebrae/vertebras
dwarf	dwarfs/dwarves	ox	oxen	wife	wives
elf	elves			woman	women

* fishes = different species of fish
** a people = an ethnic group

ABSTRACTIONS

advice	integrity
anarchy	love
behavior	luck
chance	momentum
decay	oppression
democracy	peace
energy	pollution
entertainment	responsibility
evil	slavery
freedom	socialism
fun	spontaneity
good	stupidity
happiness	time
hate	totalitarianism
hatred	truth
honesty	violence
inertia	

ACTIVITIES

badminton	hockey
baseball	judo
basketball	karate
biking	reading
billiards	sailing
bowling	singing
boxing	skating
canoeing	soccer
cards	surfing
conversation	tae kwon do
cycling	talking
dancing	tennis
football	volleyball
golf	wrestling
hiking	

DISEASES

AIDS
appendicitis
bronchitis
cancer
chicken pox
cholera
diabetes
diphtheria
flu (influenza)
heart disease
malaria
measles
mumps
pneumonia
polio
smallpox
strep throat
tuberculosis (TB)

FOODS

barley
beef
bread
broccoli
cake
candy
chicken
corn
fish
meat
oats
pie
rice
wheat

GASES

carbon dioxide
helium
hydrogen
neon
nitrogen
oxygen

LIQUIDS

coffee
gasoline
juice
milk
oil
soda
tea
water

NATURAL PHENOMENA

air
cold
electricity
fog
hail
heat
ice
lightning
mist
rain
sleet
slush
smog
smoke
snow
steam
thunder
warmth
wind

OCCUPATIONS

banking
computer
  technology
construction
dentistry
engineering
farming
fishing
law
manufacturing
medicine
nursing
retail
sales
teaching
writing
work

PARTICLES

dust
gravel
pepper
salt
sand
spice
sugar

SOLID ELEMENTS

calcium
carbon
copper
gold
iron
lead
magnesium
platinum
plutonium
radium
silver
tin
titanium
uranium

SUBJECTS

accounting
art
astronomy
biology
business
chemistry
civics
computer science
economics
geography
history
linguistics
literature
mathematics
music
physics
psychology
science
sociology
speech
writing

OTHER

clothing
equipment
film
furniture
news

6 | Ways of Making Non-Count Nouns Countable

ABSTRACTIONS
a piece of advice
a matter of choice
a unit of energy
a type/form of entertainment
a piece/bit of luck

ACTIVITIES
a game of badminton/baseball/basketball/
  cards/football/golf/soccer/tennis, etc.
a badminton game/a baseball game, etc.

FOODS
a grain of barley
a cut/piece/slice of beef
a loaf of bread
a piece of cake
a piece/wedge of pie
a grain of rice
a portion/serving of . . .

LIQUIDS
a cup of coffee, tea, cocoa
a gallon/liter of gasoline
a can of oil
a glass of milk, water, juice
a can/glass of soda

NATURAL PHENOMENA
a bolt/current of electricity
a bolt/flash of lightning
a drop of rain
a clap of thunder

PARTICLES
a speck of dust
a grain of pepper, salt, sand, sugar

SUBJECTS
a branch of accounting/art/
  astronomy/biology/chemistry/
  economics/geography/literature/
  linguistics/mathematics/music/
  physics/psychology/sociology, etc.

MISCELLANEOUS
an article of clothing
a piece of equipment
a piece/article of furniture
a piece of news/a news item/an item of
  news
a period of time

7 | Nouns Often Used with the Definite Article

the air
the atmosphere
the authorities
the Bhagavad Gita
the Bible
the cosmos
the Creator

the earth
the economy
the Empire State
  Building
the environment
the flu

the gross national
  product (GNP)
the Internet
the Koran
the measles
the Milky Way
  (galaxy)

the moon
the movies
the mumps
the ocean
the police
the *Queen Mary*

the radio
the sky
the solar system
the stock market
the stratosphere
the sun

the Taj Mahal
the *Titanic*
the United Nations
the universe
the Vatican
the world

8 | Countries Whose Names Contain the Definite Article

the Bahamas
the Cayman Islands
the Central African Republic
the Channel Islands
the Comoros
the Czech Republic

the Dominican Republic
the Falkland Islands
the Gambia
the Isle of Man
the Ivory Coast
the Leeward Islands

the Maldives (the Maldive Islands)
the Marshall Islands
the Netherlands
the Netherlands Antilles
the Philippines
the Solomon Islands

the Turks and Caicos Islands
the United Arab Emirates
the United Kingdom (of Great
  Britain and Northern Ireland)
the United States (of America)
the Virgin Islands

9 | Selected Geographical Features Whose Names Contain the Definite Article

GULFS, OCEANS, SEAS, AND STRAITS

the Adriatic Sea
the Aegean Sea
the Arabian Sea
the Arctic Ocean
the Atlantic (Ocean)
the Baltic (Sea)
the Black Sea
the Caribbean (Sea)
the Caspian (Sea)
the Coral Sea
the Gulf of Aden
the Gulf of Mexico
the Gulf of Oman

the Indian Ocean
the Mediterranean (Sea)
the North Sea
the Pacific (Ocean)
the Persian Gulf
the Philippine Sea
the Red Sea
the Sea of Japan
the South China Sea
the Strait of Gibraltar
the Strait of Magellan
the Yellow Sea

MOUNTAIN RANGES

the Alps
the Andes
the Appalachians
the Atlas Mountains
the Caucasus

the Himalayas
the Pyrenees
the Rockies (the Rocky
    Mountains)
the Urals

RIVERS

(all of the following can contain the word *River*)

the Amazon
the Colorado
the Columbia
the Danube
the Don
the Euphrates
the Ganges
the Huang
the Hudson
the Indus
the Jordan
the Lena
the Mackenzie
the Mekong
the Mississippi
the Missouri
the Niger

the Nile
the Ob
the Ohio
the Orinoco
the Po
the Rhine
the Rhone
the Rio Grande
the St. Lawrence
the Seine
the Tagus
the Thames
the Tiber
the Tigris
the Volga
the Yangtze

OTHER FEATURES

the equator
the Far East
the Gobi (Desert)
the Kalahari (Desert)
the Middle East
the Near East
the North Pole
the Occident
the Orient
the Panama Canal
the Sahara (Desert)
the South Pole
the Suez Canal
the Tropic of Cancer
the Tropic of Capricorn

10 | Verbs Used in the Passive Followed by a *That* Clause

EXAMPLE: It is alleged **that** he committed the crime.

allege	believe	fear	hold	predict	theorize
assume	claim	feel	postulate	say	think

11 | Stative Passive Verbs + Prepositions

EXAMPLE: The island of Hispaniola **is divided into** two separate nations.

be bordered by	be divided into/by	be known as	be measured by
be composed of	be filled with	be listed in/as	be placed near/in
be comprised of	be found in/on, etc.	be located in/on, etc.	be positioned near/in
be connected to/with/by	be intended	be made (out) of	be related to
be covered by/with	be joined to	be made up of	be surrounded by

12 | Verbs Followed by the Gerund

EXAMPLE: Jane enjoys **playing** tennis and **gardening**.

abhor	confess	endure	give up (= stop)	postpone	resume
acknowledge	consider	enjoy	imagine	practice	risk
admit	defend	escape	keep (= continue)	prevent	shirk
advise	delay	evade	keep on	put off	shun
allow	deny	explain	mention	recall	suggest
anticipate	detest	fancy	mind (= object to)	recollect	support
appreciate	discontinue	fear	miss	recommend	tolerate
avoid	discuss	feel like	necessitate	report	understand
be worth	dislike	feign	omit	resent	urge
can't help	dispute	finish	permit	resist	warrant
celebrate	dread	forgive	picture		

13 | Adjective + Preposition Combinations

These expressions are followed by nouns, pronouns, or gerunds.

EXAMPLES: I'm not **familiar with** that writer.
I'm **amazed at** her.
We're **excited about** going.

accustomed to	capable of	fascinated with/by	intent on	ready for	suited to
afraid of	careful of	fed up with	interested in	responsible for	surprised at/about/
amazed at/by	concerned with/	fond of	intrigued by/at	sad about	by
angry at/with	about	furious with/at	mad at (=angry at/	safe from	terrible at
ashamed of	content with	glad about	with)	satisfied with	tired from
astonished at/by	curious about	good at	nervous about	shocked at/by	tired of
aware of	different from	good with	obsessed with/about	sick of	used to
awful at	excellent at	guilty of	opposed to	slow at	weary of
bad at	excited about	happy about	pleased about/with	sorry for/about	worried about
bored with/by	famous for	incapable of	poor at		

14 | Verbs Followed by the Infinitive

EXAMPLE: The Baxters **decided to sell** their house.

agree	care	determine	hurry	plan	say	swear	wait
appear	chance	elect	incline	prepare	seek	tend	want
arrange	choose	endeavor	learn	pretend	seem	threaten	wish
ask	claim	expect	manage	profess	shudder	turn out	would like
attempt	come	fail	mean (=	promise	strive	venture	yearn
beg	consent	get	intend)	prove	struggle	volunteer	
can/cannot	dare	grow (up)	need	refuse			
afford	decide	guarantee	neglect	remain			
can/cannot	demand	hesitate	offer	request			
wait	deserve	hope	pay	resolve			

15 | Verbs Followed by the Gerund or Infinitive Without a Significant Change in Meaning

EXAMPLES: Martha hates **to go** to bed early.
Martha hates **going** to bed early.

begin	can't stand	hate	love	propose
can't bear	continue	like	prefer	start

16 | Verbs Followed by the Gerund or the Infinitive with a Significant Change in Meaning

forget
I've almost **forgotten meeting** him. (= At present, I can hardly remember.)
I almost **forgot to meet** him. (= I almost didn't remember to meet him.)

go on
Jack **went on writing** novels. (= Jack continued to write novels.)
Carrie **went on to write** novels. (= Carrie ended some other activity and began to write novels.)

quit
Ella **quit working** at Sloan's. (= She isn't working there anymore.)
Frank **quit to work** at Sloan's. (= He quit another job in order to work at Sloan's.)

regret
I **regret telling** you I'd take the job. (= I'm sorry that I said I would take it.)
I **regret to tell** you that I can't take the job. (= I'm telling you now that I can't take the job, and I'm sorry I can't take it.)

remember
Velma **remembered writing** to Bill. (= Velma remembered the previous activity of writing to Bill.)
Melissa **remembered to write** to Bill. (= Melissa didn't forget to write to Bill. She wrote him.)

stop
Hank **stopped eating**. (= He stopped the activity of eating.)
Bruce **stopped to eat**. (= He stopped doing something else in order to eat.)

try
Martin **tried skiing**. (= Martin sampled the activity of skiing.)
Helen **tried to ski**. (= Helen attempted to ski but didn't succeed.)

17 | Verbs Followed by Noun / Pronoun + Infinitive

EXAMPLE: I asked Sally **to lend** me her car.

advise	choose*	forbid	invite	pay*	remind	tell	warn
allow	convince	force	need*	permit	require	urge	would like*
ask*	encourage	get*	order	persuade	teach	want*	
cause	expect*	hire					

*These verbs can also be followed by the infinitive without an object:

EXAMPLES: I **want to go**.
I **want Jerry to go**.

18 | Adjectives Followed by the Infinitive

EXAMPLE: I was **glad to hear** about that.

advisable*	careful	disappointed	essential*	happy	lucky	proud	sorry
afraid	crucial*	distressed	excited	hard	mandatory*	ready	surprised
alarmed	curious	disturbed	fascinated	hesitant	necessary*	relieved	touched
amazed	delighted	eager	fortunate	important*	nice	reluctant	unlikely
angry	depressed	easy	frightened	impossible	obligatory*	right	unnecessary*
anxious	desirable*	ecstatic	furious	interested	pleased	sad	upset
ashamed	determined*	embarrassed	glad	intrigued	possible	scared	willing
astonished	difficult	encouraged	good	likely	prepared	shocked	wrong

* These adjectives can also be followed with a noun clause containing a subjunctive verb form.

EXAMPLES: It's essential **to communicate**.
It's essential **that she communicate with her parents**.

19 | Sentence Adverbs

actually	clearly	frankly	importantly	possibly	surprisingly
amazingly	definitely	generally	mainly	probably	thankfully
apparently	essentially	happily	maybe	significantly	understandably
basically	evidently	honestly	mercifully	surely	unfortunately
certainly	fortunately	hopefully	perhaps		

20 | Words That Begin Dependent Clauses

SUBORDINATING CONJUNCTIONS (TO INTRODUCE ADVERB CLAUSES)		RELATIVE PRONOUNS (TO INTRODUCE ADJECTIVE CLAUSES)	OTHERS (TO INTRODUCE NOUN CLAUSES)
after	no matter if	that	how
although	no matter whether	when	how far
anywhere	now that	where	how long
as	on account of the fact that	which	how many
as if	once	who	how much
as long as	only if	whom	however (= the way in which)
as many as	plus the fact that	whose	if
as much as	provided (that)		that
as soon as	providing (that)		the fact that
as though	since		what
because	so that		what color
because of the fact that	so . . . that (= in order to)		whatever
before	such . . . that		what time
despite the fact that	though		when
due to the fact that	till		where
even if	unless		whether (or not)
even though	until		whichever (one)
even when	when		why
everywhere	whenever		
if	where		
if only	whereas		
inasmuch as	wherever		
in case	whether (or not)		
in spite of the fact that	while		

21 | Transitions: Sentence Connectors

TO SHOW ADDITION	TO SHOW A CONTRAST	TO SHOW AN EFFECT/ RESULT	TO SHOW TIME AND SEQUENCE
additionally	actually	accordingly	after this/that
along with this/that	anyhow	as a result	afterwards
also	anyway	because of this/that	an hour later (several hours later, etc.)
alternatively	as a matter of fact	consequently	at last
as a matter of fact	at any rate	for this/that reason	at this moment
besides	despite this/that	hence	before this/that
furthermore	even so	in consequence	from now on
in addition	however	on account of this/that	henceforth
indeed	in any case	otherwise	hitherto
in fact	in contrast	then	in the meantime
in other words	in either case	therefore	just then
in the same way	in fact	this/that being so	meanwhile
likewise	in spite of this/that	thus	next
moreover	instead (of this/that)	to this end	on another occasion
plus	nevertheless		previously
	nonetheless		then
	on the contrary		under the circumstances
	on the other hand		until then
	rather		up to now
	still		
	though		

22 | Transitions: Blocks of Text

all in all	in short	second(ly)	to conclude
nother reason/point, etc.	in sum	the most important reason/factor, etc.	to resume
finally	in summary		to return to the point
first(ly)	last(ly)	third(ly)	to summarize
in conclusion	most importantly		

23 | Reporting Verbs

EXAMPLE: "This is the best course of action," Jack **maintained**.

add	claim	maintain	point out	respond	tell
allege	comment	murmur	query	say	wonder
allow	confess	note	report	shout	yell
ask	exclaim	observe			

EXAMPLES: We **demand (that)** he **do** it.
It is **essential (that)** he **do** it.
The professor **suggested (that)** we **buy** his book.

AFTER SINGLE VERBS
ask*
demand
insist
move (= formally propose something in a meeting)
order*
prefer*
propose
recommend
request*
require*
suggest
urge*

AFTER IT + ADJECTIVE + NOUN CLAUSE
it is advisable that
it is crucial that
it is desirable that
it is essential that
it is important that
it is mandatory that
it is necessary that
it is obligatory that
it is reasonable that
it is required that
it is unnecessary that
it is unreasonable that

* These verbs also take the form verb + object pronoun + infinitive.

EXAMPLE: We **asked** that she **be** present.
We **asked her to be** present.

GLOSSARY OF GRAMMAR TERMS

action verb   A verb that describes an action.
- *The tourist **finds** a beautiful rug.*

active sentence   A sentence in which the subject acts upon the object.
- ***William Shakespeare** wrote <u>Hamlet</u>.*

adjective   A part of speech modifying a noun or pronoun.
- *The **blue** sofa is **beautiful**, but it's also **expensive**.*

adjective clause   A clause that identifies or gives additional information about a noun.
- *The man **who directed the film** won an Oscar.*

adjective phrase   A phrase that identifies or gives additional information about a noun.
- *The actress **playing the Queen** is Glenn Close.*

adverb   A part of speech modifying a verb, an adjective, another adverb, or an entire sentence.
- *Ben drives his **incredibly** valuable car **very carefully**.*

adverb clause   A dependent clause that indicates how, when, where, why, or under what conditions things happen; or which establishes a contrast. An adverb clause begins with a subordinating conjunction and modifies an independent clause.
- *We're going to leave for the airport **as soon as Jack gets home**.*

adverb/adverbial phrase   A phrase that indicates how, when, where, why, or under what conditions things happen. An adverb phrase modifies an independent clause.
- *We learned a great deal of Spanish **while traveling in Mexico**.*

An adverbial phrase performs the same functions as an adverb phrase but does not contain a subordinating conjunction.
- ***Having had the professor for a previous class**, I knew what to expect.*

auxiliary (helping) verb   A verb that occurs with and "helps" a main verb.
- ***Did** Mary contact you? No. She **should have** called at least.*

base form   The form of a verb listed in a dictionary. It has no endings (-*s*, -*ed*, etc.).
- *It is mandatory that Sally **be** there and **participate** in the discussion.*

causative   A verb construction showing that someone arranges for or causes something to happen. **Get** and **have** are the two most common causative verbs.
- *We **got** Martha to help us when we **had** the house remodeled.*

clause   A group of words with a subject and a verb that shows time. An **independent clause** can stand by itself. A **dependent clause** needs to be attached to an independent clause to be understood fully.

    independent   dependent
- *We'll go out for dinner as soon as I get back from the bank.*

comma splice   An error resulting from joining two independent clauses with only a comma.
- *I understand the point he made, however, I don't agree with it. (comma splice)*
- *I understand the point he made; however, I don't agree with it. (correction)*

common noun   A noun that does not name a particular thing or individual.
- *We bought a **turkey**, cranberry **sauce**, mashed **potatoes**, and **rolls** for the **dinner**.*

complement   A noun or adjective (phrase) that describes or explains a subject or direct object.
- *Hal is **a man with unusual tastes**. He painted his house **orange**.*

compound modifier   A modifier of a noun that is composed of more than one word. A compound modifier is usually hyphenated when it precedes a noun.

- My **five-year-old** daughter can already read.

conditional sentence   A sentence containing a dependent clause showing a condition and an independent clause showing a result. The condition may or may not be fulfilled.

    condition   result
- If I had enough time, I would visit Morocco.

coordinating conjunction   A word connecting independent clauses or items in a series. The seven coordinating conjunctions are **and**, **but**, **for**, **nor**, **or**, **so**, and **yet**.

- Mom had forgotten to buy groceries, **so** we had a supper of cold pizza, salad, **and** water.

count noun   A noun that can be counted in its basic sense. Count nouns have plural forms.

- The **students** in my **class** all have at least one **sibling**.

definite article   The article **the**; it indicates that the person or thing being talked about is unique or is known or identified to the speaker and listener.

- China is **the** most populous nation in **the** world.

definite past   The simple past form; it shows an action, state, or event at a particular time or period in the past.

- I **lived** in Spain in the '70s and **visited** there again last year.

dependent clause   A dependent clause cannot stand alone as a sentence: it requires a main clause for its meaning.

    main clause   dependent clause
- They saw the bandit, who was wearing a bandanna.

direct object   A noun or pronoun that receives the action of a verb.

- Martin discovered an autographed **copy** of the novel.

direct speech   The exact words (or thoughts) of a speaker, which are enclosed in quotation marks.

- **"Barry,"** Phyllis said, **"I want you to tell me the truth."**

embedded question   A question that is inside another sentence.

- He didn't know **what to buy his mother**.

focus adverb   An adverb that focuses attention on a word or phrase. Focus adverbs come before the word or phrase they focus on.

- **Even** I don't support that idea. It's too radical.

fragment   A group of words that is not a complete sentence. It is often considered an error.

- Because he doesn't know what to do about the situation. (fragment)
- He's asking for our help because he doesn't know what to do about the situation. (correction)

future in the past   A verb construction showing a state, action, or event now past but future from some point of time in the past.

- We **were going to help** Tim move but couldn't. Sam said he **would help** instead.

generic   Referred to in general; including all the members of the class to which something belongs.

- **The computer** has become essential in today's world.
- **Whales** are endangered.
- **An orangutan** is a primate living in Borneo and Sumatra.

gerund   A verbal noun made by adding **-ing** to a verb.

- Dad loves **cooking**, and we love **eating** what he cooks.

identifying (essential) clauses and phrases
Clauses and phrases that distinguish one person or thing from others. They are not enclosed in commas.

- The student **who is sitting at the end of the second row** is my niece.
- The film **starring Johnny Depp** is the one I want to see.

if clause   The clause in a conditional sentence that states the condition.

- **If it rains,** they will cancel the picnic.

implied condition   A condition that is suggested or implied but not stated fully. Implied conditional sentences use expressions such as *if so, if not, otherwise, with,* and *without.*

- *You may be able to get the item for half price. **If so**, please buy one for me as well. (= if you are able to get the item for half price)*

indefinite article   The articles *a* and *an*; they occur with count nouns and indicate that what is referred to is not a particular or identified person or thing.

- *In the last year I have bought **an** old **house** and **a** new **car**.*

indefinite past   The present perfect; it shows a past action, event, or state not occurring at any particular or identified time.

- *We **have seen** that movie several times.*

indirect object   A noun or pronoun that shows the person or thing that receives something as a result of the action of the verb.

- *Martin gave **Priscilla** an autographed copy of his new novel.*

indirect (reported) speech   A report of the words of a speaker. Indirect speech does not include all of a speaker's exact words and is not enclosed in quotation marks.

- *Phyllis told Barry **that she wanted him to tell her the truth**.*

infinitive   *To* + the base form of a verb.

- *Frank Jones is said **to be** the author of that article.*

inverted condition   The condition of a conditional sentence, stated without the word *if*. Inverted conditions occur with the verbs *had, were,* and *should,* which come first in the sentence and are followed by the subject.

- ***Had I** known that would happen, I never would have agreed.*

main clause   A main clause can stand alone as a sentence.

   main clause   dependent clause
- *They saw the bandit, who was wearing a bandanna.*

mixed conditional   A conditional sentence which shows the hypothetical present result of a past unreal situation or the hypothetical past result of a present unreal situation.

- *If I had taken that job, I would be living in Bucharest now.*
- *Sam would have arrived by now if he were planning to come.*

modal (auxiliary)   A type of helping verb. The modals are ***can, could, had better, may, might, must, ought to, shall, should, will,*** and ***would***. They each have one form and no endings.

- *You certainly **can** do that; the question is whether you **should** do it.*

modal-like expression   An expression with a meaning similar to that of a modal. Modal-like expressions have endings and show time.

- *Russell **has to** find a new job.*

non-action (stative) verb   A verb that in its basic sense does not show action.

- *It **seems** to me that Joe **has** a problem.*

non-count noun   A noun that in its basic sense cannot be counted.

- ***Smoke** from the **fire** filled the **air**.*

nonidentifying (nonessential) clauses and phrases   Clauses and phrases that add extra information but do not distinguish one person or thing from others. They are enclosed in commas.

- *Henry**, who is a member of the hockey team,** is also a star basketball player.*

noun clause   A dependent clause that performs the same function as a noun. Noun clauses function as subjects, objects, objects of prepositions, and complements.

- ***What I want to do** is spend a week relaxing on the beach.*

noun modifier   A noun that modifies another noun.

- *What did you buy, **milk** chocolate or **chocolate** milk?*

parallelism (parallel structure)   The placing of items in a series in the same grammatical form.

- *Marie loves **hiking, riding** horses, and **collecting** artifacts.*

participial adjective   An adjective formed from present and past participial forms of verbs.

- The **bored** students were not paying attention to the **boring** speaker.

passive causative   A verb structure formed with **have** or **get** + **object** + **past participle**. It is used to talk about services that you arrange for someone to do for you.

- I usually **have my dresses made** by Chantal.

passive sentence   A sentence that shows the subject being acted upon by the object.

- <u>Hamlet</u> was written by **William Shakespeare**.

perfect forms   Verb constructions formed with the auxiliary verbs **had**, **has**, and **have**, and a past participle. They include the **past perfect**, **present perfect**, and **future perfect**.

- I **had** never **been** to Brazil before 1990. Since then I'**ve been** there eight times. By this time next year, I'**ll have been** there ten times.

phrase   A group of related words without a subject or a verb showing time.

- **Relaxing in the hammock**, I pondered my future.

proper noun   The name of a particular individual or thing. Proper nouns are capitalized.

- **Stella** and I both think that **Rio de Janeiro** and **Paris** are the world's two most beautiful cities.

quantifier   A word or phrase showing the amount or number of something.

- Ken earned **a lot of** money selling vacuum cleaners.

relative pronoun   A pronoun used to form adjective clauses. The relative pronouns are **that**, **when**, **where**, **which**, **who**, **whom**, and **whose**.

- The fairy tale **that** always scared me when I was a child was Rumpelstiltskin.

reporting verb   A verb such as **said**, **told**, or **asked**, which introduces both direct and indirect speech. It can also come after the quotation in direct speech.

- The mayor **said**, "I've read the report." OR "I've read the report," the mayor **said**.

result clause   The clause in a conditional sentence that indicates what happens if the condition occurs.

- If it rains, **they'll cancel the picnic**.

run-on sentence   An error resulting from the joining of two independent clauses with no punctuation.

- I think therefore, I am. (run-on sentence)
- I think; therefore, I am. (correction)

sentence adverb   An adverb that modifies an entire sentence. It can occur at the beginning, in the middle, or at the end of a sentence.

- **Fortunately**, Sarah was not hurt badly in the accident.

stative passive   A passive form used to describe situations or states.

- North and South America **are connected** by the Isthmus of Panama.

subjunctive   A verb form using the base form of a verb and normally following a verb or expression showing advice, necessity, or urgency. The verb be has the special subjunctive form were used for all persons.

- We always **insist** that our daughter **do** her homework before watching TV.
- If I **were** you, I would pay off my mortgage as soon as possible.

subordinating conjunction   A connecting word used to begin an adverb clause.

- We were relieved **when** Jack finally called at 1 A.M.

tag question   A statement + tag. The **tag** is a short question that follows the statement. Tag questions are used to check information or comment on a situation.

- She's an actor, **isn't she?**

transition   A word or phrase showing a connection between sentences or between larger blocks of text.

- Global warming is a serious problem. **However,** it is not as serious as the problem of poverty.

unreal conditional sentence   A sentence that talks about untrue, imagined, or impossible conditions and their results.

- If I were you, I would study a lot harder.

zero article   The absence of a definite or indefinite article. The zero article occurs before unidentified plurals or non-count nouns.

- **Whales** are endangered. **Water** is necessary for survival.

REVIEW TESTS ANSWER KEY

Note: In this answer key, where the contracted verb form is given, it is the preferred form, though the full form is also acceptable. Where the full verb form is given, it is the preferred form, though the contracted form is also acceptable.

PART I

I (Units 1 and 2)
2. was going to
3. 're going to
4. he was going to
5. we'll eat, we're going to eat
6. Weren't you going to turn over
7. we'd try
8. he'll take

II (Unit 2)
1. **b.** 'd smoke
   c. used to smoke
   d. 'd smoke
2. **e.** would take
   f. 'd go
   g. used to own
   h. 'd spend
   i. used to be
3. **j.** used to be
   k. used to live
   l. would go
   m. 'd have
   n. used to be
   o. would start
   p. 'd feel

III (Units 1 and 2)
2. stayed
3. toured
4. 've seen
5. 've been walking
6. haven't gone
7. 're taking
8. 'll be arriving / 'll arrive
9. 're spending / 're going to spend / 'll be spending
10. 'll have returned
11. fly /'re flying

IV (Unit 3)
1. **a.** are   **b.** 're being
2. **a.** has written   **b.** has been writing
3. **a.** are having   **b.** have
4. **a.** has been developing **b.** has developed

V (Units 1–3)
2. A   7. B
3. C   8. A
4. D   9. B
5. D   10. B
6. C

VI (Units 1–3)
2. isn't going   6. did
   (to go)   7. terrible
3. you   8. had
4. was taking   9. didn't use to
5. It smells   10. visited

PART II

I (Unit 4)
1. **c.** 'm
   d. 'm not
   e. am
2. **a.** didn't earn
   b. did earn
3. **a.** haven't lived
   b. have traveled
4. **a.** isn't
   b. is
   c. does have
   d. would like

II (Unit 4)
2. So did   6. Neither would
3. hasn't either   7. hadn't either
4. Neither will   8. So does
5. am too

III (Unit 5)
2. 're supposed to
3. shouldn't have
4. aren't supposed to
5. 're supposed to
6. should have
7. should have brought
8. don't have to
9. must
10. shouldn't
11. is supposed to do

IV (Units 5 and 6)

Possible answers:

2.	could	8.	can't
3.	must have	9.	might
4.	may have	10.	should have
5.	might have	11.	could have
6.	should	12.	may
7.	's got		

V (Units 5 and 6)

Possible answers:

2. They must have forgotten to put gas in the tank.
3. They'd better slow down.
4. Drivers are supposed to carry their driver's license with them.
5. Jerry might have missed his flight. / Jerry might have decided to take a different flight.
6. Jerry could have called his parents to tell them what he was going to do.
7. It may rain.
8. They should have brought their umbrellas. / They shouldn't have tried to play tennis today.

VI (Units 4–6)

2.	B	7.	C
3.	B	8.	C
4.	C	9.	D
5.	A	10.	C
6.	D		

VII (Units 4–6)

2.	too	7.	mustn't / can't
3.	set	8.	should
4.	be	9.	won't
5.	are	10.	neither
6.	have		

PART III

I (Unit 8)

2.	no article	18.	an
3.	no article	19.	a
4.	the	20.	the
5.	the	21.	an
6.	no article	22.	a
7.	no article	23.	no article
8.	no article	24.	no article
9.	no article	25.	no article
10.	no article	26.	the
11.	no article	27.	no article
12.	no article	28.	no article
13.	the	29.	no article
14.	A	30.	the
15.	a	31.	the
16.	no article	32.	no article
17.	no article		

II (Unit 8)

2. . . . not birds . . .
3. . . . a humanlike ape . . .
4. . . . was the third of . . .
5. The Jurassic period . . .
6. . . . the official currency . . .
7. A meltdown is . . .
8. The statues on Easter Island
9. . . . for raising cattle.
10. The telephone . . .

III (Unit 7)

Possible answers:

2. Several pieces of furniture are for sale.
3. *Gabriela, Clove* and *Cinnamon* is a literary work by Jorge Amado.
4. Let me give you a piece of advice.
5. The Shan are a people of northern Myanmar.
6. There are several spices on the rack.
7. The tree was hit by a bolt of lightning.
8. Camembert is a cheese produced in France.

IV (Unit 10)

1. b. chilly winter
2. a. new pink silk
   b. handsome, young European
3. a. beautiful new brick
   b. dirty little old

V (Unit 9)

2. a. any
   b. some
3. a. many
   b. amount
   c. less
   d. fewer
4. a. a few
   b. any
   c. a few
5. a. much
   b. a great many
   c. any
   d. a great deal of
   e. little
   f. Few

VI (Units 7–10)

2.	C	7.	B
3.	A	8.	C
4.	D	9.	B
5.	B	10.	C
6.	D		

VII (Units 7–10)

2. a beautiful condominium
3. The plan
4. the wheel

5. first two
6. the scientific community
7. the Canadian Southwest
8. beans
9. 10-year-old
10. lightning / a bolt of lightning

PART IV

I (Unit 11)

I   I work with in my secretarial job
NI whom I'll call "Jennifer"
I   who always greet you in a friendly manner and never have an unkind word to say
NI whom I'll call "Myrtle"
I   who rarely gives compliments and can sometimes be critical
I   who was my friend
NI which is why I didn't seek out her friendship
I   when all three of us, Jennifer, Myrtle, and I, were working together
NI who tends to jump to conclusions
I   whose name he wouldn't reveal
NI whom I expected to stand up for me
NI which was a lie
I   who had stolen the money
I   who took the money
I   that tells us not to judge a book by its cover

II (Unit 11)

2. where	**7.** whose
3. that	**8.** whose
4. which	**9.** who
5. whom	**10.** whose
6. who	

III (Unit 11)

2. no omission	**7.** no omission
3. no omission	**8.** (that)
4. (that)	**9.** no omission
5. no omission	**10.** no omission
6. (that)	

IV (Unit 12)

2. A film starring Jamie Foxx will probably be a blockbuster.
3. *Seabiscuit*, featuring Chris Cooper in a supporting role, is a heartwarming movie.
4. *Cats*, written by Andrew Lloyd Webber and Tim Rice, was a long-running Broadway musical.
5. Several James Cameron films, including the *Terminator* movies and *Titanic*, have earned a great deal of money.

V (Unit 11)

Possible answers:

2. The man who is looking at one of the posters has a toothache.
3. The girl, whose father is talking to the receptionist, doesn't want to visit her dentist.
4. The boy, whose mother is reading him a story, is named Jerry.
5. The poster that is to the left of the receptionist is about gum disease.
6. The poster that is to the left of the door is about brushing properly.
7. The woman who is reading a story to her son is wearing a big hat.
8. The woman who is reading a magazine has her dog with her.

VI (Units 11 and 12)

2. B	**7.** B
3. C	**8.** A
4. C	**9.** D
5. A	**10.** D
6. D	

VII (Units 11 and 12)

2. of whom
3. committed
4. suggesting
5. who
6. which
7. which
8. an extrovert who loves
9. in which case
10. the people with whom he works / the people he works with

PART V

I (Unit 13)

1. **b.** was discovered
2. will get beaten
3. got hit
4. **a.** we've been getting overcharged
   b. have the company investigated
5. **a.** Aren't they cleaned
   b. didn't get done
6. **a.** are fed
   b. Are they being fed
   c. won't be fed

II (Unit 13)

2. he has learned his lesson
3. He parked his motorcycle
4. he discovered
5. his motorcycle had been removed
6. It had been placed
7. No one had been noticed
8. Mason commented

III (Unit 14)
2. was located
3. were found
4. are assumed
5. is believed
6. should not be considered

IV (Units 13 and 14)
Suggested answers:
2. Mrs. Riley just got stopped.
3. Two months ago a building was being torn down.
4. Now a new building is being built.
5. Mrs. Platt is going to have her toaster repaired.
6. Once a month, Mr. Platt gets his hair and beard cut and trimmed.
7. The yeti is thought to live in the Himalayas.
8. The lost continent of Atlantis is said to have been located in the Atlantic Ocean.

V (Units 13 and 14)
2. A
3. B
4. C
5. B
6. B
7. D
8. C
9. D
10. C

VI (Units 13 and 14)
2. was
3. said
4. reported
5. being
6. suspended
7. started
8. are being / are to be / are going to be
9. be launched
10. staffed

PART VI

I (Units 15 and 16)
1. b. going
2. a. to tell
   b. lying
3. a. to defend
   b. defending
4. a. to major
   b. being / to be
   c. doing

II (Unit 15)
2. Seward's having perceived
3. Court's having outlawed
4. Parks's deciding
5. her refusing
6. John F. Kennedy's having agreed
7. his having been warned
8. The reformers' having misjudged
9. protesters' seizing the moment and demanding

III (Units 15 and 16)
2. using
3. slowing
4. to have been completed
5. causing / having caused
6. to be finished
7. to be cleared
8. taking
9. switching

IV (Unit 16)
2. was supposed to
3. planning to
4. ought to
5. didn't have time to
6. don't want to

V (Units 15 and 16)
Possible answers:
1. (second verb) to read
2. driving, getting
3. working / to work
4. staying
5. working
6. reading

VI (Units 15 and 16)
2. C
3. A
4. A
5. B
6. D
7. B
8. C
9. D
10. C

PART VII

I (Unit 18)
1. **B:** OK. We can leave <u>as soon as you back the car out of the garage</u>.
2. **A:** Harry is a lot more responsible <u>since he's been class president</u>.
   B: Yes, I know. He never used to do his chores <u>unless I threatened him</u>.
3. **A:** I'll call you <u>when the plane gets in</u>.
   B: OK, but you'd better take down Harriet's number <u>in case I'm not home</u>.
4. **A:** Wasn't that a great dinner? It won't surprise me <u>if I'm five pounds heavier tomorrow</u>.
   B: Yeah. <u>Whenever I come home to visit</u>, I gain weight. Mom is a such a great cook.
5. **A:** There were better TV shows <u>before there were so many channels</u>.
   B: I don't agree. <u>Now that cable is available</u>, we have access to some impressive programming.

6. **A:** Joe, <u>since you didn't turn in your term paper</u>, you didn't pass the course—<u>even though you did well on the tests</u>.

  B: Yes, I know. I didn't do the term paper . <u>because I couldn't think of anything to write about</u>.

7. **A:** Is your new house going to be finished <u>by the time you leave on your big trip</u>?

  B: I think so. <u>Once they've laid the foundation</u>, they can start building.

II **(Unit 20)**

2. However
3. therefore
4. otherwise
5. on the contrary
6. Moreover

III **(Unit 18)**

Suggested answers:

2. Though they had been leaving the children with Sarah's mother, this wasn't a satisfactory solution. OR They had been leaving the children with Sarah's mother, though this wasn't a satisfactory solution.

3. One of them was going to have to quit working unless they could find a solution to the problem.

4. When one of their neighbors proposed the creation of a daycare co-op involving five families, their problem was solved.

5. Each day, one of the parents in the co-op cares for all the children while the other parents are working.

IV **(Unit 17)**

Dear Samantha,

  I wanted to thank you again for your hospitality while we were in Vancouver. Not only *did you and Michael show* ~~you and Michael showed~~ us a wonderful time, but we also got to reestablish the close ties we used to have. *Even the kids* ~~The even kids~~ enjoyed the trip, and you know how kids are on vacations. *I only hope* ~~Only I hope~~ that Dan and I can reciprocate sometime.

  The drive back to Edmonton was something else; *we almost didn't* ~~almost we didn't~~ make it back in one piece. About 4:30 on the day we left, there was an ice storm near Calgary that turned the highway into a sheet of ice. Little did we know that it would take us four hours to get through the city. Rarely *have I* ~~I have~~ been in such an awful traffic jam. By the time we got off the freeway, it was 11:30 at night, and the kids were crying. We stopped at a motel to try to get a room; they were full up, but when we asked

the proprietors if *we could just* ~~just we could~~ spend the night in their lobby, they took pity on us and made us up a bed in their living room. People can be so kind sometimes. Never again *will I* ~~I will~~ think twice about helping people when they need it. By the next morning, the roads had been cleared, and we made it safely back to Edmonton.

  Well, here *come the kids* ~~the kids come~~ to get their afternoon snack. Please write soon. Thanks again.

Love,
Barb

V **(Units 18 and 20)**

2. They tried combinations of threats, punishments, and rewards; however, nothing seemed to work.

3. Tim and Zeya both got home about 5:30 P.M., and they needed to occupy the children's attention while they were fixing dinner.

4. Though they felt so much TV watching wasn't good, they allowed it because they had no alternative.

5. Their children weren't getting enough exercise; in addition, they weren't interacting with the other children in the neighborhood.

6. Since a lot of their neighbors were having similar problems with their children, someone came up with the idea of starting a neighborhood activity club.

7. The club met every afternoon from 5:00 until 6:30, and two parents from different families supervised activities.

8. The club has been a big success; none of the children have watched very much television lately.

VI **(Units 17–20)**

2. A
3. D
4. C
5. B
6. B
7. C
8. A
9. D
10. D

VII **(Units 17–20)**

2. Feeling
3. even if
4. is capital punishment
5. but
6. clearly
7. obviously
8. Having landed
9. he doesn't even
10. he comes

PART VIII

I (Unit 21)

1. A: I don't know what we should do
tonight.
B: <u>Whatever you want to do</u> is fine with
me.
2. A: We haven't decided <u>where we want to
go on vacation</u>.
B: Don't you think <u>Hawaii would be nice</u>?
3. A: How do we decide <u>who wins the prize</u>?
B: Give it to <u>whoever gets the most points</u>.
4. A: Do you think <u>she's guilty</u>?
B: Well, <u>the fact that she waited so long to
contact the police</u> doesn't help her case.
5. A: I can't believe <u>what I'm seeing</u>. The
Bengals might even win this game.
B: Yeah, I know. I'm amazed <u>that they're
doing this well</u>.
6. A: Mr. Brown, I'm sorry to report <u>that I
need more time to complete the
assignment</u>.
B: That's all right. Take <u>whatever time you
need</u>. I want the job done well.
7. A: As for the problem of stopping violence
in schools, I don't know <u>what the
answer is</u>.
B: I think <u>that we need to ban weapons of
all kinds</u>.
8. A: Do you know <u>what Samantha's problem
is</u>?
B: No, but it's clear <u>that she's very
unhappy</u>.

II (Unit 21)

November 28
Dear Manny,

Well, my first month as a literacy volunteer is
over, and I feel exhilarated!

What
~~The fact that~~ I like best is the chance to work
what's
with real people. In the mornings I report to ~~it's~~
called "Open Classroom." I'm assigned to tutor
whoever
~~whomever~~ comes in and asks for help. Most of the
students are wonderful; sometimes I'm amazed
[that]
~~what~~ they're so motivated to learn. In the
afternoons I tutor my regular students. I often
work with a lady from Vietnam named Mrs.
Tranh. When I started working with her, she could
hardly read at all. Now I'm really impressed by
what
~~whichever~~ she's learned. At first I chose the

whatever / what
assignments, but now we work on ~~whomever~~ Mrs.
Tranh chooses. If she wants to practice oral
what
reading, that's ~~which~~ we do. If she wants to work
on comprehension, we do that for as long as she
likes. Sometimes we spend all afternoon on one
the fact that / that
thing, but that's OK; ~~what~~ she's so motivated is
very rewarding.

Well, that's all for now. Write soon, and I'll do
the same.

Best,
Diane

III (Unit 21)

2. where she is
3. a. that Bill is
 b. the fact that he is ill a great deal
4. a. that we need to do
 b. whatever is necessary
5. a. whoever it is
 b. that it isn't
6. a. how far it is
 b. that it's

IV (Units 21 and 22)

Possible answers:

2. The Martins wondered if they could
afford a bigger house.
3. Mrs. Martin's father asked where the
house was located.
4. Mrs. Martin's mother said it was
important that they have the house they
needed.
5. Mrs. Martin's father told them that they
would help them with the down payment.
6. The Martins were thrilled that they got
their new house.

V (Unit 21)

2. C		**7.** A
3. A		**8.** D
4. C		**9.** D
5. A		**10.** B
6. B		

PART IX

I (Units 23 and 24)

2. F		**7.** P
3. F		**8.** PR
4. PR		**9.** F
5. P		**10.** PR
6. PR		

II (Unit 23)

2. If he had changed the oil, the engine wouldn't have seized.
3. If the engine hadn't seized, the other car wouldn't have rear-ended him.
4. He wouldn't have had to pay a towing bill.
5. He wouldn't have had to replace the engine.
6. He could have made it to the job interview if all this hadn't happened.
7. If he had made it to the interview, he might have a job now.
8. Brandon wishes he had listened to his inner voice.

III (Unit 24)

2. that Mary not lose her temper
3. that her neighbor keep the dog in at night
4. that the neighbor get rid of the animal
5. that Mary call the animal control bureau

IV (Unit 23)

2. we'd realized
3. he keeps
4. there were
5. we could contact
6. it weren't
7. we had
8. this isn't / this won't be
9. we knew
10. it is

V (Units 23 and 24)

Possible answers:

2. Karen insisted that they leave.
3. If they hadn't stayed up late, Sam wouldn't have overslept.
4. If Sam had already gotten some gas, he wouldn't have run out.
5. If he had taken a taxi, he could have made it to the interview.
6. If he had listened to Karen's advice, he might have gotten the job / he might have a job now.

VI (Units 23 and 24)

2. B	7. A
3. A	8. D
4. A	9. C
5. B	10. D
6. C	

INDEX

This Index is for the full and split editions. All entries are in the full book. Entries for Volume A of the split edition are in black. Entries for Volume B are in color.